DATE			

© THE BAKER & TAYLOR CO.

The Oxford Book
of American
Light Verse

The
Oxford Book
of
American
Light Verse

Chosen and Edited by

WILLIAM HARMON

New York   Oxford
OXFORD UNIVERSITY PRESS
1979

Copyright ©1979 by Oxford University Press, Inc.

Library of Congress Cataloging in Publication Data
Main entry under title:
The Oxford book of American light verse.
Includes index.
1. American poetry.   2. Humorous poetry, American.
I. Harmon, William, 1938–
PS586.095   811'.07   78-12356   ISBN 0-19-502509-1

Since this page cannot legibly accommodate all the copyright notices, the pages following constitute an extension of the copyright page.

Printed in the United States of America

To
Richard Harter Fogle
and
Robert Haig

INTRODUCTION

I

Those *o*'s look out from *Oxford Book* so owlishly and solemnly that any editor ought to recall the words of Daniel H. H. Ingalls, the distinguished Orientalist: "Sanskrit anthologies usually begin with a considerable number of benedictory verses, distributed in groups according to the god addressed, the personal god of the anthologist coming first." Although I do not in any way resemble the Abbot Vidyākara or even Sir Arthur Quiller-Couch, I can readily understand any anthologist's recognition of the need for benedictory preliminaries. The comforting sound of "the personal god of the anthologist" makes me wish I could, like Vidyākara, invoke the names of powerful bodhisattvas or, like Quiller-Couch, mention "the President, Fellows, and Scholars of Trinity College, Oxford." But this is a book of *American Light Verse*, from which no *o*'s look out, so that any solemn name I call is likely to be taken in vain.

Even so, an anthologist needs all the help he can get, and it may do some good if I invoke, as a provisional muse, one of the lesser figures among the "self-born mockers of man's enterprise": Mary, Mary, Quite Contrary. I do this, first, for fun (her epithet does share the initials of Sir Arthur's excellent family name), but also for a rhetorical purpose, which is to suggest that the spirit of comedy, which pervades all of the many species of light verse, is a spirit of contrariness, opposing disorder to rigidity ("raising hell") but in virtually the next breath correcting disorder with regularity ("blowing the whistle"). Comedy, that is, polices. Corrective policing is itself neutral, indefinite, and flexible. Since verse—even *vers libre*—is an uncommonly organized entity, light verse tends to carry out its policing function by asserting its implicit symmetry, courtesy, and urbanity as surgical procedures to get rid of the embarrassing disorder of clowns, hicks, braggarts, crooks, and fools.

Just as soon as you commit yourself to the position that such a category of comedy as ordinary light verse ought to be *invariably* reactionary and conservative, however, you are overwhelmed by exceptions and idiosyncratic variations. Each time I have tried to codify the principles governing the selection of pieces for this anthology, I have not been able to go four steps without meeting a case that required at least some modest bending of the rules and, as often as not, the complete abandonment of them. When I think about definition, I remember how E. M. Forster's essay on Ronald Firbank handles critics of a certain sort: "With quiet eyes and cool fingers they pass from point to point, they define fantasy as 'the unserious treatment of the unusual'— an impeccable definition, the only objection to it being that it defines."

II

I got the idea for this anthology one day six or seven years ago. I was in the university office of my friend Forrest Read, an accomplished scholar and critic specializing in the work of Ezra Pound, whose anthology *Confucius to Cummings* we had been discussing. "Have you seen this?" Mr. Read asked, handing me a quaint and curious volume that he had borrowed from the university library: the 1894 edition of *Ben King's Verse* with Nixon Waterman's fantastic introduction and (amid many other treats) the whole text of "The Pessimist," of which Pound had included only a part in his dogmatic anthology. I borrowed the King book, and later as I read through it I began to recognize how little I knew about the general climate of popular art that had prevailed around the turn of the century when the great masters of modern American literature were just growing up. The prose and poetry of those masters had impressed me as difficult, obscure, cerebral, violent, exotic, esoteric, and rather odd; the fact was that I had seldom given much thought to their writings in their original cultural settings. The more I thought about Ben King, the more I remembered some of Pound's own occasional doggerel and by-the-way references to verse like "The Little Peach in the Orchard Grew," and I began to consider the unkind reference to Cole Porter in (of all places) Hemingway's "The Snows of Kilimanjaro" and, closer to my own study of poetry, Eliot's lifelong and steadfast devotion to informal ditties, children's verses, the music hall, the Higher Nonsense of certain eccentric Victorians, and the achievement of Groucho Marx. And then it was—with Ring Lardner's parodies of "Night and Day" drumming in my head— that I began to think that the world needed an anthology of American light verse. The verses themselves are enjoyable, they have meant a lot to a lot of people, and they can even matter in the study of heavy verse. But the operative word is "enjoyable."

III

This anthology complements four earlier collections: *The Oxford Book of Light Verse* (1938), edited by W. H. Auden; *The Oxford Book of American Verse* (1950), edited by F. O. Matthiessen; *The New Oxford Book of American Verse* (1976), edited by Richard Ellmann; and *The New Oxford Book of English Light Verse* (1978), edited by Kingsley Amis. As admirable and comprehensive as these collections may be—and all four are very admirable and comprehensive indeed—they exclude, almost completely, a considerable body of verse. The books of light verse contain almost nothing American, and the books of American verse contain almost nothing light. I aim, then, to furnish a handy collection of enjoyable verses, which, as a mass, may remind the reader of certain durable features of the American people. The senses of adventure and fun combine with a practical turn of mind to produce works that deflate the hifalutin, debunk the hypocritical, abridge the sesquipedalian, praise the praiseworthy, and even make fun of the stated or implicit ideals of the Republic itself. Yankee Doodle remains, after all, at bottom a yokel: his attempt at Italianate elegance—sticking a barnyard feather in his rustic hat and naïvely calling the effect "macaroni"—parodies the manners of the dandy. Because of its celebrity and liveliness, the rebels of 1776 could appropriate "Yankee Doodle" despite its ostensibly anti-American denotation. A little later, Francis Scott Key, who was not a poet but a devoted patriot, could produce what was eventually to become the national anthem by appropriating the meter and rhyme scheme of a flamboyant

"Anacreontic" drinking song in aristocratic disregard (or ignorance) of its ostensibly iconoclastic connotation. The rituals of nature and culture both behave economically, so that one structure or symbol may serve many purposes at once.

Even so, such paradoxical heroes as Yankee Doodle and Anacreon endure in American iconography too consistently and too strongly to be dismissed as accidents or as simple projections of some essential psychic contradiction. "Mighty Casey," hero of one of the most genuinely popular of American popular verses, does strike out, after all, and remains forever a failure and a loser, redeemed, if at all, only by the splendor of his stubborn pride and stoical understatement. It may be that Americans, even after touring the alabaster monuments in Washington and the stupendous towers of commerce in New York and Chicago, know somewhere deep inside that one home they come back to again and again is Casey's joyless Mudville. But that judgment is too solemn. The comedy in "Casey at the Bat" is created by a release of ironic energy in the surprising shift of viewpoint at the very end of the poem, so that the reader finds himself in the position, not of a Mudville fan reduced to woe by a loss, but of a cultivated citizen of a larger community given stability and justice by the harmless punishment of a disruptive braggart.

Such failures, profanations, and punishments are not the whole fabric of American light verse; they just seem to be, early and late, the lightest and the most popular. Other strands in the fabric include routine poems for children, prosodic tours de force, nonsense rhymes, flytings, satires, curses, word games, and the modest accounts of daily life that Auden included in his broad threefold definition of light verse: "1. Poetry written for performance, to be spoken or sung before an audience. . . . 2. Poetry intended to be read, but having for its subject-matter the everyday social life of its period or the experiences of the poet as an ordinary human being. . . . 3. Such nonsense poetry as, through its properties and technique, has a general appeal." To that capacious definition one can add Matthiessen's criterion for Americanness of poets—"poets whose lives have been deeply shaped by American experience"—and get a fair idea of the scope of this anthology.

With a small number of poets the question of Americanness can become problematic. Edgar A. Guest was born in England but came to this country as a child and flourished as a thoroughly American poet; I include a few of his verses because they seem amiable enough and have been too often misquoted and ridiculed. I include some poems written by T. S. Eliot before he gave up American citizenship and took on the wholly British idiom of *Old Possum's Book of Practical Cats*, which is fine light verse but not American. Of Auden's verse I include only pieces written after he had become an American citizen (a policy that applies also to Vladimir Nabokov). Bliss Carman was a Canadian, but he did live awhile in the United States, so that one can say fairly that his life was "deeply shaped by American experience." Some anonymous works tend to be anomalous as to nationality, and I have as a rule included only pieces that are somehow distinctly American in setting, subject, or style. I have left out some fine filthy pieces of folklore that would belong in an anthology of international light verse in English but could not be justified in a distinctly American collection.

A fastidious reader may notice that my principles of inclusion differ a good bit from those stated by Mr. Amis in *his* Oxford anthology. Mr. Amis's Introduction is admirably and deceptively relaxed, so that the reader begins to feel that he is in on a pleasantly casual conversation that ambles and rambles from one old thing to another, with no more shocks or surprises than one encounters in any genuine conversation, and only when he finishes the whole piece does he recognize that Mr. Amis, with an impressive fund of ingenuity and courage, has painstakingly committed himself quite clearly as being on one or another side of every single question of definition or taste that may come up in a proper discussion of light verse. If we can disagree with Mr. Amis on this or that point, it is largely because we know so well what he thinks. He has said *so*, and his authoritative clarity permits us to say *not-so* with, we may hope, equal force.

If Mr. Amis and I seem to disagree on some point of philosophy or policy, it is probably because we have had to deal with bodies of verse that are more divergent than one might think. American and English light verse are written in approximately the same language and in the same broad tradition, but there are so many points of separation and paths of divergence that the two bodies of literature may almost as well have been in wholly different languages. Mr. Amis rejects just plain bad verse, for example, because it is dull and its writers were not in fact writing or trying to write light verse, at least by their own estimate. But Mr. Amis, confined to the likes of Whur and McGonigal, was denied the pleasure of dealing with Thomas Holley Chivers, Julia Moore, and J. Gordon Coogler. That collection of Americans could not be dismissed as plain lousy writers. They are Prismatics. A Prismatic—and Mrs. Moore is such a writer *par excellence* and *sui generis*—is a writer so transcendently, surpassingly, superlatively bad that he or she belongs in a special genre in which normal rules and habits of judgment are magically suspended. The Prismatics do not write light verse; they write lighter verse, lightest verse, something that belongs on the moon.

On political grounds (revolution versus reaction) that apply more to a small country divided into Whigs and Tories than to a much larger one much less tidily divided into Democrats and Republicans, Mr. Amis excludes verses and whole types of verse and schools of versifiers that I have seen fit to include. My principles of inclusion, such as they are, seek to comprehend as much as possible, with room for parodies, burlesques, travesties, satires, nonsense, *vers de société*, occasional poems, and verse that used to be called "familiar." I exclude only such works as are not fit for any collection and those that find their way normally into collections and textbooks of serious, official, canonical literature. In the matter of obscenity, I have been distressed by only one word: "Nigger." I am sorry that that word, or some synonym thereof, occurs in our language or literature at all, but it would do no good for me now to pretend that it never existed. For other offensive terms, I have left the text of any given work in the state that I found it and not attempted to sanitize or modernize. There's something quaint and delicate about those dots and dashes. In the general problem of editing I have settled for a diplomatic text that represents the best version I could find or create, with very few annotations other than those furnished by the authors themselves. Some of these verses have never been published before, and some others have not been published during this century. It has been my pleasure to know some of the authors who appear in these pages, and in three instances—poems by Jonathan Williams, George Starbuck, and Kathleen Norris—I have the honor to offer revised versions newer and better than those appearing in print elsewhere.

With many song lyrics I have found that we murder to dissect: without the music to buoy them up, even clever words may sink and drown, so that I have not included quite as much of this kind of verse as one might expect. In a few cases—works by Ambrose Bierce, George Ade, and Ring Lardner—I have had to include some prose to explain what the verse is about.

IV

The presence of three names in the table of contents of this anthology —John Quincy Adams, John Hay, Joseph W. Stilwell—gives me special pleasure. It is encouraging to note that we do not take ourselves too seriously and that the production of fine light verse is not incompatible with the execution of the sort of public responsibility entrusted to a distinguished President, an admirable Secretary of State, and a courageous Army General. Lincoln's sense of humor was probably more developed than that of any other President, but it did not find its way into verse. Woodrow Wilson wrote a few lines of tolerable collegiate doggerel, but the limerick attributed to him by his biographer Josephus Daniels—

> For beauty I am not a star;
> There are others handsomer, far;
> But my face, I don't mind it,
> For I am behind it;
> 'Tis the people in front that I jar.

—seems to have been the work of the unfortunate Anthony Euwer (whose original version is smoother than that quoted by Daniels). But it is to Wilson's credit that he *had* a favorite limerick and, moreover, could quote it when a friendly voice from the gallery of a political rally cried out, "Go it, Woody. You are all right. But you ain't no beaut."

That truthful statement expresses a grand democratic toughness and honesty along with an acute sense of the vanity of some human wishes. Under such toughness lies a soil of human cheer and sweet persistence that can be seen time and again in American history. Below the ironic puzzles ("The sun so hot I froze to death") and the skeptical axioms—

> You may talk of your learning and brag of your sense:
> 'Twill all be forgotten a hundred years hence.

—lies the subsoil of Mudville, supporting a flourishing crop: the animated jingles that come out of a collective custom of facing facts, telling the truth, and saying what's what:

> Logic is logic.

> Rose is a rose is a rose.

> Men seldom make passes
> At girls who wear glasses.

> Candy
> Is dandy
> But liquor
> Is quicker.

> a politician is an arse upon
> which everyone has sat except a man.

> Bravery runs in my family.

That sort of utterance—like "But you ain't no beaut"—impresses me as the heart of the recurrent message passing between America and Americans.

V

When Henry Adams, a humorist of sorts, spoke of himself as a "conservative Christian anarchist," he was recording an extraordinarily clear trace of the divided spirit of American comedy. Some years later, another comedian of sorts, Norman Mailer (who has more than one quality in common with Adams), was pleased to register himself as a "left conservative," an ostensible oxymoron that again records the old division of spirit, at least among aesthetes. The conservative or conservationist attitude, expressed in habits of detection, exposure, and judgment of excessive folly and equally implicit in the habits of regular and even ornate verse-forms, favors consolidation, stability, tradition, convention, continuity, and "normalcy." (That last word is usually attributed to a Republican President, Warren Harding; as with Wilson's limerick, however, "normalcy" existed, as one might expect, before the Harding of folklore supposedly misread what was written in a prepared statement.)

In such a conservative spirit, the journalistic light verse that prevailed for decades between the administrations of Lincoln and Franklin Roosevelt flourished largely because it stood foursquare for nothing more advanced than some imaginary status quo and rejected, sometimes brutally, anything different: Colenso's revisionist theology, telephones, foreigners, modern art, the New Deal. (In 1920, Forster described *Punch* as the Britannic counterpart of this conservatism: "There is neither wit, laughter, nor satire in our national jester—only the snigger of a suburban householder who can understand nothing that does not resemble himself. Week after week, under Mr. Punch's supervision, a man falls off his horse, or a colonel misses a golf ball, or a little girl makes a mistake in her prayers. Week after week ladies show not too much of their legs, foreigners are deprecated, originality condemned. Week after week a bricklayer does not do as much work as he ought and a futurist does more than he need.") Comedy of this sort, on both sides of the Atlantic, bracketed its favorite targets in punitively straitlaced stanzas that besought the audience to remember and adhere to the values of whatever Good Old Days seemed worth recollecting. By now—with 1984 rearing its poor foredoomed head—this spirit has become manifest in a bizarre fashion that misapplies "nostalgia" to a rather gummy longing for *early* television when the abominable programs had at least the virtue of being "live."

The other side of the spirit of comedy, fortunately, acts internally to correct silly excesses. This is the "anarchist" or "left" side (and, according to Mr. Amis, the side occupied by Auden's *Oxford Book of Light Verse*; but, with the distance afforded by the passage of time, I can see little in Auden's anthology that deserves to be called "revolutionary" and almost as little in Mr. Amis's that deserves to be called "reactionary"). Conservative comedy, with traditional attitudes and instruments, attacks aberrations and eccentricities with a scarcely civil arsenal of radically disorderly weapons, for on the dark side of conservatism there lurks a demonic Punch (*not* Mr. Punch of the magazine), a wild old man who wickedly destroys everything and everybody: his child, his wife, the hangman, even the very Devil. This Dionysian, anarchic id-spirit of misrule seems to represent the pre-social and pre-logical Individual—as dear to American conservatives as to Jean-Jacques Rousseau—the Individual who can turn every solemn civic utterance into rude and incult parody. That most conservative of serious poems, Gray's "Elegy," has begotten a great American line of bastards, most entertainingly as handled by Bierce ("The cur foretells the knell of parting day") and Morley ("The short and simple flannels of the poor"). Much the same fate has befallen Longfellow's "Psalm of Life."

VI

The study of comedy sometimes suggests a formula no more troublesome than "Comedy is culture" and sometimes even seems to work as a mysterious branch of immunology. A social organism, let us say, makes its choices and mistakes, forever shifting and adjusting; and, as the organism goes along, a practically automatic endocrine system secretes substances that either confirm or correct the creature's behavior. The most crystalline and most powerful form of comedy is symmetrical light verse, which flows through the system at all times, through all of the media, formal and informal—now with the perishable status of scratchings on a public bathroom wall, now with the more nearly permanent tenure of a clothbound book—but flowing anyhow to keep the culture-creature alive and alert. One set of enzymes releases a couple of cubic centimeters of romantic ecstasy—

> It's spring! It's spring! It's spring!
> The bird is on the wing!

—and immediately another set of enzymes, neoclassically exact, releases a countervailing measure of corrective Pyrrhonism—

> Absurd, absurd, absurd:
> The wing is on the bird.

These immunizing processes are most conspicuous in the zone where the social creature's life is most public: politics. The great beast makes a move, and the next morning some local embodiment of the spirit of comedy—some Will Rogers or Mark Russell, say—exposes the vice or folly.

A good deal of such humor has to be topical and occasional, so that, as the topics fade and the occasions pass, much of the comedy likewise perishes. For any piece of light verse that we may remember, there are probably on the same topic a thousand pieces that everybody has forgotten. Journalism in general is meant to be diurnal, expendable; and every new day demands its own allotted quota of disposable cartoons, songs, gags, and stories, which quickly become yesterday's, then history's, then prehistory's. Even the bucket of ashes perishes as the ashes are recycled. In the case of wit, in which novelty is critical, the process is accelerated vertiginously.

To read any number of the surviving verses of two centuries of American national history is to see fashions and crises come and go and to witness a striking concentration of much comic light on a fairly limited diachronic array of subjects. The boundaries are marked, on one side, by the coquette in her chemisette, on the other, by the institution that many people speak of as "the feral government." Since many of the poems in this anthology are only typical or representative, it is not possible here to demonstrate the full wealth of wit that has been spent on a handful of perennials: The Good Old Days, Country versus City, Men versus Women, The Habits of Animals, A Nation of Immigrants, Elegance, Evolution, Prohibition, Abhorrent Modernity, Political Ethics, and The Morning After.

We seem never to grow tired of these preferred subjects—our totems and taboos, as it were—at least not in small samples. I have found that the only major fashion that I consider utterly contemptible and unamusing is the "dialect" writing that enjoyed mountainous popularity through much of the nineteenth century and is not altogether dead even yet. (After President Nixon's resignation, a scholar suggested that a certain poet write something in the fine old *De Casibus* tradition; the poet refused, offering as his reason one line drawn from the old-time minstrel mode: "De casibus ain't what dey used to be.")

But, for the sake of including a few characteristic poems of all of the important modes or conventions, I have chosen two works by Fred Emerson Brooks (whom I nominate for the title of America's Most Loathsome Versifier) because each contains several different attempts at the representation of dialect. But I do not have to like the poems.

I confess one other failure of taste. Something keeps me from liking the "cruel" infanticidal verses that have been moving in and out of favor and fashion all through this century on both sides of the Atlantic. These "Little Willy" pieces, mostly quatrains, probably serve as a corrective balance to certain excessively sentimental *Kindertotenlieder*, but I find my patience and sympathy very limited with such things. Most of them, in the fashion of Graham's *Ruthless Rhymes for Heartless Homes*, are distinctly British, and I have judged only a few American specimens—such as some of Edward Gorey's neat limericks—worthy of inclusion.

VII

It concerns me—it may even *alarm* me—that I do not know everything. More than once in my life I have found that every single person in this world seems to know, as common knowledge, something of which I have been unaware. Several years ago, in a similar hot seat (the Introduction to his Modern Library *Anthology of Light Verse*), the distinguished critic Louis Kronenberger said something that I find, for sheer professional comfort, most soothing: "I know . . . that I have undoubtedly omitted everybody's favorite poem. Every anthologist does." Some omissions of mine can be attributed to the author's or the author's estate's not furnishing permission for use, some other omissions are oversights, some were caused by a discovery or realization that came too late, some represent blind spots. To certain charges of error I enter the classic plea, "Ignorance, Madam, pure ignorance."

Whatever the causes of my shortcomings, I certainly have not starved for good advice and good companionship. With rare generosity, an extraordinary number of people—some of them perfect strangers, some perfect old friends—have talked with me, told me stories, lent me books, sung me songs, scanned the drafts of my table of contents, and found me copies of certain obscure items that I never could have tracked down on my own. Some, assigned to me as Graduate Assistants in the Department of English of the University of North Carolina at Chapel Hill, worked for many hours; some simply "turned in the hall, one hand on the door" and mentioned the name of some entertaining versifier of whom I had not heard before. But I ought to linger no more over distinctions of degree here in recording my thanks, for help of every kind, to these people: Cynthia Clay Adams, Raymond Adams, A. R. Ammons, Joellyn Ausanka, Robert Bain, Michael Benedikt, Helen Bevington, Walter Blair, the late Richmond Bond, Cleanth Brooks, Leona Capeless, William Carroll, Curtis Church, William Rossa Cole, Susan DeFrancesco, the late Dennis Donovan, Theresa Eliot, Anne Evers, Richard Harter Fogle, Nancy Frazier, James Gaskin, Bruce Geyer, Albert Goldbarth, Carol Griffith, Pamela Gurney, Robert Haig, Lynn Harmon, Sally Harmon, Virginia Harmon, Will Harmon, Cheryl Herr, George Hitchcock, Hugh Holman, John Hollander, Carroll Hollis, Mary Ishaq, Blyden Jackson, George Kane, Carolyn Kizer, Lewis Leary, Gershon Legman, George Lensing, Allan Life, Norman Maclean, Frankie McCormick, Michael McFee, Pattie McIntyre, Dougald McMillan, Sheldon Meyer, Polly Melson, Jerry Mills, Max Morath, Martie Murray, Daniel Patterson, John Postell, James Raimes, Forrest Read, Mark Reed, Louis D. Rubin, Jr., Richard Rust, Linda Scott, Walter Scott, James Seay, John Seelye, Harold Shapiro, Susan Shillinglaw, Jodi Sigmon, Susan Smock, Susan Solomon, Douglas Stalker, Hugh Staples, George Starbuck, Thomas Stumpf, Garren Tate, Joan Tate, Eli Waldron, Helen Jane Wettach, Dallas Wiebe, Jonathan Williams, and Charles Zug.

VIII

This sort of collection of verses shows how and how much things may have changed and, moreover, how and how much nothing has changed. We seem to have possessed from the beginning in America a rough vulgar humor and at the same time a smooth aristocratic humor, with a melancholy and cockeyed surrealism trafficking between them. We have had bold dirty songs and sweet dainty verses from the beginning, and the virtual tides of fashion simply shift the same water back and forth: now sentimental elegies, now sick jokes; now drawing-room persiflage, now laborers' scatology; now patriotic bombast, now the private soldier's immemorial bitching; and so on and so forth. We may, if we like, face and use our collective past in any way that suits us, as, say, John Barth does in *The Sot-Weed Factor* or John Seelye in *The Kid*. But we do not need to be self-conscious about it, really. No matter what we do or think we are doing, if our invention should sing and appeal to any number of people at all, it must be because it resonates with certain rhythmic pulses already deep in our spirits, stored there in the beginning and capable of being summoned by the right combination of plot, person, notion, feeling, word, and song. History, insofar as it matters, and whether we like it or not, is now and England, now and New England, now and wherever we are now. Willy-nilly, it makes a pattern, and light verse is going to remain an important set of symbols in that pattern.

W. H.

Chapel Hill
March, 1979

CONTENTS

CONTENTS

CONTENTS

CONTENTS

CONTENTS

CONTENTS

CONTENTS

CONTENTS

CONTENTS

CONTENTS

CONTENTS

CONTENTS

CONTENTS

CONTENTS

CONTENTS

CONTENTS

CONTENTS

l

The Oxford Book
of American
Light Verse

ANONYMOUS

Yankee Doodle

Yankee Doodle went to town
    Riding on a pony,
Stuck a feather in his cap
    And called it "macaroni."

      Yankee Doodle, keep it up,
      Yankee Doodle, dandy,
      Mind the music and the step,
      And with the girls be handy.

Father and I went down to camp,
    Along with Captain Gooding,
And there we see the men and boys,
    As thick as hasty pudding.

And there we see a thousand men,
    As rich as 'Squire David;
And what they wasted every day,
    I wish it could be saved.

The 'lasses they eat every day,
    Would keep a house in winter;
They have so much that, I'll be bound,
    They eat it when they're a mind to.

And there we see a swamping gun,
    Large as a log of maple,
Upon a deuced little cart,
    A load for father's cattle.

And every time they shoot it off,
    It takes a horn of powder,
And makes a noise like father's gun,
    Only a nation louder.

I went as nigh to one myself
    As Siah's underpinning;
And father went as nigh again,
    I thought the deuce was in him.

Cousin Simon grew so bold
   I thought he would have cock'd it;
It scared me so, I shrink'd it off,
   And hung by father's pocket.

And Captain Davis had a gun,
   He kind of clapped his hand on't,
And stuck a crooked stabbing iron
   Upon the little end on't.

And there I see a pumpkin shell
   As big as mother's basin;
And every time they touch'd it off,
   They scampered like the nation.

I see a little barrel too,
   The heads were made of leather,
They knock'd upon't with little clubs
   And call'd the folks together.

And there was Captain Washington
   And gentlefolks about him;
They say he's grown so 'tarnal proud
   He will not ride without 'em.

He got him on his meeting clothes,
   Upon a slapping stallion,
He set the world along in rows,
   In hundreds and in millions.

The flaming ribbons in his hat,
   They look'd so tearing fine, ah!
I wanted pockily to get
   To give to my Jemimah.

I see another snarl of men
   A-digging graves, they told me,
So 'tarnal long, so 'tarnal deep,
   They 'tended they should hold me.

It scar'd me so, I hook'd it off,
   Nor stopp'd, as I remember,
Nor turned about, till I got home,
   Lock'd up in mother's chamber.

． ． ．

[Earlier stanzas]

Brother Ephraim sold his cow
   And bought him a commission,
And then he went to Canada
   To fight for the nation.

But when Ephraim he came home
   He proved an arrant coward,
He wouldn't fight the Frenchmen there
   For fear of being devour'd.

Sheep's head and vinegar,
   Buttermilk and tansy,
Boston is a Yankee town —
   Sing Hey Doodle Dandy.

First we'll take a pinch of snuff,
   And then a drink of water,
And then we'll say, "How do you do" —
   And that's a Yankee's supper.

Aminadab is just come home,
   His eyes all greas'd with bacon,
And all the news that he could tell
   Is Cape Breton is taken.

Stand up, Jonathan,
   Figure in thy neighbor;
Vathen, stand a little off
   And make the room some wider.

Christmas is a-coming, boys,
   We'll go to Mother Chase's,
And there we'll get a sugar dram
   Sweetened with molasses.

Heigh ho for our Cape Cod,
   Heigh ho Nantasket,
Do not let the Boston wags
   Feel your oyster basket.

Punkin' pie is very good
  And so is apple lantern,
Had you been whipp'd as oft as I
  You'd not have been so wanton.

Uncle is a Yankee man,
  I' faith, he pays us all off,
And he has got a fiddle
  As big as Daddy's hog trough.

Seth's mother went to Lynn
  To buy a pair of breeches,
The first time Vathen put them on
  He tore out all the stitches.

Dolly Bushel let a fart,
  Jenny Jones she found it,
Ambrose carried it to mill
  Where Doctor Warren ground it.

Our Jemimah's lost her mare
  And can't tell where to find her,
But she'll come trotting by and by
  And bring her tail behind her.

Two and two may go to bed,
  Two and two together;
And if there is not room enough,
  Lie one atop o' t'other.

FRANCIS HOPKINSON

1737–1791

The Battle of the Kegs

Gallants attend, and hear a friend
  Trill forth harmonious ditty;
Strange things I'll tell, which late befel
  In Philadelphia city.

6

'Twas early day, as Poets say,
    Just when the sun was rising;
A soldier stood on a log of wood
    And saw a sight surprising.

As in a maze he stood to gaze,
    The truth can't be deny'd, Sir;
He spy'd a score of kegs, or more,
    Come floating down the tide, Sir.

A sailor too, in jerkin blue,
    This strange appearance viewing,
First damn'd his eyes in great surprize,
    Then said — "Some mischief's brewing:

"These kegs now hold the rebels bold
    Pack'd up like pickl'd herring,
And they're come down t'attack the town
    In this new way of ferrying."

The soldier flew, the sailor too,
    And scar'd almost to death, Sir,
Wore out their shoes to spread the news,
    And ran 'til out of breath, Sir.

Now up and down throughout the town
    Most frantic scenes were acted;
And some ran here and others there,
    Like men almost distracted.

Some fire cry'd, which some deny'd,
    But said the earth had quaked;
And girls and boys, with hideous noise,
    Ran thro' the streets half naked.

Sir *William* he, snug as a flea,
    Lay all this time a snoring;
Nor dreamt of harm, as he lay warm
    In bed with Mrs. *Loring*.

Now in a fright he starts upright,
    Awak'd by such a clatter;
First rubs his eyes, then boldly cries,
    "For God's sake, what's the matter?"

7

At his bed side he then espy'd
Sir Erskine at command, Sir;
Upon one foot he had one boot
And t'other in his hand, Sir.

"Arise, arise," Sir Erskine cries,
"The rebels — more's the pity!
Without a boat, are all afloat
And rang'd before the city.

"The motley crew, in vessels new,
With Satan for their guide, Sir,
Pack'd up in bags, and wooden kegs,
Come driving down the tide, Sir.

"Therefore prepare for bloody war,
These kegs must all be routed,
Or surely we despis'd shall be,
And British valour doubted."

The royal band now ready stand,
All rang'd in dread array, Sir,
On every slip, in every ship,
For to begin the fray, Sir.

The cannons roar from shore to shore,
The small arms make a rattle;
Since wars began I'm sure no man
E'er saw so strange a battle.

The rebel dales — the rebel vales,
With rebel trees surrounded;
The distant woods, the hills and floods,
With rebel echoes sounded.

The fish below swam to and fro,
Attack'd from ev'ry quarter;
Why sure, thought they, the De'il's to pay
'Mong folks above the water.

The kegs, 'tis said, tho' strongly made
Of rebel staves and hoops, Sir,
Could not oppose their pow'rful foes,
The conqu'ring British troops, Sir.

From morn to night these men of might
    Display'd amazing courage;
And when the sun was fairly down,
    Retir'd to sup their porridge.

One hundred men, with each a pen
    Or more, upon my word, Sir,
It is most true, would be too few
    Their valour to record, Sir.

Such feats did they perform that day
    Against these wicked kegs, Sir,
That years to come, *if they get home,*
    They'll make their boasts and brag, Sir.

ST. GEORGE TUCKER
1752–1827

The Cynic

Whoever to finding fault inclines
Still misconceives the best designs:
Praxiteles in vain might try
To form a statue for his eye;
Appelles too would pain in vain,
And Titian's colors give him pain,
Palladio's best designs displease him,
And Handel's water piece would freeze him,
Not Tully's eloquence can charm,
Nor e'en old Homer's fire warm:
On all occasions still a beast
He frowns upon the genial feast,
Swears that Falernian wine was sour,
And rails at champagne for an hour,
Not Heliogabalus's cook
Could drop a dish at which he'd look.
    Anticipating time and fate
He views all things when past their date,
Destruction in his noodle brewing
Turns palaces to instant ruin:
Speak but of Paris or of London
He tells how Babylon was undone:

Ask him, with Thais if he'll sup,
He cries — "The worms will eat her up."
   Once at a merry wedding feast
A cynic chanced to be a guest;
Rich was the father of the bride
And hospitality his pride.
The guests were numerous and the board
With dainties plentifully stored.
There mutton, beef, and vermicelli,
Here venison stewed with currant jelly,
Here turkeys robbed of bones and lungs
Are crammed with oysters and with tongues.
There pickled lobsters, prawn, and salmon
And there a stuffed Virginia gammon.
Here custards, tarts, and apple pies
There syllabubs and jellies rise,
Ice creams, and ripe and candied fruits
With comfits and eryngo roots.
Now entered every hungry guest
And all prepared to taste the feast.
Our cynic cries — "How damned absurd
To take such pains to make a — !"

The Discontented Student

A True Story

Returned from college R —— gets a wife
To be the joy and comfort of his life:
But ere the honeymoon was in the wane
He sighs for college, and his books again
To his thought on all occasions flock:
Like Madam Shandy, thinking of the clock.
But, sad mishap! when Phoebus gilds the skies,
If to his favorite authors he applies,
Bright Venus throws her cestus o'er the book;
In vain he tries upon the page to look;
As Cupid blind, the classic page no more
Delights his raptured sight as heretofore.
Like that sagacious beast, who placed between
Two cocks of hay — one dry, the other green,
Can neither taste; our scholar every night
Thinks of his books; and of his bride by light.

Untasted joys breed always discontents;
Thus to his sire, his rage the scholar vents.
"Would that in Italy I had been born,
And, early, of each vile encumbrance shorn,
Which now seduces all my thoughts away
From Classic studies or by night, or day.
Uninterrupted then I might have read
Or in my elbow chair, or in my bed;
Till drowsy grown, and nodding o'er the book
Upon the enchanting page I craved to look
And then in rapturous dreams renewed the joy
Till taking, I resumed the blest employ.
But now in vain I quit the genial bed,
My wife — a plague! — keeps running in my head
In ev'ry page I read my raging fires
Portray her yielding to my fierce desires."
   "G— d— your books!" the testy father said,
   "I'd not give —— for all you've read."

The Judge with the Sore Rump

*"Serva tibi minas!"**
   To a judge who was seated on high;
As (for some fatal crime)
He devoted some time
   To prepare the poor culprit to die.

"What's that about mine a—e?"
   (Says the judge to Aquinas,
   And turned up his rump as he spoke)
"I've a boil on my bum,
Thrice as large as my thumb:
   And see here! — the boil has just broke!"

Says Aquinas — "I find
That your tortures behind,
   Are more than you threaten, by far:
So here end your farce,
And take care of your a—e;
   And let me get out of the bar."

* *"Serva tibi minas"*: "Keep your threats for yourself" (Tucker).

JOEL BARLOW
1754–1812

The Hasty-Pudding

Canto I

Ye Alps audacious, thro' the Heavens that rise,
To cramp the day and hide me from the skies;
Ye Gallic flags, that o'er their heights unfurl'd,
Bear death to kings, and freedom to the world,
I sing not you. A softer theme I chuse,
A virgin theme, unconscious of the Muse,
But fruitful, rich, well suited to inspire
The purest frenzy of poetic fire.
  Despise it not, ye Bards to terror steel'd,
Who hurl'd your thunders round the epic field;
Nor ye who strain your midnight throats to sing
Joys that the vineyard and the still-house bring;
Or on some distant fair your notes employ,
And speak of raptures that you ne'er enjoy.
I sing the sweets I know, the charms I feel,
My morning incense, and my evening meal,
The sweets of Hasty-Pudding. Come, dear bowl,
Glide o'er my palate, and inspire my soul.
The milk beside thee, smoking from the kine,
Its substance mingled, married in with thine,
Shall cool and temper thy superior heat,
And save the pains of blowing while I eat.

.   .   .

  Assist me first with pious toil to trace
Thro' wrecks of time thy lineage and thy race;
Declare what lovely squaw, in days of yore,
(Ere great Columbus sought thy native shore)
First gave thee to the world; her works of fame
Have liv'd indeed, but liv'd without a name.
Some tawny Ceres, goddess of her days,
First learn'd with stones to crack the well-dry'd maize,
Thro' the rough sieve to shake the golden show'r,
In boiling water stir the yellow flour.
The yellow flour, bestrew'd and stir'd with haste,
Swells in the flood and thickens to a paste,
Then puffs and wallops, rises to the brim,

Drinks the dry knobs that on the surface swim:
The knobs at last the busy ladle breaks,
And the whole mass its true consistence takes.

    Could but her sacred name, unknown so long,
Rise like her labors, to the sons of song,
To her, to them, I'd consecrate my lays,
And blow her pudding with the breath of praise.
If 'twas Oella, whom I sang before,
I here ascribe her one great virtue more.
Not thro' the rich Peruvian realms alone
The fame of Sol's sweet daughter should be known,
But o'er the world's wide climes should live secure,
Far as his rays extend, as long as they endure.

    Dear Hasty-Pudding, what unpromis'd joy
Expands my heart, to meet thee in Savoy!
Doom'd o'er the world thro' devious paths to roam,
Each clime my country, and each house my home,
My soul is sooth'd, my cares have found an end,
I greet my long-lost, unforgotten friend.

    For thee thro' Paris, that corrupted town,
How long in vain I wandered up and down,
Where shameless Bacchus, with his drenching hoard
Cold from his cave usurps the morning board.
London is lost in smoke and steep'd in tea;
No Yankey there can lisp the name of thee:
The uncouth word, a libel on the town,
Would call a proclamation from the crown.*
For climes oblique, that fear the sun's full rays,
Chill'd in their fogs, exclude the generous maize;
A grain whose rich luxuriant growth requires
Short gentle showers, and bright etherial fires.

    But here tho' distant from our native shore,
With mutual glee we meet and laugh once more,
The same! I know thee by that yellow face,
That strong complexion of true Indian race,
Which time can never change, nor soil impair,
Nor Alpine snows, nor Turkey's morbid air;
For endless years, thro' every mild domain,
Where grows the maize, there thou art sure to reign.

    But man, more fickle, the bold licence claims,
In different realms to give thee different names.

* A certain king, at the time when this was written, was publishing proclamations to prevent American principles from being propagated in his country.

Thee the soft nations round the warm Levant
Palanta call, the French of course *Polante;*
E'en in thy native regions, how I blush
To hear the Pennsylvanians call thee *Mush!*
On Hudson's banks, while men of Belgic spawn
Insult and eat thee by the name *suppawn.*
All spurious appellations, void of truth:
I've better known thee from my earliest youth,
Thy name is *Hasty-Pudding!* thus our sires
Were wont to greet thee fuming from their fires;
And while they argu'd in thy just defence
With logic clear, they thus explained the sense: —
"In *haste* the boiling cauldron o'er the blaze,
Receives and cooks the ready-powder'd maize;
In *haste* 'tis serv'd, and then in equal *haste,*
With cooling milk, we make the sweet repast.
No carving to be done, no knife to grate
The tender ear, and wound the stony plate;
But the smooth spoon, just fitted to the lip,
And taught with art the yielding mass to dip,
By frequent journies to the bowl well stor'd,
Performs the hasty honors of the board."
Such is thy name, significant and clear,
A name, a sound to every Yankey dear,
But most to me, whose heart and palate chaste
Preserve my pure hereditary taste.

There are who strive to stamp with disrepute
The luscious food, because it feeds the brute;
In tropes of high-strain'd wit, while gaudy prigs
Compare thy nursling man to pamper'd pigs;
With sovereign scorn I treat the vulgar jest,
Nor fear to share thy bounties with the beast.
What though the generous cow gives me to quaff
The milk nutritious; am I then a calf?
Or can the genius of the noisy swine,
Tho' nurs'd on pudding, thence lay claim to mine?
Sure the sweet song, I fashion to thy praise,
Runs more melodious than the notes they raise.

.   .   .

Some talk of Hoe-cake, fair Virginia's pride,
Rich Johnny-cake this mouth has often tri'd;
Both please me well, their virtues much the same;

Alike their fabric, as allied their fame,
Except in dear New-England, where the last
Receives a dash of pumpkin in the paste,
To give it sweetness and improve the taste.
But place them all before me, smoaking hot,
The big round dumplin rolling from the pot;
The pudding of the bag, whose quivering breast,
With suet lin'd leads on the Yankey feast;
The Charlotte brown, within whose crusty sides
A belly soft the pulpy apple hides;
The yellow bread, whose face like amber glows,
And all of Indian that the bake-pan knows —
You tempt me not — my fav'rite greets my eyes,
To that lov'd bowl my spoon by instinct flies.

.   .   .

Canto III
The days grow short; but tho' the falling sun
To the glad swain proclaims his day's work done,
Night's pleasing shades his various task prolong,
And yield new subjects to my various song.
For now, the corn-house fill'd, the harvest home,
Th' invited neighbours to the *Husking* come;
A frolic scene, where work, and mirth, and play,
Unite their charms, to chace the hours away.
   Where the huge heap lies center'd in the hall,
The lamp suspended from the cheerful wall,
Brown corn-fed nymphs, and strong hard-handed beaux,
Alternate rang'd, extend in circling rows,
Assume their seats, the solid mass attack;
The dry husks rustle, and the corn-cobs crack;
The song, the laugh, alternate notes resound,
And the sweet cider trips in silence round.
   The laws of Husking ev'ry wight can tell;
And sure no laws he ever keeps so well:
For each red ear a general kiss he gains,
With each smut ear she smuts the luckless swains;
But when to some sweet maid a prize is cast,
Red as her lips, and taper as her waist,
She walks the round, and culls one favor'd beau,
Who leaps, the luscious tribute to bestow.
Various the sport, as are the wits and brains
Of well pleas'd lasses and contending swains:

Till the vast mound of corn is swept away,
And he that gets the last ear, wins the day.
  Meanwhile the house-wife urges all her care,
The well-earn'd feast to hasten and prepare.
The sifted meal already waits her hand,
The milk is strain'd, the bowls in order stand,
The fire flames high; and, as a pool (that takes
The headlong stream that o'er the mill-dam breaks)
Foams, roars and rages with incessant toils,
So the vext cauldron rages, roars and boils.
  First with clean salt she seasons well the food,
Then strews the flour and thickens all the flood.
Long o'er the simmering fire she lets it stand:
To stir it well demands a stronger hand;
The husband takes his turn; and round and round
The ladle flies; at last the toil is crown'd;
When to the board the thronging huskers pour,
And take their seats as at the corn before.
  I leave them to their feast. There still belong
More copious matters to my faithful song.
For rules there are, tho' ne'er unfolded yet,
Nice rules and wise, how pudding should be ate.
  Some with molasses line the luscious treat,
And mix, like Bards, the useful with the sweet.
A wholesome dish, and well-deserving praise,
A great resource in those bleak wintry days,
When the chill'd earth lies buried deep in snow,
And raging Boreas drives the shivering cow.
  Blest cow! thy praise shall still my notes employ,
Great source of health, the only source of joy;
How oft thy teats these pious hands have prest!
How oft thy bounties prove my only feast!
How oft I've fed thee with my fav'rite grain!
And roar'd, like thee, to find thy children slain!
  Ye swains who know her various worth to prize,
Ah! house her well from Winter's angry skies.
Potatoes, Pumpkins, should her sadness cheer,
Corn from your crib, and mashes from your beer;
When Spring returns she'll well acquit the loan,
And nurse at once your infants and her own.
  Milk then with pudding I should always chuse;

To this in future I confine my Muse,
Till she in haste some farther hints unfold,
Well for the young, nor useless to the old.
First in your bowl the milk abundant take,
Then drop with care along the silver lake
Your flakes of pudding; these at first will hide
Their little bulk beneath the swelling tide;
But when their growing mass no more can sink,
When the soft island looms above the brink,
Then check your hand: you've got the portion's due,
So taught our sires, and what they taught is true.
    There is a choice in spoons. Tho' small appear
The nice distinction, yet to me 'tis clear,
The deep bowl'd Gallic spoon, contriv'd to scoop
In ample draughts the thin diluted soup,
Performs not well in those substantial things,
Whose mass adhesive to the metal clings;
Where the strong labial muscles must embrace,
The gentle curve, and sweep the hollow space,
With ease to enter and discharge the freight,
A bowl less concave but still more dilate,
Becomes the pudding best. The shape, the size,
A secret rests unknown to vulgar eyes.
Experienc'd feeders can alone impart
A rule so much above the lore of art.
These tuneful lips, that thousand spoons have tried,
With just precision could the point decide,
Tho' not in song; the muse but poorly shines
In cones, and cubes, and geometric lines.
Yet the true form, as near as she can tell,
Is that small section of a goose-egg-shell,
Which in two equal portions shall divide
The distance from the centre to the side.
    Fear not to slaver; 'tis no deadly sin,
Like the free Frenchman, from your joyous chin
Suspend the ready napkin; or, like me,
Poise with one hand your bowl upon your knee;
Just in the zenith your wise head project,
Your full spoon, rising in a line direct,
Bold as a bucket, heeds no drops that fall,
The wide mouth'd bowl will surely catch them all.

ROYALL TYLER
1757–1826

Anacreontic to Flip

Stingo! to thy bar-room skip,
Make a foaming mug of Flip;
Make it our country's staple,
Rum New England, Sugar Maple,
Beer, that's brewed from hops and Pumpkin,
Grateful to the thirsty Bumkin.
Hark! I hear thy poker fizzle,
And o'er the mug the liquor drizzle;
All against the earthen mug,
I hear the horn-spoon's cheerful dub;
I see thee, STINGO, take the Flip,
And sling thy cud from under lip,
Then pour more rum, and, bottle stopping,
Stir it again, and swear 'tis topping.
    Come quickly bring the humming liquor,
Richer than ale of British vicar;
Better than usquebaugh Hibernian,
Or than Flaccus' famed Falernian;
More potent, healthy, racy, frisky,
Than Holland's gin, or Georgia whisky.
Come, make a ring around the fire,
And hand the mug unto the Squire;
Here, Deacon, take the elbow chair,
And Ensign, Holiday, sit there:
You take the dye-tub, you the churn,
And I'll the double corner turn.
    See the mantling liquor rise!
And burn their cheeks, and close their eyes,
See the sideling mug incline —
Hear them curse their dull divine,
Who, on Sunday, dared to rail,
At *Brewster's* flip, or *Downer's* ale.
— Quick, Stingo, fly and bring another,
The Deacon here shall pay for t'other,
Ensign and I the third will share,
It's due on swop, for pie-bald mare.

The Widower

Happy the man, who free as air,
　By nuptial ties no longer bound,
With dearest wife lays every care
　Low under ground.

While he with fops, sips tea with toasts;
　Airy, and gay, in his attire;
Whose pride, in age, and winter's frost,
　Can yield him fire.

Blest, who can unconcernedly find
　Days, hours, and years, glide soft away;
Who jokes, and laughs, with vacant mind,
　Though hairs grow grey.

No sleep by night — dancing and drink
　Together mixt, sweet recreation!
And making love, which witlings think
　Gives reputation.

Thus let me live, thus dance through life,
　Thus, unconnected, let me die;
Steal from the world, without a wife
　To LAUGH — *or* CRY!

Original Epitaph on a Drunkard

Pray who lies here? why don't you know,
'Tis stammering, staggering, boozy Joe;
What, dead at last? I thought that death
Could never stop his long long breath.
True, death ne'er threw his dart at him,
But kill'd, like David, with a *sling:*
Whither he's gone we do not know,
With spirits above or spirits below: —
But, if he former taste inherits,
He's quaffing in a world of spirits.

SAMUEL LOW
1765–?

To a Segar

Sweet antidote to sorrow, toil and strife,
Charm against discontent and wrinkled care,
Who knows thy power can never know despair;
Who knows thee not, one solace lacks of life:
When cares oppress, or when the busy day
Gives place to tranquil eve, a single puff
Can drive ev'n want and lassitude away,
And give a mourner happiness enough.
From thee when curling clouds of incense rise,
They hide each evil that in prospect lies;
But when in evanescence fades thy smoke,
Ah! what, dear sedative, my cares shall smother?
If thou evaporate, the charm is broke,
Till I, departing taper, light another.

JOHN QUINCY ADAMS
1767–1848

The Wants of Man

I

"MAN wants but little here below,
Nor wants that little long."
'Tis not with ME exactly so,
But 'tis so in the song.
My wants are many, and if told
Would muster many a score;
And were each wish a mint of gold,
I still should long for more.

II

What first I want is daily bread,
And canvas backs and wine;
And all the realms of nature spread
Before me when I dine.

20

Four courses scarcely can provide
    My appetite to quell,
With four choice cooks from France, beside,
    To dress my dinner well.

III

What next I want, at heavy cost,
    Is elegant attire; —
Black sable furs, for winter's frost,
    And silks for summer's fire,
And Cashmere shawls, and Brussels lace
    My bosom's front to deck,
And diamond rings my hands to grace,
    And rubies for my neck.

IV

And then I want a mansion fair,
    A dwelling house, in style,
Four stories high, for wholesome air —
    A massive marble pile;
With halls for banquets and balls,
    All furnished rich and fine;
With stabled studs in fifty stalls,
    And cellars for my wine.

V

I want a garden and a park,
    My dwelling to surround —
A thousand acres (bless the mark),
    With walls encompassed round —
Where flocks may range and herds may low,
    And kids and lambkins play,
And flowers and fruits commingled grow,
    All Eden to display.

VI

I want, when summer's foliage falls,
    And autumn strips the trees,
A house within the city's walls,
    For comfort and for ease.
But here, as space is somewhat scant,
    And acres somewhat rare,
My house in town I only want
    To occupy — a square.

VII

I want a steward, butler, cooks;
  A coachman, footman, grooms,
A library of well-bound books,
  And picture-garnished rooms;
Corregios, Magdalen, and Night,
  The matron of the chair;
Guido's fleet coursers in their flight,
  And Claudes at least a pair.

. . .

XIV

And when my bosom's darling sings,
  With melody divine,
A pedal harp of many strings
  Must with her voice combine.
A piano, exquisitely wrought,
  Must open stand, apart,
That all my daughters may be taught
  To win the stranger's heart.

XV

My wife and daughters will desire
  Refreshment from perfumes,
Cosmetics for the skin require,
  And artificial blooms.
The civit fragrance shall dispense,
  And treasur'd sweets return;
Cologne revive the flagging sense,
  And smoking amber burn.

XVI

And when at night my weary head
  Begins to droop and dose,
A southern chamber holds my bed,
  For nature's soft repose;
With blankets, counterpanes, and sheet,
  Mattrass, and bed of down,
And comfortables for my feet,
  And pillows for my crown.

XVII

I want a warm and faithful friend,
  To cheer the adverse hour,
Who ne'er to flatter will descend,
  Nor bend the knee to power;
A friend to chide me when I'm wrong,
  My inmost soul to see;
And that my friendship prove as strong
  For him, as his for me.

XVIII

I want a kind and tender heart,
  For others wants to feel;
A soul secure from Fortune's dart,
  And bosom arm'd with steel;
To bear divine chastisement's rod.
  And mingling in my plan,
Submission to the will of God,
  With charity to man.

XIX

I want a keen, observing eye,
  An ever-listening ear,
The truth through all disguise to spy,
  And wisdom's voice to hear;
A tongue, to speak at virtue's need,
  In Heaven's sublimest strain;
And lips, the cause of man to plead,
  And never plead in vain.

XX

I want uninterrupted health,
  Throughout my long career,
And streams of never-failing wealth,
  To scatter far and near;
The destitute to clothe and feed,
  Free bounty to bestow;
Supply the helpless orphan's need,
  And soothe the widow's woe.

XXI

I want the genius to conceive,
  The talents to unfold,

Designs, the vicious to retrieve,
  The virtuous to uphold;
Inventive power, combining skill,
  A persevering soul,
Of human hearts to mould the will,
  And reach from pole to pole.

XXII

I want the seals of power and place,
  The ensigns of command,
Charged by the people's unbought grace,
  To rule my native land.
Nor crown, nor sceptre would I ask
  But from my country's will,
By day, by night, to ply the task
  Her cup of bliss to fill.

XXIII

I want the voice of honest praise
  To follow me behind,
And to be thought in future days
  The friend of human kind;
That after ages, as they rise,
  Exulting may proclaim,
In choral union to the skies,
  Their blessings on my name.

XXIV

These are the wants of mortal man;
  I cannot want them long,
For life itself is but a span,
  And earthly bliss a song.
My last great want, absorbing all,
  Is, when beneath the sod,
And summon'd to my final call,
  The mercy of my God.

XXV

And oh! while circles in my veins
  Of life the purple stream,
And yet a fragment small remains
  Of nature's transient dream,

My soul, in humble hope unscar'd,
   Forget not thou to pray,
That this thy WANT may be prepared
   To meet the Judgment Day.

To Sally

The man in righteousness array'd,
   A pure and blameless liver,
Needs not the keen Toledo blade,
   Nor venom-freighted quiver.
What though he wind his toilsome way
   O'er regions wild and weary —
Through Zara's burning desert stray;
    Or Asia's jungles dreary:

What though he plough the billowy deep
   By lunar light, or solar,
Meet the resistless Simoon's sweep,
   Or iceberg circumpolar.
In bog or quagmire deep and dank,
   His foot shall never settle;
He mounts the summit of Mont Blanc,
   Or Popocatapetl.

On Chimborazo's breathless height,
   He treads o'er burning lava;
Or snuffs the Bohan Upas blight,
   The deathful plant of Java.
Through every peril he shall pass,
   By Virtue's shield protected;
And still by Truth's unerring glass
   His path shall be directed.

Else wherefore was it, Thursday last,
   While strolling down the valley
Defenceless, musing as I pass'd
   A canzonet to Sally;
A wolf, with mouth protruding snout,
   Forth from the thicket bounded —
I clapped my hands and raised a shout —
   He heard — and fled — confounded.

Tangier nor Tunis never bred
   An animal more crabbed;
Nor Fez, dry nurse of lions, fed
   A monster half so rabid.
Nor Ararat so fierce a beast
   Has seen, since days of Noah;
Nor strong, more eager for a feast,
   The fell constrictor boa.

Oh! place me where the solar beam
   Has scorch'd all verdure vernal;
Or on the polar verge extreme,
   Block'd up with ice eternal —
Still shall my voice's tender lays
   Of love remain unbroken;
And still my charming SALLY praise,
   Sweet smiling, and sweet spoken.

CLEMENT MOORE
1779–1863

A Visit from Saint Nicholas

'Twas the night before Christmas, when all through the house
Not a creature was stirring, not even a mouse;
The stockings were hung by the chimney with care,
In hopes that St. Nicholas soon would be there;
The children were nestled all snug in their beds,
While visions of sugar-plums danced in their heads;
And mamma in her kerchief, and I in my cap,
Had just settled our brains for a long winter's nap,
When out on the lawn there arose such a clatter,
I sprang from the bed to see what was the matter.
Away to the window I flew like a flash,
Tore open the shutters, and threw up the sash.
The moon on the breast of the new-fallen snow
Gave a luster of mid-day to objects below,
When, what to my wondering eyes should appear,
But a miniature sleigh, and eight tiny reindeer,
With a little old driver, so lively and quick,
I knew in a moment it must be St. Nick.

More rapid than eagles his coursers they came,
And he whistled, and shouted, and called them by name;
"Now, *Dasher!* now, *Dancer!* now, *Prancer* and *Vixen!*
On, *Comet!* on, *Cupid!* on, *Dunder* and *Blitzen!*
To the top of the porch! To the top of the wall!
Now, dash away! Dash away! Dash away all!"
As dry leaves that before the wild hurricane fly,
When they meet with an obstacle, mount to the sky;
So up to the housetop the coursers they flew,
With the sleigh full of toys, and St. Nicholas, too.
And then in a twinkling, I heard on the roof
The prancing and pawing of each little hoof.
As I drew in my head, and was turning around,
Down the chimney St. Nicholas came with a bound.
He was dressed all in fur, from his head to his foot,
And his clothes were all tarnished with ashes and soot;
A bundle of toys he had flung on his back,
And he looked like a peddler just opening his pack.
His eyes — how they twinkled! — his dimples how merry!
His cheeks were like roses, his nose like a cherry!
His droll little mouth was drawn up like a bow,
And the beard of his chin was as white as the snow;
The stump of a pipe he held tight in his teeth,
And the smoke it encircled his head like a wreath;
He had a broad face and a round little belly,
That shook when he laughed like a bowlful of jelly.
He was chubby and plump, a right jolly old elf,
And I laughed when I saw him, in spite of myself;
A wink of his eye and a twist of his head,
Soon gave me to know I had nothing to dread;
He spoke not a word, but went straight to his work,
And filled all the stockings; then turned with a jerk,
And laying his finger aside of his nose,
And giving a nod, up the chimney he rose;
He sprang to his sleigh, to his team gave a whistle,
And away they all flew like the down of a thistle;
But I heard him exclaim, ere he drove out of sight,
"Happy Christmas to all, and to all a good night!"

FRANCIS SCOTT KEY
1780–1843

To My Cousin Mary,
for Mending My Tobacco Pouch

My conscience has given me several twitches
For not having thanked my fair coz. for her stitches;
The pouch that contains the best part of my riches
She has made safe and sound by her excellent stitches;
And whenever I take it from waistcoat or breeches,
I enjoy my quid and admire the stitches.
She has sent me a note all in rhyme also, which is
Still more to be praised than these praise-worthy stitches.
I sometimes have seen "few and far between" stitches,
The stitchers of which should be thrown in the ditches,
For no one need care where such vile things he pitches,
And nothing's more vile than such stitchers and stitches;
Such stitchers were taught in a time scarce of switches,
Or they ne'er would have stitched such detestable stitches;
For this saying, I'm told, a sort of distich is
Among the most eminent teachers of stitches:
That experience proves "few and far between" switches
Will always produce "few and far between" stitches.
But my sweet cousin's skill so much me bewitches,
I must give her a sonnet in praise of her stitches:

Thy stitches are not "few and far between,"
    As other stitches very often are,
And many things beside, as I have seen,
    In this sad world where good things are so rare;
But they are even, neat, and close enough
    My treasured sweets to hold in purest plight;
To keep tobacco safe, and even snuff,
    And thus at once eyes, nose, and mouth delight.

They're like thy smiles, fair cousin, frequent, bright,
    They're like the rows of pearl those smiles display;
They're like the fingers that did make them, white
    And delicate, but not so long as they.

OR

They're like thy smiles, fair cousin, frequent, bright,
And ever bringing pleasure in their train;
They're like thy teeth of pearl, and their pure white,
Like them, shall never know tobacco's stain.

Then let me view my stores, and all the while
Look on thy stitches, thinking on thy smile —
But ah! those smiles in distance far are hid,
But here the stitches are — and I will take a quid.

Written at the White Sulphur Springs

A word of advice about matters and things
May be useful to people who come to these springs:
First, there's a bell in the morning that rings
To awaken the people who come to the springs,
And the folks fix their ribbons and tie up their strings,
And look very beautiful here at the springs.

There's an insect or two, called a flea, that here stings
The skins of the people who stay at the springs;
There's a broom and a half here, for nobody brings
Such implements here, to sweep out the springs;
There's a maid and a half, too, for one of them swings
Rather much to one side; for she's lame at the springs.

There's a bawling all day — but the ball at night clings
The most to my fancy of all at the springs —
To conclude, though some things here might do e'en for kings,
If you wish to fare well, say farewell to the springs.

FITZ-GREENE HALLECK
1790–1867

Fanny

XLVI

We owe the ancients something. You have read
    Their works, no doubt — at least in a translation;
Yet there was argument in what he said,
    I scorn equivocation or evasion,

And own it must, in candour, be confess'd,
They were an ignorant set of men at best.

XLVII

'Twas their misfortune to be born too soon
    By centuries, and in the wrong place too;
They never saw a steamboat, or balloon,
    Velocipede or Quarterly Review;
Or wore a pair of Baehr's black satin breeches,
Or read an Almanac, or Clinton's Speeches.

XLVIII

In short, in every thing we far outshine them, —
    Art, science, taste, and talent; and a stroll
Through this enlighten'd city would refine them
    More than ten years hard study of the whole
Their genius has produced of rich and rare —
God bless the Corporation and the Mayor!

XLIX

In sculpture, we've a grace the Grecian master,
    Blushing, had own'd his purest model lacks;
We've Mr. Bogart in the best of plaster,
    The Witch of Endor in the best of wax,
Besides the head of Franklin on the roof
Of Mr. Lang, both jest and weather proof.

L

And on our City Hall a Justice stands;
    A neater form was never made of board,
Holding majestically in her hands
    A pair of steelyards and a wooden sword;
And looking down with complaisant civility —
Emblem of dignity and durability.

LI

In painting, we have Trumbull's proud *chef d'œuvre*,
    Blending in one the funny and the fine:
His "Independence" will endure for ever,
    And so will Mr. Allen's lottery sign;
And all that grace the Academy of Arts,
From Dr. Hosack's face to Bonaparte's.

LII

In architecture, our unrivall'd skill
    Cullen's magnesian shop has loudly spoken
To an admiring world; and better still
    Is Gautier's fairy palace at Hoboken.
In music, we've the Euterpian Society,
And amateurs, a wonderful variety.

LIII

In physic, we have Francis and M'Neven,
    Famed for long heads, short lectures, and long bills;
And Quackenboss and others, who from heaven
    Were rain'd upon us in a shower of pills;
They'd beat the deathless Esculapius hollow,
And make a starveling druggist of Apollo.

LIV

And who, that ever slumber'd at the Forum,
    But owns the first of orators we claim;
Cicero would have bow'd the knee before 'em —
    And for law eloquence, we've Doctor Graham.
Compared with him, their Justins and Quintillians
Had dwindled into second-rate civilians.

LV

For purity and chastity of style,
    There's Pell's preface, and puffs by Horne and Waite.
For penetration deep, and learned toil,
    And all that stamps an author truly great,
Have we not Bristed's ponderous tomes? a treasure
For any man of patience and of leisure.

LVI

Oxonian Bristed! many a foolscap page
    He, in his time, hath written, and moreover
(What few will do in this degenerate age)
    Hath read his own works, as you may discover
By counting his quotations from himself —
You'll find the books on any auction shelf.

LVII

I beg Great Britain's pardon; 'tis not meant
    To claim this Oxford scholar as our own:

That he was shipp'd off here to represent
    Her literature among us, is well known;
And none could better fill the lofty station
Of Learning's envoy from the British nation.

LVIII

We fondly hope that he will be respected
    At home, and soon obtain a place or pension.
We should regret to see him live neglected,
    Like Fearon, Ashe, and others we could mention;
Who paid us friendly visits to abuse
Our country, and find food for the reviews.

LIX

But to return. — The Heliconian waters
    Are sparkling in their native fount no more,
And after years of wandering, the nine daughters
    Of poetry have found upon our shore
A happier home, and on their sacred shrines
Glow in immortal ink, the polish'd lines

LX

Of Woodworth, Doctor Farmer, Moses Scott —
    Names hallow'd by their reader's sweetest smile;
And who that reads at all has read them not?
    "That blind old man of Scio's rocky isle,"
Homer, was well enough; but would he ever
Have written, think ye, the Backwoodsman? Never.

LXI

Alas! for Paulding — I regret to see
    In such a stanza one whose giant powers,
Seen in their native element, will be
    Known to a future age, the pride of ours.
There is none breathing who can better wield
The battle-axe of satire. On its field

LXII

The wreath he fought for he has bravely won,
    Long be its laurel green around his brow!
It is too true, I'm somewhat fond of fun
    And jesting; but for once I'm serious now.

Why is he sipping weak Castalian dews?
The muse has damn'd him — let him damn the muse.

LXIII

But to return once more: the ancients fought
    Some tolerable battles. Marathon
Is still a theme for high and holy thought,
    And many a poet's lay. We linger on
The page that tells us of the brave and free,
And reverence thy name, unmatch'd Thermopylæ.

LXIV

And there were spirited troops in other days —
    The Roman legion and the Spartan band,
And Swartwout's gallant corps, the Iron Grays —
    Soldiers who met their foemen hand to hand,
Or swore, at least, to meet them undismay'd;
Yet what were these to General Laight's brigade

LXV

Of veterans? nursed in that Free School of glory,
    The New-York State Militia. From Bellevue,
E'en to the Battery flagstaff, the proud story
    Of their manœuvres at the last review
Has rang; and Clinton's "order" told afar
He never led a better corps to war.

LXVI

What, Egypt, was thy magic, to the tricks
    Of Mr. Charles, Judge Spencer, or Van Buren?
The first with cards, the last in politics,
    A conjuror's fame for years have been securing.
And who would now the Athenian dramas read
When he can get "Wall-street," by Mr. Mead.

LXVII

I might say much about our letter'd men,
    Those "grave and reverend seigniors," who compose
Our learn'd societies — but here my pen
    Stops short; for they themselves, the rumour goes,
The exclusive privilege by patent claim,
Of trumpeting (as the phrase is) their own fame.

LXVIII

And, therefore, I am silent. It remains
    To bless the hour the Corporation took it
Into their heads to give the rich in brains,
    The worn-out mansion of the poor in pocket,
Once "the old almshouse," now a school of wisdom,
Sacred to Scudder's shells and Dr. Griscom.

Song

There's a barrel of porter at Tammany Hall,
    And the bucktails are swigging it all the night long;
In the time of my boyhood 'twas pleasant to call
    For a seat and segar, mid the jovial throng.

That beer and those bucktails I never forget;
    But oft, when alone, and unnoticed by all,
I think, is the porter cask foaming there yet?
    Are the bucktails still swigging at Tammany Hall?

No! the porter was out long before it was stale,
    But some blossoms on many a nose brightly shone;
And the speeches inspired by the fumes of the ale,
    Had the fragrance of porter when porter was gone.

How much Cozzens will draw of such beer ere he dies,
    Is a question of moment to me and to all;
For still dear to my soul, as 'twas then to my eyes,
    Is that barrel of porter at Tammany Hall.

LYDIA HUNTLEY SIGOURNEY
1791–1865

God Save the Plough

See, — how the shining share
Maketh earth's bosom fair,
    Crowning her brow, —
Bread in its furrow springs,
Health and repose it brings,
Treasures unknown to kings,
    God save the plough!

Look to the warrior's blade,
While o'er the tented glade,
     Hate breathes his vow, —
Strife its unsheathing wakes,
Love at its lightning quakes,
Weeping and wo it makes,
     God save the plough!

Ships o'er the deep may ride,
Storms wreck their banner'd pride,
     Waves whelm their prow,
But the well-loaded wain
Garnereth the golden grain,
Gladdening the household train,
     God save the plough!

Who are the truly great?
Minions of pomp and state,
     Where the crowd bow?
Give us hard hands and free,
Culturers of field and tree,
Best friends of liberty —
     God save the plough!

GEORGE MOSES HORTON
?1797–?1883

New Fashions

There was a time when death was terror,
     Something harsh in every ear,
The tear left on the cheek a furrow,
     And every breath was drawn with fear;
Now the pall soon dies away,
Bury the dead and all be gay.

There was a time 'twas rare to marry,
     Wedding was a strange delight,
And the bride became a fairy,
     And the bridegroom an oddly sight;
Now the comic scenes are o'er,
And wedding flows from door to door.

35

There was a time that rare was danger,
   Dirks and pistols slept profound,
Thus sustain the harmless stranger,
   And the peasant was renowned;
Now all cry take care cut throat,
Long moustaches, caps and boots.

There was a time when rules were riches,
   Wives and husbands knew their own;
Women seldom wore the breeches,
   Left their husbands' ploughs alone;
Now tobacco rules have crossed,
And no one knows which chaws the most.

There was a time when peace was plenty,
   All the world could harmonize;
Few complained, not one in twenty,
   Of good peas and pumpkin pies;
Soda shortens now the meal,
Else you'll hear a dreadful peal.

There was a time when debts were paid up,
   Money was not then to make,
Nor for distant fortune laid up,
   Down the credit or the break;
Now insolvent pleas are made,
Take once the oath the debt is paid.

There was a time when health was nourished,
   And brandy was not but a name,
Thrifty men by labor flourished,
   And prudence mounted into fame;
Now large drinks all health oppose,
Man drinks awhile and down he goes.

There was a time when ladies swore not,
   Teasing their husbands for a dram,
Draughts of gin their bosoms bore not,
   Effusing from their lips a damn;
Now they swear, they drink and boast,
And the fairest drink the most.

There was a time when girls were fearful,
  Slow and backward truly proud,
Men in conversation careful,
  True they laughed but seldom loud;
Now their fear they all have lost,
And they solicit far the most.

Snaps for Dinner, Snaps for Breakfast, and Snaps for Supper

Come into dinner squalls the dame,
  You need it now perhaps;
But hear the husband's loud exclaim,
  I do not like your snaps;
'Tis snaps when at your breakfast meal,
  And snaps when at your spinning wheel,
Too many by a devilish deal,
  For all your words are snaps.

Why do you tarry, tell me why?
  The chamber door she taps,
Eat by yourself, my dear, for I
  Am surfeited with snaps;
For if I cough it is the cry,
  You always snap at supper time,
I'd rather lave in vats of lime,
  Than face you with your snaps.

How gladly would I be a book,
  To your long pocket flaps,
That you my face may read and look,
  And learn the worth of snaps;
I'm sorry that I learning lack,
  To turn you to an almanac;
Next year I'll hang you on the rack,
  And end the date of snaps.

RALPH WALDO EMERSON
1803–1882

Fable

The mountain and the squirrel
Had a quarrel,
And the former called the latter "Little Prig";
Bun replied,
"You are doubtless very big;
But all sorts of things and weather
Must be taken in together,
To make up a year
And a sphere.
And I think it no disgrace
To occupy my place.
If I'm not so large as you,
You are not so small as I,
And not half so spry.
I'll not deny you make
A very pretty squirrel track;
Talents differ; all is well and wisely put;
If I cannot carry forests on my back,
Neither can you crack a nut."

The Test

I hung my verses in the wind,
Time and tide their faults may find.
All were winnowed through and through,
Five lines lasted sound and true;
Five were smelted in a pot
Than the South more fierce and hot;
These the siroc could not melt,
Fire their fiercer flaming felt,
And the meaning was more white
Than July's meridian light.
Sunshine cannot bleach the snow,
Nor time unmake what poets know.
Have you eyes to find the five
Which five hundred did survive?

RALPH WALDO EMERSON

Solution

I am the Muse who sung alway
By Jove, at dawn of the first day.
Star-crowned, sole-sitting, long I wrought
To fire the stagnant earth with thought:
On spawning slime my song prevails,
Wolves shed their fangs, and dragons scales;
Flushed in the sky the sweet May-morn,
Earth smiled with flowers, and man was born.
Then Asia yeaned her shepherd race,
And Nile substructs her granite base, —
Tented Tartary, columned Nile, —
And, under vines, on rocky isle,
Or on wind-blown sea-marge bleak,
Forward stepped the perfect Greek:
That wit and joy might find a tongue,
And earth grow civil, HOMER sung.

Flown to Italy from Greece,
I brooded long and held my peace,
For I am wont to sing uncalled,
And in days of evil plight
Unlock doors of new delight;
And sometimes mankind I appalled
With a bitter horoscope,
With spasms of terror for balm of hope.
Then by better thought I lead
Bards to speak what nations need;
So I folded me in fears,
And DANTE searched the triple spheres,
Moulding Nature at his will,
So shaped, so colored, swift or still,
And, sculptor-like, his large design
Etched on Alp and Apennine.

Seethed in mists of Penmanmaur,
Taught by Plinlimmon's Druid power,
England's genius filled all measure
Of heart and soul, of strength and pleasure,
Gave to the mind its emperor,
And life was larger than before:

Nor sequent centuries could hit
Orbit and sum of SHAKSPEARE'S wit.
The men who lived with him became
Poets, for the air was fame.

Far in the North, where polar night
Holds in check the frolic light,
In trance upborne past mortal goal
The Swede EMANUEL leads the soul.
Through snows above, mines underground,
The inks of Erebus he found;
Rehearsed to men the damnèd wails
On which the seraph music sails.
In spirit-worlds he trod alone,
But walked the earth unmarked, unknown.
The near bystander caught no sound, —
Yet they who listened far aloof
Heard rendings of the skyey roof,
And felt, beneath, the quaking ground;
And his air-sown, unheeded words,
In the next age, are flaming swords.

In newer days of war and trade,
Romance forgot, and faith decayed,
When Science armed and guided war,
And clerks the Janus-gates unbar,
When France, where poet never grew,
Halved and dealt the globe anew,
GOETHE, raised o'er joy and strife,
Drew the firm lines of Fate and Life
And brought Olympian wisdom down
To court and mart, to gown and town.
Stooping, his finger wrote in clay
The open secret of to-day.

So bloom the unfading petals five,
And verses that all verse outlive.

Prudence

Theme no poet gladly sung,
Fair to old and foul to young;
Scorn not thou the love of parts,
And the articles of arts.
Grandeur of the perfect sphere
Thanks the atoms that cohere.

NATHANIEL PARKER WILLIS
1806–1867

The Lady Jane: A Humorous Novel in Rhyme

Canto I

. . .

XIX

Some men, 'tis said, prefer a woman fat.
   Lord Byron did. Some like her very spare.
Some like a lameness. (I have known one that
   Would go quite far enough for your despair,
And *halt* in time.) Some like them delicate
   As lilies, and with some "the only wear"
Is one whose sex has spoil'd a midshipman.
Some only like what pleased another man.

XX

I like one that *likes me*. But there's a kind
   Of women, very dangerous to poets,
Whose hearts beat with a truth that seems like mind —
   A nature that, though passionate, will show its
Devotion by not being rash or blind;
   But by sweet study grows to love. And so it's
Not odd if they are counted cold, though handsome,
And never meet a man who understands 'em.

XXI

By *never*, I mean late in life. But ah!
   How exquisite their love and friendship then!
Perennial of soul such women are,
   And readers of the hearts of gifted men;

And as the deep well mourns the hidden star,
  And mirrors the first ray that beams again,
They — be the loved light lost or dimly burning,
Feel all its clouds, and trust its bright returning.

XXII

In outward seeming tranquil and subdued,
  Their hearts beneath beat youthfully and fast.
Time and imprison'd love make not a prude;
  And warm the gift we know to be the last;
And pure is the devotion that must brood
  Upon *your* hopes alone — for *hers* are past!
Trust me, "a rising man" rose seldom higher,
But some dear, sweet old maid has pull'd the wire.

.   .   .

XCI

If, in well-bred society, ("hear! hear!")
  If, in this "wrong and pleasant" world of ours
There beats a pulse that seraphs may revere —
  If Eden's birds, when frighted from its flowers,
Clung to one deathless seed, still blooming here —
  If Time cut ever down, 'mid blighted hours,
A bliss that will spring up in bliss again —
'Tis woman's love. This I believe. Amen.

To the Lady in the Chemisette
with Black Buttons

I know not who thou art, oh lovely one!
Thine eyes were droop'd, thy lips half sorrowful.
Yet thou didst eloquently smile on me
While handing up thy sixpence through the hole
Of that o'er-freighted omnibus! Ah me!
The world is full of meetings such as this —
A thrill, a voiceless challenge and reply —
And sudden partings after! We may pass,
And know not of each other's nearness now —
Thou in the Knickerbocker Line, and I,
Lone, in the Waverley! Oh, life of pain!
And even should I pass where thou dost dwell —
Nay — see thee in the basement taking tea —
So cold is this inexorable world,

I must glide on! I dare not feast mine eye!
I dare not make articulate my love,
Nor o'er the iron rails that hem thee in
Venture to fling to thee my innocent card —
Not knowing thy papa!

                 Hast thou papa?
Is thy progenitor alive, fair girl?
And what doth he for lucre? Lo again!
A shadow o'er the face of this fair dream!
For thou mayst be as beautiful as Love
Can make thee, and the ministering hands
Of milliners, incapable of more,
Be lifted at thy shapeliness and air,
And still 'twixt me and thee, invisibly,
May rise a wall of adamant. My breath
Upon my pale lip freezes as I name
Manhattan's orient verge, and eke the west
In its far down extremity. Thy sire
May be the signer of a temperance pledge,
And clad all decently may walk the earth —
Nay — may be number'd with that blessed few
Who never ask for discount — yet, alas!
If, homeward wending from his daily cares,
He go by Murphy's Line, thence eastward tending —
Or westward from the Line of Kipp & Brown, —
My vision is departed! Harshly falls
The doom upon the ear, "She's not genteel!"
And pitiless is woman who doth keep
Of "good society" the golden key!
And gentlemen are bound, as are the stars,
To stoop not after rising!

                But farewell,
And I shall look for thee in streets where dwell
The passengers by Broadway Lines alone!
And if my dreams be true, and thou, indeed,
Art only not more lovely than genteel —
Then, lady of the snow-white chemisette,
The heart which vent'rously cross'd o'er to thee
Upon that bridge of sixpence, may remain —
And, with up-town devotedness and truth,
My love shall hover round thee!

The Declaration

'Twas late, and the gay company was gone,
And light lay soft on the deserted room
From alabaster vases, and a scent
Of orange leaves, and sweet verbena came
Through the unshutter'd window on the air,
And the rich pictures with their dark old tints
Hung like a twilight landscape, and all things
Seem'd hush'd into a slumber. Isabel,
The dark-eyed, spiritual Isabel
Was leaning on her harp, and I had stay'd
To whisper what I could not when the crowd
Hung on her look like worshippers. I knelt,
And with the fervor of a lip unused
To the cool breath of reason, told my love.
There was no answer, and I took the hand
That rested on the strings, and press'd a kiss
Upon it unforbidden — and again
Besought her, that this silent evidence
That I was not indifferent to her heart,
Might have the seal of one sweet syllable.
I kiss'd the small white fingers as I spoke,
And she withdrew them gently, and upraised
Her forehead from its resting-place, and look'd
Earnestly on me — *She had been asleep!*

To Helen in a Huff

Nay, lady, one frown is enough
　　In a life as soon over as this —
And though minutes seem long in a huff,
　　They're minutes 'tis pity to miss!
The smiles you imprison so lightly
　　Are reckon'd, like days in eclipse;
And though you may smile again brightly,
　　You've lost so much light from your lips!
　　　　Pray, lady, smile!

The cup that is longest untasted
　　May be with our bliss running o'er,

And, love when we will, we have wasted
  An age in not loving before!
Perchance Cupid's forging a fetter
  To tie us together some day,
And, just for the chance, we had better
  Be laying up love, I should say!
      Nay, lady, smile!

HENRY WADSWORTH LONGFELLOW
1807–1882

The Village Blacksmith

Under a spreading chestnut-tree
  The village smithy stands:
The smith, a mighty man is he,
  With large and sinewy hands;
And the muscles of his brawny arms
  Are strong as iron bands.

His hair is crisp, and black, and long,
  His face is like the tan;
His brow is wet with honest sweat,
  He earns whate'er he can,
And looks the whole world in the face,
  For he owes not any man.

Week in, week out, from morn till night,
  You can hear his bellows blow;
You can hear him swing his heavy sledge,
  With measured beat and slow,
Like a sexton ringing the village bell,
  When the evening sun is low.

And children coming home from school
  Look in at the open door;
They love to see the flaming forge,
  And hear the bellows roar,
And catch the burning sparks that fly
  Like chaff from a threshing-floor.

He goes on Sunday to the church,
    And sits among his boys;
He hears the parson pray and preach,
    He hears his daughter's voice,
Singing in the village choir,
    And it makes his heart rejoice.

It sounds to him like her mother's voice,
    Singing in Paradise!
He needs must think of her once more,
    How in the grave she lies;
And with his hard, rough hand he wipes
    A tear out of his eyes.

Toiling, — rejoicing, — sorrowing,
    Onward through life he goes;
Each morning sees some task begin,
    Each evening sees it close;
Something attempted, something done,
    Has earned a night's repose.

Thanks, thanks to thee, my worthy friend,
    For the lesson thou hast taught!
Thus at the flaming forge of life
    Our fortunes must be wrought;
Thus on its sounding anvil shaped
    Each burning deed and thought.

The Children's Hour

Between the dark and the daylight,
    When the night is beginning to lower,
Comes a pause in the day's occupations,
    That is known as the Children's Hour.

I hear in the chamber above me
    The patter of little feet,
The sound of a door that is opened,
    And voices soft and sweet.

From my study I see in the lamplight,
    Descending the broad hall stair,
Grave Alice, and laughing Allegra,
    And Edith with golden hair.

A whisper, and then a silence:
    Yet I know by their merry eyes
They are plotting and planning together
    To take me by surprise.

A sudden rush from the stairway,
    A sudden raid from the hall!
By three doors left unguarded
    They enter my castle wall!

They climb up into my turret
    O'er the arms and back of my chair;
If I try to escape, they surround me;
    They seem to be everywhere.

They almost devour me with kisses,
    Their arms about me entwine,
Till I think of the Bishop of Bingen
    In his Mouse-Tower on the Rhine!

Do you think, O blue-eyed banditti,
    Because you have scaled the wall,
Such an old mustache as I am
    Is not a match for you all!

I have you fast in my fortress,
    And will not let you depart,
But put you down into the dungeon
    In the round-tower of my heart.

And there will I keep you forever,
    Yes, forever and a day.
Till the walls shall crumble to ruin,
    And moulder in dust away!

Paul Revere's Ride

Listen, my children, and you shall hear
Of the midnight ride of Paul Revere,
On the eighteenth of April, in Seventy-five;
Hardly a man is now alive
Who remembers that famous day and year.

He said to his friend, "If the British march
By land or sea from the town tonight,
Hang a lantern aloft in the belfry arch
Of the North Church tower as a signal light, —
One, if by land, and two, if by sea;
And I on the opposite shore will be,
Ready to ride and spread the alarm
Through every Middlesex village and farm,
For the country folk to be up and to arm."

Then he said, "Good-night!" and with muffled oar
Silently rowed to the Charlestown shore.
Just as the moon rose over the bay,
Where swinging wide at her moorings lay
The Somerset, British man-of-war;
A phantom ship, with each mast and spar
Across the moon like a prison bar,
And a huge black hulk, that was magnified
By its own reflection in the tide.

Meanwhile, his friend, through alley and street,
Wanders and watches with eager ears.
Till in the silence around him he hears
The muster of men at the barrack door,
The sound of arms, and the tramp of feet,
And the measured tread of the grenadiers,
Marching down to their boats on the shore.

Then he climbed the tower of the Old North Church,
By the wooden stairs, with stealthy tread,
To the belfry-chamber overhead,
And startled the pigeons from their perch
On the sombre rafters, that round him made
Masses and moving shapes of shade, —

By the trembling ladder, steep and tall,
To the highest window in the wall,
Where he paused to listen and look down
A moment on the roofs of the town,
And the moonlight flowing over all.

Beneath, in the churchyard, lay the dead,
In their night-encampment on the hill,
Wrapped in silence so deep and still
That he could hear, like a sentinel's tread,
The watchful night-wind, as it went
Creeping along from tent to tent.
And seeming to whisper, "All is well!"
A moment only he feels the spell
Of the place and the hour, and the secret dread
Of the lonely belfry and the dead;
For suddenly all his thoughts are bent
On a shadowy something far away,
Where the river widens to meet the bay, —
A line of black that bends and floats
On the rising tide, like a bridge of boats.

Meanwhile, impatient to mount and ride,
Booted and spurred, with a heavy stride
On the opposite shore walked Paul Revere.
Now he patted his horse's side,
Now gazed at the landscape far and near,
Then, impetuous, stamped the earth,
And turned and tightened his saddle-girth;
But mostly he watched with eager search
The belfry-tower of the Old North Church,
As it rose above the graves on the hill,
Lonely and spectral and sombre and still.
And lo! as he looks, on the belfry's height
A glimmer, and then a gleam of light!
He springs to the saddle, the bridle he turns,
But lingers and gazes, till full on his sight
A second lamp in the belfry burns!

A hurry of hoofs in a village street,
A shape in the moonlight, a bulk in the dark,
And beneath, from the pebbles, in passing, a spark
Struck out by a steed flying fearless and fleet:

That was all! And yet, through the gloom and the light,
The fate of a nation was riding that night;
And the spark struck out by that steed in his flight,
Kindled the land into flame with its heat.

He has left the village and mounted the steep,
And beneath him, tranquil and broad and deep,
Is the Mystic, meeting the ocean tides;
And under the alders that skirt its edge,
Now soft on the sand, now loud on the ledge,
Is heard the tramp of his steed as he rides.

It was twelve by the village clock,
When he crossed the bridge into Medford town.
He heard the crowing of the cock,
And the barking of the farmer's dog,
And felt the damp of the river fog
That rises after the sun goes down.

It was one by the village clock,
When he galloped into Lexington.
He saw the gilded weathercock
Swim in the moonlight as he passed,
And the meeting-house windows, blank and bare,
Gaze at him with a spectral glare,
As if they already stood aghast
At the bloody work they would look upon.

It was two by the village clock,
When he came to the bridge in Concord town.
He heard the bleating of the flock,
And the twitter of birds among the trees,
And felt the breath of the morning breeze
Blowing over the meadows brown.
And one was safe and asleep in his bed
Who at the bridge would be first to fall,
Who that day would be lying dead,
Pierced by a British musket-ball.

You know the rest. In the books you have read,
How the British Regulars fired and fled, —
How the farmers gave them ball for ball,
From behind each fence and farm-yard wall,

Chasing the red-coats down the lane,
Then crossing the fields to emerge again
Under the trees at the turn of the road,
And only pausing to fire and load.

So through the night rode Paul Revere;
And so through the night went his cry of alarm
To every Middlesex village and farm, —
A cry of defiance and not of fear,
A voice in the darkness, a knock at the door,
And a word that shall echo forevermore!
For, borne on the night-wind of the Past,
Through all our history, to the last,
In the hour of darkness and peril and need,
The people will waken and listen to hear
The hurrying hoof-beats of that steed,
And the midnight message of Paul Revere.

JOHN GREENLEAF WHITTIER
1807–1892

The Haschish

Of all that Orient lands can vaunt
    Of marvels with our own competing,
The strangest is the Haschish plant,
    And what will follow on its eating.

What pictures to the taster rise,
    Of Dervish or of Almeh dances!
Of Eblis, or of Paradise,
    Set all aglow with Houri glances!

The poppy visions of Cathay,
    The heavy beer-trance of the Suabian;
The wizard lights and demon play
    Of nights Walpurgis and Arabian!

The Mollah and the Christian dog
    Change place in mad metempsychosis;
The Muezzin climbs the synagogue,
    The Rabbi shakes his beard at Moses!

The Arab by his desert well
   Sits choosing from some Caliph's daughters,
And hears his single camel's bell
   Sound welcome to his regal quarters.

The Koran's reader makes complaint
   Of Shitan dancing on and off it;
The robber offers alms, the saint
   Drinks Tokay and blasphemes the Prophet.

Such scenes that Eastern plant awakes;
   But we have one ordained to beat it.
The Haschish of the West, which makes
   Or fools or knaves of all who eat it.

The preacher eats, and straight appears
   His Bible in a new translation;
Its angels negro overseers,
   And Heaven itself a snug plantation!

The man of peace, about whose dreams
   The sweet millennial angels cluster,
Tastes the mad weed, and plots and schemes,
   A raving Cuban filibuster!

The noisiest Democrat, with ease,
   It turns to Slavery's parish beadle;
The shrewdest statesman eats and sees
   Due southward point the polar needle.

The Judge partakes, and sits erelong
   Upon his bench a railing blackguard;
Decides off-hand that right is wrong,
   And reads the ten commandments backward.

O potent plant! so rare a taste
   Has never Turk or Gentoo gotten;
The hempen Haschish of the East
   Is powerless to our Western Cotton!

Barbara Frietchie

This poem was written in strict conformity to the account of the incident as I had it from respectable and trustworthy sources. It has since been the subject of a good deal of conflicting testimony, and the story was probably incorrect in some of its details. It is admitted by all that Barbara Frietchie was no myth, but a worthy and highly esteemed gentlewoman, intensely loyal and a hater of the Slavery Rebellion, holding her Union flag sacred and keeping it with her Bible; that when the Confederates halted before her house, and entered her dooryard, she denounced them in vigorous language, shook her cane in their faces, and drove them out; and when General Burnside's troops followed close upon Jackson's, she waved her flag and cheered them. It is stated that May Quantrell, a brave and loyal lady in another part of the city, did wave her flag in sight of the Confederates. It is possible that there has been a blending of the two incidents.

Up from the meadows rich with corn,
Clear in the cool September morn,

The clustered spires of Frederick stand
Green-walled by the hills of Maryland.

Round about them orchards sweep,
Apple and peach tree fruited deep,

Fair as the garden of the Lord
To the eyes of the famished rebel horde,

On that pleasant morn of the early fall
When Lee marched over the mountain-wall;

Over the mountains winding down,
Horse and foot, into Frederick town.

Forty flags with their silver stars,
Forty flags with their crimson bars,

Flapped in the morning wind: the sun
Of noon looked down, and saw not one.

Up rose old Barbara Frietchie then,
Bowed with her fourscore years and ten;

Bravest of all in Frederick town,
She took up the flag the men hauled down;

In her attic window the staff she set,
To show that one heart was loyal yet.

Up the street came the rebel tread,
Stonewall Jackson riding ahead.

Under his slouched hat left and right
He glanced; the old flag met his sight.

"Halt!" — the dust-brown ranks stood fast.
"Fire!" — out blazed the rifle-blast.

It shivered the window, pane and sash;
It rent the banner with seam and gash.

Quick, as it fell, from the broken staff
Dame Barbara snatched the silken scarf,

She leaned far out on the window-sill,
And shook it forth with a royal will.

"Shoot, if you must, this old gray head,
But spare your country's flag," she said.

A shade of sadness, a blush of shame,
Over the face of the leader came;

The nobler nature within him stirred
To life at that woman's deed and word;

"Who touches a hair of yon gray head
Dies like a dog! March on!" he said.

All day long through Frederick street
Sounded the tread of marching feet:

All day long that free flag tost
Over the heads of the rebel host.

Ever its torn folds rose and fell
On the loyal winds that loved it well;

And through the hill-gaps sunset light
Shone over it with a warm good-night.

Barbara Frietchie's work is o'er,
And the Rebel rides on his raids no more.

Honor to her! and let a tear
Fall, for her sake, on Stonewall's bier.

Over Barbara Frietchie's grave,
Flag of Freedom and Union, wave!

Peace and order and beauty draw
Round thy symbol of light and law;

And ever the stars above look down
On thy stars below in Frederick town!

The Barefoot Boy

Blessings on thee, little man,
Barefoot boy, with cheek of tan!
With thy turned-up pantaloons,
And thy merry whistled tunes;
With thy red lip, redder still
Kissed by strawberries on the hill;
With the sunshine on thy face,
Through thy torn brim's jaunty grace;
From my heart I give thee joy, —
I was once a barefoot boy!
Prince thou art, — the grown-up man
Only is republican.
Let the million-dollared ride!
Barefoot, trudging at his side,
Thou hast more than he can buy
In the reach of ear and eye, —
Outward sunshine, inward joy:
Blessings on thee, barefoot boy!

Oh for boyhood's painless play,
Sleep that wakes in laughing day,
Health that mocks the doctor's rules,
Knowledge never learned of schools,
Of the wild bee's morning chase,
Of the wild-flower's time and place,
Flight of fowl and habitude
Of the tenants of the wood;
How the tortoise bears his shell,
How the woodchuck digs his cell,
And the ground-mole sinks his well;
How the robin feeds her young,
How the oriole's nest is hung;
Where the whitest lilies blow,
Where the freshest berries grow,

Where the ground-nut trails its vine,
Where the wood grape's clusters shine;
Of the black wasp's cunning way,
Mason of his walls of clay,
And the architectural plans
Of gray hornet artisans!
For, eschewing books and tasks,
Nature answers all he asks:
Hand in hand with her he walks,
Face to face with her he talks,
Part and parcel of her joy, —
Blessings on the barefoot boy!

Oh for boyhood's time of June,
Crowding years in one brief moon,
When all things I heard or saw,
Me, their master, waited for.
I was rich in flowers and trees,
Humming-birds and honey-bees;
For my sport the squirrel played,
Plied the snouted mole his spade;
For my taste the blackberry cone
Purpled over hedge and stone;
Laughed the brook for my delight
Through the day and through the night,
Whispering at the garden wall,
Talked with me from fall to fall;
Mine the sand-rimmed pickerel pond,
Mine the walnut slopes beyond,
Mine, on bending orchard trees,
Apples of Hesperides!
Still as my horizon grew,
Larger grew my riches too;
All the world I saw or knew
Seemed a complex Chinese toy,
Fashioned for a barefoot boy!

Oh for festal dainties spread,
Like my bowl of milk and bread;
Pewter spoon and bowl of wood,
On the door-stone, gray and rude!
O'er me, like a regal tent,

Cloudy-ribbed, the sunset bent,
Purple-curtained, fringed with gold,
Looped in many a wind-swung fold;
While for music came the play
Of the pied frogs' orchestra;
And, to light the noisy choir,
Lit the fly his lamp of fire.
I was monarch: pomp and joy
Waited on the barefoot boy!

Cheerily, then, my little man,
Live and laugh, as boyhood can!
Though the flinty slopes be hard,
Stubble-speared the new-mown sward,
Every morn shall lead thee through
Fresh baptisms of the dew;
Every evening from thy feet
Shall the cool wind kiss the heat:
All too soon these feet must hide
In the prison cells of pride,
Lose the freedom of the sod,
Like a colt's for work be shod,
Made to tread the mills of toil,
Up and down in ceaseless moil:
Happy if their track be found
Never on forbidden ground;
Happy if they sink not in
Quick and treacherous sands of sin.
Ah! that thou couldst know thy joy,
Ere it passes, barefoot boy!

Skipper Ireson's Ride

In the valuable and carefully prepared *History of Marblehead*, published in 1879 by Samuel Roads, Jr., it is stated that the crew of Captain Ireson, rather than himself, were responsible for the abandonment of the disabled vessel. To screen themselves they charged their captain with the crime. In view of this the writer of the ballad addressed the following letter to the historian: —

OAK KNOLL, DANVERS, 5 mo. 18, 1880.

MY DEAR FRIEND; I heartily thank thee for a copy of thy *History of Marblehead*. I have read it with great interest and think good use has been made of the abundant material. No town in Essex County has a record more honorable than Marblehead; no one has done more to develop the industrial interests of our New England seaboard, and certainly none have given such evidence of self-sacrificing patriotism. I am glad the story of it has been at last told, and told so well. I have now no doubt that thy version of Skipper Ireson's ride is the correct one. My verse was founded solely on a fragment of rhyme which I heard from one of my early schoolmates, a native of Marblehead.

I supposed the story to which it referred dated back at least a century. I knew nothing of the participators, and the narrative of the ballad was pure fancy. I am glad for the sake of truth and justice that the real facts are given in thy book. I certainly would not knowingly do injustice to any one, dead or living.

I am very truly thy friend,

JOHN G. WHITTIER.

Of all the rides since the birth of time,
Told in story or sung in rhyme, —
On Apuleius's Golden Ass,
Or one-eyed Calender's horse of brass,
Witch astride of a human back,
Islam's prophet on Al-Borák, —
The strangest ride that ever was sped
Was Ireson's, out from Marblehead!
   Old Floyd Ireson, for his hard heart,
   Tarred and feathered and carried in a cart
   By the women of Marblehead!

Body of turkey, head of owl,
Wings a-droop like a rained-on fowl,
Feathered and ruffled in every part,
Skipper Ireson stood in the cart.
Scores of women, old and young,
Strong of muscle, and glib of tongue,
Pushed and pulled up the rocky lane,
Shouting and singing the shrill refrain:
   "Here's Flud Oirson, fur his horrd horrt,
   Torr'd an' futherr'd an' corr'd in a corrt
   By the women o' Morble'ead!"

Wrinkled scolds with hands on hips,
Girls in bloom of cheek and lips,
Wild-eyed, free-limbed, such as chase
Bacchus round some antique vase,
Brief of skirt, with ankles bare,
Loose of kerchief and loose of hair,
With conch-shells blowing and fish-horns' twang,
Over and over the Mænads sang:
   "Here's Flud Oirson, fur his horrd horrt,
    Torr'd an' futherr'd an' corr'd in a corrt
     By the women o' Morble'ead!"

Small pity for him! — He sailed away
From a leaking ship in Chaleur Bay, —
Sailed away from a sinking wreck,
With his own town's-people on her deck!
"Lay by! lay by!" they called to him.
Back he answered, "Sink or swim!
Brag of your catch of fish again!"
And off he sailed through the fog and rain!
   Old Floyd Ireson, for his hard heart,
    Tarred and feathered and carried in a cart
     By the women of Marblehead!

Fathoms deep in dark Chaleur
That wreck shall lie forevermore.
Mother and sister, wife and maid,
Looked from the rocks of Marblehead
Over the moaning and rainy sea, —
Looked for the coming that might not be!
What did the winds and the sea-birds say
Of the cruel captain who sailed away? —
   Old Floyd Ireson, for his hard heart,
    Tarred and feathered and carried in a cart
     By the women of Marblehead!

Through the street, on either side,
Up flew windows, doors swung wide;
Sharp-tongued spinsters, old wives gray,
Treble lent the fish-horn's bray.
Sea-worn grandsires, cripple-bound,
Hulks of old sailors run aground,
Shook head, and fist, and hat, and cane,

And cracked with curses the hoarse refrain:
"Here's Flud Oirson, fur his horrd horrt,
Torr'd an' futherr'd an' corr'd in a corrt
    By the women o' Morble'ead!"

Sweetly along the Salem road
Bloom of orchard and lilac showed.
Little the wicked skipper knew
Of the fields so green and the sky so blue.
Riding there in his sorry trim,
Like an Indian idol glum and grim,
Scarcely he seemed the sound to hear
Of voices shouting, far and near:
    "Here's Flud Oirson, fur his horrd horrt,
    Torr'd an' futherr'd an' corr'd in a corrt
    By the women o' Morble'ead!"

"Hear me, neighbors!" at last he cried, —
"What to me is this noisy ride?
What is the shame that clothes the skin
To the nameless horror that lives within?
Waking or sleeping, I see a wreck,
And hear a cry from a reeling deck!
Hate me and curse me, — I only dread
The hand of God and the face of the dead!"
    Said old Floyd Ireson, for his hard heart,
    Tarred and feathered and carried in a cart
    By the women of Marblehead!

Then the wife of the skipper lost at sea
Said, "God has touched him! why should we!"
Said an old wife mourning her only son,
"Cut the rogue's tether and let him run!"
So with soft relentings and rude excuse,
Half scorn, half pity, they cut him loose,
And gave him a cloak to hide him in,
And left him alone with his shame and sin.
    Poor Floyd Ireson, for his hard heart,
    Tarred and feathered and carried in a cart
    By the women of Marblehead!

THOMAS HOLLEY CHIVERS
1809–1858

Lily Adair

On the beryl-rimmed rebecs of Ruby,
    Brought fresh from the hyaline streams,
She played, on the banks of the Yuba,
    Such songs as she heard in her dreams.
Like the heavens, when the stars from their eyries
    Look down through the ebon night air,
Where the groves by the Ouphantic Fairies
    Lit up for my Lily Adair —
    For my child-like Lily Adair —
    For my heaven-born Lily Adair —
For my beautiful, dutiful Lily Adair.

Like two rose-leaves in sunshine when blowing,
    Just curled softly, gently apart,
Were her lips by her passion, while growing
    In perfume on the stalk of her heart.
As mild as the sweet influences
    Of the Pleiades 'pregning the air —
More mild than the throned Excellencies
    Up in heaven, was my Lily Adair —
    Was my Christ-like Lily Adair —
    Was my lamb-like Lily Adair —
Was my beautiful, dutiful Lily Adair.

At the birth of this fair virgin Vestal,
    She was taken for Venus' child;
And her voice, though like diamond in crystal,
    Was not more melodious than mild.
Like the moon in her soft silver splendor,
    She was shrined in her own past compare,
For no Angel in heaven was more tender
    Than my beautiful Lily Adair —
    Than my dove-like Lily Adair —
    Than my saint-like Lily Adair —
Than my beautiful, dutiful Lily Adair.

Thus she stood on the arabesque borders
    Of the beautiful blossoms that blew
On the banks of the crystalline waters,
    Every morn, in the diaphane dew.

The flowers, they were radiant with glory,
   And shed such perfume on the air,
That my soul, now to want them, feels sorry,
   And bleeds for my Lily Adair —
   For my much-loved Lily Adair —
   For my long-lost Lily Adair —
For my beautiful, dutiful Lily Adair.

The Moon of Mobile

The Song that she sang was all written
   In rubies that sparkled like wine,
Like the Morning Star burning, new litten
   By the tablets of diamond divine.
Like some ravishing sound made from divers
   Sweet instruments fluting in June,
From her soul flowed those musical rivers
   Of Odin, called the rivers of Rune.
Then come to my bower, sweet Angel!
   Love's Fountain of Life to unseal; *
You shall live in this amber Evangel,
   Sweet Ellen! the Pride of Mobile!
Sweet Ellen! dear Ellen! the Maid of Mobile!
My Mary, mavourneen, the Moon of Mobile!

On the rhythmical rounds of the rhyming
   Of this Lyrical Ladder she rode,
Like an Angel that sings in his climbing
   To the Gates of the City of God.
Like the Gods when they feed on the blisses
   Of the undefiled glories above;
So my soul drank delight from the kisses
   Of the lips of my beautiful love.
Then come to my bower, sweet Angel!
   Love's fountain of life to unseal;
You shall live in this amber Evangel,
   Sweet Ellen! the Pride of Mobile!
Sweet Ellen! dear Ellen! the Maid of Mobile!
My Mary, mavourneen, the Moon of Mobile!

* "A garden enclosed is my sister, my spouse;
a spring shut up, a fountain sealed."
SOLOMON'S SONGS, IV, 12

Her soul sparkled bright through the azure
    Of her violet eyes full of light,
Like young Venus, long absent from pleasure,
    When Adonis first comes in her sight.
As the Angels clomb up, late at even,
    From the Bethel of Jacob above;
So, the Angels of thought go to Heaven
    On the rounds of the Ladder of Love.
Then come to my bower, sweet Angel!
    Love's Fountain of Life to unseal;
You shall live in this amber Evangel,
    Sweet Ellen! the Pride of Mobile!
Sweet Ellen! dear Ellen! the Maid of Mobile!
My Mary, mavourneen, the Moon of Mobile!

Prester John never sent, out of duty,
    From the City of Heaven, called Cansay,*
Any maiden so rich in all beauty,
    To the Lord of the Isles of Cathay.†
Like the Moon in her soft silver azure,
    Star-engirdled, sweet Queen of the Night!
So she stood in this Palace of Pleasure,
    Circled round by the Swans of Delight.
Then come to my bower, sweet Angel!
    Love's Fountain of Life to unseal;
You shall live in this amber Evangel,
    Sweet Ellen! the Pride of Mobile!
Sweet Ellen! dear Ellen! the Maid of Mobile!
    My Mary, mavourneen, the Moon of Mobile!

* Cansay or Kin-Sai, which signifies the City of Heaven. It was the capital of Southern China, under the dynasty of the Song.
† Ghenhis Khan, whose palace was built of pure gold, and ornamented with the finest of jewels.

OLIVER WENDELL HOLMES
1809–1899

The Height of the Ridiculous

I wrote some lines once on a time
    In wondrous merry mood,
And thought, as usual, men would say
    They were exceeding good.

They were so queer, so very queer,
　　I laughed as I would die;
Albeit, in the general way,
　　A sober man am I.

I called my servant, and he came;
　　How kind it was of him
To mind a slender man like me,
　　He of the mighty limb.

"These to the printer," I exclaimed,
　　And, in my humorous way,
I added, (as a trifling jest,)
　　"There'll be the devil to pay."

He took the paper, and I watched,
　　And saw him peep within;
At the first line he read, his face
　　Was all upon the grin.

He read the next; the grin grew broad,
　　And shot from ear to ear;
He read the third; a chuckling noise
　　I now began to hear.

The fourth; he broke into a roar;
　　The fifth; his waistband split;
The sixth; he burst five buttons off,
　　And tumbled in a fit.

Ten days and nights, with sleepless eye,
　　I watched that wretched man,
And since, I never dare to write
　　As funny as I can.

Æstivation

An Unpublished Poem, by My Late Latin Tutor

Your talking Latin — said I — reminds me of an odd trick of one of my old tutors. He read so much of that language, that his English half turned into it. He got caught in town, one hot summer, in pretty close quarters, and wrote, or began to write, a series of city pastorals. Eclogues he called them, and meant to have published them by subscription. I remember some of his verses, if you want to hear them. — You, Sir (addressing myself to the divinity-student), and all such as have been through college, or what is the same thing, received an honorary degree, will understand them without a dictionary. The old man had a great deal to say about "æstivation," as he called it, in opposition, as one might say, to *hibernation*. Intramural æstivation, or townlife in summer, he would say, is a peculiar form of suspended existence, or semi-asphyxia. One wakes up from it about the beginning of the last week in September. This is what I remember of his poem: —

> In candent ire the solar splendor flames;
> The foles, languescent, pend from arid rames;
> His humid front the cive, anheling, wipes,
> And dreams of erring on ventiferous ripes.
>
> How dulce to vive occult to mortal eyes,
> Dorm on the herb with none to supervise,
> Carp the suave berries from the crescent vine,
> And bibe the flow from longicaudate kine!
>
> To me, alas! no verdurous visions come,
> Save yon exiguous pool's conferva-scum, —
> No concave vast repeats the tender hue
> That laves my milk-jug with celestial blue!
>
> Me wretched! Let me curr to quercine shades!
> Effund your albid hausts, lactiferous maids!
> Oh, might I vole to some umbrageous clump, —
> Depart, — be off, — excede, — evade, — erump!

The Deacon's Masterpiece

Or, the wonderful "One-Hoss Shay"

A logical story

[The following note was prefaced to the poem when it appeared in an illustrated edition.]

"The Wonderful One-Hoss Shay" is a perfectly intelligible conception, whatever material difficulties it presents. It is conceivable that a being of an order superior to humanity should so understand the conditions of matter that he could construct a machine which should go to pieces, if not into its constituent atoms, at a given moment of the future. The mind may take a certain pleasure in this picture of the impossible. The event follows as a logical consequence of the presupposed condition of things.

There is a practical lesson to be got out of the story. Observation shows us in what point any particular mechanism is most likely to give way. In a wagon, for instance, the weak point is where the axle enters the hub or nave. When the wagon breaks down, three times out of four, I think, it is at this point that the accident occurs. The workman should see to it that this part should never give way; then find the next vulnerable place, and so on, until he arrives logically at the perfect result attained by the deacon.

Have you heard of the wonderful one-hoss shay,
That was built in such a logical way
It ran a hundred years to a day,
And then, of a sudden, it — ah, but stay,
I'll tell you what happened without delay,
Scaring the parson into fits,
Frightening people out of their wits, —
Have you ever heard of that, I say?

Seventeen hundred and fifty-five.
Georgius Secundus was then alive, —
Snuffy old drone from the German hive.
That was the year when Lisbon-town
Saw the earth open and gulp her down,
And Braddock's army was done so brown,
Left without a scalp to its crown.
It was on the terrible Earthquake-day
That the Deacon finished the one-hoss shay.

Now in building of chaises, I tell you what,
There is always *somewhere* a weakest spot, —
In hub, tire, felloe, in spring or thill,
In panel, or crossbar, or floor, or sill,
In screw, bolt, thoroughbrace, — lurking still,
Find it somewhere you must and will, —
Above or below, or within or without, —
And that's the reason, beyond a doubt,
That a chaise *breaks down*, but does n't *wear out.*

But the Deacon swore (as Deacons do,
With an "I dew vum," or an "I tell *yeou*")

He would build one shay to beat the taown
'N' the keounty 'n' all the kentry raoun';
It should be so built that it *could n'* break daown:
"Fur," said the Deacon, " 't's mighty plain
Thut the weakes' place mus' stan' the strain;
'N' the way t' fix it, uz I maintain, is only jest
T' make that place uz strong uz the rest."

So the Deacon inquired of the village folk
Where he could find the strongest oak,
That could n't be split nor bent nor broke, —
That was for spokes and floor and sills;
He sent for lancewood to make the thills;
The crossbars were ash, from the straightest trees,
The panels of white-wood, that cuts like cheese,
But lasts like iron for things like these;
The hubs of logs from the "Settler's ellum," —
Last of its timber, — they couldn't sell 'em.

Never an axe had seen their chips,
And the wedges flew from between their lips,
Their blunt ends frizzled like celery-tips;
Step and prop-iron, bolt and screw,
Spring, tire, axle, and linchpin too,
Steel of the finest, bright and blue;
Thoroughbrace bison-skin, thick and wide;
Boot, top, dasher, from tough old hide
Found in the pit when the tanner died.
That was the way he "put her through."
"There!" said the Deacon, "naow she'll dew!"

Do! I tell you, I rather guess
She was a wonder, and nothing less!
Colts grew horses, beards turned gray,
Deacon and deaconess dropped away,
Children and grandchildren — where were they?
But there stood the stout old one-hoss shay
As fresh as on Lisbon-earthquake-day!

Eighteen hundred; — it came and found
The Deacon's masterpiece strong and sound.
Eighteen hundred increased by ten; —
"Hahnsum kerridge" they called it then.

Eighteen hundred and twenty came; —
Running as usual; much the same.
Thirty and forty at last arrive,
And then come fifty, and FIFTY-FIVE.

Little of all we value here
Wakes on the morn of its hundredth year
Without both feeling and looking queer.
In fact, there's nothing that keeps its youth,
So far as I know, but a tree and truth.
(This is a moral that runs at large;
Take it. — You're welcome. — No extra charge.)

FIRST OF NOVEMBER, — the Earthquake day, —
There are traces of age in the one-hoss shay.
A general flavor of mild decay,
But nothing local, as one may say.
There couldn't be, — for the Deacon's art
Had made it so like in every part
That there was n't a chance for one to start.
For the wheels were just as strong as the thills,
And the floor was just as strong as the sills,
And the panels just as strong as the floor,
And the whipple-tree neither less nor more,
And the back crossbar as strong as the fore,
And spring and axle and hub *encore*.
And yet, *as a whole*, it is past a doubt
In another hour it will be *worn out!*

First of November, 'Fifty-five!
This morning the parson takes a drive.
Now, small boys, get out of the way!
Here comes the wonderful one-hoss shay,
Drawn by a rat-tailed, ewe-necked bay.
"Huddup!" said the parson. — Off went they.
The parson was working his Sunday's text, —
Had got to *fifthly*, and stopped perplexed
At what the — Moses — was coming next.
All at once the horse stood still,
Close by the meet'n'-house on the hill.
First a shiver, and then a thrill,
Then something decidedly like a spill, —
And the parson was sitting upon a rock,

At half past nine by the meet'n'-house clock, —
Just the hour of the Earthquake shock!
What do you thing the parson found,
When he got up and stared around?
The poor old chaise in a heap or mound,
As if it had been to the mill and ground!
You see, of course, if you're not a dunce,
How it went to pieces all at once, —
All at once, and nothing first, —
Just as bubbles do when they burst.

End of the wonderful one-hoss shay.
Logic is logic. That's all I say.

Ode for a Social Meeting

With Slight Alterations by a Teetotaler

Here is a little poem I sent a short time since to a committee for a certain celebration. I understood that it was to be a festive and convivial
occasion, and ordered myself accordingly. It seems the president of the
day was what is called a "teetotaler." I received a note from him in the
following words, containing the copy subjoined, with the emendations
annexed to it.

"Dear Sir, — Your poem gives good satisfaction to the committee.
The sentiments expressed with reference to liquor are not, however,
those generally entertained by this community. I have therefore con-
sulted the clergyman of this place, who has made some slight changes,
which he thinks will remove all objections, and keep the valuable portions of the poem. Please to inform me of your charge for said poem.
Our means are limited, etc., etc., etc.

"Yours with respect."

Here it is with the slight alterations.

Come! fill a fresh bumper, for why should we go
       logwood
While the ~~nectar~~ still reddens our cups as they flow?
       decoction
Pour out the ~~rich juices~~ still bright with the sun,
       dye-stuff
Till o'er the brimmed crystal the ~~rubies~~ shall run.

half-ripened apples
The ~~purple-globed clusters~~ their life-dews have bled;
     taste   sugar of lead.
How sweet is the ~~breath~~ of the ~~fragrance they shed!~~
    rank poisons   *wines! ! !*
For summer's ~~last roses~~ lie hid in the ~~wines~~
                 stable-boys smoking long-nines.
That were garnered by ~~maidens who laughed thro' the vines.~~
   scowl   howl   scoff   sneer,
Then a ~~smile,~~ and a ~~glass,~~ and a ~~toast,~~ and a ~~cheer,~~
   strychnine and whiskey, and ratsbane and beer!
For all ~~the good wine, and we've some of it here!~~
In cellar, in pantry, in attic, in hall,
   Down, down with the tyrant that masters us all !
~~Long live the gay servant that laughs for us all!~~

A Sea Dialogue
November 10, 1864

CABIN PASSENGER   Friend, you seem thoughtful. I not wonder much
That he who sails the ocean should be sad.
I am myself reflective. When I think
Of all this wallowing beast, the Sea, has sucked
Between his sharp thin lips, the wedgy waves,
What heaps of diamonds, rubies, emeralds, pearls;
What piles of shekels, talents, ducats, crowns,
What bales of Tyrian mantles, Indian shawls,
Of laces that have blanked the weavers' eyes,
Of silken tissues, wrought by worm and man,
The half-starved workman, and the well-fed worm;
What marbles, bronzes, pictures, parchments, books;
What many-lobuled, thought-engendering brains;
Lie with the gaping sea-shells in his maw, —
I, too, am silent; for all language seems
A mockery, and the speech of man is vain.
O mariner, we look upon the waves
And they rebuke our babbling. "Peace!" they say, —
"Mortal, be still!" My noisy tongue is hushed,
And with my trembling finger on my lips
My soul exclaims in ecstasy —

MAN AT WHEEL   Belay!

CABIN PASSENGER   Ah yes! "Delay," — it calls, "nor haste to break
The charm of stillness with an idle word!"
O mariner, I love thee, for thy thought
Strides even with my own, nay, flies before.
Thou art a brother to the wind and wave;
Have they not music for thine ear as mine,
When the wild tempest makes thy ship his lyre,
Smiting a cavernous basso from the shrouds
And climbing up his gamut through the stays,
Through buntlines, bowlines, ratlines, till it shrills
An alto keener than the locust sings,
And all the great Æolian orchestra
Storms out its mad sonata in the gale?
Is not the scene a wondrous and —

MAN AT WHEEL   Avast!

CABIN PASSENGER   Ah yes, a vast, a vast and wondrous scene!
I see thy soul is open as the day
That holds the sunshine in its azure bowl
To all the solemn glories of the deep.
Tell me, O mariner, dost thou never feel
The grandeur of thine office, — to control
The keel that cuts the ocean like a knife
And leaves a wake behind it like a seam
In the great shining garment of the world?

MAN AT WHEEL   Belay y'r jaw, y' swab! y' hoss-marine!

(To the Captain.)

Ay, ay, Sir! Stiddy, Sir! Sou'wes'b'sou'!

EDGAR ALLAN POE
1809–1849

The Bells

I
Hear the sledges with the bells —
Silver bells!
What a world of merriment their melody foretells!
How they tinkle, tinkle, tinkle,
In the icy air of night!

While the stars that oversprinkle
All the heavens, seem to twinkle
With a crystalline delight;
Keeping time, time, time,
In a sort of Runic rhyme,
To the tintinnabulation that so musically wells
From the bells, bells, bells, bells,
Bells, bells, bells —
From the jingling and the tinkling of the bells.

II

Hear the mellow wedding bells
Golden bells!
What a world of happiness their harmony foretells!
Through the balmy air of night
How they ring out their delight! —
From the molten-golden notes,
And all in tune,
What a liquid ditty floats
To the turtle-dove that listens, while she gloats
On the moon!
Oh, from out the sounding cells,
What a gush of euphony voluminously wells!
How it swells!
How it dwells
On the Future! — how it tells
Of the rapture that impels
To the swinging and the ringing
Of the bells, bells, bells —
Of the bells, bells, bells, bells,
Bells, bells, bells —
To the rhyming and the chiming of the bells!

III

Hear the loud alarum bells —
Brazen bells!
What a tale of terror, now their turbulency tells!
In the startled ear of night
How they scream out their affright!
Too much horrified to speak,
They can only shriek, shriek,
Out of tune,
In a clamorous appealing to the mercy of the fire,

In a mad expostulation with the deaf and frantic fire,
Leaping higher, higher, higher,
With a desperate desire,
And a resolute endeavour
Now — now to sit, or never,
By the side of the pale-faced moon.
Oh, the bells, bells, bells!
What a tale their terror tells
Of Despair!
How they clang, and clash, and roar!
What a horror they outpour
On the bosom of the palpitating air!
Yet the ear, it fully knows,
By the twanging,
And the clanging,
How the danger ebbs and flows;
Yet the ear distinctly tells,
In the jangling,
And the wrangling,
How the danger sinks and swells,
By the sinking or the swelling in the anger of the bells —
Of the bells —
Of the bells, bells, bells, bells,
Bells, bells, bells —
In the clamor and the clanging of the bells!

IV
Hear the tolling of the bells —
Iron bells!
What a world of solemn thought their monody compels!
In the silence of the night,
How we shiver with affright
At the melancholy menace of their tone!
For every sound that floats
From the rust within their throats
Is a groan.
And the people — ah, the people —
They that dwell up in the steeple,
All alone,
And who, tolling, tolling, tolling,
In that muffled monotone,
Feel a glory in so rolling
On the human heart a stone —

They are neither man nor woman —
They are neither brute nor human —
   They are Ghouls: —
And their king it is who tolls: —
And he rolls, rolls, rolls,
     Rolls
   A pæan from the bells;
And his merry bosom swells
   With the pæan of the bells!
And he dances, and he yells;
Keeping time, time, time,
In a sort of Runic rhyme,
   To the pæan of the bells: —
    Of the bells:
Keeping time, time, time
In a sort of Runic rhyme,
   To the throbbing of the bells —
Of the bells, bells, bells —
   To the sobbing of the bells: —
Keeping time, time, time,
   As he knells, knells, knells,
In a happy Runic rhyme,
   To the rolling of the bells —
   Of the bells, bells, bells: —
   To the tolling of the bells —
Of the bells, bells, bells, bells,
   Bells, bells, bells —
To the moaning and the groaning of the bells.

JAMES THOMAS FIELDS
1817–1881

The Owl Critic

"Who stuffed that white owl?" No one spoke in the shop:
The barber was busy, and he couldn't stop;
The customers, waiting their turns, were all reading
The "Daily," the "Herald," the "Post," little heeding
The young man who blurted out such a blunt question;
Not one raised a head, or even made a suggestion;
   And the barber kept on shaving.

"Don't you see, Mister Brown,"
Cried the youth, with a frown,
"How wrong the whole thing is,
How preposterous each wing is,
How flattened the head is, how jammed down the neck is —
In short, the whole owl, what an ignorant wreck 't is!
I make no apology;
I've learned owl-eology.
I've passed days and nights in a hundred collections,
And cannot be blinded to any deflections
Arising from unskilful fingers that fail
To stuff a bird right, from his beak to his tail.
Mister Brown! Mister Brown!
Do take that bird down,
Or you'll soon be the laughing-stock all over town!"
              And the barber kept on shaving.

"I've *studied* owls,
And other night fowls,
And I tell you
What I know to be true:
An owl cannot roost
With his limbs so unloosed;
No owl in this world
Ever had his claws curled,
Ever had his legs slanted,
Ever had his bill canted,
Ever had his neck screwed
Into that attitude.
He can't *do* it, because
'T is against all bird-laws.
Anatomy teaches,
Ornithology preaches
An owl has a toe
That *can't* turn out so!
I've made the white owl my study for years,
And to see such a job almost moves me to tears!
Mister Brown, I'm amazed
You should be so gone crazed
As to put up a bird
In that posture absurd!
To *look* at that owl really brings on a dizziness;
The man who stuffed *him* don't half know his business!"
              And the barber kept on shaving.

75

"Examine those eyes.
I'm filled with surprise
Taxidermists should pass
Off on you such poor glass;
So unnatural they seem
They'd make Audubon scream,
And John Burroughs laugh
To encounter such chaff.
Do take that bird down;
Have him stuffed again, Brown!"
                    And the barber kept on shaving.

"With some sawdust and bark
I could stuff in the dark
An owl better than that.
I could make an old hat
Look more like an owl
Than that horrid fowl,
Stuck up there so stiff like a side of coarse leather.
In fact, about *him* there's not one natural feather."

Just then, with a wink and a sly normal lurch,
The owl, very gravely, got down from his perch,
Walked round, and regarded his fault-finding critic
(Who thought he was stuffed) with a glance analytic,
And then fairly hooted, as if he should say:
"Your learning's at fault *this* time, any way;
Don't waste it again on a live bird, I pray.
I'm an owl; you're another. Sir Critic, good-day!"
                    And the barber kept on shaving.

Jupiter and Ten

Mrs. Chub was rich and portly,
    Mrs. Chub was very grand,
Mrs. Chub was always reckoned
    A lady in the land.

You shall see her marble mansion
    In a very stately square, —
Mr. C. knows what it cost him,
    But that's neither here nor there.

Mrs. Chub was so sagacious,
  Such a patron of the arts,
And she gave such foreign orders,
  That she won all foreign hearts.

Mrs. Chub was always talking,
  When she went away from home,
Of a prodigious painting
  Which had just arrived from Rome.

"Such a treasure," she insisted,
  "One might never see again!"
"What's the subject?" we inquired.
  "It is Jupiter and Ten!"

"Ten *what?*" we blandly asked her,
  For the knowledge we did lack.
"Ah! that I cannot tell you,
  But the name is on the back.

"There it stands in printed letters.
  Come to-morrow, gentlemen,
Come and see our splendid painting,
  Our fine *Jupiter and Ten.*"

When Mrs. Chub departed,
  Our brains we all did rack, —
She could not be mistaken,
  For the name was on the back.

So we begged a great Professor
  To lay aside his pen,
And give some information
  Touching "Jupiter and Ten."

And we pondered well the subject,
  And our Lemprière we turned,
To discover what the *Ten* were;
  But we could not, though we burned!

But when we saw the picture, —
  Oh, Mrs. Chub! Oh, fie! Oh!
We perused the printed label,
  And 't was *Jupiter and Io!*

JAMES RUSSELL LOWELL
1819–1891

In an Album

The misspelt scrawl, upon the wall
By some Pompeian idler traced,
In ashes packed (ironic fact!)
Lies eighteen centuries uneffaced,
While many a page of bard and sage,
Deemed once mankind's immortal gain,
Lost from Time's ark, leaves no more mark
Than a keel's furrow through the main.

O Chance and Change! our buzz's range
Is scarcely wider than a fly's;
Then let us play at fame to-day,
To-morrow be unknown and wise;
And while the fair beg locks of hair,
And autographs, and Lord knows what,
Quick! let us scratch our moment's match,
Make our brief blaze, and be forgot!

Too pressed to wait, upon her slate
Fame writes a name or two in doubt;
Scarce written, these no longer please,
And her own finger rubs them out:
It may ensue, fair girl, that you
Years hence this yellowing leaf may see,
And put to task, your memory ask
In vain, "This Lowell, who was he?"

A Misconception

B, taught by Pope to do his good by stealth,
'Twixt participle and noun no difference feeling,
In office placed to serve the Commonwealth,
Does himself all the good he can by stealing.

78

The Boss

Skilled to pull wires, he baffles Nature's hope,
Who sure intended him to stretch a rope.

from *The Biglow Papers*

The Courtin'

God makes sech nights, all white an' still
    Fur 'z you can look or listen,
Moonshine an' snow on field an' hill,
    All silence an' all glisten.

Zekle crep' up quite unbeknown
    An' peeked in thru' the winder,
An' there sot Huldy all alone,
    'Ith no one nigh to hender.

A fireplace filled the room's one side
    With half a cord o' wood in —
There warn't no stoves (tell comfort died)
    To bake ye to a puddin'.

The wa'nut logs shot sparkles out
    Towards the pootiest, bless her,
An' leetle flames danced all about
    The chiny on the dresser.

Agin the chimbley crook-necks hung,
    An' in amongst 'em rusted
The ole queen's-arm thet gran'ther Young
    Fetched back f'om Concord busted.

The very room, coz she was in,
    Seemed warm f'om floor to ceilin',
An' she looked full ez rosy agin
    Ez the apples she was peelin'.

'T was kin' o' kingdom-come to look
 On sech a blessed cretur,
A dogrose blushin' to a brook
 Ain't modester nor sweeter.

He was six foot o' man, A 1,
 Clear grit an' human natur',
None couldn't quicker pitch a ton
 Nor dror a furrer straighter.

He'd sparked it with full twenty gals,
 He'd squired 'em, danced 'em, druv 'em,
Fust this one, an' then thet, by spells —
 All is, he could n't love 'em.

But long o' her his veins 'ould run
 All crinkly like curled maple,
The side she breshed felt full o' sun
 Ez a south slope in Ap'il.

She thought no v'ice hed sech a swing
 Ez hisn in the choir;
My! when he made Ole Hunderd ring,
 She *knowed* the Lord was nigher.

An' she'd blush scarlit, right in prayer,
 When her new meetin'-bunnet
Felt somehow thru' its crown a pair
 O' blue eyes sot upon it.

Thet night, I tell ye, she looked *some!*
 She seemed to 've gut a new soul,
For she felt sartin-sure he'd come,
 Down to her very shoe-sole.

She heered a foot, an' knowed it tu,
 A-raspin' on the scraper, —
All ways to once her feelins flew
 Like sparks in burnt-up paper.

He kin' o' l'itered on the mat
 Some doubtfle o' the sekle,
His heart kep' goin' pity-pat,
 But hern went pity Zekle.

An' yit she gin her cheer a jerk
  Ez though she wished him furder,
An' on her apples kep' to work,
  Parin' away like murder.

"You want to see my Pa, I s'pose?"
  "Wal . . . no . . . I come dasignin' " —
"To see my Ma? She's sprinklin' clo'es
  Agin to-morrer's i'nin'. "

To say why gals act so or so,
  Or don't, 'ould be persumin';
Mebby to mean *yes* an' say *no*
  Comes nateral to women.

He stood a spell on one foot fust,
  Then stood a spell on t' other,
An' on which one he felt the wust
  He could n't ha' told ye nuther.

Says he, "I'd better call agin;"
  Says she, "Think likely, Mister."
Thet last word pricked him like a pin,
  An' . . . Wal, he up an' kist her.

When Ma bimeby upon 'em slips,
  Huldy sot pale ez ashes,
All kin' o' smily roun' the lips
  An' teary roun' the lashes.

For she was jes' the quiet kind
  Whose naturs never vary,
Like streams that keep a summer mind
  Snowhid in Jenooary.

The blood clost roun' her heart felt glued
  Too tight for all expressin',
Tell mother see how metters stood,
  An' gin 'em both her blessin'.

Then her red come back like the tide
  Down to the Bay o' Fundy,
An' all I know is they was cried
  In meetin' come nex' Sunday.

Rev. Homer Wilbur's "Festina Lente"

Once on a time there was a pool
Fringed all about with flag-leaves cool
And spotted with cow-lilies garish,
Of frogs and pouts the ancient parish.
Alders the creaking redwings sink on,
Tussocks that house blithe Bob o' Lincoln
Hedged round the unassailed seclusion,
Where muskrats piled their cells Carthusian;
And many a moss-embroidered log,
The watering-place of summer frog,
Slept and decayed with patient skill,
As watering-places sometimes will.

Now in this Abbey of Theleme,
Which realized the fairest dream
That ever dozing bull-frog had,
Sunned on a half-sunk lily-pad,
There rose a party with a mission
To mend the polliwogs' condition,
Who notified the sélectmen
To call a meeting there and then.
"Some kind of steps," they said, "are needed;
They don't come on so fast as we did:
Let's dock their tails; if that don't make 'em
Frogs by brevet, the Old One take 'em!
That boy, that came the other day
To dig some flag-root down this way,
His jack-knife left, and 't is a sign
That Heaven approves of our design:
'T were wicked not to urge the step on,
When Providence has sent the weapon."

Old croakers, deacons of the mire,
That led the deep batrachian choir,
Uk! Uk! Caronk! with bass that might
Have left Lablache's out of sight,
Shook nobby heads, and said, "No go!
You'd better let 'em try to grow:
Old Doctor Time is slow, but still
He does know how to make a pill."

But vain was all their hoarsest bass,
Their old experience out of place,
And spite of croaking and entreating,
The vote was carried in marsh-meeting.

"Lord knows," protest the polliwogs,
"We're anxious to be grown-up frogs;
But don't push in to do the work
Of Nature till she prove a shirk;
'T is not by jumps that she advances,
But wins her way by circumstances:
Pray, wait awhile, until you know
We're so contrived as not to grow;
Let Nature take her own direction,
And she'll absorb our imperfection;
You might n't like 'em to appear with,
But we must have the things to steer with."

"No," piped the party of reform,
"All great results are ta'en by storm;
Fate holds her best gifts till we show
We've strength to make her let them go;
The Providence that works in history,
And seems to some folks such a mystery,
Does not creep slowly on *incog.*,
But moves by jumps, a mighty frog;
No more reject the Age's chrism,
Your queues are an anachronism;
No more the Future's promise mock,
But lay your tails upon the block,
Thankful that we the means have voted
To have you thus to frogs promoted."

The thing was done, the tails were cropped,
And home each philotadpole hopped,
In faith rewarded to exult,
And wait the beautiful result.
Too soon it came; our pool, so long
The theme of patriot bull-frog's song,
Next day was reeking, fit to smother,
With heads and tails that missed each other, —
Here snoutless tails, there tailless snouts:
The only gainers were the pouts.

Moral

From lower to the higher next,
Not to the top, is Nature's text;
And embryo Good, to reach full stature,
Absorbs the Evil in its nature.

HERMAN MELVILLE
1819–1891

In a Garret

Gems and jewels let them heap —
Wax sumptuous as the Sophi:
For me, to grapple from Art's deep
One dripping trophy!

The Bench of Boors

In bed I muse on Tenier's boors,
Embrowned and beery losels all:
   A wakeful brain
   Elaborates pain:
Within low doors the slugs of boors
Laze and yawn and doze again.

In dreams they doze, the drowsy boors,
Their hazy hovel warm and small:
   Thought's ampler bound
   But chill is found:
Within low doors the basking boors
Snugly hug the ember-mound.

Sleepless, I see the slumberous boors
Their blurred eyes blink, their eyelids fall:
   Thought's eager sight
   Aches — overbright!
Within low doors the boozy boors
Cat-naps take in pipe-bowl light.

The Attic Landscape

Tourist, spare the avid glance
    That greedy roves the sight to see:
Little here of "Old Romance,"
    Or Picturesque of Tivoli.

No flushful tint the sense to warm —
Pure outline pale, a linear charm.
The clear-cut hills carved temples face,
Respond, and share their sculptural grace.

The Lover and the Syringa-Bush

Like a lit-up Christmas Tree,
    Like a grotto pranked with spars,
Like white corals in green sea,
    Like night's sky of crowded stars —
To me like these you show, Syringa
    Such heightening power has love, believe,
While here by Eden's gate I linger
    Love's tryst to keep, with truant Eve.

The New Ancient of Days

The man of bone confirms his throne
    In cave where fossils be;
Outdating every mummy known,
Not older Cuvier's mastodon,
    Nor older much the sea:
    Old as the Glacial Period, he;
And claims he calls to mind the day
When Thule's king, by reindeer drawn,
His sleigh-bells jingling in icy morn,
Slid clean from the Pole to the Wetterhorn
Over frozen waters in May!
    Oh, the man of the cave of Engihoul,
    With Eld doth he dote and drule?

A wizard one, his lore is none
  Ye spell with A. B. C.;
But *do-do* tracks, all up and down
That slate he poreth much upon,
  His algebra may be: —
Yea, there he cyphers and sums it free;
To ages ere Indus met ocean's swell
Addeth æons ere Satan or Saturn fell.
His totals of time make an awful schism,
And old Chronos he pitches adown the abysm
Like a pebble down Carisbrook well.
  Yea, the man of the cave of Engihoul
  From Moses knocks under the stool.

In *bas-relief* he late has shown
  A horrible show, agreed —
Megalosaurus, iguanodon,
Palæotherium Glypthæcon,
  A Barnum-show raree;
  The vomit of slimy and sludgey sea:
Purposeless creatures, odd inchoate things
Which splashed thro' morasses on fleshly wings;
The cubs of Chaos, with eyes askance,
Preposterous griffins that squint at Chance
And Anarch's cracked decree!
  Oh the showman who dens in Engihoul,
  Would he fright us, or quit us, or fool?

But, needs to own, he takes a tone,
  Satiric on nobs, pardee!
"Though in ages whose term is yet to run,
Old Adam a seraph may have for son,
  His gran'ther's a crab, d'y'see!
And why cut your kinsman the ape?" adds he:
"Your trick of scratching is borrowed from him,
Grimace and cunning, with many a whim,
Your fidgets and hypoes, and each megrim —
All's traced in the family tree!"
  Ha, the wag of the cave of Engihoul:
  Buss me, gorilla and ghoul!

Obstreperous grown he'd fain dethrone
  Joe Smith, and e'en Jones Three;

Against even Jos and great Mahone
He flings his fossiliffer's stone
   And rattles his shanks for glee.
   I'll settle these parvenu fellows, he-he!
Diluvian Jove of Ducalion's day —
A parting take to the Phocene clay!
He swears no Ens that takes a name
Commensurate is with the vasty claim
Of the protoplastic Fegee.
   O, the spook of the cave of Engihoul
   He flogs us and sends us to school.

Hyena of bone! Ah, beat him down,
   Great Pope, with Peter's key,
Ere the Grand Pan-Jam be overthrown
With Joe and Jos and great Mahone,
   And the firmament mix with the sea;
And then, my masters, where should we be?
But the ogre of bone he snickers alone,
He grins for his godless glee:
"I have flung my stone, my fossil stone,
And your gods, how they scamper," saith he.
   Imp! imp of the cave of Engihoul,
   Shall he grin like the Gorgon and rule?

WALT WHITMAN
1819–1892

A Boston Ballad

To get betimes in Boston town I rose this morning early,
Here's a good place at the corner, I must stand and see the show.

Clear the way there Jonathan!
Way for the President's marshal — way for the government cannon!
Way for the Federal foot and dragoons, (and the apparitions copiously
   tumbling.)

I love to look on the Stars and Stripes, I hope the fifes will play Yankee
   Doodle.
How bright shine the cutlasses of the foremost troops!
Every man holds his revolver, marching stiff through Boston town.

A fog follows, antiques of the same come limping,
Some appear wooden-legged, and some appear bandaged and bloodless.
Why this is indeed a show — it has called the dead out of the earth!
The old graveyards of the hills have hurried to see!

Phantoms! phantoms countless by flank and rear!
Cock'd hats of mothy mould — crutches made of mist!
Arms in slings — old men leaning on young men's shoulders.

What troubles you Yankee phantoms? what is all this chattering of bare
    gums?
Does the ague convulse your limbs? do you mistake your crutches for
    firelocks and level them?

If you blind your eyes with tears you will not see the President's marshal,
If you groan such groans you might balk the government cannon.

For shame old maniacs — bring down those toss'd arms, and let your
    white hair be,
Here gape your great grandsons, their wives gaze at them from the
    windows,
See how well dress'd, see how orderly they conduct themselves.

Worse and worse — can't you stand it? are you retreating?
Is this hour with the living too dead for you?

Retreat then — pell-mell!
To your graves — back — back to the hills old limpers!
I do not think you belong here anyhow.

But there is one thing that belongs here — shall I tell you what it is,
    gentlemen of Boston?

I will whisper it to the Mayor, he shall send a committee to England,
They shall get a grant from the Parliament, go with a cart to the royal
    vault,
Dig out King George's coffin, unwrap him quick from the grave-clothes,
    box up his bones for a journey,
Find a swift Yankee clipper — here is freight for you, black-bellied
    clipper,
Up with your anchor — shake out your sails — steer straight toward
    Boston bay.

Now call for the President's marshal again, bring out the government
    cannon,
Fetch home the roarers from Congress, make another procession, guard
    it with foot and dragoons.

This centre-piece for them;
Look, all orderly citizens — look from the windows, women!

The committee open the box, set up the regal ribs, glue those that will
    not stay,
Clap the skull on top of the ribs, and clap a crown on top of the skull.

You have got your revenge, old buster — the crown is come to its own,
    and more than its own.

Stick your hands in your pockets, Jonathan — you are a made man from
    this day,
You are mighty cute — and here is one of your bargains.

CHARLES GODFREY LELAND
1824–1903

Hans Breitmann's Party

Hans Breitmann gife a barty;
    Dey had biano-blayin':
I felled in lofe mit a Merican frau,
    Her name was Madilda Yane.
She hat haar as prown ash a pretzel,
    Her eyes vas himmel-plue,
Und ven dey looket indo mine,
    Dey shplit mine heart in two.

Hans Breitmann gife a barty:
    I vent dere, you'll pe pound.
I valtzet mit Madilda Yane
    Und vent shpinnen round und round.
De pootiest Fräulein in de house,
    She vayed 'pout dwo hoondred pound,
Und efery dime she gife a shoomp
    She make de vindows sound.

Hans Breitmann gife a barty:
 I dells you it cost him dear.
Dey rolled in more ash sefen kecks
 Of foost-rate Lager Beer,
Und venefer dey knocks de shpicket in
 De Deutschers gifes a cheer.
I dinks dat so vine a barty
 Nefer coom to a het dis year.

Hans Breitmann gife a barty:
 Dere all vas Souse und Brouse;
Ven de sooper comed in, de gompany
 Did make demselfs to house.
Dey ate das Brot und Gensy broost,
 De Bratwurst und Braten fine,
Und vash der Abendessen down
 Mit four parrels of Neckarwein.

Hans Breitmann gife a barty.
 We all cot troonk ash bigs.
I poot mine mout to a parrel of bier,
 Und emptied it oop mit a schwigs.
Und denn I gissed Madilda Yane
 Und she shlog me on de kop,
Und de gompany fited mit daple-lecks
 Dill be coonshtable made oos shtop.

Hans Breitmann gife a barty —
 Where ish dat barty now!
Where ish de lofely golden cloud
 Dat float on de moundain's prow?
Where ish de himmelstrahlende Stern —
 De shtar of de shpirit's light?
All goned afay mit de Lager Beer —
 Afay in de Ewigkeit!

Breitmann in Politics

VII

Dere's a liddle fact in hishdory vitch few hafe oondershtand,
Deutschers are, *de jure*, de owners of dis land,
Und I brides mineself oonshpeak-barly dat I foorst make beknown,
De primordial cause dat Columbus vas derivet from Cologne.

For ash his name vas Colon it fisiply does shine,
Dat his Eldern are geboren been in Cologne on der Rhein,
Und Colonia peing a colony, it sehr bemerkbar ist,
Dat Columbus in America was der firster colonist.

Und ash Columbus ish a tove, id ish wort' de drople to mark
Dat an bidgeon foorst tiscofer land a-vlyin' from de ark;
Und shtill wider — in de peginnin', mitout de leastest toubt,
A tofe vas vly ofer de wassers und pring de vorldt herout.

Ash mein goot oldt teacher der Kreutzer to me tid ofden shbeak,
De mythus of name rebeats itself — vhitch see in his "Symbolik,"
So also de name America, if we a liddle look,
Vas coom from der oldt King Emerich in de Deutsche Heldenbuch.

Und id vas from dat fery Heldenbuch — how voonderful id ron —
Dat I shdole de "Song of Hildebrand, or der Vater und der Sohn,"
Und dishtripude it to Breitmann for a reason vhitch now ish plain,
Dat dis Sagen Cyclus, full-endet, pring me round to der Hans again.

Dese laws of un-endly un-windoong ish so teep and broad and tall
Dat nopody boot a Deutscher hafe a het to versteh dem at all,
Und should I write mine dinks all out, I tont peliefe, inteed,
Dat I mineself vould versteh de half of dis here Breitmann's Lied.

Ash der Hegel say of his system — dat only von mans knew
Vot der tyfel id meant — und *he* could n't tell — und der Jean Paul
    Richter, too,
Who saidt: "Gott knows I meant somedings vhen foorst dis buch
    I writ,
Boot Gott only wise vot das buch means now — for I hafe fergotten
    it."

And all of dis be-wises so blain ash de face on your nose
Dat der Deutscher hafe efen more intellects dan he himself soopose,
Und his tifference mit de over-again vorldt, as I really do soospect,
Ish dat oder volk hafe more *soopose* — und lesser intellect.

Yet oop-rightly I confess it, mitout ashkin' vhy or vhence,
Dere ish also dimes vhen Amerigans hafe shown sharp-pointet sense,
Und a fery outsigned exemple of genius in dis line
Vas dishblayed in dis elegdion py Mishder Hiram Twine.

PHOEBE CARY
1824–1871

Samuel Brown

It was many and many a year ago,
 In a dwelling down in town,
That a fellow there lived whom you may know,
 By the name of Samuel Brown;
And this fellow he lived with no other thought
 Than to our house to come down.

I was a child, and he was a child,
 In that dwelling down in town,
But we loved with a love that was more than love,
 I and my Samuel Brown, —
With a love that the ladies coveted,
 Me and Samuel Brown.

And this was the reason that, long ago,
 To that dwelling down in town,
A girl came out of her carriage, courting
 My beautiful Samuel Brown;
So that her high-bred kinsmen came,
 And bore away Samuel Brown,
And shut him up in a dwelling house,
 In a street quite up in the town.

The ladies not half so happy up there,
 Went envying me and Brown;
Yes! that was the reason (as all men know,
 In this dwelling down in town),
That the girl came out of the carriage by night,
 Coquetting and getting my Samuel Brown.

But our love is more artful by far than the love
 Of those who are older than we, —
 Of many far wiser than we, —
And neither the girls that are living above,
 Nor the girls that are down in town,
Can ever dissever my soul from the soul
 Of the beautiful Samuel Brown.

For the morn never shines, without bringing me lines
　　From my beautiful Samuel Brown;
And the night's never dark, but I sit in the park
　　With my beautiful Samuel Brown.
And often by day, I walk down in Broadway,
With my darling, my darling, my life and my stay,
　　To our dwelling down in town,
　　To our house in the street down town.

The Day Is Done

The day is done, and darkness
　　From the wing of night is loosed,
As a feather is wafted downward,
　　From a chicken going to roost.

I see the lights of the baker,
　　Gleam through the rain and mist,
And a feeling of sadness comes o'er me,
　　That I cannot well resist.

A feeling of sadness and longing
　　That is not like being sick,
And resembles sorrow only
　　As a brickbat resembles a brick.

Come, get for me some supper, —
　　A good and regular meal —
That shall soothe this restless feeling,
　　And banish the pain I feel.

Not from the pastry bakers,
　　Not from the shops for cake;
I wouldn't give a farthing
　　For all that they can make.

For, like the soup at dinner,
　　Such things would but suggest
Some dishes more substantial,
　　And to-night I want the best.

Go to some honest butcher,
　　Whose beef is fresh and nice,
As any they have in the city
　　And get a liberal slice.

Such things through days of labor,
　　And nights devoid of ease,
For sad and desperate feelings,
　　Are wonderful remedies.

They have an astonishing power
　　To aid and reinforce,
And come like the "finally, brethren,"
　　That follows a long discourse.

Then get me a tender sirloin
　　From off the bench or hook,
And lend to its sterling goodness
　　The science of the cook.

And the night shall be filled with comfort,
　　And the cares with which it begun
Shall fold up their blankets like Indians,
　　And silently cut and run.

Jacob

He dwelt among "Apartments let,"
　　About five stories high;
A man, I thought, that none would get,
　　And very few would try.

A boulder, by a larger stone
　　Half hidden in the mud,
Fair as a man when only one
　　Is in the neighborhood.

He lived unknown, and few could tell
　　When Jacob was not free;
But he has got a wife — and O!
　　The difference to me!

WILLIAM ALLEN BUTLER
1825–1902

Nothing To Wear

Miss Flora McFlimsey, of Madison Square,
Has made three separate journeys to Paris;
And her father assures me, each time she was there,
That she and her friend Mrs. Harris
(Not the lady whose name is so famous in history,
But plain Mrs. H., without romance or mystery)
Spent six consecutive weeks without stopping,
In one continuous round of shopping; —
Shopping alone, and shopping together,
At all hours of the day, and in all sorts of weather:
For all manner of things that a woman can put
On the crown of her head or the sole of her foot,
Or wrap round her shoulders, or fit round her waist,
Or that can be sewed on, or pinned on, or laced,
Or tied on with a string, or stitched on with a bow,
In front or behind, above or below;
For bonnets, mantillas, capes, collars, and shawls;
Dresses for breakfasts, and dinners, and balls;
Dresses to sit in, and stand in, and walk in,
Dresses to dance in, and flirt in, and talk in;
Dresses in which to do nothing at all;
Dresses for winter, spring, summer, and fall, —
All of them different in color and pattern,
Silk, muslin, and lace, crape, velvet, and satin,
Brocade, and broadcloth, and other material
Quite as expensive and much more ethereal:
In short, for all things that could ever be thought of,
Or milliner, modiste, or tradesman be bought of,
From ten-thousand-francs robes to twenty-sous frills;
    In all quarters of Paris, and to every store:
    While McFlimsey in vain stormed, scolded, and swore,
They footed the streets, and he footed the bills.

The last trip, their goods shipped by the steamer *Argo*
Formed, McFlimsey declares, the bulk of her cargo,
Not to mention a quantity kept from the rest,
Sufficient to fill the largest-sized chest,
Which did not appear on the ship's manifest,

But for which the ladies themselves manifested
Such particular interest that they invested
Their own proper persons in layers and rows
Of muslins, embroideries, worked underclothes,
Gloves, handkerchiefs, scarfs, and such trifles as those;
Then, wrapped in great shawls, like Circassian beauties,
Gave good by to the ship, and go-by to the duties.
Her relations at home all marvelled, no doubt,
Miss Flora had grown so enormously stout
    For an actual belle and a possible bride;
But the miracle ceased when she turned inside out,
    And the truth came to light, and the dry-goods beside,
Which, in spite of collector and custom-house sentry,
Had entered the port without any entry.
And yet, though scarce three months have passed since the day
The merchandise went, on twelve carts, up Broadway,
This same Miss McFlimsey, of Madison Square,
The last time we met, was in utter despair,
Because she had nothing whatever to wear!

Nothing to wear! Now, as this is a true ditty,
    I do not assert — this you know is between us —
That she's in a state of absolute nudity,
    Like Powers's Greek Slave, or the Medici Venus;
But I do mean to say I have heard her declare,
    When at the same moment she had on a dress
    Which cost five hundred dollars, and not a cent less,
    And jewelry worth ten times more, I should guess,
That she had not a thing in the wide world to wear!
I should mention just here, that out of Miss Flora's
Two hundred and fifty or sixty adorers,
I had just been selected as he who should throw all
The rest in the shade, by the gracious bestowal
On myself, after twenty or thirty rejections
Of those fossil remains which she called her "affections,"
And that rather decayed but well-known work of art,
Which Miss Flora persisted in styling "her heart."
So we were engaged. Our troth had been plighted
    Not by moonbeam or starbeam, by fountain or grove;
But in a front parlor, most brilliantly lighted,
    Beneath the gas-fixtures we whispered our love —
Without any romance, or raptures, or sighs,
Without any tears in Miss Flora's blue eyes,

Or blushes, or transports, or such silly actions;
It was one of the quietest business transactions,
With a very small sprinkling of sentiment, if any,
And a very large diamond imported by Tiffany.
On her virginal lips while I printed a kiss,
She exclaimed, as a sort of parenthesis,
And by way of putting me quite at my ease,
"You know, I'm to polka as much as I please,
And flirt when I like, — now stop, — don't you speak, —
And you must not come here more than twice in the week,
Or talk to me either at party or ball;
But always be ready to come when I call:
So don't prose to me about duty and stuff, —
If we don't break this off, there will be time enough
For that sort of thing; but the bargain must be,
That as long as I choose I am perfectly free:
For this is a sort of engagement, you see,
Which is binding on you, but not binding on me."

Well, having thus wooed Miss McFlimsey, and gained her,
With the silks, crinolines, and hoops that contained her,
I had, as I thought, a contingent remainder
At least in the property, and the best right
To appear as its escort by day and by night;
And it being the week of the Stuckups' grand ball, —
    Their cards had been out for a fortnight or so,
    And set all the Avenue on the tiptoe, —
I considered it only my duty to call
    And see if Miss Flora intended to go.
I found her — as ladies are apt to be found
When the time intervening between the first sound
Of the bell and the visitor's entry is shorter
Than usual — I found — I won't say I caught — her
Intent on the pier-glass, undoubtedly meaning
To see if perhaps it didn't need cleaning.
She turned as I entered — "Why, Harry, you sinner,
I thought that you went to the Flashers' to dinner!"
"So I did," I replied; "but the dinner is swallowed,
    And digested, I trust; for 'tis now nine or more:
So being relieved from that duty, I followed
    Inclination, which led me, you see, to your door.
And now will your Ladyship so condescend
As just to inform me if you intend

Your beauty and graces and presence to lend
(All of which, when I own, I hope no one will borrow)
To the Stuckups, whose party, you know, is to-morrow?"
  The fair Flora looked up with a pitiful air,
And answered quite promptly, "Why, Harry, *mon cher*,
I should like above all things to go with you there;
But really and truly — I've nothing to wear."

"Nothing to wear? Go just as you are:
  Wear the dress you have on, and you'll be by far,
  I engage, the most bright and particular star
    On the Stuckup horizon —" I stopped, for her eye,
Notwithstanding this delicate onset of flattery,
Opened on me at once a most terrible battery
    Of scorn and amazement. She made no reply,
But gave a slight turn to the end of her nose
    (That pure Grecian feature), as much as to say,
"How absurd that any sane man should suppose
  That a lady would go to a ball in the clothes,
    No matter how fine, that she wears every day!"
So I ventured again — "Wear your crimson brocade."
  (Second turn-up of nose) — "That's too dark by a shade." —
"Your blue silk —" "That's too heavy." — "Your pink —" "That's too
    light." —
"Wear tulle over satin." "I can't endure white." —
"Your rose-colored, then, the best of the batch —"
"I haven't a thread of point lace to match." —
"Your brown moire-antique —" "Yes, and look like a Quaker." —
"The pearl colored —" "I would, but that plaguy dressmaker
  Has had it a week." — "Then that exquisite lilac,
  In which you would melt the heart of a Shylock."
  (Here the nose took again the same elevation) —
"I wouldn't wear that for the whole of creation." —
    "Why not? It's my fancy, there's nothing could strike it
  As more *comme il faut*" — "Yes, but, dear me, that lean
    Sophronia Stuckup has got one just like it,
  And I won't appear dressed like a chit of sixteen." —
"Then that splendid purple, that sweet mazarine,
  That superb *point d'aiguille*, that imperial green,
  That zephyr-like tarlatan, that rich grenadine —"
    "Not one of all which is fit to be seen,"
  Said the lady, becoming excited and flushed.
"Then wear," I exclaimed, in a tone which quite crushed

Opposition, "that gorgeous toilette which you sported
   In Paris last spring, at the grand presentation,
   When you quite turned the head of the head of the nation;
And by all the grand court were so very much courted."
The end of the nose was portentously tipped up,
   And both the bright eyes shot forth indignation,
   As she burst upon me with the fierce exclamation,
   "I have worn it three times at the least calculation,
And that and most of my dresses are ripped up!"
Here I *ripped out* something, perhaps rather rash —
   Quite innocent, though; but to us an expression
More striking than classic, it "settled my hash,"
   And proved very soon the last act of our session.
"Fiddlesticks, is it, sir? I wonder the ceiling
Doesn't fall down and crush you! — oh, you men have no feeling.
You selfish, unnatural, illiberal creatures,
Who set yourselves up as patterns and preachers,
Your silly pretence — why, what a mere guess it is!
Pray, what do you know of a woman's necessities?
I have told you and shown you I've nothing to wear,
And it's perfectly plain you not only don't care,
But you do not believe" (here the nose went still higher):
"I suppose if you dared you would call me a liar.
Our engagement is ended, sir — yes, on the spot;
You're a brute, and a monster, and — I don't know what."
I mildly suggested the words Hottentot,
Pickpocket, and cannibal, Tartar, and thief,
As gentle expletives which might give relief:
But this only proved as a spark to the powder,
And the storm I had raised came faster and louder;
It blew, and it rained, thundered, lightened, and hailed
Interjections, verbs, pronouns, till language quite failed
To express the abusive, and then its arrears
Were brought up all at once by a torrent of tears;
And my last faint, despairing attempt at an obs-
Ervation was lost in a tempest of sobs.

Well, I felt for the lady, and felt for my hat too,
Improvised on the crown of the latter a tatoo,
In lieu of expressing the feelings which lay
Quite too deep for words, as Wordsworth would say:
Then, without going through the form of a bow,
Found myself in the entry, — I hardly knew how, —

On doorstep and sidewalk, past lamp-post and square,
At home and up-stairs, in my own easy-chair;
   Poked my feet into slippers, my fire into blaze,
And said to myself, as I lit my cigar, —
Supposing a man had the wealth of the Czar
   Of the Russias to boot, for the rest of his days,
On the whole do you think he would have much time to spare
If he married a woman with nothing to wear?

BAYARD TAYLOR
1825–1878

The Ballad of Hiram Hover

Where the Moosatockmaguntic
Pours its waters in the Skuntic,
   Met, along the forest side
   Hiram Hover, Huldah Hyde.

She, a maiden fair and dapper,
He, a red-haired, stalwart trapper,
   Hunting beaver, mink, and skunk
   In the woodlands of Squeedunk.

She, Pentucket's pensive daughter,
Walked beside the Skuntic water
   Gathering, in her apron wet,
   Snake-root, mint, and bouncing-bet.

"Why," he murmured, loth to leave her,
"Gather yarbs for chills and fever,
   When a lovyer bold and true,
   Only waits to gather you?"

"Go," she answered, "I'm not hasty,
I prefer a man more tasty;
   Leastways, one to please me well
   Should not have a beasty smell."

"Haughty Huldah!" Hiram answered,
"Mind and heart alike are cancered;
   Jest look here! these peltries give
   Cash, wherefrom a pair may live.

"I, you think, am but a vagrant,
Trapping beasts by no means fragrant;
  Yet, I'm sure it's worth a thank —
  I've a handsome sum in bank."

Turned and vanished Hiram Hover,
And, before the year was over,
  Huldah, with the yarbs she sold,
  Bought a cape, against the cold.

Black and thick the furry cape was,
Of a stylish cut the shape was;
  And the girls, in all the town,
  Envied Huldah up and down.

Then at last, one winter morning,
Hiram came without a warning.
  "Either," said he, "you are blind,
  Huldah, or you've changed your mind.

"Me you snub for trapping varmints,
Yet you take the skins for garments;
  Since you wear the skunk and mink,
  There's no harm in me, I think."

"Well," said she, "we will not quarrel,
Hiram; I accept the moral,
  Now the fashion's so I guess
  I can't hardly do no less."

Thus the trouble all was over
Of the love of Hiram Hover.
  Thus he made sweet Huldah Hyde
  Huldah Hover as his bride.

Love employs, with equal favor,
Things of good and evil savor;
  That which first appeared to part,
  Warmed, at last, the maiden's heart.

Under one impartial banner,
Life, the hunter, Love the tanner,
  Draw, from every beast they snare,
  Comfort for a wedded pair!

Palabras Grandiosas

I lay i' the bosom of the sun,
Under the roses dappled and dun.
I thought of the Sultan Gingerbeer,
In his palace beside the Bendemeer,
With his Afghan guards and his eunuchs blind,
And the harem that stretched for a league behind.

The tulips bent i' the summer breeze,
Under the broad chrysanthemum-trees,
And the minstrel, playing his culverin,
Made for mine ears a merry din.
If I were the Sultan, and he were I,
Here i' the grass he should loafing lie,
And I should bestride my zebra steed,
And ride to the hunt of the centipede:
While the pet of the harem, Dandeline,
Should fill me a crystal bucket of wine,
And the kislar aga, Up-to-Snuff,
Should wipe my mouth when I sighed, "Enough!"
And the gay court poet, Fearfulbore,
Should sit in the hall when the hunt was o'er,
And chant me songs of silvery tone,
Not from Hafiz, but — mine own!

Ah, wee sweet love, beside me here,
I am not the Sultan Gingerbeer,
Nor you the odalisque Dandeline,
Yet I am yourn, and you are mine!

Nauvoo

This is the place: be still for a while, my high-pressure steamboat!
Let me survey the spot where the Mormons builded their temple.
Much have I mused on the wreck and ruin of ancient religions,
Scandinavian, Greek, Assyrian, Zend, and the Sanskrit,
Yea, and explored the mysteries hidden in Talmudic targums,
Caught the gleam of Chrysaor's sword and occulted Orion,
Backward spelled the lines of the Hebrew graveyard at Newport,
Studied Ojibwa symbols and those of the Quarry of Pipestone,

Also the myths of the Zulus whose questions converted Colenso,
So, methinks, it were well I should muse a little at Nauvoo.

Fair was he not, the primitive Prophet, nor he who succeeded,
Hardly for poetry fit, though using the Urim and Thummim.
Had he but borrowed Levitical trappings, the girdle and ephod,
Fine-twined linen, and ouches of gold, and bells and pomegranates,
That, indeed, might have kindled the weird necromancy of fancy.
Had he but set up mystical forms, like Astarte or Peor,
Balder, or Freya, Quetzalcoatl, Perun, Manabozho,
Verily, though to the sense theologic it might be offensive,
Great were the gain to the pictured, flashing speech of the poet.
Yet the Muse that delights in Mesopotamian numbers,
Vague and vast as the roar of the wind in a forest of pine-trees,
Now must tune her strings to the names of Joseph and Brigham.
Hebrew, the first; and a Smith before the Deluge was Tubal,
Thor of the East, who first made iron ring to the hammer;
So on the iron heads of the people about him, the latter,
Striking the sparks of belief and forging their faith in the Good Time
Coming, the Latter Day, as he called it, — the Kingdom of Zion.
Then, in the words of Philip the Eunuch unto Belshazzar,
Came to him multitudes wan, diseased and decrepit of spirit,
Came and heard and believed, and builded the temple at Nauvoo.

All is past; for Joseph was smitten with lead from a pistol,
Brigham went with the others over the prairies to Salt Lake.
Answers now to the long, disconsolate wail of the steamer,
Hoarse, inarticulate, shrill, the rolling and bounding of ten-pins, —
Answers the voice of the bartender, mixing the smash and the julep,
Answers, precocious, the boy, and bites a chew of tobacco.
Lone as the towers of Afrasiab now is the seat of the Prophet,
Mournful, inspiring to verse, though seeming utterly vulgar:
Also — for each thing now is expected to furnish a moral —
Teaching innumerable lessons for whoso believes and is patient.
Thou, that readest, be resolute, learn to be strong and to suffer!
Let the dead Past bury its dead and act in the Present!
Bear a banner of strange devices, "Forever" and "Never!"
Build in the walls of time the fane of a permanent Nauvoo,
So that thy brethren may see it and say, "Go thou and do likewise!"

STEPHEN COLLINS FOSTER
1826–1864

Gwine To Run All Night;
or, De Camptown Races

De Camptown ladies sing dis song
Doo dah! doo dah!
De Camptown racetrack five miles long
Oh! doo dah day!
I come down dah wid my hat caved in
Doo dah! doo dah!
I go back home wid a pocket full of tin
Oh! doo dah day!

> *Gwine to run all night!*
> *Gwine to run all day!*
> *I'll bet my money on de bobtail nag,*
> *Somebody bet on de bay.*

De long tail filly, and de big black hoss
Doo dah! doo dah!
Dey fly de track, and dey both cut across
Oh! doo dah day!
De blind hoss sticken in a big mud hole
Doo dah! doo dah!
Can't touch bottom wid a ten foot pole
Oh! doo dah day!

Old muley cow come on to de track
Doo dah! doo dah!
De bobtail fling her ober his back
Oh! doo dah day!
Den fly along like a railroad car
Doo dah! doo dah!
Runnin' a race wid a shootin' star
Oh! doo dah day!

See dem flyin' on a ten mile heat
Doo dah! doo dah!
Round de race track, den repeat
Oh! doo dah day!
I win my money on de bobtail nag
Doo dah! doo dah!
I keep my money in an old tow bag
Oh! doo dah day!

Oh! Susanna

I come from Alabama,
Wid my banjo on my knee,
I'm g'wan to Lousiana,
My true love for to see.
It rain'd all night the day I left,
The weather it was dry;
The sun so hot I froze to death;
Susanna, don't you cry.

> *Oh! Susanna,*
> *Don't you cry for me,*
> *I come from Alabama*
> *Wid my banjo on my knee.*

I jumped aboard de telegraph,
And trabbeled down de ribber,
De lectric fluid magnified,
And killed five hundred nigger;
De bullgine bust, de horse run off,
I really thought I'd die;
I shut my eyes to hold my breath;
Susanna, don't you cry.

I had a dream de udder night,
When eb'ryting was still;
I thought I saw Susanna,
A coming down de hill;
De buckwheat-cake was in her mouth,
De tear was in her eye;
Says I, I'm coming from de South,
Susanna, don't you cry.

I soon will be in New Orleans,
And den I'll look all round,
And when I find Susanna,
I'll fall upon the ground.
But if I do not find her,
Dis darkey'l surely die;
And when I'm dead and buried,
Susanna, don't you cry.

ANONYMOUS

The Little Brown Jug

My wife and I live all alone,
In a little hut we call our own,
She loves gin and I love rum,
Tell you what it is, don't we have fun?

> *Ha, ha, ha! 'Tis you and me,*
> *Little brown jug, don't I love thee?*
> *Ha, ha, ha! 'Tis you and me,*
> *Little brown jug, don't I love thee?*

If I had a cow that gave such beer,
I'd dress her in the finest sheer,
Feed her on the choicest hay,
And milk her twenty times a day.

'Tis gin that makes my friends my foes,
'Tis gin that makes me wear old clothes,
But seeing you are so near my nose,
Tip her up and down she goes.

When I go toiling on my farm,
Take little brown jug under my arm,
Set it under some shady tree,
Little brown jug, don't I love thee?

Then came the landlord tripping in,
Round top hat and a peaked chin,
In his hand he carried a cup,
Says I, "Old fellow, give us a sup."

If all the folks in Adam's race
Were put together in one place,
Then I'd prepare to drop a tear
Before I'd part with you, my dear.

Sweet Betsey from Pike

Oh, don't you remember sweet Betsey from Pike,
Who crossed the big mountains with her lover Ike,
With two yoke of cattle, a large yellow dog,
A tall shanghai rooster and one spotted hog.

Singing, goodbye, Pike County, farewell for awhile,
We'll come back again when we've panned out our pile,
Singing tooral lal, looral lal, looral lal lay,
Singing tooral lal, looral lal, looral lal lay.

One evening quite early they camped on the Platte,
'Twas near by the road on a green shady flat,
Where Betsey, sore-footed, lay down to repose,
While with wonder Ike gazed on his Pike County rose.

Their wagon broke down with a terrible crash,
And out on the prairie rolled all kinds of trash;
A few little baby clothes done up with great care —
'Twas rather suspicious, though all on the square.

The shanghai ran off and the cattle all died;
That morning the last piece of bacon was fried;
Poor Ike was discouraged, and Betsey got mad,
The dog drooped his tail and looked wondrously sad.

They stopped at Salt Lake to inquire the way,
When Brigham declared that sweet Betsey should stay;
But Betsey got frightened and ran like a deer,
While Brigham stood pawing the ground like a steer.

They soon reached the desert, where Betsey gave out,
And down in the sand she lay rolling about;
While Ike, half distracted, looked on with surprise,
Saying, "Betsey, get up, you'll get sand in your eyes."

Sweet Betsey got up in a great deal of pain,
Declared she'd go back to Pike County again;
But Ike gave a sigh, and they fondly embraced,
And they traveled along with his arm round her waist.

They suddenly stopped on a very high hill,
With wonder looked down upon old Placerville;
Ike sighed when he said, and he cast his eyes down,
"Sweet Betsey, my darling, we've got to Hangtown."

Long Ike and sweet Betsey attended a dance,
Ike wore a pair of his Pike County pants;
Sweet Betsey was covered with ribbons and rings;
Says Ike, "You're an angel, but where are your wings?"

A miner said, "Betsey, will you dance with me?"
"I will that, old hoss, if you don't make too free;
But don't dance me hard, do you want to know why?
Dog on you! I'm chock full of strong alkali!"

This Pike County couple got married, of course,
And Ike became jealous — obtained a divorce;
Sweet Betsey, well satisfied, said with a shout,
"Goodbye, you big lummox, I'm glad you've backed out!"

Clementine

In a cavern in a canyon, excavating for a mine,
Dwelt a miner, forty-niner, and his daughter, Clementine.

> *Oh, my darling, oh, my darling, oh, my darling Clementine,*
> *You are lost and gone forever, dreadful sorry, Clementine.*

Light she was and like a fairy, and her shoes were number nine,
Herring boxes without topses, sandals were for Clementine.

Drove her ducklings to the water, every morning just at nine,
Hit her foot against a splinter, fell into the foaming brine.

Ruby lips above the water, blowing bubbles soft and fine,
Alas, for me! I was no swimmer, so I lost my Clementine.

In a churchyard, near the canyon, where the myrtle doth entwine,
There grow roses and other posies fertilized by Clementine.

Then the miner, forty-niner, soon began to droop and pine,
Thought he ought to join his daughter, now he's with his Clementine.

In my dreams she still doth haunt me, robed in garments soaked in brine,
Though in life I used to kiss her, now she's dead, I draw the line.

ANONYMOUS

Starving to Death on a Government Claim

My name is Frank Taylor, a bachelor I am,
I'm keeping old batch on an elegant plan,
You'll find me out West in the county of Lane
A-starving to death on a Government claim.

Hurrah for Lane County, the land of the free,
The home of the bedbug, grasshopper and flea,
I'll sing of its praises and boast of its fame
A-starving to death on a Government claim.

My clothes they are ragged, my language is rough,
My bread is case-hardened and solid and tough,
But I have a good time and live at my ease
On common sop-sorghum and old bacon grease.

How happy am I when I crawl into bed,
With rattlesnakes rattling just under my head,
And the gay little bedbug, so cheerful and bright,
He keeps me a-going two-thirds of the night.

How happy am I on my Government claim,
I've nothing to lose and I've nothing to gain,
I've nothing to eat and I've nothing to wear,
And nothing from nothing is honest and fair.

Oh, come to Lane County, there's room for you all,
Where the wind never stops and the rains never fall,
Oh, join in the chorus and sing of her fame,
A-starving to death on a Government claim.

Oh, don't be downhearted, you poor hungry men,
We're all just as free as the pigs in the pen,
Just stick to your homestead and fight with your fleas,
And pray to your Maker to send some more breeze.

Now all you poor sinners, I hope you will stay
And chaw on your hardtack till you're toothless and grey,
But as for myself I don't aim to remain
And slave like a dog on no Government claim.

Farewell to Lane County, the pride of the West,
I'm going back East to the girl I love best,
I'll stop in Missouri and get me a wife,
And live on corn dodgers the rest of my life.

The Factory Girl's Come-All-Ye

Come all ye Lewiston fact'ry girls,
I want you to understand,
I'm a-going to leave this factory,
And return to my native land.
　　Sing dum de whickerty, dum de way.

No more will I take my Shaker* and shawl
And hurry to the mill;
No more will I work so pesky hard
To earn a dollar bill.

No more will I take the towel and soap
To go to the sink and wash;
No more will the overseer say
"You're making a terrible splosh!"

No more will I take the comb and go
To the glass to comb my hair;
No more the overseer will say
"You're weaving your cloth too thin!"

No more will I eat cold pudding,
No more will I eat hard bread,
No more will I eat those half-baked beans,
For I vow! They're killing me dead!

I'm going back to Boston town
And live on Tremont Street;
And I want all you fact'ry girls
To come to my house and eat!
　　Sing dum de whickerty, dum de way.

* Bonnet.

An Ode on Gas

A country town having been recently lighted with gas,
the local editor electrifies the community with an ode:

Luminous blaze!
I never seen the like in all my born days!
Tallow candles ain't no mor'n tar
When you're about;
And spirit lamps is no whar,
Bein clean dun out.

Sparkling lite!
I think I never seen anything half so brite;
Everything is amazing clear;
The hidjus glume
Is defunct; and every cheer
Is apparient in the rume!

Gloryous halo!
Your skintelashuns make a surprising display;
You don't need no snuffers,
But you are just scrude out;
When you are squenched by puffers,
Ojus fumes aryse.

Brillyant flame!
The nites was next to darkness when you came;
But candles has vanisht
Before you, and lard oil gone to grass;
Every greasy nuisance has been banisht —
Hurraw for Gass!

JOHN TOWNSEND TROWBRIDGE
1827–1916

Darius Greene and His Flying-Machine

If ever there lived a Yankee lad,
Wise or otherwise, good or bad,
Who, seeing the birds fly, didn't jump
With flapping arms from stake or stump,

Or, spreading the tail
Of his coat for a sail,
Take a soaring leap from post or rail,
And wonder why
He couldn't fly,
And flap and flutter and wish and try —
If ever you knew a country dunce
Who didn't try that as often as once,
All I can say is, that's a sign
He never would do for a hero of mine.

An aspiring genius was D. Green:
The son of a farmer, age fourteen;
His body was long and lank and lean —
Just right for flying, as will be seen;
He had two eyes as bright as a bean,
And a freckled nose that grew between,
A little awry — for I must mention
That he had riveted his attention
Upon his wonderful invention,
Twisting his tongue as he twisted the strings,
And working his face as he worked the wings,
And with every turn of gimlet and screw
Turning and screwing his mouth round too,
Till his nose seemed bent
To catch the scent,
Around some corner, of new-baked pies,
And his wrinkled cheeks and his squinting eyes
Grew puckered into a queer grimace,
That made him look very droll in the face,
And also very wise.

And wise he must have been, to do more
Than ever a genius did before,
Excepting Dædalus of yore
And his son Icarus, who wore
Upon their backs
Those wings of wax
He had read of in the old almanacs.
Darius was clearly of the opinion
That the air is also man's dominion,
And that, with paddle or fin or pinion,
We soon or late shall navigate

The azure as now we sail the sea.
The thing looks simple enough to me;
   And if you doubt it,
Hear how Darius reasoned about it.

  "The birds can fly an' why can't I?
   Must we give in," says he with a grin,
  "That the bluebird an' phœbe
   Are smarter'n we be?
Jest fold our hands an' see the swaller
An' blackbird an' catbird beat us holler?
Doos the little chatterin', sassy wren,
No bigger'n my thumb, know more than men?
   Just show me that!
   Ur prove 't the bat
Hez got more brains than's in my hat.
An' I'll back down, an' not till then!"
He argued further: "Nur I can't see
What's th' use o' wings to a bumble-bee,
Fur to git a livin' with, more'n to me; —
   Ain't my business
   Important's his'n is?
   That Icarus
   Made a perty muss —
Him an' his daddy Dædalus
They might 'a' knowed wings made o' wax
Wouldn't stand sun-heat an' hard whacks.
   I'll make mine o' luther,
   Ur suthin' ur other."

And he said to himself, as he tinkered and planned:
"But I ain't goin' to show my hand
To mummies that never can understand
The fust idee that's big an' grand."
So he kept his secret from all the rest,
Safely buttoned within his vest;
And in the loft above the shed
Himself he locks, with thimble and thread
And wax and hammer and buckles and screws
And all such things as geniuses use; —
Two bats for patterns, curious fellows!
A charcoal-pot and a pair of bellows;
Some wire, and several old umbrellas;

A carriage-cover, for tail and wings;
A piece of harness; and straps and strings;
    And a big strong box,
    In which he locks
These and a hundred other things.
His grinning brothers, Reuben and Burke
And Nathan and Jotham and Solomon, lurk
Around the corner to see him work —
Sitting cross-legged, like a Turk,
Drawing the waxed-end through with a jerk,
And boring the holes with a comical quirk
Of his wise old head, and a knowing smirk.
But vainly they mounted each other's backs,
And poked through knot-holes and pried through cracks;
With wood from the pile and straw from the stacks
He plugged the knot-holes and caulked the cracks;
And a dipper of water, which one would think
He had brought up into the loft to drink
    When he chanced to be dry,
    Stood always nigh,
    For Darius was sly!
And whenever at work he happened to spy
At chink or crevice a blinking eye.
He let the dipper of water fly.
"Take that! an' ef ever ye git a peep,
Guess ye'll ketch a weasel asleep!"
    And he sings as he locks
    His big strong box: —

  "The weasel's head is small an' trim,
  An' he is little an' long an' slim,
  An' quick of motion an' nimble of limb
    An' ef you'll be
    Advised by me
  Keep wide awake when ye're ketchin' him !"

    So day after day
He stitched and tinkered and hammered away,
    Till at last 'twas done —
The greatest invention under the sun!
"An' now," says Darius, "hooray fur some fun!"

    'Twas the Fourth of July,
    And the weather was dry,
And not a cloud was on all the sky,
Save a few light fleeces, which here and there,

Half mist, half air,
Like foam on the ocean went floating by —
Just as lovely a morning as ever was seen
For a nice little trip in a flying-machine.
Thought cunning Darius: "Now I shan't go
Along 'ith the fellers to see the show.
I'll say I've got sich a terrible cough!
An' then, when the folks 'ave all gone off,
I'll hev full swing fur to try the thing,
An' practise a little on the wing."
"Ain't goin' to see the celebration?"
Says brother Nate. "No; botheration!
I've got sich a cold — a toothache — I —
My gracious! — feel's though I should fly!"
    Said Jotham, "Sho!
    Guess ye better go."
    But Darius said, "No!
Shouldn't wonder 'f you might see me, though,
'Long 'bout noon, ef I git red
O' this jumpin', thumpin' pain 'n my head."
For all the while to himself he said: —

"I tell ye what!
I'll fly a few times around the lot,
To see how 't seems, then soon's I've got
The hang o' the thing, ez likely's not,
    I'll astonish the nation,
    An' all creation,
By flyin' over the celebration!
Over their heads I'll sail like an eagle;
I'll balance myself on my wings like a sea-gull:
I'll dance on the chimbleys; I'll stand on the steeple;
I'll flop up to winders an' scare the people!
I'll light on the liberty-pole, an' crow;
An' I'll say to the gawpin' fools below,
    'What world's this 'ere
    That I've come near?'
Fur I'll make 'em b'lieve I'm a chap f'm the moon;
An' I'll try to race 'ith their ol' balloon!"
    He crept from his bed;
And, seeing the others were gone, he said,
"I'm gittin' over the cold 'n my head."
    And away he sped,
To open the wonderful box in the shed.

His brothers had walked but a little way,
When Jotham to Nathan chanced to say,
"What is the feller up to, hey!"
"Don'o' — the 's suthin' ur other to pay,
Ur he wouldn't 'a' stayed tu hum to-day."
Says Burke, "His toothache's all 'n his eye!
He never 'd missed a Fo'th-o'-July,
Ef he hedn't got some machine to try."
Then Sol, the little one, spoke: "By darn!
Le's hurry back an' hide 'n the barn,
An' pay him fur tellin' us that yarn!"
"Agreed!" Through the orchard they creep back
Along by the fences, behind the stack,
And one by one, through a hole in the wall,
In under the dusty barn they crawl,
Dressed in their Sunday garments all;
And a very astonishing sight was that,
When each in his cobwebbed coat and hat
Came up through the floor like an ancient rat
    And there they hid;
    And Reuben slid
The fastenings back, and the door undid.
    "Keep dark!" said he,
"While I squint an' see what the' is to see."

As knights of old put on their mail —
    From head to foot an iron suit,
Iron jacket and iron boot,
Iron breeches, and on the head
No hat, but an iron pot instead,
    And under the chin the bail,
(I believe they called the thing a helm,)
Then sallied forth to overwhelm
The dragons and pagans that plagued the earth
    So this *modern* knight
    Prepared for flight,
Put on his wings and strapped them tight
Jointed and jaunty, strong and light —
Buckled them fast to shoulder and hip;
Ten feet they measured from tip to tip
And a helm had he, but that he wore,
Not on his head, like those of yore,
    But more like the helm of a ship.

"Hush!" Reuben said,
"He's up in the shed!
He's opened the winder — I see his head!
He stretches it out, an' pokes it about,
Lookin' to see 'f the coast is clear,
    An' nobody near; —
Guess he don' o' who's hid in here!
He's riggin' a spring-board over the sill!
Stop laffin', Solomon! Burke, keep still!
He's a climbin' out now — Of all the things!
What's he got on? I vum, it's wings!
An' that 'tother thing? I vum, it's a tail!
An' there he sits like a hawk on a rail!
Steppin' careful, he travels the length
Of his spring-board, and teeters to try its strength.
Now he stretches his wings, like a monstrous bat;
Peeks over his shoulder; this way an' that,
Fur to see 'f the' 's any one passin' by;
But the' 's on'y a caf an' goslin nigh.
They turn up at him a wonderin' eye,
To see — The dragon! he's goin' to fly!
Away he goes! Jimminy! what a jump!
    Flop — flop — an' plump
    To the ground with a thump!
Flutt'rin' an' flound'rin' all 'n a lump!"

As a demon is hurled by an angel's spear,
Heels over head, to his proper sphere —
Heels over head, and head over heels,
Dizzily down the abyss he wheels —
So fell Darius. Upon his crown,
In the midst of the barn-yard, he came down,
In a wonderful whirl of tangled strings,
Broken braces and broken springs,
Broken tail and broken wings,
Shooting-stars, and various things;
Barn-yard litter of straw and chaff,
And much that wasn't so sweet by half.
Away with a bellow fled the calf,
And what was that? Did the gosling laugh?
'Tis a merry roar from the old barn-door.
And he hears the voice of Jotham crying,
"Say, D'rius! how do you like flyin'?"

Slowly, ruefully, where he lay,
Darius just turned and looked that way,
As he stanched his sorrowful nose with his cuff.
"Wal, I like flyin' well enough,"
He said; "but the' ain't such a thunderin' sight
O' fun in 't when ye come to light."

I just have room for the MORAL here:
And this is the moral — Stick to your sphere.
Or if you insist, as you have the right,
On spreading your wings for a loftier flight,
The moral is — Take care how you light.

Recollections of "Lalla Rookh"

Read at the Moore banquet in Boston, May 27, 1879.

When we were farm-boys, years ago,
    I dare not tell how many,
When, strange to say, the fairest day
    Was often dark and rainy;

No work, no school, no weeds to pull,
    No picking up potatoes,
No copy-page to fill with blots,
    With little o's or great O's;

But jokes and stories in the barn
    Made quiet fun and frolic;
Draughts, fox-and-geese, and games like these,
    Quite simple and bucolic;

Naught else to do, but just to braid
    A lash, or sing and whittle,
Or go, perhaps, and set our traps,
    If it "held up" a little;

On one of those fine days, for which
    We boys were always wishing,
Too wet to sow, or plant, or hoe,
    Just right to go a fishing, —

I found, not what I went to seek,
    In the old farmhouse gable, —
Nor line, nor hook, but just a book
    That lay there on the table,

Beside my sister's candlestick
    (The wick burned to the socket);
A handy book to take to bed,
    Or carry in one's pocket.

I tipped the dainty cover back,
    With little thought of finding
Anything half so bright within
    The red morocco binding;

And let by chance my careless glance
    Range over song and story;
When from between the magic leaves
    There streamed a sudden glory, —

As from a store of sunlit gems,
    Pellucid and prismatic, —
That edged with gleams the rough old beams,
    And filled the raftered attic.

I stopped to read; I took no heed
    Of time or place, or whether
The window-pane was streaked with rain,
    Or bright with clearing weather.

Of chore-time or of supper-time
    I had no thought or feeling;
If calves were bleating to be fed,
    Or hungry pigs were squealing.

The tangled web of tale and rhyme,
    Enraptured, I unraveled;
By caravan, through Hindostan,
    Toward gay Cashmere, I traveled.

Before the gate of Paradise
    I pleaded with the Peri;
And even of queer old Fadladeen
    I somehow did not weary;

119

Until a voice called out below:
   "Come, boys! the rain is over!
It's time to bring the cattle home!
   The lambs are in the clover!"

My dream took flight; but day or night,
   It came again, and lingered.
I kept the treasure in my coat,
   And many a time I fingered

Its golden leaves among the sheaves
   In the long harvest nooning;
Or in my room, till fell the gloom,
   And low boughs let the moon in.

About me beamed another world,
   Refulgent, oriental;
Life all aglow with poetry,
   Or sweetly sentimental.

My hands were filled with common tasks,
   My head with rare romances;
My old straw hat was bursting out
   With light locks and bright fancies.

In field or wood, my thoughts threw off
   The old prosaic trammels;
The sheep were grazing antelopes,
   The cows, a train of camels.

Under the shady apple-boughs,
   The book was my companion;
And while I read, the orchard spread
   One mighty branching banyan.

To mango-trees or almond-groves
   Were changed the plums and quinces.
I was the poet, Feramorz,
   And had, of course, my Princess.

The well-curb was her canopied,
   Rich palanquin; at twilight,
'T was her pavilion overhead,
   And not my garret skylight.

Ah, Lalla Rookh! O charmèd book!
   First love, in manhood slighted!
To-day we rarely turn the page
   In which our youth delighted.

Moore stands upon our shelves to-day,
   I fear a trifle dusty;
With Scott, beneath a cobweb wreath,
   And Byron, somewhat musty.

But though his orient cloth-of-gold
   Is hardly now the fashion,
His tender melodies will live
   While human hearts have passion.

The centuries roll; but he has left,
   Beside the ceaseless river,
Some flowers of rhyme untouched by Time,
   And songs that sing forever.

Filling an Order

Read at the Holmes breakfast, Boston, Dec. 3, 1879.

To Nature, in her shop one day, at work compounding simples,
Studying fresh tints for Beauty's cheeks, or new effects in dimples,
An order came: she wiped in haste her fingers and unfolded
The scribbled scrap, put on her specs, and read it, while she scolded.

"From Miss Columbia! I declare! of all the upstart misses!
What will the jade be asking next? Now what an order this is!
Where's Boston? Oh, that one-horse town out there beside the ocean!
She wants — of course, she always wants — another little notion!

"This time, three geniuses, A 1, to grace her favorite city:
The first a bard; the second wise; the third supremely witty;
None of the staid and hackneyed sort, but some peculiar flavor,
Something unique and fresh for each, will be esteemed a favor!
Modest demands! as if my hands had but to turn and toss over
A Poet veined with dew and fire, a Wit, and a Philosopher!

"But now let's see!" She put aside her old, outworn expedients,
And in a quite unusual way began to mix ingredients, —

Some in the fierce retort distilled, some pounded by the pestle, —
And set the simmering souls to steep, each in its glowing vessel.
In each, by turns, she poured, she stirred, she skimmed the shining
    liquor,
Threw laughter in, to make it thin, or thought, to make it thicker.
But when she came to choose the clay, she found, to her vexation,
That, with a stock on hand to fill an order for a nation,
Of that more finely tempered stuff, electric and ethereal,
Of which a genius must be formed, she had but scant material —
For three? For one! What should be done? A bright idea struck her;
Her old witch-eyes began to shine, her mouth began to pucker.

Says she, "The fault, I'm well aware, with genius is the presence
Of altogether too much clay, with quite too little essence,
And sluggish atoms that obstruct the spiritual solution;
So now, instead of spoiling these by over-much dilution,
With their fine elements I'll make a single, rare phenomenon,
And of three common geniuses concoct a most uncommon one,
So that the world shall smile to see a soul so universal,
Such poesy and pleasantry, packed in so small a parcel."

So said, so done; the three in one she wrapped, and stuck the label:
Poet, Professor, Autocrat of Wit's own Breakfast-Table.

SEPTIMUS WINNER
1827–1902

Ten Little Injuns

Ten little Injuns standin' in a line,
One toddled home and then there were nine;
Nine little Injuns swingin' on a gate,
One tumbled off and then there were eight.

    One little, two little, three little,
        four little, five little Injun boys;
    Six little, seven little, eight little,
        nine little, ten little Injun boys.

Eight little Injuns never heard of heav'n,
One kick'd the bucket and then there were seven;
Seven little Injuns cuttin' up their tricks,
One broke his neck and then there were six.

Six little Injuns kickin' all alive,
One went to sleep and then there were five;
Five little Injuns on a cellar door,
One tumbled in and then there were four.

Four little Injuns out upon a spree,
One dead drunk and then there were three;
Three little Injuns out in a canoe,
One tumbled overboard and then there were two.

Two little Injuns foolin' with a gun,
One shot t'other and then there was one;
One little Injun livin' all alone,
He got married and then there was none.

This little Injun, with his little wife,
Lived in a wigwam the balance of his life;
One daddy Injun and a mommy Squaw
Brought up a family of Ten Injuns more.

> *One little, two little, three little,*
> > *four little, five little Injuns more;*
> *Six little, seven little, eight little,*
> > *nine little, ten little Injuns more.*

The Coolie Chinee

You have heard, I suppose, of the man in the moon,
And the mermaids that live in the sea,
Of Baron Munchausen and John Chinaman,
Better known as the Coolie Chinee.
He shaves half his head and then raises a queue
That reaches way down to his knee,
He carries a fan, and there's much he can do,
This elegant Coolie Chinee.

> *Hong-Kong, Oolong;*
> *Hari-Kari, ding-a-dong.*
> *Hong-Kong, Souchoung;*
> *Hari-Kari, sound the gong.*

We sent off our Biddy, and also our cook,
Because their wages were high,
And as a domestic we went for, and took
A coolie their place to supply.
For dinner he gave us our little pet cat
And a cup of steaming hot tea;
Our supper he made from a cussed old rat,
This troublesome Coolie Chinee.

His skin was the color of coffee and milk,
And his feet were delightfully small;
His trowsers were made of the finest of silk,
But some things he had not at all.
He never would sit like the rest of us did,
But down on the floor squatted he:
I never could tell all the trouble we had
With this wonderful Coolie Chinee.

This cunning old chap, from the nation of flow'rs,
Would cheat as you couldn't believe:
He'd "go for" the game with the aces and bowers
He'd manage to hide in his sleeve;
He had the most innocent kind of a look
That any one ever did see;
But he'd "shut up your eye" by hook or by crook,
This terrible Coolie Chinee.

We bought a silk hat and a duster so neat
To keep off the sun and the dirt,
But the hat for a basket to market he took,
And the duster he wore for a shirt.
Oh never be foolish, dear people, I pray,
Oh never be silly like me,
And if you need help, in the future, I pray,
Engage not a Coolie Chinee.

Lilliputian's Beer Song

If you wish to pull a cork,
It's no work in New York,
Ev'ry house of good renown,
Well is known 'round the town;

All you wish your thirst to slake
You can take for its sake,
To refresh yourself, "you bet"
Or to treat a friend you've met.

> Lager beer, Lager beer,
> Light and foamy, bright and clear,
> Lager beer, Lager beer,
> Sure to give your heart good cheer.
> Glass of beer, glass of beer,
> To the thirsty one so dear,
> Lager beer, Lager beer,
> Lager, Lager beer.
> Kronen beer, Franken beer,
> Light and foamy, bright and clear,
> Leisten beer, Bürger beer,
> Sure to give your heart good cheer.
> Glass of beer, glass of beer,
> To the thirsty one so dear,
> German beer, German beer,
> German, German beer.

If in Phil-a-del-phia too,
Feeling blue, as we do,
Where the license is so high
Do not sigh, if you're dry.
For you need not try in vain
If in pain, try again
As it all is very plain
Just *speak easy* to obtain.

If you go to Manayunk
Full of spunk, don't get drunk,
For the natives on the hills,
And the mills, fill the tills.
Full of fight both day and night,
Take delight, I am right,
They are sure to make it hot
At that spot no matter what.

If to Jersey you should go
Be it so, don't you know?

Tackle Glos'ter for your drink
So I think, so *we* think.
But you need not travel far
For a bar, or segar,
And you never need to fret
All you want, why you can get.

If you go to Boston town
Of renown, sit you down
For you dare not stand to sip
With your nip, at your lip.
You must also take a bite
Very light, if I'm right
When you wish to take a drink
Give the knowing ones a wink.

If to Baltimore you go,
Be not slow, don't you know
You will find just all you need
Yes indeed! drink and feed.
Ask the first one that you meet
On the street, he will treat,
For the people that you find
In the South are just that kind.

When you wander in the West
Take a rest, it is best,
Till they show in ninety-two
Something new, they can do.
If you need a jolly treat
When you meet on the street,
Give the Hoosier boys a show
It's a go, that you must know.

Well, I'm out of wind you see
All agree, pity me,
And I'm getting awful dry
Very dry, that's no lie.
I must go and see a man
If I can, that's my plan,
Let me wind up with my rhyme
And I'll sing some other time.

EMILY DICKINSON
1830–1886

A bird came down the walk

A bird came down the walk:
He did not know I saw;
He bit an angle-worm in halves
And ate the fellow, raw.

And then he drank a dew
From a convenient grass,
And then hopped sidewise to the wall
To let a beetle pass.

He glanced with rapid eyes
That hurried all abroad, —
They looked like frightened beads, I thought
He stirred his velvet head

Like one in danger; cautious,
I offered him a crumb,
And he unrolled his feathers
And rowed him softer home

Than oars divide the ocean,
Too silver for a seam,
Or butterflies, off banks of noon,
Leap, plashless, as they swim.

I like to see it lap the miles

I like to see it lap the miles,
And lick the valleys up,
And stop to feed itself at tanks;
And then, prodigious, step

Around a pile of mountains,
And, supercilious, peer
In shanties by the sides of roads;
And then a quarry pare

To fit its sides, and crawl between,
Complaining all the while
In horrid, hooting stanza;
Then chase itself down hill

And neigh like Boanerges;
Then, punctual as a star,
Stop — docile and omnipotent —
At its own stable door.

His Mansion in the Pool

His Mansion in the Pool
The Frog forsakes —
He rises on a Log
And statements makes —
His Auditors two Worlds
Deducting me —
The Orator of April
Is hoarse Today —
His Mittens at his Feet
No Hand hath he —
His eloquence a Bubble
As Fame should be —
Applaud him to discover
To your chagrin
Demosthenes has vanished
In Waters Green —

MARY MAPES DODGE
1830–1905

The Zealless Xylographer

A xylographer started to cross the sea
By means of a Xanthic Xebec;
But, alas! he sighed for the Zuyder Zee,
And feared he was in for a wreck.

He tried to smile, but all in vain,
    Because of a Zygomatic pain;
And as for singing, his cheeriest tone
    Reminded him of a Xylophone —
Or else, when the pain would sharper grow,
    His notes were as keen as a Zuffolo.
And so it is likely he did not find
    On board Xenodochy to his mind.
The fare was poor, and he was sure
    Xerofphagy he could not endure;
Zoöphagous surely he was, I aver,
    This dainty and starving Xylographer.
Xylophagous truly he could not be —
    No sickly vegetarian he!
He'd have blubbered like any old Zeuglodon
    Had Xerophthalmia not come on.
And the end of it was he never again
    In a Xanthic Xebec went sailing the main.

EDMUND CLARENCE STEDMAN
1833–1908

The Ballad of Lager Bier

In fallow college days, Tom Harland,
    We both have known the ways of Yale,
And talked of many a nigh and far land,
    O'er many a famous tap of ale.
There still they sing their Gaudeamus,
    And see the road to glory clear;
But taps, that in our day were famous,
    Have given place to Lager Bier.

Now, settled in this island-city,
    We let new fashions have their weight;
Though none too lucky — more's the pity! —
    Can still beguile our humble state
By finding time to come together,
    In every season of the year,
In sunny, wet, or windy weather,
    And clink our mugs of Lager Bier.

On winter evenings, cold and blowing,
    'Tis good to order " 'alf-and-'alf";
To watch the fire-lit pewter glowing,
    And laugh a hearty English laugh;
Or even a sip of mountain whiskey
    Can raise a hundred phantoms dear
Of days when boyish blood was frisky,
    And no one heard of Lager Bier.

We've smoked in summer with Oscanyan,
    Cross-legged in that defunct bazaar,
Until above our heads the banyan
    Or palm-tree seemed to spread afar;
And, then and there, have drunk his sherbet,
    Tinct with the roses of Cashmere:
That Orient calm! who would disturb it
    With Norseland calls for Lager Bier?

There's Paris chocolate, — nothing sweeter,
    At midnight, when the dying strain,
Just warbled by La Favorita,
    Still hugs the music-haunted brain;
Yet of all bibulous compoundings,
    Extracts or brewings, mixed or clear,
The best, in substance and surroundings,
    For frequent use, is Lager Bier.

Karl Schaeffer is a stalwart brewer,
    Who has above his vaults a hall,
Where — fresh-tapped, foaming, cool, and pure —
    He serves the nectar out to all.
Tom Harland, have you any money?
    Why, then, we'll leave this hemisphere,
This western land of milk and honey,
    For one that flows with Lager Bier.

Go, flaxen-haired and blue-eyed maiden,
    My German Hebe! hasten through
Yon smoke-cloud, and return thou laden
    With bread and cheese and bier for two.
Limburger suits this bearded fellow;
    His brow is high, his taste severe:
But I'm for Schweitzer, mild and yellow,
    To eat with bread and Lager Bier.

Ah, yes! the Schweitzer hath a savor
   Of marjoram and mountain thyme,
An odoriferous, Alpine flavor;
   You almost hear the cow-bells chime
While eating it, or, dying faintly,
   The *Ranz-des-vaches* entrance the ear,
Until you feel quite Swiss and saintly,
   Above your glass of Lager Bier.

Here comes our drink, froth-crowned and sunlit,
   In goblets with high-curving arms,
Drawn from a newly opened runlet,
   As bier must be, to have its charms.
This primal portion each shall swallow
   At one draught, for a pioneer;
And thus a ritual usage follow
   Of all who honor Lager Bier.

Glass after glass in due succession,
   Till, borne through midriff, heart, and brain,
He mounts his throne and takes possession, —
   The genial Spirit of the grain!
Then comes the old Berserker madness
   To make each man a priest and seer,
And, with a Scandinavian gladness,
   Drink deeper draughts of Lager Bier!

Go, maiden, fill again our glasses!
   While, with anointed eyes, we scan
The blouse Teutonic lads and lasses,
   The Saxon — Pruss — Bohemian,
The sanded floor, the cross-beamed gables,
   The ancient Flemish paintings queer,
The rusty cup-stains on the tables,
   The terraced kegs of Lager Bier.

And is it Göttingen, or Gotha,
   Or Munich's ancient Wagner Brei,
Where each Bavarian drinks his quota,
   And swings a silver tankard high?
Or some ancestral Gast-Haus lofty
   In Nuremberg — of famous cheer
When Hans Sachs lived, and where, so oft, he
   Sang loud the praise of Lager Bier?

For even now some curious glamour
   Has brought about a misty change!
Things look, as in a moonlight dream, or
   Magician's mirror, quaint and strange.
Some weird, phantasmagoric notion
   Impels us backward many a year,
And far across the northern ocean,
   To Fatherlands of Lager Bier.

As odd a throng I see before us
   As ever haunted Brocken's height,
Carousing, with unearthly chorus,
   On any wild Walpurgis-night;
I see the wondrous art-creations!
   In proper guise they all appear,
And, in their due and several stations,
   Unite in drinking Lager Bier.

I see in yonder nook a trio:
   There's Doctor Faust, and, by his side,
Not half so love-distraught as Io,
   Is gentle Margaret, heaven-eyed;
That man in black beyond the waiter —
   I know him by his fiendish leer —
Is Mephistophiles, the traitor!
   And how he swigs his Lager Bier!

Strange if great Goethe should have blundered,
   Who says that Margaret slipt and fell
In Anno Domini Sixteen Hundred,
   Or thereabout; and Faustus, — well,
We won't deplore his resurrection,
   Since Margaret is with him here,
But, under her serene protection,
   May boldly drink our Lager Bier.

That bare-legged gypsy, small and lithy,
   Tanned like an olive by the sun,
Is little Mignon; sing us, prithee,
   Kennst Du das Land, my pretty one!

Ah, no! she shakes her southern tresses,
  As half in doubt and more in fear;
Perhaps the elvish creature guesses
  We've had too much of Lager Bier.

There moves, full-bodiced, ripe, and human,
  With merry smiles to all who come,
Karl Schaeffer's wife, — the very woman
  Whom Rubens drew his Venus from!
But what a host of tricksome graces
  Play round our fairy Undine here,
Who pouts at all the bearded faces,
  And, laughing, brings the Lager Bier.

"Sit down, nor chase the vision farther,
  You're tied to Yankee cities still!"
I hear you, but so much the rather
  Should Fancy travel where she will.
Yet let the dim ideals scatter;
  One puff, and lo! they disappear;
The comet, next, or some such matter,
  We'll talk about our Lager Bier.

Now, then, your eyes begin to brighten,
  And marvellous theories to flow;
A philosophic theme you light on,
  And, spurred and booted, off you go!
If e'er — to drive Apollo's phaeton —
  I need an earthly charioteer,
This tall-browed genius I will wait on,
  And prime him first with Lager Bier.

But higher yet, in middle Heaven,
  Your steed seems taking flight, my friend;
You read the secret of the Seven,
  And on through trackless regions wend!
Don't vanish in the Milky Way, for
  This afternoon you're wanted here;
Come back! come back! and help me pay for
  The bread and cheese and Lager Bier.

GEORGE ARNOLD
1834–1865

Beer

Here,
   With my beer
I sit,
While golden moments flit:
   Alas!
   They pass
Unheeded by:
And, as they fly,
I,
Being dry,
   Sit, idly sipping here
   My beer.

O, finer far
Than fame, or riches, are
The graceful smoke-wreaths of this free cigar!
   Why
   Should I
   Weep, wail, or sigh?
   What if luck has passed me by?
What if my hopes are dead, —
My pleasures fled?
   Have I not still
   My fill
Of right good cheer, —
Cigars and beer?

   Go, whining youth,
   Forsooth!
Go, weep and wail,
Sigh and grow pale,
   Weave melancholy rhymes
   On the old times,
Whose joys like shadowy ghosts appear, —
But leave to me my beer!
   Gold is dross, —
   Love is loss, —

So, if I gulp my sorrows down,
Or see them drown
In foamy draughts of old nut-brown,
Then do I wear the crown,
   Without the cross!

CHARLES H. WEBB ("JOHN PAUL")
1834–1905

Autumn Leaves

The melancholy days have come,
   Which Mr. Bryant sings,
Of wailing winds and naked woods,
   And other cheerful things.

The robin from the glen has flown,
   And there Matilda J.
Now roams in quest of autumn leaves
   To press and put away.

Leaves in the sere, to school-girls dear,
   Are found where'er one looks,
On hill, in vale, in wood, in field,
   But mostly in my books.

If I take up my Unabridged
   Some curious word to scan,
Rare leaves are sped of green and red,
   Or maybe black and tan.

The book of books — my Bible — now
   I scarcely dare to touch,
Lest it bring grief to some rare leaf —
   Ash, maple, oak, or such.

And if upon the lounge I lie
   To read while I repose,
Lo! arid leaves in dusty sheaves
   Sift down upon my clothes.

No more I swear in empty air,
    But straight invoke a broom,
And soon St. Bridget comes and sweeps
    The rubbish from the room.

O autumn leaves, rare autumn leaves,
    So lovely out-of-doors,
Strew the wild wood (you could or should),
    But muss not Christian floors!

Too late I know a solemn truth
    I did suspect before:
These leaves that autumn branches bear
    Are an autumnal bore.

At the Ball!

Is the ball very stupid, *ma mignonne?*
    Pauvre petite, you look ennuied to death —
There is *Bête — n'est-ce pas?* in your eye,
    And a *soupçon* of yawn in your breath.

Of a truth it is stupid, *ma mignonne;*
    The giver is wrinkled and gray!
The dances are older than Rome,
    And the dancers as well are *passé.*

The wine that they give us, *ma mignonne,*
    Is but *vin ordinaire,* thin and poor, —
It comes from a shop in *Rue Jacques,*
    And it cost but ten *sous,* I am sure.

There's a ghost stirring somewhere, *ma mignonne;*
    The lamps all burn dimly and low,
And the music would do for *La Morgue* —
    Allons!. . . . not quite yet. . . . I won't go.

Come sit on this *fauteuil, ma mignonne,*
    And show me the make of that glove.
It is *Jouvin,* I think. . . . now you're wicked!
    Reste tranquille un moment, that's a love.

Who called the ball stupid, *ma mignonne?*
   'Tis the best we have had for a week;
The dances are lively enough,
   And for music — *j'attends*, please to speak!

One glass *à ta santé, ma mignonne;*
   On the rim of my cup print a kiss —
Never tell me again of Bordeaux;
   There's no red wine in life like to this!

Who said lamps burned dimly, *ma mignonne?*
   Look, the *salon* is lighter than day —
It was queer, to find fault with the light!
   Not enough! there's too much, *verité.*

At what time did *ta maman, ma mignonne,*
   Suggest that the carriage should call?
Sainte Vierge! it is striking the hour —
   Do you wish to go home from the ball?

SAMUEL LANGHORNE CLEMENS ("MARK TWAIN")
1835–1910

The Aged Pilot Man

On the Erie Canal, it was,
   All on a summer's day,
I sailed forth with my parents
   Far away to Albany.

From out the clouds at noon that day
   There came a dreadful storm,
That piled the billows high about,
   And filled us with alarm.

A man came rushing from a house,
   Saying, "Snub up your boat, I pray,
Snub up your boat, snub up, alas,
   Snub up while yet you may."

Our captain cast one glance astern,
    Then forward glancèd he,
And said, "My wife and little ones
    I never more shall see."

Said Dollinger the pilot man,
    In noble words, but few —
"Fear not, but lean on Dollinger,
    And he will fetch you through."

The boat drove on, the frightened mules
    Tore through the rain and wind,
And bravely still, in danger's post,
    The whip-boy strode behind.

"Come 'board, come 'board," the captain cried,
    "Nor tempt so wild a storm";
But still the raging mules advanced,
    And still the boy strode on.

Then said the captain to us all,
    "Alas, 'tis plain to me,
The greater danger is not there,
    But here upon the sea.

"So let us strive, while life remains,
    To save all souls on board,
And then if die at last we must,
    Let . . . I *cannot* speak the word!"

Said Dollinger the pilot man,
    Tow'ring above the crew,
"Fear not, but trust in Dollinger,
    And he will fetch you through."

"Low bridge! low bridge!" all heads went down,
    The laboring bark sped on;
A mill we passed, we passed a church,
    Hamlets, and fields of corn;
And all the world came out to see,
    And chased along the shore

Crying, "Alas, alas, the sheeted rain,
    The wind, the tempest's roar!
Alas, the gallant ship and crew,
    Can *nothing* help them more?"

And from our deck sad eyes looked out
    Across the stormy scene;
The tossing wake of billows aft,
    The bending forests green,

The chickens sheltered under carts,
    In lee of barn the cows,
The scurrying swine with straw in mouth,
    The wild spray from our bows!

      "She balances!
      She wavers!
Now let her go about!
  If she misses stays and broaches to,
We're all" — [then with a shout]
     "Huray! huray!
     Avast! belay!
     Take in more sail!
     Lord, what a gale!
Ho, boy, haul taut on the hind mule's tail!"

"Ho! lighten ship! ho! man the pump!
    Ho, hostler, heave the lead!
And count ye all, both great and small,
    As numbered with the dead!
For mariner for forty year
    On Erie, boy and man,
I never yet saw such a storm,
    Or one 't with it began!"

So overboard a keg of nails
    And anvils three we threw,
Likewise four bales of gunny-sacks,
    Two hundred pounds of glue,
Two sacks of corn, four ditto wheat,
    A box of books, a cow,
A violin, Lord Byron's works,
    A rip-saw and a sow.

A curve! a curve! the dangers grow!
"Labbord! — stabbord! — s-t-e-a-d-y! — so! —
Hard-a-port, Dol! — hellum-a-lee!
Haw the head mule! — the aft one gee!
Luff! — bring her to the wind!"

"A quarter-three! — 'tis shoaling fast!
    Three feet large! — t-h-r-e-e feet! —
Three feet scant!" I cried in fright.
    "Oh, is there no retreat?"

Said Dollinger the pilot man,
    As on the vessel flew,
"Fear not, but trust in Dollinger,
    And he will fetch you through."

A panic struck the bravest hearts,
    The boldest cheek turned pale;
For plain to all, this shoaling said
A leak had burst the ditch's bed!
And, straight as bolt from crossbow sped,
Our ship swept on with shoaling lead,
    Before the fearful gale!

"Sever the tow-line! Cripple the mules!"
    Too late! . . . There comes a shock!

    .   .   .   .   .   .

Another length, and the fated craft
    Would have swum in the saving lock!

Then gathered together the shipwrecked crew
    And took one last embrace,
While sorrowful tears from despairing eyes
    Ran down each hopeless face;
And some did think of their little ones
    Whom they never more might see,
And others of waiting wives at home,
    And mothers that grieved would be.

But of all the children of misery there
    On that poor sinking frame,
But one spake words of hope and faith,
    And I worshiped as they came:

140

Said Dollinger the pilot man —
   (O brave heart, strong and true!) —
"Fear not, but trust in Dollinger,
   For he will fetch you through."

Lo! scarce the words have passed his lips
   The dauntless prophet say'th,
When every soul about him seeth
   A wonder crown his faith!

For straight a farmer brought a plank —
   (Mysteriously inspired) —
And laying it unto the ship,
   In silent awe retired.
Then every sufferer stood amazed
   That pilot man before;
A moment stood. Then wondering turned,
   And speechless walked ashore.

Imitation of Julia A. Moore

Come forth from thy oozy couch,
   O Ornithorhyncus dear!
And greet with a cordial claw
   The stranger that longs to hear

From thy own lips the tale
   Of thy origin all unknown:
Thy misplaced bone where flesh should be
   And flesh where should be bone;

And fishy fin where should be paw,
   And beaver-trowel tail,
And snout of beast equip'd with teeth
   Where gills ought *to* prevail.

Come, Kangaroo, the good and true!
   Foreshortened as to legs,
And body tapered like a churn,
   And sack marsupial, i' fegs,

And tell us why you linger here,
    Thou relic of a vanished time,
When all your friends as fossils sleep,
    Immortalized in lime!

Emmeline Grangerford's
"Ode to Stephen Dowling Bots, Dec'd"

And did young Stephen sicken,
    And did young Stephen die?
And did the sad hearts thicken,
    And did the mourners cry?

No; such was not the fate of
    Young Stephen Dowling Bots;
Though sad hearts round him thickened,
    'Twas not from sickness' shots.

No whooping-cough did rack his frame,
    Nor measles drear with spots;
Not these impaired the sacred name
    Of Stephen Dowling Bots.

Despised love struck not with woe
    That head of curly knots,
Nor stomach troubles laid him low,
    Young Stephen Dowling Bots.

O no. Then list with tearful eye,
    Whilst I his fate do tell.
His soul did from this cold world fly
    By falling down a well.

They got him out and emptied him;
    Alas it was too late;
His spirit was gone for to sport aloft
    In the realms of the good and great.

THOMAS BAILEY ALDRICH
1836–1907

Fannie

Fannie has the sweetest foot
Ever in a gaiter boot!
And the hoyden knows it,
And, of course, she shows it, —
Not the knowledge, but the foot, —
Yet with such a modest grace,
Never seems it out of place,
      Ah, there are not many
         Half so sly, or sad, or mad,
        Or wickeder than Fannie.

Fannie has the blackest hair
  Of any of the village girls;
It does not shower on her neck
  In silken or coquettish curls.
It droops in folds around her brow,
  As clouds, at night, around the moon,
Looped with lilies here and there,
  In many a dangerous festoon.
And Fannie wears a gipsy hat,
Saucily — yes, all of that!
      Ah, there are not many
         Half so sly, or sad, or mad,
        Or wickeder than Fannie.

Fannie wears an open dress —
  Ah! the charming chemisette!
Half concealing, half revealing
  Something far more charming yet.
Fannie drapes her breast with lace,
As one would drape a costly vase
To keep away mischievous flies;
But lace can't keep away one's eyes,
For every time her bosom heaves,
  Ah, it peepeth through it;
Yet Fannie looks the while as if
  Never once she knew it.
      Ah, there are not many
         Half so sly, or sad, or mad,
        Or innocent as Fannie.

Fannie lays her hand in mine;
  Fannie speaks with *naïveté*,
Fannie kisses me, she does!
  In her own coquettish way.
Then softly speaks and deeply sighs,
With angels nestled in her eyes.
In the merrie month of May,
  Fannie swears sincerely
She will be my own, my wife,
  And love me dearly, dearly
Ever after all her life.
      Ah, there are not many
        Half so sly, or sad, or mad,
        As my true-hearted Fannie.

At a Reading

The spare Professor, grave and bald,
Began his paper. It was called,
I think, "A brief Historic Glance
At Russia, Germany, and France."
A glance, but to my best belief
'Twas almost anything but brief —
A wide survey, in which the earth
Was seen before mankind had birth;
Strange monsters basked them in the sun,
Behemoth, armored glyptodon,
And in the dawn's unpractised ray
The transient dodo winged its way;
Then, by degrees, through silt and slough,
We reached Berlin — I don't know how.
The good Professor's monotone
Had turned me into senseless stone
Instanter, but that near me sat
Hypatia in her new spring hat,
Blue-eyed, intent, with lips whose bloom
Lighted the heavy-curtained room.
Hypatia — ah, what lovely things
Are fashioned out of eighteen springs!
At first, in sums of this amount,
The blighting winters do not count.

Just as my eyes were growing dim
With heaviness, I saw that slim,
Erect, elastic figure there,
Like a pond-lily taking air.
She looked so fresh, so wise, so neat,
So altogether crisp and sweet,
I quite forgot what Bismarck said,
And why the Emperor shook his head,
And how it was Von Moltke's frown
Cost France another frontier town.
The only facts I took away
From the Professor's theme that day
Were these: a forehead broad and low,
Such as the antique sculptures show;
A chin to Greek perfection true;
Eyes of Astarte's tender blue;
A high complexion without fleck
Or flaw, and curls about her neck.

ANONYMOUS

The Young Woman from Aenos

There was a young woman from Aenos
Who came to our party as Venus.
　　We told her how rude
　　'Twas to come there quite nude,
And we brought her a leaf from the green-h'us.

BRET HARTE
1836–1902

Colenso Rhymes for Orthodox Children

A smart man was Bishop Colenso —
'T were better he never had been so —
　　He said, "A queer book
　　Is that same Pentateuch!"
Said the clergy, "You mus n't tell men so."

There once was a Bishop of Natal
Who made this admission most fatal;
He said: "Between us
I fear *Exodus*
Is a pretty tough yarn for Port Natal."

Shall I believe that Noah's Ark
    Rode on the waters blue?
Or must I, with Colenso, say
    The story is untrue?

What then becomes of all my joys —
    That ark I loved so well —
Those tigers — dear to little boys —
    Shall they this error swell?

There once was a Bishop, and what do you think!
He talked with a Zulu, who says with a wink,
"Folks say that the Pentateuch's true. — I deny it."
And never since then has this Bishop been quiet.

Schemmelfennig

Brave Teuton, though thy awful name
    Is one no common rhyme can mimic,
Though in despair the trump of Fame
    Evades thy painful patronymic —
Though orators forego thy praise,
    And timid bards by tongue or pen ig-
Nore thee — thus alone I raise
    Thy name in song, my Schemmelfennig!

What though no hecatombs may swell
    With mangled forms thy path victorious;
Though Charleston to thee bloodless fell,
    Wert thou less valiant or less glorious?
Thou took'st tobacco — cotton — grain —
    And slaves — they say a hundred and ten nig-
Gers were captives in thy train
    And swelled thy pomp, my Schemmelfennig!

Let Asboth mourn his name unsung,
And Schurz his still unwritten story;
Let Blenker grieve the silent tongue,
And Zagonyi forego his glory;
Ye are but paltry farthing lamps,
Your lights the fickle marsh or fen ig-
Nus fatuus of Southern swamps,
Beside the sun of Schemmelfennig!

Plain Language from Truthful James

Which I wish to remark,
And my language is plain,
That for ways that are dark
And for tricks that are vain,
The heathen Chinee is peculiar,
Which the same I would rise to explain.

Ah Sin was his name;
And I shall not deny,
In regard to the same,
What that name might imply;
But his smile it was pensive and childlike,
As I frequent remarked to Bill Nye.

It was August the third,
And quite soft was the skies;
Which it might be inferred
That Ah Sin was likewise;
Yet he played it that day upon William
And me in a way I despise.

Which we had a small game,
And Ah Sin took a hand:
It was Euchre. The same
He did not understand;
But he smiled as he sat by the table,
With the smile that was childlike and bland.

Yet the cards they were stocked
 In a way that I grieve,
And my feelings were shocked
 At the state of Nye's sleeve,
Which was stuffed full of aces and bowers,
 And the same with intent to deceive.

But the hands that were played
 By that heathen Chinee,
And the points that he made, —
 Were quite frightful to see, —
Till at last he put down a right bower,
 Which the same Nye had dealt unto me.

Then I looked up at Nye,
 And he gazed upon me;
And he rose with a sigh,
 And said, "Can this be?
We are ruined by Chinese cheap labor," —
 And he went for that heathen Chinee.

In the scene that ensued
 I did not take a hand,
But the floor it was strewed
 Like the leaves on the strand
With the cards that Ah Sin had been hiding,
 In the game "he did not understand."

In his sleeves, which were long,
 He had twenty-four jacks, —
Which was coming it strong,
 Yet I state but the facts;
And we found on his nails, which were taper,
 What is frequent in tapers, — that's wax.

Which is why I remark,
 And my language is plain,
That for ways that are dark
 And for tricks that are vain,
The heathen Chinee is peculiar, —
 Which the same I am free to maintain.

The Society upon the Stanislaus

I reside at Table Mountain, and my name is Truthful James;
I am not up to small deceit, or any sinful games;
And I'll tell in simple language what I know about the row
That broke up our society upon the Stanislow.

But first I would remark, that it is not a proper plan
For any scientific man to whale his fellow-man,
And, if a member don't agree with his peculiar whim,
To lay for that same member for to "put a head" on him.

Now, nothing could be finer or more beautiful to see
Than the first six months' proceedings of that same society,
Till Brown of Calaveras brought a lot of fossil bones
That he found within a tunnel near the tenement of Jones.

Then Brown he read a paper, and he reconstructed there,
From those same bones, an animal that was extremely rare;
And Jones then asked the Chair for a suspension of the rules,
Till he could prove that those same bones was one of his lost mules.

Then Brown he smiled a bitter smile and said he was at fault,
It seemed he had been trespassing on Jones's family vault;
He was a most sarcastic man, this quiet Mr. Brown,
And on several occasions he had cleaned out the town.

Now, I hold it is not decent for a scientific gent
To say another is an ass — at least, to all intent;
Nor should the individual who happens to be meant
Reply by heaving rocks at him to any great extent.

Then Abner Dean of Angel's raised a point of order, when
A chunk of old red sandstone took him in the abdomen,
And he smiled a kind of sickly smile, and curled up on the floor,
And the subsequent proceedings interested him no more.

For, in less time than I write it, every member did engage
In a warfare with the remnants of a palæozoic age;
And the way they heaved those fossils in their anger was a sin,
Till the skull of an old mammoth caved the head of Thompson in.

R. H. NEWELL ("ORPHEUS C. KERR")

And this is all I have to say of these improper games
For I live at Table Mountain, and my name is Truthful James;
And I've told, in simple language, what I know about the row
That broke up our society upon the Stanislow.

R. H. NEWELL ("ORPHEUS C. KERR")
1836–1901

The Rejected "National Hymns"

National Hymn

BY H——Y W. L–NGF——W

Back in the years when Phlagstaff, the Dane, was monarch
Over the sea-ribb'd land of the fleet-footed Norsemen,
Once there went forth young Ursa to gaze at the heavens —
Ursa, the noblest of all the Vikings and horsemen.

Musing, he sat in his stirrups and viewed the horizon,
Where the Aurora lapt stars in a North-polar manner,
Wildly he started, — for there in the heavens before him
Flutter'd and flam'd the original Star-Spangled Banner.

National Hymn

BY THE HON. CH——S S–MN–R

Pond'rous projectiles, hurl'd by heavy hands,
Fell on our Liberty's poor infant head,
Ere she a stadium had well advanced
On the great path that to her greatness led;
Her temple's propylon was shatteréd;
Yet, thanks to saving Grace and Washington,
Her incubus was from her bosom hurl'd;
And, rising like a cloud-dispelling sun,
She took the oil with which her hair was curl'd
To grease the "Hub" round which revolves the world.

R. H. NEWELL ("ORPHEUS C. KERR")

National Hymn

BY J—HN GR——NL—F WH—T———R

My Native Land, thy Puritanic stock
Still finds its roots firm-bound in Plymouth Rock,
And all thy sons unite in one grand wish —
To keep the virtues of Preservéd Fish.

Preservéd Fish, the Deacon stern and true,
Told our New England what her sons should do,
And if they swerve from loyalty and right,
Then the whole land is lost indeed in night.

National Hymn

BY DR. OL—V—R W—ND——L H—LMES

A diagnosis of our hist'ry proves
Our native land a land its native loves;
Its birth a deed obstetric without peer,
Its growth a source of wonder far and near.
To love it more behold how foreign shores
Sink into nothingness beside its stores;
Hyde Park at best — though counted ultra-grand —
The "Boston Common" of Victoria's land.

National Hymn

BY R—LPH W—LDO EM—R——N

Source immaterial of material naught,
Focus of light infinitesimal,
Sum of all things by sleepless Nature wrought,
Of which the normal man is decimal.

Refract, in prism immortal, from thy stars
To the stars blent incipient on our flag,
The beam translucent, neutrifying death;
And raise to immortality the rag.

National Hymn

BY W—LL—M C—LL—N B—Y—NT

The sun sinks softly to his ev'ning post,
   The sun swells grandly to his morning crown;
Yet not a star our Flag of Heav'n has lost,
   And not a sunset stripe with him goes down.

So thrones may fall, and from the dust of those
   New thrones may rise, to totter like the last;
But still our Country's nobler planet glows
   While the eternal stars of Heaven are fast.

National Hymn

BY G—RGE P. M—RR—S

In the days that tried our fathers,
   Many years ago,
Our fair land achieved her freedom,
   Blood-bought, you know.
Shall we not defend her ever
   As we'd defend
That fair maiden, kind and tender,
   Calling us friend?

Yes! Let all the echoes answer,
   From hill and vale;
Yes! Let other nations, hearing,
   Joy in the tale.
Our Columbia is a lady,
   High-born and fair;
We have sworn allegiance to her —
   Touch her who dare.

National Hymn

BY N. P. W—LL—S

One hue of our Flag is taken
   From the cheeks of my blushing Pet.
And its stars beat time and sparkle
   Like the studs on her chemisette.

Its blue is the ocean shadow
    That hides in her dreamy eyes,
It conquers all men, like her,
    And still for a Union flies.

National Hymn

BY TH—M—S B—IL—Y ALD—CH

The little brown squirrel hops in the corn,
    The cricket quaintly sings,
The emerald pigeon nods his head,
    And the shad in the river springs,
The dainty sunflow'r hangs its head
    On the shore of the summer sea;
And better far that I were dead,
    If Maud did not love me.

I love the squirrel that hops in the corn,
    And the cricket that quaintly sings;
And the emerald pigeon that nods his head,
    And the shad that gayly springs.
I love the dainty sunflow'r, too,
    And Maud with her snowy breast;
I love them all; — but I love — I love —
    I love my country best.

National Hymn

BY R. H. ST—D—RD

Behold the flag! Is it not a flag?
    Deny it, man, if you dare;
And midway spread, 'twixt earth and sky,
    It hangs like a written pray'r.

Would impious hand of foe disturb
    Its memories' holy spell,
And blight it with a dew of blood?
    Ha, tr-r-aitor! ! . . . . It is well.

R. H. NEWELL ("ORPHEUS C. KERR")

The American Traveller

To Lake Aghmoogenegamook,
　All in the State of Maine,
A man from Wittequergaugaum came
　One evening in the rain.

"I am a traveller," said he,
　"Just started on a tour,
And go to Nomjamskillicook
　To-morrow morn at four."

He took a tavern bed that night,
　And with the morrow's sun,
By way of Sekledobskus went,
　With carpet-bag and gun.

A week pass'd on; and next we find
　Our native tourist come
To that sequester'd village call'd
　Genasagarnagum.

From thence he went to Absequoit,
　And there — quite tired of Maine —
He sought the mountains of Vermont,
　Upon a railroad train.

Dog Hollow, in the Green Mount State,
　Was his first stopping-place,
And then Skunk's Misery display'd
　It sweetness and its grace.

By easy stages then he went
　To visit Devil's Den;
And Scrabble Hollow, by the way,
　Did come within his ken.

Then, *via* Nine Holes and Goose Green
　He travell'd through the State,
And to Virginia, finally,
　Was guided by his fate.

R. H. NEWELL ("ORPHEUS C. KERR")

Within the Old Dominion's bounds
   He wandered up and down;
To-day, at Buzzard Roost ensconced,
   To-morrow, at Hell Town.

At Pole Cat, too, he spent a week,
   Till friends from Bull Ring came,
And made him spend a day with them
   In hunting forest game.

Then, with his carpet-bag in hand,
   To Dog Town next he went;
Though stopping at Free Negro Town,
   Where half a day he spent.

From thence, into Negationburg
   His route of travel lay,
Which having gain'd, he left the State
   And took a southward way.

North Carolina's friendly soil
   He trod at fall of night,
And, on a bed of softest down,
   He slept at Hell's Delight.

Morn found him on the road again,
   To Lazy Level bound;
At Bull's Tail, and Lick Lizzard, too,
   Good provender he found.

But the plantations near Burnt Coat
   Were even finer still,
And made the wond'ring tourist feel
   A soft, delicious thrill.

At Tear Shirt, too, the scenery
   Most charming did appear,
With Snatch It in the distance far,
   And Purgatory near.

But, 'spite of all these pleasant scenes,
   The tourist stoutly swore,
That home is brightest, after all,
   And travel is a bore.

So back he went to Maine, straightway,
  A little wife he took;
And now is making nutmegs at
  Moosehicmagunticook.

Columbia's Agony

BY MARTIN FARQUHAR TUP—R

I hold it good — as who shall hold it bad?
  To lave Columbia in the boiling tears
I shed for Freedom when my soul is sad,
  And having shed proceed to shed again:
For *human sadness sad to all appears*,
  And tears men sometimes shed are shed by men.

The normal nation lives until it dies,
  As men may die when they have ceased to live;
But when abnormal, by a foe's surprise,
  It may not reach its first-appointed goal;
For *what we have not is not ours to give*,
  And if we miss it all we miss the whole.

Columbia, young, a giant baby born,
  Aim'd at a manhood ere the child had been,
And, slipping downward in a strut forlorn,
  Learns, to its sorrow, what 't is good to know,
That *babes who walk too soon, too soon begin
  To walk*, in this dark vale of life below.

When first the State of Charleston did secede,
  And Morrill's tariff was declared repeal'd,
The soul of Freedom ev'rywhere did bleed
  For that which, having seen, it sadly saw;
So true it is, *death wounds are never heal'd,
  And law defied is not unquestion'd law*.

The mother-poet, England, sadly view'd
  The strife unnatural across the wave,
And with maternal tenderness renew'd
  Her sweet assurances of neutral love;
A *mother's love may not its offspring save;
  But mother's love is still a mother's love*.

R. H. NEWELL ("ORPHEUS C. KERR")

Learn thou, Columbia, in thine agony,
   That England loves thee, with a love as deep
As my "Proverbial Philosophy"
   Has won for me from her approving breast;
The love that never slumbers cannot sleep,
   And all for highest good is for the best.

Thy Freedom fattens on the work of slaves,
   Her Grace of Sutherland informeth me;
And all thy South Amboy is full of graves,
   Where tortured bondmen snatch a dread repose;
Learn, then, *the race enslaved is never free,*
   And in thy woes incurr'd, behold thy woes.

Thy pride is humbled, humbled is thy pride,
   And now misfortunes come upon thee, thick
With dark reproaches for the right defied,
   And cloud thy banner in a dim eclipse;
Sic transit gloria, gloria transit sic,
   The mouth that speaketh useth its own lips.

Thus speeds the world, and thus our planet speeds;
   What is, must be; and what can't be, is not;
Our acts unwise are not our wisest deeds,
   And what we do is what ourselves have done;
Mistakes remember'd are not faults forgot,
   And we must wait for day to see the sun.

The Editor's Wooing

We love thee, Ann Maria Smith,
   And in thy condescension,
We see a future full of joys
   Too numerous to mention.

There's Cupid's arrow in thy glance,
   That by thy love's coercion
Has reach'd our melting heart of hearts,
   And ask'd for one insertion.

With joy we feel the blissful smart,
    And ere our passion ranges,
We freely place thy love upon
    The list of our exchanges.

There's music in thy lowest tone,
    And silver in thy laughter;
And truth — but we will give the full
    Particulars hereafter.

Oh! we could tell thee of our plans
    All obstacles to scatter;
But we are full just now, and have
    A press of other matter.

Then let us marry, Queen of Smiths,
    Without more hesitation;
The very thought doth give our blood
    A larger circulation!

The Neutral British Gentleman

Incrusted in his island home that lies beyond the sea,
Behold the great original and genuine 'T is HE;
A paunchy, fuming Son of Beef, with double weight of chin,
And eyes that were benevolent, — but for their singular tendency to
    turn green whenever it is remarked that his irrepressible American
    cousins have made another Treaty with China ahead of him, —
    and taken Albion in.
This Neutral British Gentleman, one of the modern time.

With William, Duke of Normandy, his ancestors, he boasts,
Came over from the shores of France to whip the Saxon hosts;
And this he makes a source of pride; but wherefore there should be
Such credit to an Englishman — in the fact that he is descended from
    a nation which England is forever pretending to regard as slightly
    her inferior in everything, and particularly behind her in military
    and naval affairs — we really cannot see.
This Neutral British Gentleman, one of the modern time.

He deals in Christianity, Episcopalian brand,
And sends his missionaries forth to bully heathen land;
Just mention "Slavery" to him, and with a pious sigh
He'll say it's 'orrid, scandalous — although he's ready to fight for the
Cotton raised by slaves, and forgets how he butchered the Chinese
to make them take Opium, and blew the Sepoys from the guns
because the poor devils refused to be enslaved by the East India
Company — or his phi-lan-thro-py.
This Neutral British Gentleman, one of the modern time.

He yields to Brother Jonathan a love that passeth show, —
"We're Hanglo-Saxons, both of us, and carn't be foes, you know."
But as a Christian Englishman, he cannot, cannot hide
His horror of the spectacle — of four millions of black beings boldly
held in bondage by a nation professing the largest liberty in the
world, though in case of an anti-slavery crusade the interests of his
Manchester factors would imperatively forbid him to — take part
on either side.
This Neutral British Gentleman, one of the modern time.

Now seeing the said Jonathan by base rebellion stirr'd,
And battling with pro-slavery, it might be thence inferr'd
That British sympathy, at last, would spur him on to strife;
But, strange to say, this sympathy — is labelled "NEUTRALITY," and
consigned to any rebel port not too closely blockaded to permit
English vessels, loaded with munitions, to slip in. And when you
ask Mr. Bull what he means by this inconsistent conduct, he becomes virtuously indignant, rolls up his eyes, and says: "I carn't
endure to see brothers murdering each other and keeping me out
of my cotton — I carn't, upon my life!"
This Neutral British Gentleman, one of the modern time.

Supposing Mr. Bull should die, the question might arise:
Will he be wanted down below, or wafted to the skies?
Allowing that he had his choice, it really seems to me
The moral British Gentleman — would choose a front seat with his
Infernal Majesty; since Milton, in his blank verse correspondence
with old *Times*, more than once hinted the possibility of Nick's
rebellion against Heaven succeeding; and as the Lower Secessia
cottoned to England through numerous Hanoverian reigns, such a
choice on the part of the philanthropical Britisher would be simply
another specimen — of his NEUTRAL–I–TY!
This Neutral British Gentleman, one of the modern time.

R. H. NEWELL ("ORPHEUS C. KERR")

Tuscaloosa Sam

There was a man in Arkansaw
    As let his passions rise,
And not unfrequently pick'd out
    Some other varmint's eyes.

His name was Tuscaloosa Sam,
    And often he would say,
"There's not a cuss in Arkansaw
    I can't whip any day."

One morn, a stranger passin' by,
    Heard Sammy talkin' so,
When down he scrambled from his hoss,
    And off his coat did go.

He sorter kinder shut one eye,
    And spit into his hand,
And put his ugly head one side,
    And twitch'd his trousers' band.

"My boy," says he, "it's my belief,
    Whomever you may be,
That I kin make you screech, and smell
    Pertikler agony."

"I'm thar," says Tuscaloosa Sam,
    And chuck'd his hat away;
"I'm thar," says he, and button'd up
    As far as buttons may.

They clinch'd like two rampageous bears,
    And then went down a bit;
They swore a stream of six-inch oaths
    And fit, and fit, and fit.

When Sam would try to work away,
    And on his pegs to git,
The stranger'd pull him back; and so,
    They fit, and fit, and fit!

Then like a pair of lobsters, both
  Upon the ground were knit,
And yet the varmints used their teeth,
  And fit, and fit, and fit! !

The sun of noon was high above,
  And hot enough to split,
But only riled the fellers more,
  That fit, and fit, and fit! ! !

The stranger snapp'd at Sammy's nose,
  And shorten'd it a bit;
And then they both swore awful hard,
  And fit, and fit, and fit! ! ! !

The mud it flew, the sky grew dark,
  And all the litenins lit;
But still them critters roll'd about
  And fit, and fit, and fit! ! ! ! !

First Sam on top, then t'other chap;
  When one would make a hit,
The other'd smell the grass; and so,
  They fit, and fit, and fit! ! ! ! ! !

The night came on, the stars shone out
  As bright as wimmen's wit;
And still them fellers swore and gouged,
  And fit, and fit, and fit ! ! ! ! ! ! !

The neighbors heard the noise they made,
  And thought an earthquake lit;
Yet all the while 't was him and Sam
  As fit, and fit, and fit! ! ! ! ! ! ! !

For miles around the noise was heard;
  Folks could n't sleep a bit,
Because them two rantank'rous chaps
  Still fit, and fit, and fit! ! ! ! ! ! ! ! !

But jist at cock-crow, suddently,
  There came an awful pause,
And I and my old man run out
  To ascertain the cause.

The sun was rising in the yeast,
    And lit the hull concern;
But not a sign of either chap
    Was found at any turn.

Yet, in the region where they fit,
    We found, to our surprise,
One pint of buttons, two big knives,
    Some whiskers, and four eyes!

Dear Father, Look Up

(Illustrative of American domestic Discipline and paternal Veracity.)

Dear Father, look up,
    Away from the cup,
And tell me what aileth ma's forehead.
    It's all black-and-blue;
    O, what could she do
To cause a contusion so horrid?

"Your mother, Jane Ann,
    A newspaper man
Admired, till I warn'd her she'd catch it;
    Like Washington, I
    Cannot tell a lie —
I did it with my little hachet."

When Your Cheap Divorce Is Granted

(From a Child in the Eastern States to her mother, temporarily absent
from Home on a supposed visit to relatives in the West.)

When your cheap divorce is granted,
    Mother, and you leave the West,
Shall I stay with you or father?
    Tell me, mother, which the best?
He'll be much surprised, I fear me,
    When he knows what you have filed,
And, unless you hover near me,
    He'll appropriate your child.

Mother, if the move was needful;
    If the income you and he
Shared so long, at last has bred an
    Incompatibility;
If you'll be his wife no longer,
    When returning from the West,
Which am I to love the stronger?
    Tell me, mother, which the best?

O, Be Not Too Hasty, My Dearest

(Descriptive of a Morning-Call between fashionable sisters-in-law; as
suggested by what the American "Round Table" and the English "Saturday Review" have revealed concerning the most respectable Women of
Society.)

O, be not too hasty, my dearest,
    That cloth o'er the flagon to draw,
But pour in the goblet that's nearest
    A swig for your sister-in-law.
I know that I've taken already
    As much as beginner should stand;
But soda at home will soon steady
    The tremulous nerves of my hand.

"Pour out for yourself, my dear Bella,
    A couple of fingers, or so;
And don't you be getting too 'meller,'
    If home you have early to go.
Already the tint of our noses
    The pace is betraying, my dear;
And, after we've taken our doses,
    Suppose we swear off, for a year."

INNES RANDOLPH
1837–1887

The Rebel

Oh, I'm a good old Rebel,
    Now that's just what I am;
For this "fair Land of Freedom"
    I do not care a dam.

I'm glad I fit against it —
    I only wish we'd won,
And I don't want no pardon
    For anything I've done.

I hates the Constitution,
    This great Republic, too;
I hates the Freedmen's Buro,
    In uniforms of blue.
I hates the nasty eagle,
    With all his brag and fuss;
The lyin', thievin' Yankees,
    I hates 'em wuss and wuss.

I hate the Yankee Nation
    And everything they do;
I hate the Declaration
    Of Independence, too.
I hates the glorious Union,
    'Tis dripping with our blood;
I hates the striped banner —
    I fit it all I could.

I followed old Mars' Robert
    For four year, near about,
Got wounded in three places,
    And starved at Pint Lookout.
I cotch the roomatism
    A-campin' in the snow,
But I killed a chance of Yankees —
    I'd like to kill some mo'.

Three hundred thousand Yankees
    Is stiff in Southern dust;
We got three hundred thousand
    Before they conquered us.
They died of Southern fever
    And Southern steel and shot;
I wish it was three millions
    Instead of what we got.

I can't take up my musket
  And fight 'em now no more,
But I ain't agoin' to love 'em,
  Now that is sartin sure.
And I don't want no pardon
  For what I was and am;
I won't be reconstructed,
  And I don't care a dam.

ANONYMOUS

Two Appeals to John Harralson, Agent,
Nitre and Mining Bureau, C. S. A.

[To provide saltpetre for making gunpowder, the Confederates resorted
to many devices and stationed agents in every town to maintain artificial beds of all sorts of nitrogenous refuse. The following notice appeared in the newspapers of Selma, Alabama, signed "John Harralson,
Agent, Nitre and Mining Bureau": "The Ladies of Selma are respect-
fully requested to preserve the chamber lye collected about their premises
for the purpose of making nitre. A barrel will be sent around daily to
collect it." The notice prompted a Rebel verse and a Union reply.
—W.H.]

An Appeal to John Harralson

John Harralson, John Harralson, you are a wretched creature,
You've added to this bloody war a new and awful feature.
You'd have us think while every man is bound to be a fighter,
The ladies, bless the pretty dears, should save their p—— for nitre.

John Harralson, John Harralson, where did you get this notion,
To send your barrel round the town to gather up the lotion?
We thought the girls had work enough in making shirts and kissing,
But you have put the pretty dears to patriotic p————.

John Harralson, John Harralson, do pray invent a neater
And somewhat less immodest mode of making your saltpetre:
For 'tis an awful idea, John, gunpowdery and cranky,
That when a lady lifts her shift she's killing off a Yankee.

A *Yankee View*

John Harralson, John Harralson, we've read in song and story
How woman's tears through all the years have moistened fields of glory,
But never was it told before how, mid such scenes of slaughter,
Your southern beauties dried their tears and went to making water.

No wonder that your boys are brave! Who couldn't be a fighter,
If every time he shot his gun he used his sweetheart's nitre?
And, vice-versa, what could make a Yankee soldier sadder
Than dodging bullets fired by a pretty woman's bladder?

They say there was a subtle smell that lingered in that powder,
That as the smoke grew thicker and the din of battle louder,
That there was found to this compound one serious objection:
No soldier could sniff it without having an erection.

JOHN HAY
1838–1905

The Pledge at Spunky Point

A Tale of Earnest Effort and Human Perfidy

It's all very well for preachin',
    But preachin' and practice don't gee:
I've give the thing a fair trial,
    And you can't ring it in on me.
So toddle along with your pledge, Squire,
    Ef that's what you want me to sign;
Betwixt me and you, I've been thar,
    And I'll not take any in mine.

A year ago last Fo'th July
    A lot of the boys was here.
We all got corned and signed the pledge
    For to drink no more that year.
There was Tilmon Joy and Sheriff McPhail
    And me and Abner Fry,
And Shelby's boy Leviticus
    And the Golyers, Luke and Cy.

And we anteed up a hundred
　　In the hands of Deacon Kedge
For to be divided the follerin' Fo'th
　　'Mongst the boys that kep' the pledge.
And we knowed each other so well, Squire,
　　You may take my scalp for a fool,
Ef every man when he signed his name
　　Didn't feel cock-sure of the pool.

Fur a while it all went lovely;
　　We put up a job next day
Fur to make Joy b'lieve his wife was dead,
　　And he went home middlin' gay;
Then Abner Fry he killed a man
　　And afore he was hung McPhail
Jest bilked the widder outen her sheer
　　By getting him slewed in jail.

But Chris'mas scooped the Sheriff,
　　The egg-nogs gethered him in;
And Shelby's boy Leviticus
　　Was, New Year's, tight as sin;
And along in March the Golyers
　　Got so drunk that a fresh-biled owl
Would 'a' looked 'long-side o' them two young men,
　　Like a sober temperance fowl.

Four months alone I walked the chalk,
　　I thought my heart would break;
And all them boys a-slappin' my back
　　And axin', "What'll you take?"
I never slep' without dreamin' dreams
　　Of Burbin, Peach, or Rye,
But I chawed at my niggerhead and swore
　　I'd rake that pool or die.

At last — the Fo'th — I humped myself
　　Through chores and breakfast soon,
Then scooted down to Taggart's store —
　　For the pledge was off at noon;
And all the boys was gethered thar,
　　And each man hilt his glass —
Watchin' me and the clock quite solemn-like
　　Fur to see the last minute pass.

The clock struck twelve! I raised the jug
    And took one lovin' pull —
I was holler clar from skull to boots,
    It seemed I could n't git full.
But I was roused by a fiendish laugh
    That might have raised the dead —
Them ornary sneaks had sot the clock
    A half an hour ahead!

"All right!" I squawked. "You've got me,
    Jest order your drinks agin,
And we'll paddle up to the Deacon's
    And scoop the ante in."
But when we got to Kedge's,
    What a sight was that we saw!
The Deacon and Parson Skeeters
    In the tail of a game of Draw.

They had shook 'em the heft of the mornin',
    The Parson's luck was fa'r,
And he raked, the minute we got thar,
    The last of our pool on a pa'r.
So toddle along with your pledge, Squire,
    I 'low it's all very fine,
But ez fur myself, I thank ye,
    I'll not take any in mine.

Good and Bad Luck

After Heine

Good Luck is the gayest of all gay girls,
    Long in one place she will not stay,
Back from your brow she strokes the curls,
    Kisses you quick and flies away.

But Madame Bad Luck soberly comes
    And stays, — no fancy has she for flitting, —
Snatches of true love-songs she hums,
    And sits by your bed, and brings her knitting.

CHARLES E. CARRYL

1841–1920

A *Nautical Ballad*

A capital ship for an ocean trip
   Was the "Walloping Window-blind";
No gale that blew dismayed her crew
   Or troubled the captain's mind.
The man at the wheel was taught to feel
   Contempt for the wildest blow,
And it often appeared, when the weather had cleared,
   That he'd been in his bunk below.

"The boatswain's mate was very sedate,
   Yet fond of amusement, too;
And he played hop-scotch with the starboard watch,
   While the captain tickled the crew.
And the gunner we had was apparently mad,
   For he sat on the after rail,
And fired salutes with the captain's boots,
   In the teeth of the booming gale.

"The captain sat in a commodore's hat
   And dined in a royal way
On toasted pigs and pickles and figs
   And gummery bread each day.
But the cook was Dutch and behaved as such;
   For the diet he gave the crew
Was a number of tons of hot-cross buns
   Prepared with sugar and glue.

"All nautical pride we laid aside,
   And we cast the vessel ashore
On the Gulliby Isles, where the Poohpooh smiles,
   And the Rumbletumbunders roar.
And we sat on the edge of a sandy ledge
   And shot at the whistling bee;
And the cinnamon-bats wore water-proof hats
   As they danced in the sounding sea.

"On rubgub bark, from dawn to dark,
  We fed, till we all had grown
Uncommonly shrunk, — when a Chinese junk
  Came by from the torriby zone.
She was stubby and square, but we didn't much care,
  And we cheerily put to sea;
And we left the crew of the junk to chew
  The bark of the rubgub tree."

CHARLES HEBER CLARK ("MAX ADELER")
1841–1915

Mr. Slimmer's Funeral Verses
for the Morning Argus

ALEXANDER MCGLUE

The death-angel smote Alexander McGlue,
  And gave him protracted repose;
He wore a checked shirt and a Number Nine shoe,
  And he had a pink wart on his nose.
No doubt he is happier dwelling in space
  Over there on the evergreen shore.
His friends are informed that his funeral takes place
  Precisely at quarter-past four.

WILLIE

Willie had a purple monkey climbing on a yellow stick,
And when he sucked the paint all off it made him deathly sick;
And in his latest hours he clasped that monkey in his hand,
And bade good-bye to earth and went into a better land.

Oh! no more he'll shoot his sister with his little wooden gun;
And no more he'll twist the pussy's tail and make her yowl, for fun.
The pussy's tail now stands out straight; the gun is laid aside;
The monkey doesn't jump around since little Willie died.

JOHNNY SMITH

Four doctors tackled Johnny Smith —
  They blistered and they bled him;
With squills and anti-bilious pills
  And ipecac. they fed him.
They stirred him up with calomel,
  And tried to move his liver;

But all in vain — his little soul
Was wafted o'er The River.

HANNER

We have lost our little Hanner in a very painful manner,
    And we often asked, How can her harsh sufferings be borne?
When her death was first reported, her aunt got up and snorted
    With the grief that she supported, for it made her feel forlorn.

She was such a little seraph that her father, who is sheriff,
    Really doesn't seem to care if he ne'er smiles in life again.
She has gone, we hope, to heaven, at the early age of seven
    (Funeral starts off at eleven), where she'll nevermore have pain.

MRS. MCFADDEN

Mrs. McFadden has gone from this life;
    She has left all its sorrows and cares;
She caught the rheumatics in both of her legs
    While scrubbing the cellar and stairs.
They put mustard-plasters upon her in vain;
    They bathed her with whisky and rum;
But Thursday her spirit departed, and left
    Her body entirely numb.

ALEXANDER

Little Alexander's dead;
    Jam him in a coffin;
Don't have as good a chance
    For a fun'ral often.
Rush his body right around
    To the cemetery;
Drop him in the sepulchre
    With his Uncle Jerry.

CHARLES FOLLEN ADAMS
1842–1918

To Bary Jade

The bood is beabig brighdly, love;
    The sdars are shidig too;
While I ab gazig dreabily,
    Add thigkig, love, of you.

You caddot, oh! you caddot kdow,
    By darlig, how I biss you —
(Oh, whadt a fearful cold I've got! —
    Ck-*tish*-u! Ck-ck-*tish*-u!)

I'b sittig id the arbor, love,
    Where you sat by by side,
Whed od that calb, autubdal dight
    You said you'd be by bride.
Oh! for wud bobedt to caress
    Add tederly to kiss you;
Budt do! we're beddy biles apart —
    (Ho-*rash*-o! Ck-ck-*tish*-u!)

This charbig evedig brigs to bide
    The tibe whed first we bet:
It seebs budt odly yesterday;
    I thigk I see you yet.
Oh! tell me, ab I sdill your owd?
    By hopes — oh, do dot dash theb!
(Codfoud by cold, 'tis gettig worse —
    Ck-*tish*-u! Ck-ck-*thrash*-eb!)

Good-by, by darlig Bary Jade!
    The bid-dight hour is dear;
Add it is hardly wise, by love,
    For be to ligger here.
The heavy dews are fallig fast:
    A fod good-dight I wish you.
(Ho-*rash*-o! — there it is agaid —
    Ck-*thrash*-ub! Ck-ck-*tish*-u!)

Repartée

One Mr. B———,
    A joker he,
While in a jovial mood,
    Tried to explain
    To neighbor N———
A joke which he thought good.

His hearer, Neff,
Was very deaf,
And couldn't catch the joke;
Whereat B——— smiled,
Though slightly "riled,"
And thus to him he spoke: —

" 'Tis plain to *me*
As A B C,
My dear friend, Mr. Neff!"
"Oh, yes! but then,"
Says Mr. N———,
"You know *I'm D E F!*"

John Barley-Corn, My Foe

John Barley-Corn, my foe, John,
The song I have to sing
Is not in praise of you, John,
E'en though you are a king.
Your subjects they are legion, John,
I find where'er I go:
They wear your yoke upon their necks,
John Barley-Corn, my foe.

John Barley-Corn, my foe, John,
By your despotic sway
The people of our country, John,
Are suffering to-day.
You lay the lash upon their backs:
Yet willingly they go
And pay allegiance at the polls,
John Barley-Corn, my foe.

John Barley-Corn, my foe, John,
You've broken many a heart,
And caused the bitter tear, John,
From many an eye to start,

The widow and the fatherless
From pleasant homes to go,
And lead a life of sin and shame,
John Barley-Corn, my foe.

John Barley-Corn, my foe, John,
May Heaven speed the hour,
When Temperance shall wear the crown
And Rum shall lose its power;
When from the East unto the West
The people all shall know
Their greatest curse has been removed,
John Barley-Corn, my foe!

Misplaced Sympathy

Little Benny sat one evening,
Looking o'er his picture-book:
Suddenly his mother noticed
On his face a troubled look.

He was gazing on a picture, —
"Christians in the early days,"
When the cruel tyrant Nero
Harassed them in various ways.

'Twas a family of Christians,
Torn by lions fierce and wild,
In the horrible arena,
Which had thus distressed the child.

Thinking it a golden moment
To impress his youthful mind
With our freedom, dearly purchased,
And by martyrs' blood refined,

His good mother told the story
Of their persecutions sore,
While he listened, all attention,
And the picture pondered o'er.

"See, my child, those hungry lions,
How upon the group they fall!
'Tis a sight, my precious darling,
That the bravest might appall."

Then, with little lip a-quiver,
"Mamma, look!" says little Benny:
"Little lion in the corner,
Mamma, *isn't gettin' any!*"

My Infundibuliform Hat

The scenes of my childhood, how oft I recall!
The sports of my youth, with my kite, top, and ball;
And that happy day when, with spirits elate,
I took my first step towards manhood's estate,
With a new coat and vest, bosom shirt and cravat,
And *début* with my infundibuliform hat.

How I stooped beneath awnings full seven feet high,
To the no small delight of my friends passing by;
And the sport that I made for the boys at the store
When I "chalked" at the height of my "tile" on the door;
One foot and two inches — I think it was that —
My guess on that infundibuliform hat.

Then my maiden attempt as a maiden's gallant
When I proffered my elbow, with glances aslant;
And the walk to her dwelling that evening so fair,
Not to speak of the *tête-à-tête* when we got there,
The forfeit I claimed, as together we sat,
When she tried on my infundibuliform hat.

. . .

Well! boys will be boys, and we men, after all,
Would gladly be freed from Time's pitiless thrall,
And live those days over, when, single and free —
Zounds! wife's looking over my shoulder to see
What I have been writing. . . . Well, we've had a spat,
And she smashed my infundibuliform hat.

AMBROSE BIERCE

1842–?1914

from *The Devil's Dictionary*

BODY-SNATCHER, *n*. A robber of grave-worms. One who supplies the young physicians with that which the old physicians have supplied the undertaker. The hyena.

> "One night," a doctor said, "last fall,
> I and my comrades, four in all,
>   When visiting a graveyard stood
> Within the shadow of a wall.
>
> "While waiting for the moon to sink
> We saw a wild hyena slink
>   About a new-made grave, and then
> Begin to excavate its brink!
>
> "Shocked by the horrid act, we made
> A sally from our ambuscade,
>   And, falling on the unholy beast,
> Dispatched him with a pick and spade."
>   BETTEL K. JHONES

CORPORAL, *n*. A man who occupies the lowest rung of the military ladder.

> Fiercely the battle raged and, sad to tell,
> Our corporal heroically fell!
> Fame from her height looked down upon the brawl
> And said: "He hadn't very far to fall."
>   GIACOMO SMITH

EGOTIST, *n*. A person of low taste, more interested in himself than in me.

> Megaceph, chosen to serve the State
> In the halls of legislative debate,
> One day with all his credentials came
> To the capitol's door and announced his name.
> The doorkeeper looked, with a comical twist
> Of the face, at the eminent egotist,

And said: "Go away, for we settle here
All manner of questions, knotty and queer,
And we cannot have, when the speaker demands
To be told how every member stands,
A man who to all things under the sky
Assents by eternally voting 'I'. "

ELEGY, *n.* A composition in verse, in which, without employing any of the methods of humor, the writer aims to produce in the reader's mind the dampest kind of dejection. The most famous English example begins somewhat like this:

The cur foretells the knell of parting day;
The loafing herd winds slowly o'er the lea;
The wise man homeward plods; I only stay
To fiddle-faddle in a minor key.

LEAD, *n.* A heavy blue-gray metal much used in giving stability to light lovers — particularly to those who love not wisely but other men's wives. Lead is also of great service as a counterpoise to an argument of such weight that it turns the scale of debate the wrong way. An interesting fact in the chemistry of international controversy is that at the point of contact of two patriotisms lead is precipitated in great quantities.

Hail, holy Lead! — of human feuds the great
And universal arbiter; endowed
With penetration to pierce any cloud
Fogging the field of controversial hate,
And with a swift, inevitable, straight,
Searching precision find the unavowed
But vital point. Thy judgment, when allowed
By the chirurgeon, settles the debate.
O useful metal! — were it not for thee
We'd grapple one another's ears alway:
But when we hear thee buzzing like a bee
We, like old Muhlenberg, "care not to stay."
And when the quick have run away like pullets
Jack Satan smelts the dead to make new bullets.

NOSE, *n.* The extreme outpost of the face. From the circumstance that great conquerors have great noses, Getius, whose writings antedate the age of humor, calls the nose the organ of quell. It has been observed that one's nose is never so happy as when thrust into the affairs of another, from which some physiologists have drawn the inference that the nose is devoid of the sense of smell.

> There's a man with a Nose,
> And wherever he goes
> The people run from him and shout:
> "No cotton have we
> For our ears if so be
> He blow that interminous snout!"
>
> So the lawyers applied
> For injunction. "Denied,"
> Said the Judge: "the defendant prefixion,
> Whate'er it portend,
> Appears to transcend
> The bounds of this court's jurisdiction."
>
> ARPAD SINGINY

ORTHOGRAPHY, n. The science of spelling by the eye instead of the ear. Advocated with more heat than light by the outmates of every asylum for the insane. They have had to concede a few things since the time of Chaucer, but are none the less hot in defence of those to be conceded hereafter.

> A spelling reformer indicted
> For fudge was before the court cicted.
> The judge said: "Enough —
> His candle we'll snough,
> And his sepulchre shall not be whicted."

PROSPECT, n. An outlook, usually forbidding. An expectation, usually forbidden.

> Blow, blow, ye spicy breezes —
> O'er Ceylon blow your breath,
> Where every prospect pleases,
> Save only that of death.
>
> BISHOP SHEBER

SAFETY-CLUTCH, n. A mechanical device acting automatically to prevent the fall of an elevator, or cage, in case of an accident to the hoisting apparatus.

> Once I seen a human ruin
> In a elevator-well,
> And his members was bestrewin'
> All the place where he had fell.

And I says, apostrophisin'
    That uncommon woful wreck:
"Your position's so surprisin'
    That I tremble for your neck!"

Then that ruin, smilin' sadly
    And impressive, up and spoke:
"Well, I wouldn't tremble badly,
    For it's been a fortnight broke."

Then, for further comprehension
    Of his attitude, he begs
I will focus my attention
    On his various arms and legs —

How they all are contumacious;
    Where they each, respective, lie;
How one trotter proves ungracious,
    T'other one an *alibi*.

These particulars is mentioned
    For to show his dismal state,
Which I wasn't first intentioned
    To specifical relate.

None is worser to be dreaded
    That I ever have heard tell
Than the gent's who there was spreaded
    In that elevator-well.

Now this tale is allegoric —
    It is figurative all,
For the well is metaphoric
    And the feller didn't fall.

I opine it isn't moral
    For a writer-man to cheat,
And despise to wear a laurel
    As was gotten by deceit.

For 'tis Politics intended
    By the elevator, mind,
It will boost a person splendid
    If his talent is the kind.

Col. Bryan had the talent
  (For the busted man is him)
And it shot him up right gallant
  Till his head begun to swim.

Then the rope it broke above him
  And he painful comes to earth
Where there's nobody to love him
  For his detrimented worth.

Though he's livin' none would know him,
  Or at leastwise not as such.
Moral of this woful poem:
  Frequent oil your safety-clutch.

ANONYMOUS

Willie the Weeper

Listen to the story of Willie the Weeper.
Willie the Weeper was a chimney sweeper.
He had the hop habit and he had it bad;
Listen and I'll tell you of a dream he had.

He went to a hop joint the other night,
Where he knew the lights were always shining bright,
And, calling for a chink to bring some hop,
He started in smoking like he wasn't gonna stop.

After he'd smoked about a dozen pills,
He said, "This ought to cure all my aches and ills."
And turning on his side he fell asleep,
And dreamt he was a sailor on the ocean deep.

He played draw poker as they left the land,
And won a million dollars on the very first hand.
He played and he played till the crew went broke.
Then he turned around and took another smoke.

He came to the island of Siam,
Rubbed his eyes and said, "I wonder where I am,"
Played craps with the king and won a million more,
But had to leave the island 'cause the king got sore.

He went to Monte Carlo where he played roulette,
And couldn't lose a penny but won every bet —
Played and he played till the bank went broke.
Then he turned around and took another smoke.

Then he thought he'd better be sailing for home,
And chartered a ship and sailed away alone.
Ship hit a rock. He hit the floor.
Money was gone and the dream was o'er.

Now this is the story of Willie the Weeper;
Willie the Weeper was a chimney sweeper.
Someday a pill too many he'll take,
And dreaming he's dead, he'll forget to awake.

No More Booze

There was a little man and he had a little can,
    And he used to rush the growler;
He went to the saloon on a Sunday afternoon,
    And you ought to hear the bartender holler:

    No more booze, no more booze,
    No more booze on Sunday;
    No more booze, no more booze,
    Got to get your can filled Monday.

She's the only girl I love,
    With a face like a horse and buggy.
Leaning up against the lake,
    O fireman! save my child!

The chambermaid came to my door,
    "Get up, you lazy sinner,
We need those sheets for table-cloths
    And it's almost time for dinner."
        [*Refrain*]

The Drunkard and the Pig

It was early last December,
    As near as I remember,
I was walking down the street in tipsy pride;

No one was I disturbing
As I lay down by the curbing,
And a pig came up and lay down by my side.

As I lay there in the gutter
Thinking thoughts I shall not utter,
A lady passing by was heard to say:
"You can tell a man who boozes
By the company he chooses";
And the pig got up and slowly walked away.

ROBERT JONES BURDETTE
1844–1914

Orphan Born

I am a lone, unfathered chick,
    Of artificial hatching,
A pilgrim in a desert wild,
By happier, mothered chicks reviled,
From all relationships exiled,
    To do my own lone scratching.

Fair science smiled upon my birth
    One raw and gusty morning;
But ah, the sounds of barnyard mirth
To lonely me have little worth;
Alone am I in all the earth —
    An orphan without borning.

Seek I my mother? I would find
    A heartless personator;
A thing brass-feathered, man-designed,
With steam-pipe arteries intermined,
And pulseless cotton-batting lined —
    A patent incubator.

It wearies me to think, you see —
    Death would be better, rather —
Should downy chicks be hatched of me,

By fate's most pitiless decree,
My piping pullets still would be
    With never a grandfather.

And when to earth I bid adieu
    To seek a planet greater,
I will not do as others do,
Who fly to join the ancestral crew,
For I will just be gathered to
    My incubator.

"Soldier, Rest!"

A Russian sailed over the blue Black Sea
Just when the war was growing hot,
And he shouted, "I'm Tjalikavakeree —
Karindabrolikanavandorot —
        Schipkadirova —
        Ivandiszstova —
            Sanilik —
            Danilik —
        Varagobhot!"

A Turk was standing upon the shore
    Right where the terrible Russian crossed;
And he cried, "Bismillah! I'm Abd el Kor —
Bazaroukilgonautoskobrosk —
        Getzinpravadi —
        Kilgekosladji —
            Grivido —
            Blivido —
        Jenikodosk!"

So they stood like brave men, long and well,
    And they called each other their proper names,
Till the lockjaw seized them, and where they fell
    They buried them both by the Irdosholames —
        Kalatalustchuk —
        Mischaribustchup —
            Bulgari —
            Dulgari —
        Sagharimainz.

JOHN B. TABB
1845–1909

Foot-Soldiers

'Tis all the way to Toe-town,
  Beyond the Knee-high hill,
That Baby has to travel down
  To see the soldiers drill.

One, two, three, four, five, a-row —
  A captain and his men —
And on the other side, you know,
  Are six, seven, eight, nine, ten.

Bicycles! Tricycles!

Bicycles! Tricycles! Nay, to shun laughter,
Try cycles first, and *buy* cycles after;
For surely the buyer deserves but the worst
Who would buy cycles, failing to try cycles first.

Close Quarters

Little toe, big toe, three toes between,
  All in a pointed shoe!
Never was narrower forecastle seen
  Nor so little room for the crew.

A Rub

'Twixt Handkerchief and Nose
  A difference arose;
And a tradition goes
  That they settled it by blows.

The Tryst

Potato was deep in the dark under ground,
  Tomato, above in the light.
The little Tomato was ruddy and round,
  The little Potato was white.

And redder and redder she rounded above,
  And paler and paler he grew,
And neither suspected a mutual love
  Till they met in a Brunswick stew.

JULIA A. MOORE
1847–1920

Grand Rapids

Wild roved the Indians once
  On the banks of Grand River,
And they built their little huts
  Down by that flowing river.
In a pleasant valley fair,
  Where flows the river rapid,
An Indian village once was there,
  Where now stands Grand Rapids.

Indian girls and boys were seen,
  With their bow and quiver,
Riding in their light canoes
  Up and down the river.
Their hearts were full of joy,
  Happy voices singing
Made music with forest birds,
  They kept the valley ringing.

Indians have left and gone
  Beyond the Mississippi.
They called the river Owashtenong
  Where stands this pleasant city.
Louis Campau the first white man
  Bought land in Grand Rapids.
He lived and died, an honored man
  By people of Grand Rapids.

When Campau came to the valley
　　No bridge was across the river;
Indians in their light canoes
　　Rowed them o'er the water.
Railroads now from every way
　　Run through the city, Grand Rapids;
The largest town in west Michigan
　　Is the city of Grand Rapids.

Ashtabula Disaster

Have you heard of the dreadful fate
　　Of Mr. P. P. Bliss and wife?
Of their death I will relate,
　　And also others lost their life;
Ashtabula Bridge disaster,
　　Where so many people died
Without a thought that destruction
　　Would plunge them 'neath the wheel of tide.

　　　　Swiftly passed the engine's call,
　　　　　Hastening souls on to death,
　　　　Warning not one of them all;
　　　　　It brought despair right and left.

Among the ruins are many friends,
　　Crushed to death amidst the roar;
On one thread all may depend,
　　And hope they've reached the other shore.
P. P. Bliss showed great devotion
　　To his faithful wife, his pride,
When he saw that she must perish,
　　He died a martyr by her side.

P. P. Bliss went home above —
　　Left all friends, earth and fame,
To rest in God's holy love;
　　Left on earth his work and name.
The people love his work by numbers,
　　It is read by great and small,
He by it will be remembered,
　　He has left it for us all.

186

His good name from time to time
    Will rise on land and sea;
It is known in distant climes,
    Let it echo wide and free.
One good man among the number,
    Found sweet rest in a short time,
His weary soul may sweetly slumber
    Within the vale, heaven sublime.

Destruction lay on every side,
    Confusion, fire and despair;
No help, no hope, so they died,
    Two hundred people over there.
Many ties was there broken,
    Many a heart was filled with pain,
Each one left a little token,
    For above they live again.

Little Libbie

One more little spirit to Heaven has flown,
    To dwell in that mansion above,
Where dear little angels, together roam,
    In God's everlasting love.

One little flower has withered and died,
    A bud nearly ready to bloom,
Its life on earth is marked with pride;
    Oh, sad it should die so soon.

Sweet little Libbie, that precious flower
    Was a pride in her parents' home,
They miss their little girl *every* hour,
    Those friends that are left to mourn.

Her sweet silvery voice no more is heard
    In the home where she once roamed;
Her place is *vacant* around the hearth,
    Where her friends are mourning lone.

They are mourning the loss of a little girl,
  With black eyes and auburn hair,
She was a treasure to them in this world,
  This beautiful child so fair.

One morning in April, a short time ago,
  Libbie was active and gay;
Her Saviour called her, she had to go,
  E're the close of that pleasant day.

While eating dinner, this dear little child
  Was choked on a piece of beef.
Doctors came, tried their skill awhile,
  But none could give relief.

She was ten years of age, I am told,
  And in school stood very high.
Her little form now the earth enfolds,
  In her embrace it must ever lie.

Her friends and schoolmates will not forget
  Little Libbie that is no more;
She is waiting on the shining step,
  To welcome home friends once more.

Sketch of Lord Byron's Life

"Lord Byron" was an Englishman
  A poet I believe,
His first works in old England
  Was poorly received.
Perhaps it was "Lord Byron's" fault
  And perhaps it was not.
His life was full of misfortunes,
  Ah, strange was his lot.

The character of "Lord Byron"
  Was of a low degree,
Caused by his reckless conduct,
  And bad company.
He sprung from an ancient house,
  Noble, but poor, indeed.
His career on earth, was marred
  By his own misdeeds.

Generous and tender hearted,
    Affectionate by extreme,
In temper he was wayward,
    A poor "Lord" without means;
Ah, he was a handsome fellow
    With great poetic skill,
His great intellectual powers
    He could use at his will.

He was a sad child of nature,
    Of fortune and of fame;
Also sad child to society,
    For nothing did he gain
But slander and ridicule,
    Throughout his native land.
Thus the "poet of the passions,"
    Lived, unappreciated, man.

Yet at the age of 24,
    "Lord Byron" then had gained
The highest, highest, pinacle
    Of literary fame.
Ah, he had such violent passions
    They was beyond his control,
Yet the public with its justice,
    Sometimes would him extol.

Sometimes again "Lord Byron"
    Was censured by the press,
Such obloquy, he could not endure,
    So he done what was the best.
He left his native country,
    This great unhappy man;
The only wish he had, " 'tis said,"
    He might die, sword in hand.

He had joined the Grecian Army;
    This man of delicate frame;
And there he died in a distant land,
    And left on earth his fame.
"Lord Byron's" age was 36 years,
    Then closed the sad career,
Of the most celebrated "Englishman"
    Of the nineteenth century.

JAMES WHITCOMB RILEY
1849–1916

Craqueodoom

The Crankadox leaned o'er the edge of the moon
   And wistfully gazed on the sea
Where the Gryxabodill madly whistled a tune
   To the air of "Ti-fol-de-ding-dee."
The quavering shriek of the Fly-up-the-creek
   Was fitfully wafted afar
To the Queen of the Wunks as she powdered her cheek
   With the pulverized rays of a star.

The Gool closed his ear on the voice of the Grig,
   And his heart it grew heavy as lead
As he marked the Baldekin adjusting his wing
   On the opposite side of his head,
And the air it grew chill as the Gryxabodill
   Raised his dank, dripping fins to the skies,
And plead with the Plunk for the use of her bill
   To pick the tears out of his eyes.

The ghost of the Zhack flitted by in a trance,
   And the Squidjum hid under a tub
As he heard the loud hooves of the Hooken advance
   With a rub-a-dub — dub-a-dub — dub!
And the Crankadox cried, as he lay down and died,
   "My fate there is none to bewail,"
While the Queen of the Wunks drifted over the tide
   With a long piece of crape to her tail.

A Rose in October
I

I strayed, all alone, where the Autumn
   Had swept, in her petulant wrath:
All the flowers, that had bloomed in the garden,
   She had gathered, and flung in her path.
And I saw the dead face of the lily,
   Struck down, by the rain and the sleet,
And the pink, with her lashes yet weeping,
   Drooped low in the dust, at my feet.

II

The leaves on the branches still swinging,
　　Were blanched with the crimson of death;
And the vines that still clung to the trellis,
　　Were palsied, and shook at a breath.
And I sighed: "So hath fate, like the Autumn,
　　Swept over my path, till I see,
As I walk through life's desolate garden
　　Not a rose is left blooming for me!"

III

"Heigho!" said a voice of low laughter —
　　"How blind are you poets!" And there,
At the gate, just in front of me, leaning,
　　Stood Rosalind May, I declare!
I stammered, confused, for the moment;
　　But was blest for the rest of my life,
For my Rose of October there promised
　　She'd bloom for me aye, as — my wife.

When the Frost Is on the Punkin

When the frost is on the punkin and the fodder's in the shock,
And you hear the kyouck and gobble of the struttin' turkey-cock,
And the clackin' of the guineys, and the cluckin' of the hens,
And the rooster's hallylooyer as he tiptoes on the fence;
O, it's then's the times a feller is a-feelin' at his best,
With the risin' sun to greet him from a night of peaceful rest,
As he leaves the house, bareheaded, and goes out to feed the stock,
When the frost is on the punkin and the fodder's in the shock.

They's something kindo' harty-like about the atmusfere
When the heat of summer's over and the coolin' fall is here —
Of course we miss the flowers, and the blossums on the trees,
And the mumble of the hummin'-birds and buzzin' of the bees;
But the air's so appetizin'; and the landscape through the haze
Of a crisp and sunny morning of the airly autumn days
Is a pictur' that no painter has the colorin' to mock —
When the frost is on the punkin and the fodder's in the shock.

The husky, rusty russel of the tossels of the corn,
And the raspin' of the tangled leaves, as golden as the morn;

The stubble in the furries — kindo' lonesome-like, but still
A-preachin' sermons to us of the barns they growed to fill;
The strawstack in the medder, and the reaper in the shed;
The hosses in theyr stalls below — the clover overhead! —
O, it sets my hart a-clickin' like the tickin' of a clock,
When the frost is on the punkin and the fodder's in the shock!

Then your apples all is gethered, and the ones a feller keeps
Is poured around the celler-floor in red and yeller heaps;
And your cider-makin' 's over, and your wimmern-folks is through
With their mince and apple-butter, and theyr souse and sausage, too! . . .
I don't know how to tell it — but ef sich a thing could be
As the Angels wantin' boardin', and they'd call around on *me* —
I'd want to 'commodate 'em — all the whole-indurin' flock —
When the frost is on the punkin and the fodder's in the shock!

Little Orphant Annie

To all the little children:—The happy ones; and sad ones;
The sober and the silent ones; the boisterous and glad ones;
The good ones—Yes, the good ones, too; and all the lovely bad ones.

Little Orphant Annie's come to our house to stay,
An' wash the cups an' saucers up, an' brush the crumbs away,
An' shoo the chickens off the porch, an' dust the hearth, an' sweep,
An' make the fire, an' bake the bread, an' earn her board-an'-keep;
An' all us other children, when the supper-things is done,
We set around the kitchen fire an' has the mostest fun
A-list'nin' to the witch-tales 'at Annie tells about,
An' the Gobble-uns 'at gits you
        Ef you
          Don't
            Watch
            Out!

Wunst they wuz a little boy wouldn't say his prayers, —
An' when he went to bed at night, away up-stairs,
His Mammy heerd him holler, an' his Daddy heerd him bawl,
An' when they turn't the kivvers down, he wuzn't there at all!
An' they seeked him in the rafter-room, an' cubby-hole, an' press,
An' seeked him up the chimbly-flue, an' ever'-wheres, I guess;
But all they ever found wuz thist his pants an' roundabout: —

An' the Gobble-uns 'll git you
    Ef you
       Don't
         Watch
           Out!

An' one time a little girl 'ud allus laugh an' grin,
An' make fun of ever' one, an' all her blood-an'-kin;
An' wunst, when they was "company," an' ole folks wuz there,
She mocked 'em an' shocked 'em, an' said she didn't care!
An' thist as she kicked her heels, an' turn't to run an' hide,
They wuz two great big Black Things a-standin' by her side,
An' they snatched her through the ceilin' 'fore she knowed what she's
    about!
An' the Gobble-uns 'll git you
    Ef you
       Don't
         Watch
           Out!

An' little Orphant Annie says, when the blaze is blue,
An' the lamp-wick sputters, an' the wind goes *woo-oo!*
An' you hear the crickets quit, an' the moon is gray,
An' the lightnin'-bugs in dew is all squenched away, —
You better mind yer parunts, an' yer teachurs fond an' dear,
An' churish them 'at loves you, an' dry the orphant's tear,
An' he'p the pore an' needy ones 'at clusters all about,
Er the Gobble-uns 'll git you
    Ef you
       Don't
         Watch
           Out!

The Diners in the Kitchen

    Our dog Fred
    Et the bread.

    Our dog Dash
    Et the hash.

    Our dog Pete
    Et the meat.

Our dog Davy
Et the gravy.

Our dog Toffy
Et the coffee.

Our dog Jake
Et the cake.

Our dog Trip
Et the dip.

And — the worst,
From the first, —

Our dog *Fi*do
Et the pie-dough.

RUTH McENERY STUART
?1849–1917

The Endless Song

Oh, I used to sing a song.
An' dey said it was too long,
So I cut it off de en'
To accommodate a frien'
          Nex' do', nex' do' —
To accommodate a frien' nex' do'.

But it made de matter wuss
Dan it had been at de fus,
'Ca'ze de en' was gone, an' den
Co'se it didn't have no en'
          Any mo', any mo' —
Oh, it didn't have no en' any mo'!

So, to save my frien' from sinnin',
I cut off de song's beginnin';
Still he cusses right along
Whilst I sings *about* my song
          Jes so, jes so —
While I sings *about* my song *jes so*.

How to please 'im is my riddle,
So I'll fall back on my fiddle;
For I'd stan' myself on en'
To accommodate a frien'
       Nex' do', nex' do' —
To accommodate a frien' nex' do'.

FRED EMERSON BROOKS
1850–1923

Foreigners at the Fair

Said the Englishman: "W'at's all this bloomin' wow?
An w'ere is Chicago, anyhow?
I've 'eard abeout yo'r Columbian show;
An' abeout yo'r Columbus, don' cher know!
The Prince infawmed me that 'e was the cove
Who discovahd yo'r blawsted ceountry, bah Jove!
An' cwossed the wahtaw, His 'Ighness tells,
In three little chocolate *caramels!*"

Then Italy spoke: "Greata beega show!
I sella da banan', catch da mon' to go!
I tella da peopl' I wasa descend
From Colombo; dey scratcha da nose on da end!
Man Christof Colomb' was a greata man:
He discova da world for d' American.
But they draga to preeson, chain lika da dog,
When Is'bella find out he discova Chicag'!"

"Hoot, lad! I'm fra Scootlan', but canna find oot,
Fra yer garlicky tongue what ye're ta'kin' aboot!
Ef ye canna spak English, an' spak withoot flaw,
As I do mysel', dinna spak it at a'!
Ye'll not mak' musicians by turnin' a crank;
Till ye learn on the bagpipe ye'll niver take rank.
To discoover the counthree, Columbus did well,
But ye're sp'ilin' it a', comin' over yersel'!"

"Wal, I'm from the wild an' the woolly West;
An' thar's jist one thing I wanter suggest:

That yo' call this y'ar the Chicago Fair,
An' not the Corlumbian! Neow take care!
Fur this is the biggest city on earth,
Ef yo' take it in height, er take it in girth;
We're growin' so fast we've got ter make
A petition that Providence move the lake."

"You vas beat the veorld!" said the traveling Jew;
"You vas on der beat — I vas onto you!
It vas called der 'Vindy Cidy,' I know,
Because der beoble vas on der blow.
Der greatest cidy for hogs un' porok!
Dat's vy der Hebrew remains in Ny-Yorok.
I discover dis fact ven I pays my bill —
You vas keep some hogs vich you neffer kill!"

"It's wuth a heap, stranger, 'twixt me an' yeou,
A-gittin' the best of a New York Jew!
We've got the push, an' we've got the go;
An' we're showin' New York how a city should grow.
We taught them dude Knickerbockers a trick
By gittin' the Fair, an' a-gittin' 'er slick;
An' a-bringin' 'er up to the present stage —
'Twas the greatest feat of the modern age!"

Said Patrick: "I've heard all about yer big feet!
But Oi'll not mintion that ef ye'll promise to treat!
They charged me fur wather out here at the Fair;
Oi've been howldin' me breath lest they charge me fur air.
But why they should wish to be fillin' the land
Wid those half-grown Oitalians, I can't understhand;
They discovered the counthry at others' expinse;
But they niver discovered a single thing since."

"You'll excuse me, Cunnel, ef I use my mouf,
I'se a cullud gemman fum away down Souf.
I was nuffin' but a niggah befo' de wah;
But now I rides in de palace caw!
Who say Marse C'lumbus done 'scovah dees earf?
Don' yo' know dey was Injuns heah on de turf,
A-raisin' terbac' an' de Injun cawn,
Befo' Marse C'lumbus he gwine to be bawn."

"I'm ze French gentlemon'! I come ovair to see
Ze Fair, an' ze statue of French Libairtee:
I ask ze bronze Lady, weez smile debonair,
Vich enlighten ze voorld an' ze way to ze Fair,
How she like ze great peopal? Vair well, but, my face,
Turn black 'ven I try me to speak ze Englais!
Mon Dieu! what a countree zes would have become
Ef discovair by Frenchman instead of Colomb'!"

"Me heap sabe you! You heap sabe me,
Me Melican-citizen-heathen-Chinee:
Me heap sabe C'lumbus; him velley smart man —
No sabe lay egg — heap sabe makee stan'.
Heap sabe George Washman; him velley lenoun';
No likee climb chelly tlee, heap cut 'em down.
Me alle same 'Washman,' him 'Georgee,' me 'John,'
Him tellee no lie, gottee pigtail on."

Barnyard Melodies

Delightful change from the town's abode,
Is a charming drive on a country road;
From the stifling air of the city's street
To the perfumed breath of the daisies sweet.

You halt your team at the farmer's gate,
He comes to open it; while you wait,
Old Rover comes bounding down the hill
In spite of his master's "Rover, be still!" —
His barking shakes his thick shaggy coat,
While these notes roll from his deep-toned throat: —
    Bow-wow-wow-wow!
    Bow-wow-wow-wow!

On either side the fat hens take leg,
While others announce a new-laid egg: —
    Cut-cut-cut — cu-da-cut!
    Cut-cut-cut — cu-da-cut!
The rooster, shrill spokesman for the brood,
Says — one-third polite and two-thirds rude: —
    I'm Cock-a-doodle-do!
    And who the deuce are you?

The ducks and drakes have the self-same quack —
They're just alike, save the curl at the back;
For "*divers*" reasons they go to the pond,
For "*sun-dry*" reasons they strut around,
And waddle off like sailors a-spreeing.
And talk like doctors when disagreeing: —
   Quack-quack-quack-quack!
   Quack-quack-quack-quack!

The turkey gobbler comes charging round
With ruffled temper and wings aground;
For fear he might his foe overtake
He gives alarm, then puts on the brake: —
   Plip-gobble-obble-obble!
   Plip-gobble-obble-obble!

The hog in the trough, with dirty feet;
The more you give him the more he'll eat;
This gourmand finds nothing to desire
When half asleep in the half-dried mire: —
   R-r-r-ough-ff! — *r-r-r-ough-ff!*
   R-r-r-ough-ff! — *r-r-r-ough-ff!*
The sow is teaching her litter of shoats
To speak *hog-Latin* with guttural throats: —
   Ugh-ee! ugh-ee! ugh-ee! ugh-ee!
   Ugh-ee! ugh-ee! ugh-ee! ugh-ee!

The calf and lamb at distance dispute
The right of bin with the hornèd brute;
Their blat and bleat the hard-headed scorns
Where right and wrong's a question of horns: —
   Bah! bah! — *Beh-eh-eh-eh-eh!*
   Bah! bah! — *Beh-eh-eh-eh-eh!*

The barefoot boy, from the tender rows
Of corn, is driving the "pesky crows";
He stubs his toe, and they mock his pain: —
He throws a stone and they're off again: —
   Caw-caw-caw-caw!
   Caw-caw-caw-caw!

From out the meadow the lowing kine,
Treading the buttercups, come in line;
Come with their soft tread through the grass,
Answer the call of the farmer's lass: —
    Co'boss! co'boss! co'boss! — moo!
    Co'boss! co'boss! co'boss! — moo!

They stand there meekly chewing their cud,
Whacking their sides with a sudden thud
To battle the flies; the swinging tail
Meanwhile drops down in the frothing pail;
    So boss! so boss! so! so! so!
    Stand still, Brindle! Heist! so! so!

The king of the herd, imprisoned afield,
Is hooking the bars, quite loath to yield!
He paws up the earth with muscles tense,
And then, pacing down the long line-fence,
On neighboring chief, with haughty mien
And challenge hoarse, he vents his spleen: —
    Mow-ow-ush! mow-ow-ush!
    Mow-oo! mow-oo! ow-ush!

The mare, knee deep in the clover bed,
Caresses her nursing thoroughbred;
The well-fed oxen in stanchions meek;
The plowboy grooming his horses sleek;
They whisk their tails and nip at his back,
While down the curry-comb comes a-whack;
    "Whoa, Dan! you rascal, stand still!
    Cxh! cxh! cxh! Gee up thar, Bill!"

The barn well filled with the bursting sheaves;
The swallows twittering 'neath the eaves
Their song of plenty. The farmer's heart
And barn are full! — while he walks apart
And chants his thankfulness as he goes
By whistling the only tune he knows: —
    "Yankee Doodle!"

EUGENE FIELD
1850–1895

The Little Peach

A little peach in the orchard grew,
A little peach of emerald hue:
Warmed by the sun, and wet by the dew,
          It grew.

One day, walking the orchard through,
That little peach dawned on the view
Of Johnny Jones and his sister Sue —
          Those two.

Up at the peach a club they threw:
Down from the limb on which it grew,
Fell the little peach of emerald hue —
          Too true!

John took a bite, and Sue took a chew,
And then the trouble began to brew, —
Trouble the doctor couldn't subdue, —
          Paregoric too.

Under the turf where the daisies grew,
They planted John and his sister Sue;
And their little souls to the angels flew —
          Boo-hoo!

But what of the peach of emerald hue,
Warmed by the sun, and wet by the dew?
Ah, well! its mission on earth is through —
          Adieu!

Wynken, Blynken, and Nod
(Dutch Lullaby)

Wynken, Blynken, and Nod one night
    Sailed off in a wooden shoe —
Sailed on a river of crystal light,
    Into a sea of dew.

"Where are you going, and what do you wish?"
    The old moon asked the three.
"We have come to fish for the herring fish
    That live in this beautiful sea;
    Nets of silver and gold have we!"
            Said Wynken,
            Blynken,
            And Nod.

The old moon laughed and sang a song,
    As they rocked in the wooden shoe,
And the wind that sped them all night long
    Ruffled the waves of dew.
The little stars were the herring fish
    That lived in that beautiful sea —
"Now cast your nets wherever you wish —
    Never afeard are we";
    So cried the stars to the fishermen three:
            Wynken,
            Blynken,
            And Nod.

All night long their nets they threw
    To the stars in the twinkling foam —
Then down from the skies came the wooden shoe,
    Bringing the fishermen home;
'Twas all so pretty a sail it seemed
    As if it could not be,
And some folks thought 'twas a dream they'd dreamed
    Of sailing that beautiful sea —
    But I shall name you the fishermen three:
            Wynken,
            Blynken,
            And Nod.

Wynken and Blynken are two little eyes,
    And Nod is a little head,
And the wooden shoe that sailed the skies
    Is a wee one's trundle-bed.

So shut your eyes while mother sings
    Of wonderful sights that be,
And you shall see the beautiful things
    As you rock in the misty sea,
    Where the old shoe rocked the fishermen three:
          Wynken,
          Blynken,
          And Nod.

Little Boy Blue

The little toy dog is covered with dust,
    But sturdy and stanch he stands;
And the little toy soldier is red with rust,
    And the musket moulds in his hands.
Time was when the little toy dog was new,
    And the soldier was passing fair;
And that was the time when our Little Boy Blue
    Kissed them and put them there.

"Now, don't you go till I come," he said,
    "And don't you make any noise!"
So, toddling off to his trundle-bed,
    He dreamt of the pretty toys;
And, as he was dreaming, an angel song
    Awakened our Little Boy Blue —
Oh! the years are many, the years are long,
    But the little toy friends are true!

Aye, faithful to Little Boy Blue they stand,
    Each in the same old place —
Awaiting the touch of a little hand,
    The smile of a little face;
And they wonder, as waiting the long years through
    In the dust of that little chair,
What has become of our Little Boy Blue,
    Since he kissed them and put them there.

The Duel

The gingham dog and the calico cat
Side by side on the table sat;
'Twas half-past twelve, and (what do you think)
Nor one nor t'other had slept a wink!
    The old Dutch clock and the Chinese plate
    Appeared to know as sure as fate
There was going to be a terrible spat.
    (I wasn't there; I simply state
    What was told me by the Chinese plate!)

The gingham dog went "bow-wow-wow!"
And the calico cat replied "mee-ow!"
The air was littered, an hour or so,
With bits of gingham and calico,
    While the old Dutch clock in the chimney place
    Up with its hands before its face,
For it always dreaded a family row!
    (Now mind: I'm only telling you
    What the old Dutch clock declares is true!)

The Chinese plate looked very blue,
And wailed, "Oh, dear! what shall we do?"
But the gingham dog and the calico cat
Wallowed this way and tumbled that,
    Employing every tooth and claw
    In the awfullest way you ever saw —
And, oh! how the gingham and calico flew!
    (Don't fancy I exaggerate!
    I got my news from the Chinese plate!)

Next morning, where the two had sat,
They found no trace of dog or cat;
And some folks think unto this day
That burglars stole that pair away!
    But the truth about the cat and pup
    Is this: they ate each other up!
Now what do you really think of that!
    (The old Dutch clock it told me so,
    And that is how I came to know.)

SAMUEL C. BUSHNELL
1852–1930

Boston

I come from the city of Boston,
The home of the bean and the cod,
Where Cabots speak only to Lowells,
And Lowells speak only to God.

SAMUEL MINTURN PECK
1854–1938

A Kiss in the Rain

One stormy morn I chanced to meet
  A lassie in the town;
Her locks were like the ripened wheat,
  Her laughing eyes were brown.
I watched her as she tripped along
  Till madness filled my brain,
And then — and then — I know 'twas wrong —
  I kissed her in the rain!

With rain-drops shining on her cheek,
  Like dew-drops on a rose,
The little lassie strove to speak
  My boldness to oppose;
She strove in vain, and quivering
  Her fingers stole in mine;
And then the birds began to sing,
  The sun began to shine.

Oh, let the clouds grow dark above,
  My heart is light below;
'Tis always summer when we love,
  However winds may blow;
And I'm as proud as any prince,
  All honors I disdain:
She says I am her *rain beau* since
  I kissed her in the rain.

JOHN PHILIP SOUSA
1854–1932

The Feast of the Monkeys

In days of old,
So I've been told,
The monkeys gave a feast.
They sent out cards,
With kind regards,
To every bird and beast.
The guests came dressed,
In fashion's best,
Unmindful of expense;
Except the whale,
Whose swallowtail,
Was "soaked" for fifty cents.

The guests checked wraps,
Canes, hats and caps;
And when that task was done,
The footman he
With dignitee,
Announced them one by one.
In Monkey Hall,
The host met all,
And hoped they'd feel at ease,
"I scarcely can,"
Said the Black and Tan,
"I'm busy hunting fleas."

"While waiting for
A score or more
Of guests," the hostess said,
"We'll have the Poodle
Sing *Yankee Doodle*,
A-standing on his head.
And when this is through,
Good Parrot, you,
Please show them how you swear."
"Oh, dear; don't cuss,"
Cried the Octopus,
And he walked off on his ear.

The Orang-Outang
A sea-song sang,
About a Chimpanzee
Who went abroad,
In a drinking gourd,
To the coast of Barbaree.
Where he heard one night,
When the moon shone bright,
A school of mermaids pick
Chromatic scales
From off their tails,
And did it mighty slick.

"All guests are here,
To eat the cheer,
And dinner's served, my Lord."
The butler bowed;
And then the crowd
Rushed in with one accord.
The fiddler-crab
Came in a cab,
And played a piece in C;
While on his horn,
The Unicorn
Blew, *You'll Remember Me.*

"To give a touch
Of early Dutch
To this great feast of feasts,
I'll drink ten drops
Of Holland's schnapps,"
Spoke out the King of Beasts.
"That must taste fine,"
Said the Porcupine,
"Did you see him smack his lip?"
"I'd smack mine, too,"
Cried the Kangaroo,
"If I didn't have the pip."

The Lion stood,
And said: "Be good
Enough to look this way;
Court Etiquette

Do not forget,
And mark well what I say:
My royal wish
Is ev'ry dish
Be tasted first by me."
"Here's where I smile,"
Said the Crocodile,
And he climbed an axle-tree.

The soup was brought,
And quick as thought,
The Lion ate it all.
"You can't beat that,"
Exclaimed the Cat,
"For monumental gall."
"The soup," all cried.
"Gone," Leo replied,
" 'Twas just a bit too thick."
"When we get through,"
Remarked the Gnu,
"I'll hit him with a brick."

The Tiger stepped,
Or, rather, crept,
Up where the Lion sat.
"O, mighty boss
I'm at a loss
To know where I am at.
I came to-night
With appetite
To drink and also eat;
As a Tiger grand,
I now demand,
I get there with both feet."

The Lion got
All-fired hot
And in a passion flew.
"Get out," he cried,
"And save your hide,
You most offensive *You*."
"I'm not afraid,"
The Tiger said,

"I know what I'm about."
But the Lion's paw
Reached the Tiger's jaw,
And he was good and out.

The salt-sea smell
Of Mackerel,
Upon the air arose;
Each hungry guest
Great joy expressed,
And "sniff!" went every nose.
With glutton look
The Lion took
The spiced and sav'ry dish.
Without a pause
He worked his jaws,
And gobbled all the fish.

Then ate the roast,
The quail on toast,
The pork, both fat and lean;
The jam and lamb,
The potted ham,
And drank the kerosene.
He raised his voice:
"Come, all rejoice,
You've seen your monarch dine."
"Never again,"
Clucked the Hen,
And all sang *Old Lang Syne*.

Have You Seen the Lady?

"Have I told you the name of a lady?
Have I told you the name of a dear?
  'Twas known long ago,
  And ends with an O;
You don't hear it often round here.

Have I talked of the eyes of a lady?
Have I talked of the eyes that are bright?
  Their color, you see,
  Is B-L-U-E;
They're the gin in the cocktail of light.

Have I sung of the hair of a lady?
Have I sung of the hair of a dove?
 What shade do you say?
 B-L-A-C-K;
It's the fizz in the champagne of love.

Can you guess it — the name of the lady?
She is sweet, she is fair, she is coy.
 Your guessing forego,
 It's J-U-N-O;
She's the mint in the julep of joy."

H. C. BUNNER
1855–1896

Poetry and the Poet

(Found on the Poet's desk.)

Weary, I open wide the antique pane
I ope to the air
I ope to
I open to the air the antique pane
 And gaze $\begin{Bmatrix} \text{beyond?} \\ \text{across} \end{Bmatrix}$ the thrift-sown fields of
 wheat, [commonplace?]
A-shimmering green in breezes born of heat;
And lo!
And high
And my soul's eyes behold $\begin{Bmatrix} \text{a?} \\ \text{the} \end{Bmatrix}$ billowy main
Whose further shore is Greece   strain
                                          again
                                          vain
[Arcadia — mythological allusion. — Mem.: Lemprière.]
 I see thee, Atalanta, vestal fleet,
 And look! with doves low-fluttering round her feet,
 Comes Venus through the golden $\begin{Bmatrix} \text{fields of?} \\ \text{bowing} \end{Bmatrix}$ grain

(Heard by the Poet's neighbor.)

Venus be bothered — it's Virginia Dix!

(Found on the Poet's door.)

> Out on important business — back at 6.

"Home, Sweet Home," with Variations

I
The Original Theme, as John Howard Payne Wrote It:

'Mid pleasures and palaces though we may roam,
Be it ever so humble, there's no place like home!
A charm from the skies seems to hallow us there,
Which, seek through the world, is not met with elsewhere.

> Home, Home! Sweet, Sweet Home!
> There's no place like Home!

An exile from home, splendor dazzles in vain!
Oh, give me my lowly thatched cottage again!
The birds singing gayly that came at my call!
Give me them! and the peace of mind dearer than all.

> Home, Home! Sweet, Sweet Home!
> There's no place like Home!

II
As Algernon Charles Swinburne Might Have
Wrapped It Up in Variations:

['Mid pleasures and palaces —]

As sea-foam blown of the winds, as blossom of brine that is drifted
    Hither and yon on the barren breast of the breeze,
Though we wander on gusts of a god's breath shaken and shifted,
    The salt of us stings and is sore for the sobbing seas.
For home's sake hungry at heart, we sicken in pillared porches.
    Of bliss made sick for a life that is barren of bliss,
For the place whereon is a light out of heaven that sears not nor
    scorches,
    Nor elsewhere than this.

[*An exile from home, splendor dazzles in vain —*]

For here we know shall no gold thing glisten,
   No bright thing burn, and no sweet thing shine;
Nor Love lower never an ear to listen
   To words that work in the heart like wine.
     What time we are set from our land apart,
     For pain of passion and hunger of heart,
Though we walk with exiles fame faints to christen,
   Or sing at the Cytherean's shrine.

[VARIATION: *An exile from home —*]

   Whether with him whose head
   Of gods is honorèd,
With song made splendent in the sight of men —
   Whose heart most sweetly stout,
   From ravished France cast out,
Being firstly hers, was hers most wholly then —
   Or where on shining seas like wine
   The dove's wings draw the drooping Erycine.

[*Give me my lowly thatched cottage —*]

     For Joy finds Love grow bitter,
     And spreads his wings to quit her,
     At thought of birds that twitter
       Beneath the roof-tree's straw —
      Of birds that come for calling,
      No fear or fright appalling,
      When dews of dusk are falling,
     Or daylight's draperies draw.

[*Give me them, and the peace of mind —*]

Give me these things then back, though the giving
   Be at cost of earth's garner of gold;
There is no life without these worth living,
   No treasure where these are not told.
For the heart give the hope that it knows not,
   Give the balm for the burn of the breast —
For the soul and the mind that repose not,
   O, give us a rest!

III

*As Mr. Francis Bret Harte Might Have Woven It into a
Touching Tale of a Western Gentleman in a Red Shirt:*

Brown o' San Juan,
    Stranger, I'm Brown.
Come up this mornin' from 'Frisco —
    Be'n a-saltin' my specie-stacks down.

Be'n a-knockin' around,
    Fer a man from San Juan,
Putty consid'able frequent —
    Jes' catch onter that streak o' the dawn!

Right thar lies my home —
    Right thar in the red —
I could slop over, stranger, in po'try
    Would spread out old Shakspoke cold dead.

Stranger, you freeze to this: there ain't no kinder gin-palace,
Nor no variety-show lays over a man's own rancho.
Maybe it hain't no style, but the Queen in the Tower o' London
Ain't got naathin' I 'd swop for that house over thar on the hillside.

Thar is my ole gal, 'n' the kids, 'n' the rest o' my livestock;
Thar my Remington hangs, and thar there's a griddlecake br'ilin' —
For the two of us, pard — and thar, I allow, the heavens
Smile more friendly-like than on any other locality.

Stranger, nowhere else I don't take no satisfaction.
Gimme my ranch, 'n' them friendly old Shanghai chickens —
I brung the original pair f'm the States in eighteen-'n'-fifty —
Gimme them and the feelin' of solid domestic comfort.

Yer parding, young man —
    But this landscape a kind
Er flickers — I 'low 'twuz the po'try —
    I thought thet my eyes hed gone blind.

. . .

Take that pop from my belt!
    Hi, thar — gimme yer han' —
Or I'll kill myself — Lizzie! — she's left me —
    Gone off with a purtier man!

Thar, I'll quit — the ole gal
  An' the kids — run away!
I be derned! Howsomever, come in, pard —
  The griddle-cake's thar, anyway.

IV

As Austin Dobson Might Have Translated It from Horace, If It Had Ever Occurred to Horace To Write It:

Rondeau

Palatiis in remotis voluptates
Si quæris . . .
— Flaccus, Q. Horatius, *Carmina, Lib.* V: 1.

At home alone, O Nomades,
Although Mæcenas' marble frieze
  Stand not between you and the sky,
  Nor Persian luxury supply
Its rosy surfeit, find ye ease.

Tempt not the far Ægean breeze;
With home-made wine and books that please,
  To duns and bores the door deny
    At home, alone.

Strange joys may lure. Your deities
Smile here alone. Oh, give me these:
  Low eaves, where birds familiar fly,
  And peace of mind, and, fluttering by,
My Lydia's graceful draperies,
    At home, *alone.*

V

As It Might Have Been Constructed in 1744, Oliver Goldsmith, at 19, Writing the First Stanza, and Alexander Pope, at 52, the Second:

Home! at the word, what blissful visions rise;
Lift us from earth, and draw toward the skies!
'Mid mirag'd towers, or meretricious joys,
Although we roam, one thought the mind employs:
Or lowly hut, good friend, or loftiest dome,
Earth knows no spot so holy as our Home.
There, where affection warms the father's breast,
There is the spot of heav'n most surely blest.

Howe'er we search, though wandering with the wind
Through frigid Zembla, or the heats of Ind,
Not elsewhere may we seek, nor elsewhere know,
The light of heav'n upon our dark below.

When from our dearest hope and haven reft,
Delight nor dazzles, nor is luxury left,
We long, obedient to our nature's law,
To see again our hovel thatched with straw:
See birds that know our avenaceous store
Stoop to our hand, and thence repleted soar:
But, of all hopes the wanderer's soul that share,
His pristine peace of mind's his final prayer.

VI
As Walt Whitman Might Have Written All Around It:

1

You over there, young man with the guide-book, red-bound, covered
flexibly with red linen,
Come here, I want to talk with you; I, Walt, the Manhattanese, citizen
of these States, call you.
Yes, and the courier, too, smirking, smug-mouthed, with oil'd hair; a
garlicky look about him generally; him, too, I take in, just as I would
a coyote, or a king, or a toad-stool, or a ham-sandwich, or anything
or anybody else in the world.
Where are you going?
You want to see Paris, to eat truffles, to have a good time; in Vienna,
London, Florence, Monaco, to have a good time; you want to see
Venice.
Come with me. I will give you a good time; I will give you all the
Venice you want, and most of the Paris.
I, Walt, I call to you. I am all on deck! Come and loafe with me! Let
me tote you around by your elbow and show you things.
You listen to my ophicleide!
Home!
Home, I celebrate. I elevate my fog-whistle, inspir'd by the thought of
home.
Come in! — take a front seat; the jostle of the crowd not minding; there
is room enough for all of you.
This is my exhibition — it is the greatest show on earth — there is no
charge for admission.
All you have to pay me is to take in my romanza.

1. The brown-stone house; the father coming home worried from a bad day's business; the wife meets him in the marble-pav'd vestibule; she throws her arms about him; she presses him close to her; she looks him full in the face with affectionate eyes; the frown from his brow disappearing.

Darling, she says, Johnny has fallen down and cut his head; the cook is going away, and the boiler leaks.

2. The mechanic's dark little third-story room, seen in a flash from the Elevated Railway train; the sewing-machine in a corner; the small cook-stove; the whole family eating cabbage around a kerosene lamp; of the clatter and roar and groaning wail of the Elevated train unconscious; of the smell of the cabbage unconscious.

Me, passant, in the train, of the cabbage not quite so unconscious.

3. The French flat; the small rooms, all right-angles, unindividual; the narrow halls; the gaudy cheap decorations everywhere.

The janitor and the cook exchanging compliments up and down the elevator-shaft; the refusal to send up more coal, the solid splash of the water upon his head, the language he sends up the shaft, the triumphant laughter of the cook, to her kitchen retiring.

4. The widow's small house in the suburbs of the city; the widow's boy coming home from his first day down town; he is flushed with happiness and pride; he is no longer a school-boy, he is earning money; he takes on the airs of a man and talks learnedly of business.

5. The room in the third-class boarding house; the mean little hard-coal fire, the slovenly Irish servant-girl making it, the ashes on the hearth, the faded furniture, the private provender hid away in the closet, the dreary back-yard out the window; the young girl at the glass, with her mouth full of hair-pins, doing up her hair to go down-stairs and flirt with the young fellows in the parlor.

6. The kitchen of the old farm-house; the young convict just return'd from prison — it was his first offense, and the judges were lenient to him.

He is taking his first meal out of prison; he has been receiv'd back, kiss'd, encourag'd to start again; his lungs, his nostrils expand with the big breaths of free air; with shame, with wonderment, with a trembling joy, his heart too expanding.

The old mother busies herself about the table; she has ready for him the dishes he us'd to like; the father sits with his back to them, reading the newspaper, the newspaper shaking and rustling much; the children hang wondering around the prodigal — they have been caution'd: *Do not ask where our Jim has been; only say you are glad to see him.*

The elder daughter is there, pale-fac'd, quiet; her young man went back on her four years ago; his folks would not let him marry a convict's sister. She sits by the window, sewing on the children's clothes, the clothes not only patching up; her hunger for children of her own invisibly patching up.

The brother looks up; he catches her eye, he fearful, apologetic; she smiles back at him, not reproachfully smiling, with loving pretense of hope smiling — it is too much for him; he buries his face in the folds of the mother's black gown.

7. The best room of the house, on the Sabbath only open'd; the smell of horse-hair furniture and mahogany varnish; the ornaments on the what-not in the corner; the wax fruit, dusty, sunken, sagged in, consumptive-looking, under a glass globe; the sealing-wax imitation of coral; the cigar boxes with shells plastered over; the perforated card-board motto.

The kitchen; the housewife sprinkling the clothes for the fine ironing to-morrow — it is Third-day night, and the plain things are already iron'd, now in cupboards, in drawers stowed away.

The wife waiting for the husband — he is at the tavern, jovial, carousing; she, alone in the kitchen sprinkling clothes — the little red wood clock with peaked top, with pendulum wagging behind a pane of gayly painted glass, strikes twelve.

The sound of the husband's voice on the still night air — he is singing: *We won't go home till morning!* — the wife arising, toward the wood-shed hastily going, stealthily entering, the voice all the time coming nearer, inebriate, chantant.

The wood-shed; the club behind the door of the wood-shed; the wife annexing the club; the husband approaching, always inebriate, chantant.

The husband passing the door of the wood-shed; the club over his head, now with his head in contact; the sudden cessation of the song; the temperance pledge signed the next morning; the benediction of peace over the domestic foyer temporarily resting.

3

I sing the soothing influences of home.

You, young man, thoughtlessly wandering, with courier, with guide-book wandering,

You hearken to the melody of my steam-calliope.

Yawp!

BEN KING
1857–1894

If I Should Die

If I should die to-night
And you should come to my cold corpse and say,
Weeping and heartsick o'er my lifeless clay —
If I should die to-night,
And you should come in deepest grief and woe —
And say: "Here's that ten dollars that I owe,"
    I might arise in my large white cravat
    And say, "What's that?"

If I should die to-night
And you should come to my cold corpse and kneel,
Clasping my bier to show the grief you feel,
    I say, if I should die to-night
And you should come to me, and there and then
Just even hint 'bout payin' me that ten,
    I might arise the while,
    But I'd drop dead again.

The Mermaid

Sweet mermaid of the incomparable eyes,
Surpassing glimpses of the April skies.
Thy form, ah, maid of the billowy deep!
So rare and fair, but to possess I'd creep
Where the old octopus deep in his briny haunts
Comes forth to feed on anything he wants;
Where mollusks crawl and cuttlefish entwine,
There on crustaceans be content to dine.
What ecstacies in some calcareous valley,
Had I but scales like thee 'tis there we'd dally,
There seek each peak and let no other bliss
Be more enchanting than one salt-sea kiss;
There sit and bask in love, and sigh, and feel
Each other's fins throb, or perhaps we'd steal
To some lone cavern. I suppose you know a
Place where we could pluck the polyzoa,

Or in your boudoir by your mirror there
I'd comb the seaweed from your auburn hair.
But hush! A red-haired mermaid sister comes this way,
And lashing with her tail the wavelets into spray.
Cometh she alone o'er yonder watery pampas?
Oh, no. By Jove! There comes the white hippocampus.

The Hair-Tonic Bottle

How dear to my heart is the old village drugstore,
    When tired and thirsty it comes to my view.
The wide-spreading sign that asks you to "Try it,"
    Vim, Vaseline, Vermifuge, Hop Bitters, too.
The old rusty stove and the cuspidor by it,
    That little back room. Oh! you've been there yourself,
And ofttimes have gone for the doctor's prescription,
    But tackled the bottle that stood on the shelf.
        The friendly old bottle,
        The plain-labeled bottle,
The "Hair-Tonic" bottle that stood on the shelf.

How oft have I seized it with hands that were glowing,
    And guzzled awhile ere I set off for home;
I owned the whole earth all that night, but next morning
    My head felt as big as the Capitol's dome.
And then how I hurried away to receive it,
    The druggist would smile o'er his poisonous pelf,
And laugh as he poured out his unlicensed bitters,
    And filled up the bottle that stood on the shelf.
        The unlicensed bottle,
        The plain-labeled bottle,
That "Hair-Tonic" bottle that stood on the shelf.

The Cultured Girl Again

She was so esthetic and culchud,
    Just doted on Wagner and Gluck;
And claimed that perfection existed
    In some foreign English bred duke.

She raved over Browning and Huxley,
   And Tyndal, and Darwin, and Taine;
And talked about flora and fauna,
   And many things I can't explain.

Of Madame Blavatski, the occult,
   Theosophy, art, and then she
Spoke of the Cunead Sibyl
   And Venus de Med-i-che.

She spoke of the why and the wherefore,
   But longed for the whither and whence;
And she said yclept, yip, yap and yonder
   Were used in alliterative sense.

Well, I like a fool sat dumfounded,
   And wondered what she did n't know
'T was 10 when I bade her good evening,
   I thought it in season to go.

I passed her house yesterday evening,
   I don't know, but it seems to me,
She was chasing around in the kitchen,
   And getting things ready for tea.

I heard her sweet voice calling: "Mother,"
   It was then that I felt quite abashed,
For she yelled, "How shall I fix the 'taters,
   Fried, lionized, baked, biled, or mashed?"

The Pessimist

Nothing to do but work,
   Nothing to eat but food,
Nothing to wear but clothes
   To keep one from going nude.

Nothing to breathe but air
   Quick as a flash 't is gone;
Nowhere to fall but off,
   Nowhere to stand but on.

219

Nothing to comb but hair,
  Nowhere to sleep but in bed,
Nothing to weep but tears,
  Nothing to bury but dead.

Nothing to sing but songs,
  Ah, well, alas! alack!
Nowhere to go but out,
  Nowhere to come but back.

Nothing to see but sights,
  Nothing to quench but thirst,
Nothing to have but what we've got;
  Thus thro' life we are cursed.

Nothing to strike but a gait;
  Everything moves that goes.
Nothing at all but common sense
  Can ever withstand these woes.

ANONYMOUS

Kentucky Moonshiner

I've been a moonshiner for seventeen long years,
I've spent all my money for whiskey and beers.
I'll go to some holler, I'll pull up my still,
I'll make you a gallon for a two-dollar bill.

I'll go to some grocery and drink with my friends,
No woman to follow to see what I spends.
God bless those pretty women, I wish they were mine,
Their breath smells as sweet as the dew on the vine.

I'll eat when I'm hungry and drink when I'm dry,
If moonshine don't kill me, I'll live till I die.
God bless those moonshiners, I wish they were mine,
Their breath smells as sweet as the good old moonshine.

Roy Bean

Cowboys, come and hear a story of Roy Bean in all his glory,
"All the law West of the Pecos," was his line:
You must let our ponies take us, to a town on Lower Pecos
Where the High Bridge spans the cañon thin and fine.

He was born one day near Toyah where he learned to be a lawyer
And a teacher and a barber for his fare,
He was cook and old shoe mender, sometimes preacher and bar-
tender:
It cost two bits to have him cut your hair.

He was certain sure a hustler and considerable a rustler
And at mixing up an egg nog he was grand.
He was lively, he was merry, he could drink a Tom and Jerry,
On occasion at a round-up took a hand.

You may find the story funny, but once he had no money
Which for him was not so very strange and rare,
And he went to help Pap Wyndid but he got so absent-minded,
Then he put his RB brand on old Pap's steer.

Now Pap was right smart angry so Roy Bean went down to Langtry
Where he opened up an office and a store.
There he'd sell you drinks or buttons or another rancher's muttons,
Though the latter made the other feller sore.

Once there came from Austin city a young dude reputed witty,
Out of Bean he thought he'd quickly take a rise:
And he got frisky as he up and called for whiskey
And he said to Bean, "Now hurry, damn your eyes."

On the counter threw ten dollars and it very quickly follers
That the bar-keep took full nine and gave back one,
Then the stranger give a holler as he viewed his single dollar,
And at that commenced the merriment and fun.

For the dude he slammed the table just as hard as he was able,
That the price of whiskey was too high he swore.
Said Roy Bean, "Cause of your fussin' and your most outrageous cussin'
You are fined the other dollar by the law.

"On this place I own a lease, sir, I'm the justice of the peace, sir,
And the Law west of the Pecos all is here,
For you've acted very badly," then the stranger went off sadly
While down his cheek there rolled a bitter tear.

Then one day they found a dead man who had been in life a Red man
So it's doubtless he was nothing else than bad.
Called on Bean to view the body, so he took a drink of toddy,
Then he listed all the things the dead man had.

Now the find it was quite rare, oh, for he'd been a "cocinero"
And his pay day hadn't been so far away.
He'd a bran' new fine white Stetson and a dandy Smith and Wesson
And a bag of forty dollars jingled gay.

Said Roy Bean, "You'll learn a lesson for I see a Smith and Wesson
And to carry implements of war is wrong,
So I fine you forty dollar," and the man gave ne'er a holler
Which concludes this very interesting song.

SAM WALTER FOSS
1858–1911

Husband and Heathen

O'er the men of Ethiopia she would pour her cornucopia,
And shower wealth and plenty on the people of Japan,
Send down jelly cake and candies to the Indians of the Andes,
And a cargo of plum pudding to the men of Hindustan;
    And she said she loved 'em so —
    Bushman, Finn and Eskimo. —
If she had the wings of eagles to their succor she would fly,
    Loaded down with jam and jelly,
    Succotash and vermicelli,
Prunes, pomegranates, plums and pudding, peaches, pineapples and pie.

She would fly with speedy succor to the natives of Molucca
With whole loads of quail and salmon, and with tons of fricassee,
    And give cake in fullest measure
    To the men of Australasia

And all the archipelagoes that dot the Southern sea;
  And the Anthropophagi,
  All their lives deprived of pie,
She would satiate and satisfy with custard, cream and mince;
  And those miserable Australians
  And the Borrioboolaghalians,
She would gorge with choicest jelly, raspberry, currant, grape and quince.

But, like old war-time hardtackers, her poor husband lived on crackers
Bought at wholesale from a baker, eaten from the mantel shelf;
  If the men of Madagascar
  And the natives of Alaska,
Had enough to sate their hunger, let him look out for himself.
  And his coat had but one tail
  And he used a shingle nail
To fasten up his "gallus" when he went out to his work;
  And she used to spend his money
  To buy sugar plums and honey
For the Terra del Fuegian and the Turcoman and Turk.

A Philosopher

Zack Bumstead uster flosserfize
About the ocean and the skies:
An' gab an' gas f'um morn till noon
About the other side the moon;
An' 'bout the natur of the place
Ten miles be-end the end of space.
An' if his wife sh'd ask the crank
Ef he wouldn't kinder try to yank
Hisself out doors an' git some wood
To make her kitchen fire good,
So she c'd bake her beans an' pies,
He'd say, "I've gotter flosserfize."

An' then he'd set an' flosserfize
About the natur an' the size
Of angels' wings, an' think, and gawp,
An' wonder how they made 'em flop.
He'd calkerlate how long a skid
'Twould take to move the sun, he did,

An' if the skid was strong an' prime,
It couldn't be moved to supper time.
An' w'en his wife 'ud ask the lout
Ef he wouldn' kinder waltz about
An' take a rag an' shoo the flies,
He'd say, "I've gotter flosserfize."

An' then he'd set an' flosserfize
'Bout schemes for fencing in the skies,
Then lettin' out the lots to rent
So's he could make an honest cent,
An' ef he'd find it pooty tough
To borry cash fer fencin' stuff?
An' if 'twere best to take his wealth
An' go to Europe for his health,
Or save his cash till he'd enough
To buy some more of fencin' stuff —
Then, ef his wife sh'd ask the gump
Ef he wouldn't kinder try to hump
Hisself to tother side the door
So she c'd come an' sweep the floor,
He'd look at her with mournful eyes,
An' say, "I've gotter flosserfize."

An' so he'd set an' flosserfize
'Bout what it wuz held up the skies,
An' how God made this earthly ball
Jest simply out er nawthin' tall,
An' 'bout the natur, shape an' form
Of nawthin' thet he made it from.
Then, ef his wife sh'd ask the freak
If he wouldn' kinder try to sneak
Out to the barn an' find some aigs,
He'd never move nor lift his laigs
An' never stir nor try to rise
But say, "I've gotter flosserfize."

An' so he'd set an' flosserfize
About the earth an' sea an' skies,
An' scratch his head an' ask the cause
Of w'at there waz before time waz,
An' w'at the universe 'ud do
Bimeby w'en time hed all got through;

An' jest how fur we'd hev to climb
Ef we sh'd travel out er time,
An' ef we'd need w'en we got there
To keep our watches in repair.
Then, ef his wife she'd ask the gawk
Ef he wouldn' kinder try to walk
To where she had the table spread
An' kinder git his stomach fed,
He'd leap for that ar kitchen door
An' say, "W'y didn't you speak afore?"

An' when he'd got his supper et,
He'd set, an' set, an' set, an' set,
An' fold his arms an' shet his eyes,
An' set, an' set, an' flosserfize.

NIXON WATERMAN
1859–1944

Cheer for the Consumer

I'm only a consumer, and it really doesn't matter
If you crowd me in the street cars till I couldn't well be flatter;
I'm only a consumer, and the strikers may go striking,
For it's mine to end my living if it isn't to my liking.
I am a sort of parasite without a special mission
Except to pay the damages — mine is a queer position:
The Fates unite to squeeze me till I couldn't well be flatter,
For I'm only a consumer, and it really doesn't matter.

The baker tilts the price of bread upon the vaguest rumor
Of damage to the wheat crop, but I'm only a consumer,
So it really doesn't matter, for there's no law that compells me
To pay the added charges on the loaf of bread he sells me.
The iceman leaves a smaller piece when days are growing hotter,
But I'm only a consumer, and I do not need iced water:
My business is to pay the bills and keep in a good humor,
And it really doesn't matter, for I'm only a consumer.

The milkman waters milk for me; there's garlic in my butter,
But I'm only a consumer, and it does no good to mutter;
I know that coal is going up and beef is getting higher,
But I'm only a consumer, and I have no need of fire;
While beefsteak is a luxury that wealth alone is needing,
I'm only a consumer, and what need have I for feeding?
My business is to pay the bills and keep in a good humor,
And it really doesn't matter, since I'm only a consumer.

The grocer sells me addled eggs; the tailor sells me shoddy,
I'm only a consumer, and I am not anybody.
The cobbler pegs me paper soles, the dairyman short-weights me,
I'm only a consumer, and most everybody hates me.
There's turnip in my pumpkin pie and ashes in my pepper,
The world's my lazaretto, and I'm nothing but a leper;
So lay me in my lonely grave and tread the turf down flatter,
I'm only a consumer, and it really doesn't matter.

If We Didn't Have To Eat

Life would be an easy matter
   If we didn't have to eat.
     If we never had to utter,
      "Won't you pass the bread and butter,
Likewise push along that platter
   Full of meat?"
     Yes, if food were obsolete
     Life would be a jolly treat,
If we didn't — shine or shower,
Old or young, 'bout every hour —
     Have to eat, eat, eat, eat, eat —
     'Twould be jolly if we didn't have to eat.

We could save a lot of money
   If we didn't have to eat.
     Could we cease our busy buying,
      Baking, broiling, brewing, frying,
Life would then be oh, so sunny
   And complete;
     And we wouldn't fear to greet
     Every grocer in the street

If we didn't — man and woman,
Every hungry, helpless human —
 Have to eat, eat, eat, eat, eat —
 We'd save money if we didn't have to eat.

All our worry would be over
 If we didn't have to eat.
  Would the butcher, baker, grocer
  Get our hard-earned dollars? No, Sir!
We would then be right in clover
 Cool and sweet.
  Want and hunger we could cheat,
  And we'd get there with both feet,
If we didn't — poor or wealthy,
Halt or nimble, sick or healthy —
 Have to eat, eat, eat, eat, eat,
 We could get there if we didn't have to eat.

HAMLIN GARLAND
1860–1940

Horses Chawin' Hay

I tell yeh whut! The chankin'
 Which the tired horses makes
When you've slipped the harness off'm,
 An' shoved the hay in flakes
From the hay-mow overhead,
 Is jest about the equal of any pi-anay;
They's nothin' soun's s' cumftabul
 As horsus chawin' hay.

I love t' hear 'em chankin',
 Jest a-grindin' slow and low,
With their snoots a-rootin' clover
 Deep as their ol' heads 'll go.
It's kind o' sort o' restin'
 To a feller's bones, I say.
It soun's s' mighty cumftabul —
 The horsus chawin' hay.

Gra-onk, gra-onk, gra-onk!
  In a stiddy kind o' tone,
Not a tail a-waggin' to 'um,
  N'r another sound 'r groan —
Fer the flies is gone a-snoozin'.
Then I loaf around an' watch 'em
  In a sleepy kind o' way,
F'r they soun' so mighty cumftabul
  As they rewt and chaw their hay.

An' it sets me thinkin' sober
  Of the days of '53,
When we pioneered the prairies —
  M' wife an' dad an' me,
In a dummed ol' prairie-schooner,
  In a rough-an'-tumble way,
Sleepin' out at nights, to music
  Of the horsus chawin' hay.

Or I'm thinkin' of my comrades
  In the fall of '63,
When I rode with ol' Kilpatrick
  Through an' through ol' Tennessee.
I'm a-layin' in m' blanket
  With my head agin a stone,
Gazin' upwards toward the North Star —
  Billy Sykes and Davy Sloan
  A-snorin' in a buck-saw kind o' way,
An' me a-layin', listenin'
  To the horsus chawin' hay.

It strikes me turrible cur'ous
  That a little noise like that,
Can float a feller backwards
  Like the droppin' of a hat;
An' start his throat a-achin',
  Make his eyes wink that a-way —
They ain't no sound that gits me
  Like horsus chawin' hay!

Goin' Back T'morrer

In the City

I tell ye, Sue, it ain't no use!
    I *can't* stay, and I won't —
W'y! a feller'd need the widder's cruse
    T' live back here an' stan' the brunt
Of all expenses, thick and thin —
    Too many men — ain't land enough
T' swing a feller's elbows in —
    I 'spose you'll take it kind a rough
But I'm goin' back t' morrer!

It ain't no use t' talk t' me
    Of whut some other feller owns,
I ain't got no grip at all,
    His fire don't warm my achin' bones,
An' then I'm ust t' walkin' where
    There ain't no p'lice 'r pavin' stones —
Of course you'll think I'm mighty sick
    But I'm goin' back t' morrer!

Fact is, folks, I *love* the West!
    They ain't no other place like home —
They ain't no other place t' *rest*,
    F'r mother 'n me but jest ol' Rome,
Cedar County, up Basswood Run —
    Lived there goin' on thirty years —
Come there spring o' sixty-one —
    An' I'm goin' back t' morrer!

I tell ye, things looked purty wild
    On that there prairie then! —
We hadn't nary chick n'r child,
    An' we buckled down to work like men —
Handsome land them two claims was
    As ever lay out doors! Rich an' clean
Of brush an' sloos. Y'r Uncle Daws
    He used t' say God done his best
On that there land — His level best.

No, I jest can't stand it here,
   Nohow — ain't room to swing my cap.
Ye're all cooped up in this ere flat
   Jest like chickens in a trap —
I'm mighty sorry, Sue, but I
   Can't stand it, an' mother can't
If *she* was willin' wy I'd try —
   But I guess we'll go t' morrer.

'N' when we jest get home agin,
   Back t' Cedar County, back t' Rome.
Back t' Basswood Run an' *home*,
   Won't the neighbors jest drop in
When we git settled down an' grin
   An' all shake han's — an' Deacon White
Drive up t' laff that laff o' hisn —
   Mother, let's start back t'night!

The corn is jest a-rampin' now —
   I c'n hear the leaves a-russlin' —
As they twist an' swing an' bow —
   I c'n see the boys a-husslin'
In the medder by the crick
   Forkin' hay f'r all in sight —
An' the birds an' bees s' thick! —
   O we *must* start back t'night!

BLISS CARMAN
1861–1929

A More Ancient Mariner

The swarthy bee is a buccaneer,
A burly velveted rover,
Who loves the booming wind in his ear
As he sails the seas of clover.

A waif of the goblin pirate crew,
With not a soul to deplore him.
He steers for the open verge of blue
With the filmy world before him.

His flimsy sails abroad on the wind
Are shivered with fairy thunder;
On a line that sings to the light of his wings
He makes for the lands of wonder.

He harries the ports of the Hollyhocks,
And levies on poor Sweetbrier;
He drinks the whitest wine of Phlox,
And the Rose is his desire.

He hangs in the Willows a night and a day;
He rifles the Buckwheat patches;
Then battens his store of pelf galore
Under the tautest hatches.

He woos the Poppy and weds the Peach,
Inveigles Daffodilly,
And then like a tramp abandons each
For the gorgeous Canada Lily.

There's not a soul in the garden world
But wishes the day were shorter,
When Mariner B. puts out to sea
With the wind in the proper quarter.

Or, so they say! But I have my doubts;
For the flowers are only human,
And the valor and gold of a vagrant bold
Were always dear to woman.

He dares to boast, along the coast,
The beauty of Highland Heather, —
How he and she, with night on the sea,
Lay out on the hills together.

He pilfers from every port of the wind,
From April to golden autumn;
But the thieving ways of his mortal days
Are those his mother taught him.

His morals are mixed, but his will is fixed;
He prospers after his kind,
And follows an instinct, compass-sure,
The philosophers call blind.

And that is why, when he comes to die,
He'll have an easier sentence
Than some one I know who thinks just so,
And then leaves room for repentance.

He never could box the compass round;
He doesn't know port from starboard;
But he knows the gates of the Sundown Straits,
Where the choicest goods are harbored.

He never could see the Rule of Three,
But he knows a rule of thumb
Better than Euclid's, better than yours,
Or the teachers' yet to come.

He knows the smell of the hydromel
As if two and two were five;
And hides it away for a year and a day
In his own hexagonal hive.

Out in the day, hap-hazard, alone,
Booms the old vagrant hummer,
With only his whim to pilot him
Through the splendid vast of summer.

He steers and steers on the slant of the gale,
Like the fiend or Vanderdecken;
And there's never an unknown course to sail
But his crazy log can reckon.

He drones along with his rough sea-song
And the throat of a salty tar,
This devil-may-care, till he makes his lair
By the light of a yellow star.

He looks like a gentleman, lives like a lord,
And works like a Trojan hero;
Then loafs all winter upon his hoard,
With the mercury at zero.

OLIVER BROOK HERFORD
1863–1935

The Fall of J. W. Beane

A Ghost Story

In all the Eastern hemisphere
You would n't find a knight, a peer,
A viscount, earl or baronet,
A marquis or a duke, nor yet
A prince, or emperor, or king,
Or sultan, czar, or anything
That could in family pride surpass
J. Wentworth Beane of Boston, Mass.
His family tree could far outscale
The bean-stalk in the fairy tale;
And Joseph's coat would pale before
The blazon'd coat-of-arms he bore,
The arms of his old ancestor,
One Godfrey Beane, "who crossed, you know,
About two hundred years ago."
He had it stamped, engraved, embossed,
Without the least regard to cost,
Upon his house, upon his gate,
Upon his table-cloth, his plate,
Upon his knocker, and his mat,
Upon his watch, inside his hat;
On scarf-pin, handkerchief, and screen,
And cards; in short, J. Wentworth Beane
Contrived to have old Godfrey's crest
On everything that he possessed.
And lastly, when he died, his will
Proved to contain a codicil
Directing that a sum be spent
To carve it on his monument.

But if you think this ends the scene
You little know J. Wentworth Beane.
To judge him by the common host
Is reckoning without his ghost.
And it is something that befell
His ghost I chiefly have to tell.

At midnight of the very day
They laid J. Wentworth Beane away,
No sooner had the clock come round
To 12 P.M. than from the ground
Arose a spectre, lank and lean,
With frigid air and haughty mien;
No other than J. Wentworth Beane,
Unchanged in all, except his pride —
If anything, intensified.
He looked about him with that air
Of supercilious despair
That very stuck-up people wear
At some society affair
When no one in their set is there.
Then, after brushing from his sleeves
Some bits of mould and clinging leaves,
And lightly dusting off his shoe,
The iron gate he floated through,
Just looking back the clock to note,
As one who fears to miss a boat.
Ten minutes later found him on
The ghost's Cunarder — "Oregon";
And ten days later by spook time
He heard the hour of midnight chime
From out the tower of Beanley Hall,
And stood within the grave-yard wall
Beside a stone, moss-grown and green,
On which these simple words were seen:

IN MEMORY
SIR GODFREY BEANE.

The while he gazed in thought serene
A little ghost of humble mien,
Unkempt and crooked, bent and spare,
Accosted him with cringing air:
"Most noble sir, 't is plain to see
You are not of the likes of me;
You are a spook of high degree."
"My good man," cried J. Wentworth B.,
"Leave me a little while, I pray,
I've travelled very far to-day,

And I desire to be alone
With him who sleeps beneath this stone.
I cannot rest till I have seen
My ancestor, Sir Godfrey Beane."

"Your ancestor! How can that be?"
Exclaimed the little ghost, "when he,
Last of his line, was drowned at sea
Two hundred years ago; this stone
Is to his memory alone.
I, and I only, saw his end.
As he, my master and my friend,
Leaned o'er the vessel's side one night
I pushed him — no, it was not right,
I own that I was much to blame;
I donned his clothes, and took the name
Of Beane — I also took his gold,
About five thousand pounds all told;
And so to Boston, Mass., I came
To found a family and name —
I, who in former times had been
Sir Godfrey's — "
     "Wretch, what do you mean!
Sir Godfrey's what?" gasped Wentworth Beane.
"Sir Godfrey's valet!"

     That same night,
When the ghost steamer sailed, you might
Among the passengers have seen
A ghost of very abject mien,
Faded and shrunk, forlorn and frayed,

The shadow of his former shade,
Who registered in steerage class,
J. W. Beane of Boston, Mass.

Now, gentle reader, do not try
To guess the family which I
Disguise as Beane — enough that they
Exist on Beacon Hill to-day,
In sweet enjoyment of their claims —
It is not well to mention names.

Eve

O dear! I cannot choose but write
To tell you of the Pure Delight
Your Little Book has given me.
While reading it I seem to be
Transported in your Fancy's train,
To my own Garden once again.
Ah me! whenever I recall
That Fatal Morning of the Fall,
Of One Thing quite convinced I am;
Had I that day, as Old Khayyám,
A Book of Verses 'neath the Bough,
I'd be in Paradise e'en now.
With your Sweet Book to entertain,
The Serpent might have talked in vain;
For is not Curiosity
The naughty Daughter of Ennui?

.   .   .

Yet, but for *my* bite into the Unknown,
Meseems *your* "Garden" never could have grown.

ERNEST LAWRENCE THAYER
1863–1940

Casey at the Bat

The outlook wasn't brilliant for the Mudville nine that day;
The score stood four to two with but one inning more to play.
So when Cooney died at second, and Burrows did the same,
A pallor wreathed the features of the patrons of the game.
A straggling few got up to go in deep despair. The rest
Clung to the hope which springs eternal in the human breast;
They thought, "If only Casey could but get a whack at that —
We'd put up even money now with Casey at the bat."
But Flynn preceded Casey, as did also Jimmy Blake,
And the former was a lulu and the latter was a fake;
So upon that stricken multitude a deathlike silence sat,
For there seemed but little chance of Casey's getting to the bat.

But Flynn let drive a single, to the wonderment of all,
And Blake, the much despis-ed, tore the cover off the ball;
And when the dust had lifted, and the men saw what had occurred,
There was Jimmy safe at second and Flynn a-hugging third.
Then from five thousand throats and more there rose a lusty yell;
It rumbled in the mountaintops, it rattled in the dell;
It knocked upon the hillside and recoiled upon the flat,
For Casey, mighty Casey, was advancing to the bat.
There was ease in Casey's manner as he stepped into his place;
There was pride in Casey's bearing and a smile on Casey's face.
And when, responding to the cheers, he lightly doffed his hat,
No stranger in the crowd could doubt 'twas Casey at the bat.
Ten thousand eyes were on him as he rubbed his hands with dirt;
Five thousand tongues applauded when he wiped them on his shirt.
Then while the writhing pitcher ground the ball into his hip,
Defiance gleamed in Casey's eye, a sneer curled Casey's lip.
And now the leather-covered sphere came hurtling through the air,
And Casey stood a-watching it in haughty grandeur there.
Close by the sturdy batsman the ball unheeded sped —
"That ain't my style," said Casey — "Strike one," the Umpire said.
From the benches black with people, there went up a muffled roar,
Like the beating of the storm-waves on a stern and distant shore.
"Kill him! kill the umpire!" shouted someone on the stand;
And it's likely they'd have killed him had not Casey raised his hand.
With a smile of Christian charity great Casey's visage shone;
He stilled the rising tumult; he bade the game go on;
He signalled to the pitcher, and once more the spheroid flew;
But Casey still ignored it, and the Umpire said, "Strike two."
"Fraud!" cried the maddened thousands, and the echo answered, "Fraud!"
But one scornful look from Casey and the multitude was awed.
They saw his face grow stern and cold, they saw his muscles strain,
And they knew that Casey wouldn't let that ball go by again.
The sneer is gone from Casey's lip, his teeth are clenched in hate;
He pounds with cruel violence his bat upon the plate.
And now the pitcher holds the ball, and now he lets it go,
And now the air is shattered by the force of Casey's blow.
Oh, somewhere in this favored land the sun is shining bright;
The band is playing somewhere, and somewhere hearts are light,
And somewhere men are laughing, and somewhere children shout;
But there is no joy in Mudville — mighty Casey has struck out.

RICHARD HOVEY
1864–1900

Eleazar Wheelock

Oh, Eleazar Wheelock was a very pious man:
He went into the wilderness to teach the Indian,
  With a *gradus ad Parnassum*, a Bible and a drum,
  And five hundred gallons of New England rum.

> *Fill the bowl! Fill the bowl!*
> *And drink to Eleazar*
> *And his primitive Alcazar,*
> *Where he mixed drinks for the heathen*
> *In the goodness of his soul.*

The big chief who met him was the Sachem of the Wah-hoo-wahs.
If he was not a big chief, there was never one you saw who was;
He had tobacco by the cord, ten squaws, and more to come,
But he never yet had tasted of New England rum.

Eleazar and the big chief harangued and gesticulated;
And they founded Dartmouth College and the big chief matriculated.
Eleazar was the faculty and the whole curriculum
Was five hundred gallons of New England rum.

Barney McGee

Barney McGee, there's no end of good luck in you,
Will-o'-the-wisp, with a flicker of Puck in you,
Wild as a bull-pup and all of his pluck in you —
Let a man tread on your coat and he'll see —
Eyes like the lakes of Killarney for clarity
Nose that turns up without any vulgarity,
Smile like a cherub, and hair that is carroty —
Wow, you're a rarity, Barney McGee!
Mellow as Tarragon,
Prouder than Aragon —
Hardly a paragon,
You will agree —
Here's all that's fine to you!
Books and old wine to you!
Girls be divine to you,
Barney McGee!

Lucky the day when I met you unwittingly,
Dining where vagabonds came and went flittingly.
Here's some Barbera to drink it befittingly,
That day at Silvio's, Barney McGee!
Many's the time we have quaffed our Chianti there,
Listened to Silvio quoting us Dante there —
Once more to drink Nebiolo spumante there,
How we'd pitch Pommery into the sea!
There where the gang of us
Met ere Rome rang of us,
They had the hang of us
To a degree.
How they would trust to you!
That was but just to you.
Here's o'er their dust to you,
Barney McGee!

Barney McGee, when you're sober you scintillate,
But when you're in drink you're the pride of the intellect;
Divil a one of us ever came in till late,
Once at the bar where you happened to be —
Every eye there like a spoke in you centering,
You with your eloquence, blarney and bantering —
All Vagabondia shouts at your entering,
King of the Tenderloin, Barney McGee!
There's no satiety
In your society
With the variety
Of your esprit.
Here's a long purse to you,
And a great thirst to you!
Fate be no worse to you,
Barney McGee!

Och, and the girls whose poor hearts you deracinate,
Whirl and bewilder and flutter and fascinate!
Faith, it's so killing you are, you assassinate —
Murder's the word for you, Barney McGee!
Bold when they're sunny and smooth when they're showery —
Oh, but the style of you, fluent and flowery!
Chesterfield's way, with a touch of the Bowery!
How would they silence you, Barney machree?
Naught can your gab allay,

Learned as Rabelais
(You in his abbey lay
Once on the spree.)
Here's to the smile of you,
(Oh, but the guile of you!)
And a long while of you,
Barney McGee!

Facile with phrases of length and Latinity,
Like *honorificabilitudinity*,
Where is the maid could resist your vicinity,
Wiled by the impudent grace of your plea?
Then your vivacity and pertinacity
Carry the day with the divil's audacity;
No mere veracity robs your sagacity
Of perspicacity, Barney McGee!
When all is new to them,
What will you do to them?
Will you be true to them?
Who shall decree?
Here's a fair strife to you!
Health and long life to you!
And a great wife to you,
Barney McGee!

Barney McGee, you're the pick of gentility;
Nothing can faze you, you've such a facility;
Nobody ever yet found your utility —
That is the charm of you, Barney McGee;
Under conditions that others would stammer in,
Still unperturbed as a cat or a Cameron,
Polished as somebody in the Decameron,
Putting the glamour on prince or Pawnee!
In your meanderin',
Love, and philanderin',
Calm as a mandarin
Sipping his tea!
Under the art of you,
Parcel and part of you,
Here's to the heart of you,
Barney McGee!

You who were ever alert to befriend a man,
You who were ever the first to defend a man,
You who had always the money to lend a man,
Down on his luck and hard up for a V!
Sure, you'll be playing a harp in beatitude
(And a quare sight you will be in that attitude) —
Some day, where gratitude seems but a platitude,
You'll find your latitude, Barney McGee.
That's not flim-flam, at all,
Just the plain — Damn it all,
Have one with me!
Here's luck and more to you,
Friends by the score to you,
True to the core to you,
Barney McGee!

J. GORDON COOGLER
1865–1901

Alas! Carolina!

Alas! Carolina! Carolina! Fair land of my birth,
   Thy fame will be wafted from the mountain to the sea
As being the greatest educational centre on earth,
   At the cost of men's blood thro' thy "one X" whiskey.

Two very large elephants* thou hast lately installed,
   Where thy sons and thy daughters are invited to come,
And learn to be physically and mentally strong,
   By the solemn proceeds of thy "innocent" rum.

* State universities.

Alas! for the South!

Alas! for the South, her books have grown fewer —
She never was much given to literature.

To Amy

I will drink to your health, sweet Amy,
 For there's nothing in this cup, I fear,
That would be suggestive of sorrow
 For my own sweet Amy, dear.

May your heart be pure and noble,
 And your arm be firm and strong,
And your hope be like the rainbow,
 Beautiful, bright and long.

May your life, like the rose of summer,
 Be fresh, and remain in its bud,
As I never was partial to whiskey, Amy,
 I'll toast you in Congaree mud.

Byron

Oh, thou immortal bard!
Men may condemn the song
 That issued from thy heart sublime,
Yet alas! its music sweet
Has left an echo that will sound
 Thro' the lone corridors of Time.

Thou immortal Byron!
Thy inspired genius
 Let no man attempt to smother —
May all that was good within thee
Be attributed to Heaven,
 All that was evil — to thy mother.

In Memorial

(To a young lady who sought publicity by attempting to belittle in public print a poem by the author, entitled "Beautiful Snow" — She has never been heard from through the press since.)

She died after the beautiful snow had melted,
 And was buried beneath the "slush";
The last sad words she breathed upon earth
Were these simple ones, "Oh, poet, do hush!"

A Mustacheless Bard

His whiskers didn't come, his mustache is gone,
  And to-day he's standing ashore
Enjoying the breeze with a cleaned shaved lip,
  Relieved of the burden it bore.

He's feeling so lonely, dull and forsaken,
  The boys they know him no more;
The girls are surprised, and speaking of him,
  Say, "He's uglier than ever before."

He can't understand why the beautiful girls
  Should thus be so cruel and rash,
Unless they believe that kisses are sweeter
  From lips that bear a mustache.

A Pretty Girl

On her beautiful face there are smiles of grace
  That linger in beauty serene,
And there are no pimples encircling her dimples
  As ever, as yet, I have seen.

GEORGE ADE
1866–1944

Il Janitoro

Mr. Tyler paid $7 for two opera tickets.

Although he slept through one duet he felt fully repaid for going, because Mrs. Tyler raved over the opera and wasted all her superlatives on it. The music was "heavenly," the prima donna "superb" and the tenor "magnificent."

There is nothing so irritates a real enthusiasm as the presence of calm scorn.

"Don't you like it?" asked Mrs. Tyler, as she settled back after the eighth recall of the motherly woman who had been singing the part of a 16-year-old maiden.

"Oh, yes; it's all right," replied Mr. Tyler, as if he were conceding something.

"All right! Oh, you iceberg! I don't believe you'd become enthusiastic over anything in the world."

"I like the music, my dear, but grand opera drags so. Then the situations are so preposterous they always appeal to my sense of humor. I can't help it. When I see Romeo and Juliet die, both singing away as if they enjoyed it, I have to laugh."

"The idea!"

"You take it in this last act. Those two fellows came out with the soldiers and announced that they were conspiring and didn't want to be heard by the people in the house, and then they shouted in chorus until they could have been heard two miles away."

"Oh, you are prejudiced."

"Not at all. I'll tell you, a grand opera's the funniest kind of a show if you only take the right view of it."

Thus they argued, and even after they arrived home she taunted him and told him he could not appreciate the dignity of the situations.

It was this nagging which induced Mr. Tyler to write an act of grand opera. He chose for his subject an alarm of fire in an apartment house. He wanted something modern and up-to-date, but in his method of treatment he resolved to reverently follow all the traditions of grand opera. The act, hitherto unpublished, and written solely for the benefit of Mrs. Tyler, is here appended:

(Mr. and Mrs. Taylor are seated in their apartment on the fifth floor of the Bohemoth residential flat building. Mrs. Taylor arises, places her hand on her heart, and moves to the center of the room. Mr. Taylor follows her, with his right arm extended.)

MRS. TAYLOR   I think I smell smoke.

MR. TAYLOR   She thinks she smells smoke.

MRS. TAYLOR   I think I smell smoke.

MR. TAYLOR   Oh. What is it? She says she thinks she smells smoke.

MRS. TAYLOR   What does it mean, what does it mean?
This smell of smoke may indicate,
That we'll be burned — oh-h-h, awful fate!

MR. TAYLOR   Behold the smell grows stronger yet,
The house is burning, I'd regret
To perish in the curling flames;
Oh, horror! horror! horror! ! !

MR. AND MRS. TAYLOR   Oh, sad is our lot, sad is our lot,
To perish in the flames so hot,
To curl and writhe and fry and sizz,
Oh, what a dreadful thing it is
To think of such a thing!

MRS. TAYLOR   We must escape!

MR. TAYLOR	Yes, yes, we must escape!
MRS. TAYLOR	We have no time to lose.
MR. TAYLOR	Ah, bitter truth, ah, bitter truth,
	We have no time to lose.
MR. AND MRS. TAYLOR	Sad is our lot, sad is our lot,
	To perish in the flames so hot.
MR. TAYLOR	Hark, what is it?
MRS. TAYLOR	Hark, what is it?
MR. TAYLOR	It is the dread alarm of fire.
MRS. TAYLOR	Ah, yes, ah, yes, it is the dread alarm.
MR. TAYLOR	The dread alarm strikes on the ear
	And chills me with an awful fear.
	The house will burn, oh, can it be
	That I must die in misery,
	That I must die in misery,
	The house will burn, oh, can it be
	That I must die in misery?
MRS. TAYLOR	Come, let us fly!
MR. TAYLOR	'Tis well. 'Tis well. We'll fly at once.

(Enter all the other residents of the fifth floor.)

MR. TAYLOR	Kind friends, I have some news to tell.
	This house is burning, it were well
	That we should haste ourselves away
	And save our lives without delay.
CHORUS	What is this he tells us?
	It must be so;
	The building is on fire
	And we must go.
	Oh, hasten, oh, hasten, oh, hasten away.
	Our terror we should not conceal,
	And language fails to express the alarm
	That in our hearts we feel.
MR. AND MRS. TAYLOR	Oh, language fails to express the alarm
	That in their hearts they feel.

(Enter the Janitor)

JANITOR	Hold, I am here.
MR. TAYLOR	Ah, it is the Janitoro.
MRS. TAYLOR	Can I believe my senses,
	Or am I going mad?
	It is the Janitoro,
	It is indeed the Janitoro.

245

JANITOR	Such news I have to tell.
MR. TAYLOR	Ah, I might have known
	He has such news to tell.
	Speak and break the awful suspense.
MRS. TAYLOR	Yes, speak.
JANITOR	I come to inform you
	That you must quickly fly.
	The fearful blaze is spreading,
	To tarry is to die.
	The floors underneath you
	Are completely burned away,
	They cannot save the building,
	So now escape I pray.
MRS. TAYLOR	Oh, awful message.
	How it chills my heart.
JANITOR	The flames are roaring loudly,
	Oh, what a fearful sound!
	You can hear the people shrieking
	As they jump and strike the ground.
	Oh, horror overtakes me,
	And I merely pause to say
	That the building's doomed for certain,
	Oh, haste, oh, haste away.
MRS. TAYLOR	Oh, awful message.
	How it chills my heart.
	Yet we will sing a few more arias
	Before we start.
MR. TAYLOR	Yes, a few more arias and then away.
CHORUS	Oh, hasten, oh, hasten, oh, hasten away.
MRS. TAYLOR	Now, e'er I retreat,
	Lest death o'ertakes me
	I'll speak of the fear
	That convulses and shakes me,
	I sicken to think what may befall,
	Oh, horror! horror! ! horror! ! !
MR. TAYLOR	The woman speaks the truth,
	And there can be no doubt
	That we will perish soon
	Unless we all clear out.
CHORUS	Oh, hasten, oh, hasten, oh, hasten away.

(But why go further? The supposition is that they continued the dilatory tactics of grand opera and perished in the flames.)

The Microbe's Serenade

A love-lorn microbe met by chance
　At a swagger bacteroidal dance,
A proud bacillian belle, and she
　Was first of the animalculae.
Of organisms saccharine,
　She was the protoplasmic queen;
The microscopical pride and pet
　Of the biological smartest set.
And so this infinitesimal swain
　Evolved a pleading low refrain:
　"O, lovely metamorphic germ!
　What futile scientific term
　Can well describe your many charms?
　Come to these embryonic arms!
　Then hie away to my cellular home
　And be my little diatom!"

His epithelium burned with love;
　He swore by molecules above,
She'd be his own gregarious mate,
　Or else he would disintegrate.
This amorous mite of a parasite
　Pursued the germ, both day and night,
And 'neath her window often played
　This Darwin-Huxley serenade —
He'd warble to her, ev'ry day,
　This rhizopodical roundelay:
　"O most primordial type of spore!
　I never met your like before;
　And, 'though a microbe has no heart,
　From you, sweet germ, I'll never part!
　We'll sit beneath some fungus growth
　Till dissolution claims us both."

R – E – M – O – R – S – E

The cocktail is a pleasant drink;
It's mild and harmless — I don't think.
When you've had one, you call for two,
And then you don't care what you do.

Last night I hoisted twenty-three
Of those arrangements into me.
My wealth increased, I swelled with pride,
I was pickled, primed, and ossified;
But R – E – M – O – R – S – E!
The water wagon is the place for me.
I think that somewhere in the game
I wept and told my real name.
At four I sought my whirling bed;
At eight I woke with such a head!
It is no time for mirth and laughter,
The cold, gray dawn of the morning after.

I wanted to pay for ev'ry round;
I talked on subjects most profound;
When all my woes I analyzed,
The barkeep softly sympathized.
The world was one kaleidoscope
Of purple bliss, transcendent hope.
But now I'm feeling mighty blue —
Three cheers for the W.C.T.U.!
R – E – M – O – R – S – E!
Those dry Martinis did the work for me;
Last night at twelve I felt immense,
Today I feel like thirty cents.
My eyes are bleared, my coppers hot,
I'll try to eat, but I cannot.
It is no time for mirth and laughter,
The cold, gray dawn of the morning after.

GELETT BURGESS
1866–1951

The Purple Cow

I never saw a Purple Cow,
    I never hope to see one;
But I can tell you, anyhow,
    I'd rather see than be one.

Cinq Ans Après

Ah, yes! I wrote the "Purple Cow" —
I'm Sorry, now, I Wrote it!
But I can Tell you, Anyhow,
I'll Kill you if you Quote it!

TOM MASSON
1866–1943

Enough

I shot a rocket in the air,
It fell to earth, I knew not where
Until next day, with rage profound,
The man it fell on came around.
In less time than it takes to tell,
He showed me where that rocket fell;
And now I do not greatly care
To shoot more rockets in the air.

My Poker Girl

Her eyes are velvet, soft and fine,
    That none can antedate;
Her hair's fine strands seem all divine,
    Her form is, oh! so

Her teeth, like driven snow, are white;
    And when she wills to blush
There is no tint can equal quite
    Her rounded cheek's fine

249

Could I but hold a hand like that
Just once, I would not care
If afterwards I stood quite pat
Forever, on a

A Tragedy

'Twas Christmas Eve, the month was May,
She wore her father's gown;
The reins beyond the horses lay,
The sleigh was upside down.

They sped across the boiling snow,
Above the sun's cold glare;
The little birds, above, below,
Were walking through the air.

The jangling sleigh-bells made no sound,
The horses backward flew;
The cows were lowing underground,
The trees all downward grew.

'Twas high noon, and the moonbeams played,
The clouds to dust all ran;
He was a winsome, pretty maid,
She was a big, strong man.

He softly said, yet did not speak:
"I hate you! Marry me."
She laughed, as tears ran down her cheek:
"I love you. No!" said she.

This sad event, which is, or was,
Or may be, must appall!
I know it happened, just because
I was not there at all.

He Took Her

She was a maid of high degree,
    And quite severely proper.
Each man she met, so proud was she,
    Would love, despair, then drop her.

But there remained without demur,
    When all the rest forsook her,
An amateur photographer,
    And finally he took her.

BERT LESTON TAYLOR ("B. L. T.")
1866–1921

Doxology

Praise Hearst, from whom all blessings flow!
Praise Hearst, who runs things here below.
Praise them who make him manifest —
Praise Andy L. and all the rest.

Praise Hearst because the world is round,
Because the seas with salt abound,
Because the water's always wet,
And constellations rise and set.

Praise Hearst because the grass is green,
And pleasant flow'rs in spring are seen;
Praise him for morning, night and noon.
Praise him for stars and sun and moon.

Praise Hearst, our nation's aim and end,
Humanity's unselfish friend;
And who remains, for all our debt,
A modest sweet white violet.

Those Flapjacks of Brown's

I'll write no more verses — plague take 'em! —
    Court neither your smiles nor your frowns,
If you'll only please tell how to make 'em,
    Those flapjacks of Brown's.

Three cupfuls of flour will do nicely,
    And toss in a teaspoon of salt;
Next add baking powder, precisely
    Two teaspoons, the stuff to exalt;
Of sugar two tablespoons, heaping —
    (All spoons should be heaping, says Neal);
Then mix it with strokes that are sweeping,
    And stir like the Deil.

Three eggs. (Tho' the missus may sputter,
    You'll pay to her protest no heed.)
A size-of-an-egg piece of butter,
    And milk as you happen to need.
Now mix the whole mess with a beater;
    Don't get it too thick or too thin.
(And I pause to remark that this meter
    Is awkward as sin.)

Of course there are touches that only
    A genius like Brown can impart;
And genius is everywhere lonely,
    And no one but Brown has the art.
I picture him stirring — a gentle
    Exponent of modern Romance,
With his shirttails, in style Oriental,
    Outside of his pants.

Upon Julia's Arctics

Whenas galoshed my Julia goes,
Unbuckled all from top to toes,
How swift the poem becometh prose!
And when I cast mine eyes and see
Those arctics flopping each way free,
Oh, how that flopping floppeth me!

Aprilly

Whan that Aprillè with hise shourès soote
The droghte of March had percèd to the roote,
I druv a motor thro' Aprillè's bliz
Somme forty mile, and dam neere lyke to friz.

EDGAR LEE MASTERS
1868–1950

Jonathan Swift Somers

After you have enriched your soul
To the highest point,
With books, thought, suffering, the understanding of many personalities,
The power to interpret glances, silences,
The pauses in momentous transformations,
The genius of divination and prophecy;
So that you feel able at times to hold the world
In the hollow of your hand;
Then, if, by the crowding of so many powers
Into the compass of your soul,
Your soul takes fire,
And in the conflagration of your soul
The evil of the world is lighted up and made clear —
Be thankful if in that hour of supreme vision
Life does not fiddle.

The Spooniad

(The late Mr. Jonathan Swift Somers, laureate of Spoon River, planned
The Spooniad as an epic in twenty-four books, but unfortunately did
not live to complete even the first book. The fragment was found
among his papers by William Marion Reedy and was for the first time
published in Reedy's Mirror of December 18th, 1914.)

Of John Cabanis' wrath and of the strife
Of hostile parties, and his dire defeat
Who led the common people in the cause
Of freedom for Spoon River, and the fall
Of Rhodes' bank that brought unnumbered woes
And loss to many, with engendered hate
That flamed into the torch in Anarch hands
To burn the court-house, on whose blackened wreck
A fairer temple rose and Progress stood —
Sing, muse, that lit the Chian's face with smiles
Who saw the ant-like Greeks and Trojans crawl
About Scamander, over walls, pursued
Or else pursuing, and the funeral pyres

And sacred hecatombs, and first because
Of Helen who with Paris fled to Troy
As soul-mate; and the wrath of Peleus' son,
Decreed, to lose Chryseis, lovely spoil
Of war, and dearest concubine.
                  Say first,
Thou son of night, called Momus, from whose eyes
No secret hides, and Thalia, smiling one,
What bred 'twixt Thomas Rhodes and John Cabanis
The deadly strife? His daughter Flossie, she,
Returning from her wandering with a troop
Of strolling players, walked the village streets,
Her bracelets tinkling and with sparkling rings
And words of serpent wisdom and a smile
Of cunning in her eyes. Then Thomas Rhodes,
Who ruled the church and ruled the bank as well,
Made known his disapproval of the maid;
And all Spoon River whispered and the eyes
Of all the church frowned on her, till she knew
They feared her and condemned.
                  But them to flout
She gave a dance to viols and to flutes,
Brought from Peoria, and many youths,
But lately made regenerate through the prayers
Of zealous preachers and of earnest souls,
Danced merrily, and sought her in the dance,
Who wore a dress so low of neck that eyes
Down straying might survey the snowy swale
Till it was lost in whiteness.
                  With the dance
The village changed to merriment from gloom.
The milliner, Mrs. Williams, could not fill
Her orders for new hats, and every seamstress
Plied busy needles making gowns; old trunks
And chests were opened for their store of laces
And rings and trinkets were brought out of hiding
And all the youths fastidious grew of dress;
Notes passed, and many a fair one's door at eve
Knew a bouquet, and strolling lovers thronged
About the hills that overlooked the river.
Then, since the mercy seats more empty showed,
One of God's chosen lifted up his voice:
"The woman of Babylon is among us; rise

Ye sons of light and drive the wanton forth!"
So John Cabanis left the church and left
The hosts of law and order with his eyes
By anger cleared, and him the liberal cause
Acclaimed as nominee to the mayoralty
To vanquish A. D. Blood.
              But as the war
Waged bitterly for votes and rumors flew
About the bank, and of the heavy loans
Which Rhodes' son had made to prop his loss
In wheat, and many drew their coin and left
The bank of Rhodes more hollow, with the talk
Among the liberals of another bank
Soon to be chartered, lo, the bubble burst
'Mid cries and curses; but the liberals laughed
And in the hall of Nicholas Bindle held
Wise converse and inspiriting debate.

High on a stage that overlooked the chairs
Where dozens sat, and where a pop-eyed daub
Of Shakespeare, very like the hired man
Of Christian Dallmann, brow and pointed beard,
Upon a drab proscenium outward stared,
Sat Harmon Whitney, to that eminence,
By merit raised in ribaldry and guile,
And to the assembled rebels thus he spake:
"Whether to lie supine and let a clique
Cold-blooded, scheming, hungry, singing psalms,
Devour our substance, wreck our banks and drain
Our little hoards for hazards on the price
Of wheat or pork, or yet to cower beneath
The shadow of a spire upreared to curb
A breed of lackeys and to serve the bank
Coadjutor in greed, that is the question.
Shall we have music and the jocund dance,
Or tolling bells? Or shall young romance roam
These hills about the river, flowering now
To April's tears, or shall they sit at home,
Or play croquet where Thomas Rhodes may see,
I ask you? If the blood of youth runs o'er
And riots 'gainst this regimen of gloom,
Shall we submit to have these youths and maids
Branded as libertines and wantons?"

Ere
His words were done a woman's voice called "No!"
Then rose a sound of moving chairs, as when
The numerous swine o'er-run the replenished troughs;
And every head was turned, as when a flock
Of geese back-turning to the hunter's tread
Rise up with flapping wings; then rang the hall
With riotous laughter, for with battered hat
Tilted upon her saucy head, and fist
Raised in defiance, Daisy Fraser stood.
Headlong she had been hurled from out the hall
Save Wendell Bloyd, who spoke for woman's rights,
Prevented, and the bellowing voice of Burchard.
Then 'mid applause she hastened toward the stage
And flung both gold and silver to the cause
And swiftly left the hall.
         Meantime upstood
A giant figure, bearded like the son
Of Alcmene, deep-chested, round of paunch,
And spoke in thunder: "Over there behold
A man who for the truth withstood his wife —
Such is our spirit — when that A. D. Blood
Compelled me to remove Dom Pedro — "
         Quick
Before Jim Brown could finish, Jefferson Howard
Obtained the floor and spake: "Ill suits the time
For clownish words, and trivial is our cause
If naught's at stake but John Cabanis' wrath,
He who was erstwhile of the other side
And came to us for vengeance. More's at stake
Than triumph for New England or Virginia.
And whether rum be sold, or for two years
As in the past two years, this town be dry
Matters but little — Oh yes, revenue
For sidewalks, sewers; that is well enough!
I wish to God this fight were now inspired
By other passion than to salve the pride
Of John Cabanis or his daughter. Why
Can never contests of great moment spring
From worthy things, not little? Still, if men
Must always act so, and if rum must be
The symbol and the medium to release
From life's denial and from slavery,

Then give me rum!"
     Exultant cries arose.
Then, as George Trimble had o'ercome his fear
And vacillation and begun to speak,
The door creaked and the idiot, Willie Metcalf,
Breathless and hatless, whiter than a sheet,
Entered and cried: "The marshal's on his way
To arrest you all. And if you only knew
Who's coming here to-morrow; I was listening
Beneath the window where the other side
Are making plans."
     So to a smaller room
To hear the idiot's secret some withdrew
Selected by the Chair; the Chair himself
And Jefferson Howard, Benjamin Pantier,
And Wendell Bloyd, George Trimble, Adam Weirauch,
Imanuel Ehrenhardt, Seth Compton, Godwin James
And Enoch Dunlap, Hiram Scates, Roy Butler,
Carl Hamblin, Roger Heston, Ernest Hyde
And Penniwit, the artist, Kinsey Keene,
And E. C. Culbertson and Franklin Jones,
Benjamin Fraser, son of Benjamin Pantier
By Daisy Fraser, some of lesser note,
And secretly conferred.
     But in the hall
Disorder reigned and when the marshal came
And found it so, he marched the hoodlums out
And locked them up.

     Meanwhile within a room
Back in the basement of the church, with Blood
Counseled the wisest heads. Judge Somers first,
Deep learned in life, and next him, Elliott Hawkins
And Lambert Hutchins; next him Thomas Rhodes
And Editor Whedon; next him Garrison Standard,
A traitor to the liberals, who with lip
Upcurled in scorn and with a bitter sneer:
"Such strife about an insult to a woman —
A girl of eighteen" — Christian Dallman too,
And others unrecorded. Some there were
Who frowned not on the cup but loathed the rule
Democracy achieved thereby, the freedom
And lust of life it symbolized.

Now morn with snowy fingers up the sky
Flung like an orange at a festival
The ruddy sun, when from their hasty beds
Poured forth the hostile forces, and the streets
Resounded to the rattle of the wheels,
That drove this way and that to gather in
The tardy voters, and the cries of chieftains
Who manned the battle. But at ten o'clock
The liberals bellowed fraud, and at the polls
The rival candidates growled and came to blows.
Then proved the idiot's tale of yester-eve
A word of warning. Suddenly on the streets
Walked hog-eyed Allen, terror of the hills
That looked on Bernadotte ten miles removed.
No man of this degenerate day could lift
The boulders which he threw, and when he spoke
The windows rattled, and beneath his brows,
Thatched like a shed with bristling hair of black,
His small eyes glistened like a maddened boar.
And as he walked the boards creaked, as he walked
A song of menace rumbled. Thus he came,
The champion of A. D. Blood, commissioned
To terrify the liberals. Many fled
As when a hawk soars o'er the chicken yard.
He passed the polls and with a playful hand
Touched Brown, the giant, and he fell against,
As though he were a child, the wall; so strong
Was hog-eyed Allen. But the liberals smiled.
For soon as hog-eyed Allen reached the walk,
Close on his steps paced Bengal Mike, brought in
By Kinsey Keene, the subtle-witted one,
To match the hog-eyed Allen. He was scarce
Three-fourths the other's bulk, but steel his arms,
And with a tiger's heart. Two men he killed
And many wounded in the days before,
And no one feared.
                But when the hog-eyed one
Saw Bengal Mike his countenance grew dark,
The bristles o'er his red eyes twitched with rage,
The song he rumbled lowered. Round and round
The court-house paced he, followed stealthily
By Bengal Mike, who jeered him every step:
"Come, elephant, and fight! Come, hog-eyed coward!

Come, face about and fight me, lumbering sneak!
Come, beefy bully, hit me, if you can!
Take out your gun, you duffer, give me reason
To draw and kill you. Take your billy out;
I'll crack your boar's head with a piece of brick!"
But never a word the hog-eyed one returned,
But trod about the court-house, followed both
By troops of boys and watched by all the men.
All day, they walked the square. But when Apollo
Stood with reluctant look above the hills
As fain to see the end, and all the votes
Were cast, and closed the polls, before the door
Of Trainor's drug store Bengal Mike, in tones
That echoed through the village, bawled the taunt:
"Who was your mother, hog-eyed?" In a trice,
As when a wild boar turns upon the hound
That through the brakes upon an August day
Has gashed him with its teeth, the hog-eyed one
Rushed with his giant arms on Bengal Mike
And grabbed him by the throat. Then rose to heaven
The frightened cries of boys, and yells of men
Forth rushing to the street. And Bengal Mike
Moved this way and now that, drew in his head
As if his neck to shorten, and bent down
To break the death grip of the hog-eyed one;
'Twixt guttural wrath and fast-expiring strength
Striking his fists against the invulnerable chest
Of hog-eyed Allen. Then, when some came in
To part them, others stayed them, and the fight
Spread among dozens; many valiant souls
Went down from clubs and bricks.

                           But tell me, Muse,
What god or goddess rescued Bengal Mike?
With one last, mighty struggle did he grasp
The murderous hands and turning kick his foe.
Then, as if struck by lightning, vanished all
The strength from hog-eyed Allen, at his side
Sank limp those giant arms and o'er his face
Dread pallor and the sweat of anguish spread.
And those great knees, invincible but late,
Shook to his weight. And quickly as the lion
Leaps on its wounded prey, did Bengal Mike

Smite with a rock the temple of his foe,
And down he sank and darkness o'er his eyes
Passed like a cloud.
                    As when the woodman fells
Some giant oak upon a summer's day
And all the songsters of the forest shrill,
And one great hawk that has his nestling young
Amid the topmost branches croaks, as crash
The leafy branches through the tangled boughs
Of brother oaks, so fell the hog-eyed one
Amid the lamentations of the friends
Of A. D. Blood.

                    Just then, four lusty men
Bore the town marshal, on whose iron face
The purple pall of death already lay,
To Trainor's drug store, shot by Jack McGuire.
And cries went up of "Lynch him!" and the sound
Of running feet from every side was heard
Bent on the

EDWIN ARLINGTON ROBINSON
1869–1935

Variations of Greek Themes

II

A Mighty Runner
(Nicarchus)

The day when Charmus ran with five
In Arcady, as I'm alive,
He came in seventh. — "Five and one
Make seven, you say? It can't be done." —
Well, if you think it needs a note,
A friend in a fur overcoat
Ran with him, crying all the while,
"You'll beat 'em, Charmus, by a mile!"
And so he came in seventh.
Therefore, good Zoilus, you see
The thing is plain as plain can be;
And with four more for company,
He would have been eleventh.

III

The Raven
(Nicarchus)

The gloom of death is on the raven's wing,
    The song of death is in the raven's cries:
But when Demophilus begins to sing,
    The raven dies.

IV

Eutychides
(Lucilius)

Eutychides, who wrote the songs,
Is going down where he belongs.
O you unhappy ones, beware:
Eutychides will soon be there!
For he is coming with twelve lyres,
And with more than twice twelve quires
Of the stuff that he has done
In the world from which he's gone.
Ah, now must you know death indeed,
For he is coming with all speed;
And with Eutychides in Hell,
Where's a poor tortured soul to dwell!

CAROLYN WELLS
1869–1942

Diversions of the Re-Echo Club

It is with pleasure that we announce our ability to offer to the public
the papers of the Re-Echo Club. This club, somewhat after the order of
the Echo Club, late of Boston, takes pleasure in trying to better what is
done. On the occasion of the meeting of which the following gems of
poesy are the result, the several members of the club engaged to write up
the well-known tradition of the Purple Cow in more elaborate form than
the quatrain made famous by Mr. Gelett Burgess:

"I never saw a Purple Cow,
    I never hope to see one;
But I can tell you, anyhow,
    I'd rather see than be one."

The first attempt here cited is the production of Mr. John Milton:

Hence, vain, deluding cows.
The herd of folly, without colour bright,
How little you delight,
Or fill the Poet's mind, or songs arouse!
But, hail! thou goddess gay of feature!
Hail, divinest purple creature!
Oh, Cow, thy visage is too bright
To hit the sense of human sight.
And though I'd like, just once, to see thee,
I never, never, never'd be thee!

MR. P. BYSSHE SHELLEY

Hail to thee, blithe spirit!
Cow thou never wert;
But in life to cheer it
Playest thy full part
In purple lines of unpremeditated art.

The pale purple colour
Melts around thy sight
Like a star, but duller,
In the broad daylight.
I'd see thee, but I would not be thee if I might.

We look before and after
At cattle as they browse;
Our most hearty laughter
Something sad must rouse.
Our sweetest songs are those that tell of Purple Cows.

MR. W. WORDSWORTH

She dwelt among the untrodden ways
Beside the springs of Dee;
A Cow whom there were few to praise
And very few to see.

A violet by a mossy stone
Greeting the smiling East
Is not so purple, I must own,
As that erratic beast.

She lived unknown, that Cow, and so
  I never chanced to see;
But if I had to be one, oh,
  The difference to me!

MR. T. GRAY

The curfew tolls the knell of parting day,
  The lowing herd winds slowly o'er the lea;
I watched them slowly wend their weary way,
  But, ah, a Purple Cow I did not see.
Full many a cow of purplest ray serene
  Is haply grazing where I may not see;
Full many a donkey writes of her, I ween,
  But neither of these creatures would I be.

MR. J. W. RILEY

There, little Cow, don't cry!
  You are brindle and brown, I know.
    And with wild, glad hues
    Of reds and blues,
  You never will gleam and glow.
But though not pleasing to the eye,
There, little Cow, don't cry, don't cry.

LORD A. TENNYSON

Ask me no more. A cow I fain would see
  Of purple tint, like a sun-soaked grape —
  Of purple tint, like royal velvet cape —
But such a creature I would never be —
  Ask me no more.

MR. R. BROWNING

All that I know
  Of a certain Cow
Is it can throw,
  Somewhere, somehow,
Now a dart of red,
  Now a dart of blue
(That makes purple, 'tis said).
  I would fain see, too.
    This Cow that darkles the red and the blue!

MR. J. KEATS

A cow of purple is a joy forever.
Its loveliness increases. I have never
Seen this phenomenon. Yet ever keep
A brave lookout; lest I should be asleep
When she comes by. For, though I would not be one,
I've oft imagined 'twould be joy to see one.

MR. D. G. ROSSETTI

The Purple Cow strayed in the glade;
　(Oh, my soul! but the milk is blue!)
She strayed and strayed and strayed and strayed
　(And I wail and I cry Wa-hoo!)

I've never seen her — nay, not I;
　(Oh, my soul! but the milk is blue!)
Yet were I that Cow I should want to die.
　(And I wail and I cry Wa-hoo!)
But in vain my tears I strew.

MR. T. ALDRICH

Somewhere in some faked nature place,
　In Wonderland, in Nonsense Land,
Two darkling shapes met face to face,
　And bade each other stand.

"And who are you!" said each to each;
　"Tell me your title, anyhow."
One said, "I am the Papal Bull,"
　"And I the Purple Cow."

MR. E. ALLAN POE

Open then I flung a shutter,
　And, with many a flirt and flutter,
In there stepped a Purple Cow which gayly tripped around my floor.
　Not the least obeisance made she,
　Not a moment stopped or stayed she,
But with mien of chorus lady perched herself above my door.
On a dusty bust of Dante perched and sat above my door.

And that Purple Cow unflitting
Still is sitting — still is sitting
On that dusty bust of Dante just above my chamber door,
And her horns have all the seeming
Of a demon's that is screaming,
And the arc-light o'er her streaming
Casts her shadow on the floor.
And my soul from out that pool of Purple shadow on the floor,
Shall be lifted Nevermore!

MR. H. LONGFELLOW

The day is done, and the darkness
Falls from the wing of night
As ballast is wafted downward
From an air-ship in its flight.

I dream of a purple creature
Which is not as kine are now;
And resembles cattle only
As Cowper resembles a cow.

Such cows have power to quiet
Our restless thoughts and rude;
They come like the Benedictine
That follows after food.

MR. A. SWINBURNE

Oh, Cow of rare rapturous vision,
Oh, purple, impalpable Cow,
Do you browse in a Dream Field Elysian,
Are you purpling pleasantly now?
By the side of wan waves do you languish?
Or in the lithe lush of the grove?
While vainly I search in my anguish,
O Bovine of mauve!

Despair in my bosom is sighing,
Hope's star has sunk sadly to rest;
Though cows of rare sorts I am buying,
Not one breathes a balm to my breast.

Oh, rapturous rose-crowned occasion,
 When I such a glory might see!
But a cow of a purple persuasion
 I never would be.

MR. A. DOBSON

I'd love to see
 A Purple Cow,
Oh, Goodness me!
I'd love to see
But not to be
 One. Anyhow,
I'd love to see
 A Purple Cow.

MR. O. HERFORD

Children, observe the Purple Cow,
You cannot see her, anyhow;
And, little ones, you need not hope
Your eyes will e'er attain such scope.
But if you ever have a choice
To be, or see, lift up your voice
And choose to see. For surely you
Don't want to browse around and moo.

MR. H. C. BUNNER

Oh, what's the way to Arcady,
 Where all the cows are purple?
Ah, woe is me! I never hope
On such a sight my eyes to ope;
But as I sing in merry glee
Along the road to Arcady,
Perchance full soon I may espy
A Purple Cow come dancing by.
 Heigho! I then shall see one.
Her horns bedecked with ribbons gay,
And garlanded with rosy may, —
 A tricksy sight. Still I must say
 I'd rather see than be one.

MR. A. SWINBURNE
(Who was so enthused that he made a second attempt.)

Only in dim, drowsy depths of a dream do I dare to delight in deliciously
dreaming
Cows there may be of a passionate purple, — cows of a violent violet
hue;

Ne'er have I seen such a sight, I am certain it is but a demi-delirious
dreaming —
Ne'er may I happily harbour a hesitant hope in my heart that my dream
may come true.

Sad is my soul, and my senses are sobbing so strong is my strenuous
spirit to see one.
Dolefully, drearily doomed to despair as warily wearily watching I wait;

Thoughts thickly thronging are thrilling and throbbing; to *see* is a glorious gain — but to *be* one!
That were a darker and direfuller destiny, that were a fearfuller, fright-
fuller fate!

MR. R. KIPLING

In the old ten-acre pasture,
    Lookin' eastward toward a tree,
There's a Purple Cow a-settin'
    And I know she thinks of me.
For the wind is in the gum-tree,
    And the hay is in the mow,
And the cow-bells are a-calling
    "Come and see a Purple Cow!"

But I am not going now,
    Not at present, anyhow,
For I am not fond of purple, and
    I can't abide a cow;
No, I shall not go to-day,
    Where the Purple Cattle play.
But I think I'd rather see one
    Than to be one, anyhow.

JOHN F. PALMER

born *c.* 1870

The Band Played On

Matt Casey formed a social club that beat the town for style,
And hired for a meeting place a hall.
When pay day came around each week they greased the floor with wax,
And danced with noise and vigor at the ball.
Each Saturday you'd see them dressed up in Sunday clothes,
Each lad would have his sweetheart by his side.
When Casey led the first grand march they all would fall in line,
Behind the man who was their joy and pride, For

> *Casey would waltz with a strawberry blonde,*
> *And the band played on,*
> *He'd glide 'cross the floor with the girl he adored,*
> *And the band played on,*
> *But his brain was so loaded, it nearly exploded,*
> *The poor girl would shake with alarm.*
> *He'd ne'er leave the girl with the strawberry curls,*
> *And the band played on.*

Such kissing in the corner and such whisp'ring in the hall,
And telling tales of love behind the stairs.
As Casey was the favorite and he that ran the ball,
Of kissing and lovemaking did his share.
At twelve o'clock exactly they all would fall in line,
Then march down to the dining hall and eat.
But Casey would not join them although ev'rything was fine,
But he stayed upstairs and exercised his feet, For [*Repeat refrain*]

Now when the dance was over and the band played "Home Sweet
Home,"
They played a tune at Casey's own request.
He thank'd them very kindly for the favors they had shown,
Then he'd waltz once with the girl that he loved best.
Most all the friends are married that Casey used to know,
And Casey too has taken him a wife.
The blonde he used to waltz and glide with on the ballroom floor,
Is happy missis Casey now for life, For [*Repeat refrain*]

268

STEPHEN CRANE
1871–1900

A man said to the universe

A man said to the universe:
"Sir, I exist!"
"However," replied the universe,
"The fact has not created in me
A sense of obligation."

Tell me not in joyous numbers

Tell me not in joyous numbers
We can make our lives sublime
By — well, at least, not by
Dabbling much in rhyme.

ANONYMOUS

The Big Rock Candy Mountains

One evening as the sun went down
And the jungle fire was burning,
Down the track came a hobo hiking.
And he said, "Boys I'm not turning,
I'm headed for a land that's far away,
Beside the crystal fountains,
So come with me, we'll go and see
The Big Rock Candy Mountains."

In the Big Rock Candy Mountains,
There's land that's fair and bright,
Where the handouts grow on bushes,
And you sleep out every night.
Where the boxcars all are empty,
And the sun shines every day
On the birds and the bees,
And the cigarette trees,
And the lemonade springs
Where the bluebird sings
In the Big Rock Candy Mountains.

In the Big Rock Candy Mountains
All the cops have wooden legs,
And the bulldogs all have rubber teeth,
And the hens lay softboiled eggs.
There the farmer's trees are full of fruit,
And the barns are full of hay,
And I'm bound to go
Where there ain't no snow,
And the rain don't fall,
And the wind don't blow
In the Big Rock Candy Mountains.

In the Big Rock Candy Mountains
You never change your socks,
And the little streams of alcohol
Come a-trickling down the rocks.
There ain't no shorthandled shovels,
No axes, spades, or picks,
And I'm bound to stay
Where they sleep all day,
Where they hung the Turk
That invented work
In the Big Rock Candy Mountains.

In the Big Rock Candy Mountains
All the jails are made of tin,
And you can walk right out again
As soon as you are in.
Where the brakemen have to tip their hats,
And the railroad bulls are blind,
There's a lake of stew,
And a gin lake, too,
You can paddle all around 'em
In a big canoe
In the Big Rock Candy Mountains.

The Four Nights' Drunk

The first night when I come home, drunk as I could be,
I found this horse in the stable, where my horse ought to be.
  "Come here, little wifey! Explain yourself to me:
  Why is there a horse in the stable, where my horse ought to be?"

"Why, you durn fool, you blame fool, can't you plainly see?
    It's only a milk cow my momma give to me."
Now, I been living in this here world forty years and more,
And I never seen a milk cow with a saddle on before.

The second night when I come home, drunk as I could be,
I found a coat in the closet, where my coat ought to be.
    "Come here, little wifey! Explain yourself to me:
    Why is there a coat in the closet, where my coat ought to be?"
        "Why, you durn fool, you blame fool, can't you plainly see?
        It's only a coverlet my momma give to me."
Now, I been living in this here world forty years and more,
And I never seen a coverlet with buttons on before.

The third night when I come home, drunk as I could be,
I found a hat hanging on the rack, where my hat ought to be.
    "Come here, little wifey! Explain yourself to me:
    Why is there a hat hanging on the rack, where my hat ought to be?"
        "Why, you durn fool, you blame fool, can't you plainly see?
        It's only a chamberpot my momma give to me."
Now, I been living in this here world forty years and more,
And I never seen a J. B. Stetson chamberpot before.

The fourth night when I come home, drunk as I could be,
I found a head lying on the bed, where my head ought to be.
    "Come here, little wifey! Explain yourself to me:
    Why is there a head lying on the bed, where my head ought to be?"
        "Why, you durn fool, you blame fool, can't you plainly see?
        It's only a cabbage head my momma give to me."
Now, I been living in this here world forty years and more,
And I never seen a cabbage head with a mustache on before.

The Frozen Logger

As I sat down one evening
In a small café,
A forty-year-old waitress
These words to a man did say:

"I see you are a logger
And not just a common bum,
Because nobody but a logger
Stirs his coffee with his thumb.

"My lover was a logger;
There's none like him today.
If you poured whiskey on it,
He would eat a bale of hay.

"He never shaved the whiskers
From off of his horny hide;
He drove them in with a hammer
And bit them off inside.

"My lover he came to see me,
'Twas on one freezing day;
He held me in a fond embrace
That broke three vertebrae.

"He kissed me when we parted
So hard that it broke my jaw;
I could not speak to tell him
He forgot his mackinaw.

"I saw my lover leaving,
Sauntering through the snow,
Going bravely homeward
At forty-eight below.

"The weather it tried to freeze him,
It tried its level best.
At a hundred degrees below zero
He buttoned up his vest.

"It froze clear through to China,
It froze to the stars above.
At a thousand degrees below zero
It froze my logger love.

"And so my lover perished.
To this café I've come,
And here I wait till someone
Stirs his coffee with his thumb."

T. A. DALY
1871–1948

Pennsylvania Places

No other State can match this (California)
for place-names rich in rhyme and rhythm.
Los Angeles Times.

Out upon you, California!
Tuneful titles do adorn ya —
More than does your megalomania —
    But, before you make your boast,
    Upstart of our Western Coast!
Lend an ear to Pennsylvania:

Philadelphia — most colonial
    Of our true Colonial Dames —
Curtsying, leads the ceremonial
    March of quaint and State-ly names:
Bethlehem, Emmaus, Kingsessing,
Lititz, Darby, Conoquenessing,
Conshohocken, Tulpehocken,
King of Prussia, Shackamaxon,
Aliquippa, Lackawaxen,
    Conestoga, Quakake, Trappe,
Punxsutawney, Hokendauqua,
Catawissa, Catasauqua,
    Lundy's Lane, Paoli, Gap.

Now, then, take another breath;
Start again with Nazareth,
Nesquehoning and Chicora,
Tomb, Two Taverns, Tuscarora,
Gipsy, Bird in Hand, Lyndora,
    Add Mauch Chunk and Equinunk:
    And the urban Manayunk;
Hickory Corners, Hickory Hill,
Juniata, Phoenixville,
Gwynedd Valley, Hazlebrook,
Maxatawney, Ontelaunee,
Sabbath Rest, Glenolden, Nook,
Gold, Lycoming,
Wissinoming,

Mustard, Muse, Morganza, Muff —
Oh, but surely that's enough!

Here are place-names "rich in rhythm" —
   And they're not so poor in rhyme;
Haven't I convinced you with 'm?
   No? I could if I had time.

ARTHUR GUITERMAN
1871–1943

Song of Hate for Eels

Oh, the slimy, squirmy, slithery eel!
He swallows your hook with malignant zeal,
He tangles your line and he gums your reel,
The slimy, squirmy, slithery eel.

Oh, the slimy, squirmy, slithery eel!
He cannot be held in a grip of steel,
And when he is dead he is hard to peel,
The slimy, squirmy, slithery eel.

Oh, the slimy, squirmy, slithery eel!
The sorriest catch in the angler's creel;
Who said he was fit for a Christian meal —
The slimy, squirmy, slithery eel!

Oh, the slimy, squirmy, slithery eel!
Malevolent serpent! who dares reveal
What eloquent fishermen say and feel
Concerning the slithery, slimy eel?

Heredity

The primitive Pithecanthropus erectus
With whom the ethnologists rightly connect us
   Defended his own
   By cudgel and stone;
Why isn't our ancestor here to protect us?

274

The arrogant Pithecanthropus erectus
Whose traits, through inheritance, deeply affect us,
    Was sure it was good
    To grab all he could,
Like some of his offspring whose morals deject us.

The ape man, the Pithecanthropus erectus,
Has many descendants prepared to dissect us;
    With them might is right,
    And if we can't fight
There's nothing at all that will make them respect us.

Brief Essay on Man

Aspiring Man, by learned pens
Once classed as Homo sapiens,
Is now, the poor, deluded chap,
Correctly labeled, Homo sap.

Everything in Its Place

The skeleton is hiding in the closet as it should,
The needle's in the haystack and the trees are in the wood,
The fly is in the ointment and the froth is on the beer,
The bee is in the bonnet and the flea is in the ear.

The meat is in the coconut, the cat is in the bag,
The dog is in the manger and the goat is on the crag,
The worm is in the apple and the clam is on the shore,
The birds are in the bushes and the wolf is at the door.

BEN HARNEY
1872–1938

You've Been a Good Old Wagon,
But You've Done Broke Down

I was standing in a crap game doing no harm, Baby!
When a Copper grabb'd me by my arm, Honey!
Took me down to the jail house door,
Place I never had been before,
I was run in.

No more will I buy my sweet thing pork chops!
And hear her lily lips go flip-flap!
The reason I'm in truble about my sweet thing
Is because this song to me she did sing.
Good bye, my Honey, if you call it gone, Darling!
Good bye, my Honey, if you call it gone, Darling!
Good bye, my Honey, if you call it gone,
You've been a good wagon, but you done broke down, Bye
Bye.

The Judge asked me what had I done, Baby!
Said standing in a crap game getting my gun, Hot Stuff!
The Judge and Jury said to me
You have kill'd three Niggers in the first degree,
No bail.

Mister Johnson

T'other eb'ning eb'ryting was still, Oh! babe,
De moon was climbin' down behind de hill, Oh! babe,
T'ought eb'ry body was a sound asleep,
But old man a Johnson was a on his beat, Oh! babe.

I went down into a Nigger crap game,
When de coons were a gambling wid a might and main,
T'ought I'd a be a sport and be dead still,
I gambled my money and I wasn't to blame.

One Nigger's point was a little, a Joe,
Bettin' six bits t'a quarter he could make de four,
He made dat point but he made no more,
Just den Johnson jump'd through de door, Oh!

> *Mister Johnson turn me loose,*
> *Got no money but a good excuse,*
> *Oh! Mister Johnson, I'll be good.*
> *Oh! Mister Johnson turn me loose,*
> *Don't take me to de calaboose,*
> *Oh! Mister Johnson, I'll be good.*

T'other eb'ning when the sun was down, Oh! babe,
I went down old man Johnson's chicken farm, Oh! babe,
Climb'd in de chicken loft on my knees,
Was a half way through when de chicken sneezed, Oh! babe.

I'll tell you, if you will only keep still,
'Bout mile and a half from Louisville,
I am so nerbous dat I can't keep still,
When I think about it I can feel a big chill.

A big black coon was a lookin' for chickens,
When a great big bulldog got to raisin' the dickens,
De coon clomb higher, de chicken got nigher,
Just den Johnson opened up fire.

> *I got no chance for to be turned loose,*
> *Got no chance for a good excuse,*
> *Oh! Mister Johnson, I'll be good.*
> *And now he's playin' seben eleben,*
> *Way up yonder in de Nigger heabn,*
> *Oh! Mister Johnson made him good.*

GUY WETMORE CARRYL
1873–1904

How a Girl Was Too Reckless of Grammar

Matilda Maud Mackenzie frankly hadn't any chin,
Her hands were rough, her feet she turned invariably in;
    Her general form was German,
        By which I mean that you
    Her waist could not determine
        Within a foot or two.
And not only did she stammer,
But she used the kind of grammar
    That is called, for sake of euphony, askew.

From what I say about her, don't imagine I desire
A prejudice against this worthy creature to inspire.
    She was willing, she was active,
        She was sober, she was kind,
    But she *never* looked attractive
        And she *hadn't* any mind.
I knew her more than slightly,
And I treated her politely
    When I met her, but of course I wasn't blind!

Matilda Maud Mackenzie had a habit that was droll,
She spent her morning seated on a rock or on a knoll,
 And threw with much composure
  A smallish rubber ball
 At an inoffensive osier
  By a little waterfall;
But Matilda's way of throwing
Was like other people's mowing,
 And she never hit the willow-tree at all!

One day as Miss Mackenzie with uncommon ardour tried
To hit the mark, the missile flew exceptionally wide,
 And, before her eyes astounded,
  On a fallen maple's trunk
 Ricochetted and rebounded
  In the rivulet, and sunk!
Matilda, greatly frightened,
In her grammar unenlightened,
 Remarked, "Well now I ast yer, who'd 'er thunk?"

But what a marvel followed! From the pool at once there rose
A frog, the sphere of rubber balanced deftly on his nose.
 He beheld her fright and frenzy
  And, her panic to dispel,
 On his knee by Miss Mackenzie
  He obsequiously fell.
With quite as much decorum
As a speaker in a forum
 He started in his history to tell.

"Fair maid," he said, "I beg you do not hesitate or wince,
If you'll promise that you'll wed me, I'll at once become a prince;
 For a fairy, old and vicious,
  An enchantment round me spun!"
 Then he looked up, unsuspicious,
  And he saw what he had won,
And in terms of sad reproach, he
Made some comments, *sotto voce*,
 (Which the publishers have bidden me to shun!)

Matilda Maud Mackenzie said, as if she meant to scold;
"I *never!* Why, you forward thing! Now, ain't you awful bold!"

Just a glance he paused to give her,
    And his head was seen to clutch,
Then he darted to the river,
    And he dived to beat the Dutch!
While the wrathful maiden panted
"I don't think he was enchanted!"
    (And he really didn't look it overmuch!)

THE MORAL

In one's language one conservative should be;
Speech is silver and it never should be free!

The Domineering Eagle and the Inventive Bratling

O'er a small suburban borough
    Once an eagle used to fly,
Making observations thorough
    From his station in the sky,
And presenting the appearance
    Of an animated V,
Like the gulls that lend coherence
    Unto paintings of the sea.

Looking downward at a church in
    This attractive little shire,
He beheld a smallish urchin
    Shooting arrows at the spire;
In a spirit of derision,
    "Look alive!" the eagle said;
And, with infinite precision,
    Dropped a feather on his head.

Then the boy, annoyed distinctly
    By the freedom of the bird,
Voiced his anger quite succinctly
    In a single scathing word;
And he sat him on a barrow,
    And he fashioned of this same
Eagle's feather such an arrow
    As was worthy of the name.

Then he tried his bow, and, stringing
   It with caution and with care,
Sent that arrow singing, winging
   Towards the eagle in the air.
Straight it went, without an error,
   And the target, bathed in blood,
Lurched, and lunged, and fell to *terra*
   Firma, landing with a thud.

"Bird of freedom," quoth the urchin,
   With an unrelenting frown,
"You shall decorate a perch in
   The menagerie in town;
But of feathers quite a cluster
   I shall first remove for Ma;
Thanks to you, she'll have a duster
   For her precious *objets d'art*."

And THE MORAL is that pride is
   The precursor of a fall.
Those beneath you to deride is
   Not expedient at all.
Howsoever meek and humble
   Your inferiors may be,
They perchance may make you tumble,
   So respect them. Q.E.D.

ROBERT FROST
1874–1963

Departmental

An ant on the tablecloth
Ran into a dormant moth
Of many times his size.
He showed not the least surprise.

His business wasn't with such.
He gave it scarcely a touch,
And was off on his duty run.
Yet if he encountered one
Of the hive's enquiry squad
Whose work is to find out God
And the nature of time and space,
He would put him onto the case.
Ants are a curious race;
One crossing with hurried tread
The body of one of their dead
Isn't given a moment's arrest —
Seems not even impressed.
But he no doubt reports to any
With whom he crosses antennae,
And they no doubt report
To the higher-up at court.
Then word goes forth in Formic:
"Death's come to Jerry McCormic,
Our selfless forager Jerry.
Will the special Janizary
Whose office it is to bury
The dead of the commissary
Go bring him home to his people.
Lay him in state on a sepal.
Wrap him for shroud in a petal.
Embalm him with ichor of nettle.
This is the word of your Queen."
And presently on the scene
Appears a solemn mortician;
And taking formal position,
With feelers calmly atwiddle,
Seizes the dead by the middle,
And heaving him high in air,
Carries him out of there.
No one stands round to stare.
It is nobody else's affair.

It couldn't be called ungentle.
But how thoroughly departmental.

The Hardship of Accounting

Never ask of money spent
Where the spender thinks it went.
Nobody was ever meant
To remember or invent
What he did with every cent.

A Considerable Speck

(Microscopic)

A speck that would have been beneath my sight
On any but a paper sheet so white
Set off across what I had written there.
And I had idly poised my pen in air
To stop it with a period of ink,
When something strange about it made me think.
This was no dust speck by my breathing blown,
But unmistakably a living mite
With inclinations it could call its own.
It paused as with suspicion of my pen,
And then came racing wildly on again
To where my manuscript was not yet dry;
Then paused again and either drank or smelt —
With loathing, for again it turned to fly.
Plainly with an intelligence I dealt.
It seemed too tiny to have room for feet,
Yet must have had a set of them complete
To express how much it didn't want to die.
It ran with terror and with cunning crept.
It faltered: I could see it hesitate;
Then in the middle of the open sheet
Cower down in desperation to accept
Whatever I accorded it of fate.
I have none of the tenderer-than-thou
Collectivistic regimenting love
With which the modern world is being swept.
But this poor microscopic item now!
Since it was nothing I knew evil of
I let it lie there till I hope it slept.

I have a mind myself and recognize
Mind when I meet with it in any guise.
No one can know how glad I am to find
On any sheet the least display of mind.

For Travelers Going Sidereal

For travelers going sidereal
The danger they say is bacterial.
I don't know the pattern
On Mars or on Saturn
But on Venus it must be venereal.

Pride of Ancestry

The Deacon's wife was a bit desirish
And liked her sex relations wild,
So she lay with one of the shanty Irish
And he begot the Deacon's child.

The Deacon himself was a man of money
And upright life and a bosom shirt;
Which made her infidelity funny
And gave her pleasure in doing him dirt.

And yet for all her romantic sneakin'
Out the back door and over the wall
How was she sure the child of the Deacon
Wasn't the Deacon's after all?

Don't question a story of high eugenics.
She lived with the Deacon and bedded with him,
But she restricted his calesthenics
To the sterile arc of her lunar rhythm.

And she only had to reverse the trick
And let the Irishman turn her turtle
When by his faith as a Catholic
A woman was almost sure to be fertile.

Her portrait hangs in the family gallery
And a family of nobodies likes to think
That their descent from such a calorie
Accounts for their genius and love of drink.

The Rose Family

The rose is a rose,
And was always a rose.
But the theory now goes
That the apple's a rose,
And the pear is, and so's
The plum, I suppose.
The dear only knows
What will next prove a rose.
You, of course, are a rose —
But were always a rose.

RUSSELL HILLARD LOINES
1874–1922

On a Magazine Sonnet

"Scorn not the sonnet," though its strength be sapped,
    Nor say malignant its inventor blundered;
The corpse that here in fourteen lines is wrapped
    Had otherwise been covered with a hundred.

AMY LOWELL
1874–1925

The Painted Ceiling

My Grandpapa lives in a wonderful house
    With a great many windows and doors,
There are stairs that go up, and stairs that go down,
    And such beautiful, slippery floors.

But of all of the rooms, even mother's and mine,
   And the bookroom, and parlour and all,
I like the green dining-room so much the best
   Because of its ceiling and wall.

Right over your head is a funny round hole
   With apples and pears falling through;
There's a big bunch of grapes all purply and sweet,
   And melons and pineapples too.

They tumble and tumble, but never come down
   Though I've stood underneath a long while
With my mouth open wide, for I always have hoped
   Just a cherry would drop from the pile.

No matter how early I run there to look
   It has always begun to fall through;
And one night when at bedtime I crept in to see,
   It was falling by candle-light too.

I am sure they are magical fruits, and each one
   Makes you hear things, or see things, or go
Forever invisible; but it's no use,
   And of course I shall just never know.

For the ladder's too heavy to lift, and the chairs
   Are not nearly so tall as I need.
I've given up hope, and I feel I shall die
   Without having accomplished the deed.

It's a little bit sad, when you seem very near
   To adventures and things of that sort,
Which nearly begin, and then don't; and you know
   It is only because you are short.

Epitaph on a Young Poet Who Died Before Having Achieved Success

Beneath this sod lie the remains
Of one who died of growing pains.

GERTRUDE STEIN
1874–1946

Sacred Emily

Compose compose beds.
Wives of great men rest tranquil.
Come go stay philip philip.
Egg be takers.
Parts of place nuts.
Suppose twenty for cent.
It is rose in hen.
Come one day.
A firm terrible a firm terrible hindering, a firm hindering have a ray nor
    pin nor.
Egg in places.
Egg in few insists.
In set a place.
I am not missing.
Who is a permit.
I love honor and obey I do love honor and obey I do.
Melancholy do lip sing.
How old is he.
Murmur pet murmur pet murmur.
Push sea push sea push sea push sea push sea push sea push sea push sea.
Sweet and good and kind to all.
Wearing head.
Cousin tip nicely.
Cousin tip.
Nicely.
Wearing head.
Leave us sit.
I do believe it will finish, I do believe it will finish.
Pat ten patent, Pat ten patent.
Eleven and eighteen.
Foolish is foolish is.
Birds measure birds measure stores birds measure stores measure birds
    measure.
Exceptional firm bites.
How do you do I forgive you everything and there is nothing to forgive.
Never the less.
Leave it to me.
Weeds without papers.

Weeds without papers are necessary.
Left again left again.
Exceptional considerations.
Never the less tenderness.
Resting cow curtain.
Resting bull pin.
Resting cow curtain.
Resting bull pin.
Next to a frame.
The only hat hair.
Leave us mass leave us. Leave us pass. Leave us. Leave us pass leave us.
Humming is.
No climate.
What is a size.
Ease all I can do.
Colored frame.
Couple of canning.
Ease all I can do.
Humming does as.
Humming does as humming is.
What is a size.
No climate.
Ease all I can do.
Shall give it, please to give it.
Like to give it, please to give it.
What a surprise.
Not sooner whether.
Cordially yours.
Pause.
Cordially yours.
Not sooner together.
Cordially yours.
In strewing, in strewing.
That is the way we are one and indivisible.
Pay nuts renounce.
Now without turning around.
I will give them to you tonight.
Cunning is and does cunning is and does the most beautiful notes.
I would like a thousand most most.
Center pricking petunia.
Electrics are tight electrics are white electrics are a button.
Singular pressing.
Recent thimble.

Noisy pearls noisy pearl coat.
Arrange.
Arrange wide opposite.
Opposite it.
Lily ice-cream.
Nevertheless.
A hand is Willie.
Henry Henry Henry.
A hand is Henry.
Henry Henry Henry.
A hand is Willie.
Henry Henry Henry.
All the time.
A wading chest.
Do you mind.
Lizzie do you mind.
Ethel.
Ethel.
Ethel.
Next to barber.
Next to barber bury.
Next to barber bury china.
Next to barber bury china glass.
Next to barber china and glass.
Next to barber and china.
Next to barber and hurry.
Next to hurry.
Next to hurry and glass and china.
Next to hurry and glass and hurry.
Next to hurry and hurry.
Next to hurry and hurry.
Plain cases for see.
Tickle tickle tickle you for education.
A very reasonable berry.
Suppose a selection were reverse.
Cousin to sadden.
A coral neck and a little song so very extra so very Susie.
Cow come out cow come out and out and smell a little.
Draw prettily.
Next to a bloom.
Neat stretch.
Place plenty.
Cauliflower.

Cauliflower.
Curtain cousin.
Apron.
Neither best set.
Do I make faces like that at you.
Pinkie.
Not writing not writing another.
Another one.
Think.
Jack Rose Jack Rose.
Yard.
Practically all of them.
Does believe it.
Measure a measure a measure or.
Which is pretty which is pretty which is pretty.
To be top.
Neglect Waldberg.
Sudden say separate.
So great so great Emily.
Sew grate sew grate Emily.
Not a spell nicely.
Ring.
Weigh pieces of pound.
Aged steps.
Stops.
Not a plan bow.
Why is lacings.
Little slam up.
Cold seam peaches.
Begging to state begging to state begging to state alright.
Begging to state begging to state begging to state alright.
Wheels stows wheels stows.
Wickedness.
Cotton could mere less.
Nevertheless.
Anne.
Analysis.
From the standpoint of all white a week is none too much.
Pink coral white coral, coral coral.
Happy happy happy.
All the, chose.
Is a necessity.
Necessity.

Happy happy happy all the.
Happy happy happy all the.
Necessity.
Remain seated.
Come on come on come on on.
All the close.
Remain seated.
Happy.
All the.
Necessity.
Remain seated.
All the, close.
Websters and mines, websters and mines.
Websters and mines.
Trimming.
Gold space gold space of toes.
Twos, twos.
Pinned to the letter.
In accompany.
In a company in.
Received.
Must.
Natural lace.
Spend up.
Spend up length.
Spend up length.
Length thoroughly.
Neatness.
Neatness Neatness.
Excellent cording.
Excellent cording short close.
Close to.
When.
Pin black.
Cough or up.
Shouting.
Shouting.
Neater pin.
Pinned to the letter.
Was it a space was it a space was it a space to see.
Neither things.
Persons.

Transition.
Say say say.
North of the calender.
Window.
Peoples rest.
Preserve pulls.
Cunning piler.
Next to a chance.
Apples.
Apples.
Apples went.
It was a chance to preach Saturday.
Please come to Susan.
Purpose purpose black.
Extra plain silver.
Furious slippers.
Have a reason.
Have a reason candy.
Points of places.
Neat Nezars.
Which is a cream, can cream.
Ink of paper slightly mine breathes a shoulder able shine.
Necessity.
Near glass.
Put a stove put a stove hoarser.
If I was surely if I was surely.
See girl says.
All the same bright.
Brightness.
When a churn say suddenly when a churn say suddenly.
Poor pour percent.
Little branches.
Pale.
Pale.
Pale.
Pale.
Pale.
Pale.
Pale.
Near sights.
Please sorts.
Example.

Example.
Put something down.
Put something down some day.
Put something down some day in.
Put something down some day in my.
In my hand.
In my hand right.
In my hand writing.
Put something down some day in my hand writing.
Needles less.
Never the less.
Never the less.
Pepperness.
Never the less extra stress.
Never the less.
Tenderness.
Old sight.
Pearls.
Real line.
Shoulders.
Upper states.
Mere colors.
Recent resign.
Search needles.
All a plain all a plain show.
White papers.
Slippers.
Slippers underneath.
Little tell.
I chance.
I chance to.
I chance to to.
I chance to.
What is a winter wedding a winter wedding.
Furnish seats.
Furnish seats nicely.
Please repeat.
Please repeat for.
Please repeat.
This is a name to Anna.
Cushions and pears.
Reason purses.

Reason purses to relay to relay carpets.
Marble is thorough fare.
Nuts are spittoons.
That is a word.
That is a word careless.
Paper peaches.
Paper peaches are tears.
Rest in grapes.
Thoroughly needed.
Thoroughly needed signs.
All but.
Relieving relieving.
Argonauts.
That is plenty.
Cunning saxon symbol.
Symbol of beauty.
Thimble of everything.
Cunning clover thimble.
Cunning of everything.
Cunning of thimble.
Cunning cunning.
Place in pets.
Night town.
Night town a glass.
Color mahogany.
Color mahogany center.
Rose is a rose is a rose is a rose.
Loveliness extreme.
Extra gaiters.
Loveliness extreme.
Sweetest ice-cream.
Page ages page ages page ages.
Wiped Wiped wire wire.
Sweeter than peaches and pears and cream.
Wiped wire wiped wire.
Extra extreme.
Put measure treasure.
Measure treasure.
Tables track.
Nursed.
Dough.
That will do.

Cup or cup or.
Excessively illegitimate.
Pussy pussy pussy what what.
Current secret sneezers.
Ever.
Mercy for a dog.
Medal make medal.
Able able able.
A go to green and a letter spoke a go to green or praise or.
Worships worships worships.
Door.
Do or.
Table linen.
Wet spoil.
Wet spoil gaiters and knees and little spools little spools or ready silk
    lining.
Suppose misses misses.
Curls to butter.
Curls.
Curls.
Settle stretches.
See at till.
Louise.
Sunny.
Sail or.
Sail or rustle.
Mourn in morning.
The way to say.
Patter.
Deal own a.
Robber.
A high b and a perfect sight.
Little things singer.
Jane.
Aiming.
Not in description.
Day way.
A blow is delighted.

ANDREW B. STERLING
1874-1955

Under the Anheuser Bush

Talk about the shade of the sheltering palms,
Praise the bamboo tree and its wide spreading charms,
There's a little bush that grows right here in town,
You know its name, it has won such renown;
Often with my sweetheart just after the play,
To this little place then my footsteps will stray,
If she hesitates when she looks at the sign,
Softly I whisper, "Now Sue don't decline."

> Come, Come, Come and make eyes with me,
> Under the Anheuser Bush.
> Come, Come, drink some "Budwise" with me
> Under the Anheuser Bush,
> Hear the old German band,
> Just let me hold your hand, Yah!
> Do, Do, Come and have a stein or two,
> Under the Anheuser Bush.

Rave about the place where your swells go to dine,
Picture Sue and me with our sandwich and stein,
Underneath the bush where the good fellows meet,
Life seems worth living, our joy is complete;
If you're sad at heart, take a trip there tonight,
You'll forget your woe and your eyes will grow bright,
There you'll surely find me with my sweetheart Sue,
Come down this ev'ning, I'll introduce you.

What You Goin' To Do
When the Rent Comes 'Round?

Who dat a-knockin' at the door below,
Who dat a-shiv'rin' in the hail and snow?
I can hear you grumblin', Mister Rufus Brown,
Just keep on a-knockin' babe, I won't come down,
I wants to tell you that you can't get in,
Have you been a-gamblin' Honey, did you win?
What's that you tell me, coon, you lost your breath?
I hope you freezes to death.

Rufus Rastus Johnson Brown,
What you goin' to do when the rent comes 'round,
What you goin' to say, how you goin' to pay?
You'll never have a bit of sense till Judgement day.
You know, I know, rent means dough,
Landlord's goin' to put us out in the snow,
Rufus Rastus Johnson Brown,
What you goin' to do when the rent comes 'round?

Keep on a-bangin' on the old front door,
In just a minute babe you'll hear me snore,
If I goes to bed without a bite or sup,
You will be an icicle when I wakes up,
Where's all the money that you said you'd bring,
Melted all away just like the snow last Spring,
Rufus! I loves you, but this serves you right,
Guess that's sifficient, "Good-night."

Meet Me in St. Louis, Louis

1

When Louis came home to the flat,
    he hung up his coat and his hat,
He gazed all around, but no wifey he found,
    so he said, "Where can Flossie be at?"
A note on the table he spied,
    he read it just once, then he cried.
It ran, "Louis dear, it's too slow for me here,
    so I think I will go for a ride.

> *"Meet me in St. Louis, Louis,*
>   *meet me at the fair,*
> *Don't tell me the lights are shining*
>   *any place but there;*
> *We will dance the Hoochee Koochee,*
>   *I will be your tootsie wootsie;*
> *If you will meet me in St. Louis, Louis,*
>   *meet me at the fair."*

2

The dresses that hung in the hall
    were gone, she had taken them all;

She took all his rings and the rest of his things;
    the picture he missed from the wall.
"What! moving!" the janitor said,
    "your rent is paid three months ahead."
"What good is the flat?" said poor Louis, "read that."
    And the janitor smiled as he read:

> *"Meet me in St. Louis, Louis,*
>   *meet me at the fair,*
> *Don't tell me the lights are shining*
>   *any place but there;*
> *We will dance the Hoochee Koochee,*
>   *I will be your tootsie wootsie;*
> *If you will meet me in St. Louis, Louis,*
>   *meet me at the fair."*

3

Lew Woods was the name of a horse,
    that ran at the New Orleans course,
I played him one day for a dollar each way,
    and I charged it to profit and loss;
He started to run in the wet,
    the son of a gun's running yet,
That crazy old skate, he made straight for the gate,
    and I hollered, "Hey Lew! don't forget."

> *Meet me in St. Louis, Louis,*
>   *meet me at the fair,*
> *Take my tip and don't stop running*
>   *until you are there;*
> *You're a wonder that's no liesky,*
>   *if you don't fall down and diesky,*
> *Meet me in St. Louis, Louis,*
>   *meet me at the fair.*

4

There came to the gay tenderloin,
    a Jay who had money to burn,
The poor simple soul, showed a girlie his roll,
    and she said, "for some wine dear, I yearn."
A bottle and bird right away,
    she touched him then said, "I can't stay."
He sighed, "Tell me, sweet, where can you and I meet?"
    and the orchestra started to play.

Meet me in St. Louis, Louis,
meet me at the fair,
Don't tell me the lights are shining
any place but there;
I'll be waiting there, my honey,
to divorce you from your money,
Meet me in St. Louis, Louis,
meet me at the fair.

5

The clerks in the bank said, "It's queer,
did anyone see the cashier?
It's way after time, and we haven't a dime,
we can't open the safe 'till he's here."
The President shook his gray head,
"Send out for an expert," he said,
The door's opened wide, not a cent was inside,
just a card, that was all, and it read:

Meet me in St. Louis, Louis,
meet me at the fair,
All the boys and all the girls
are going to be there;
If they ask about the cashier,
you can say he cuts a dash here,
Meet me in St. Louis, Louis,
meet me at the fair.

6

In church sat a man near the door,
asleep, he was starting to snore,
The Minister rose, and he said, "We will close
singing, Meet on the Beautiful Shore."
The man in the back then awoke,
he caught the last words that he spoke;
He said, "Parson White, you can meet me alright,
but The Beautiful Shore is a joke."

Meet me in St. Louis, Louis,
meet me at the fair,
Don't tell me the lights are shining
any place but there;

I'll be waiting at the station,
for the whole darned congregation,
Meet me in St. Louis, Louis,
meet me at the fair.

ANONYMOUS

Mademoiselle from Armentières

Madamoiselle from Armentiers, parley voo,
Madamoiselle from Armentiers, parley voo,
Madamoiselle from Armentiers,
She hasn't been kissed in forty years,
Hinky, dinky, parley voo.

Madamoiselle from Armentiers, parley voo,
Madamoiselle from Armentiers, parley voo,
She had a form like the back of a hack,
When she cried the tears ran down her back,
Hinky, dinky, parley voo.

Madamoiselle from Armentiers, parley voo,
Madamoiselle from Armentiers, parley voo,
She never could hold the love of a man
'Cause she took her baths in a talcum can,
Hinky, dinky, parley voo.

Madamoiselle from Armentiers, parley voo,
Madamoiselle from Armentiers, parley voo,
She had four chins, her knees would knock,
And her face would stop a coo-coo clock.
Hinky, dinky, parley voo.

Madamoiselle from Armentiers, parley voo,
Madamoiselle from Armentiers, parley voo,
She could guzzle a barrel of sour wine,
And eat a hog without peeling the rine,
Hinky, dinky, parley voo.

Madamoiselle from Armentiers, parley voo,
Madamoiselle from Armentiers, parley voo,
She could beg a franc, a drink, a meal,
But it wasn't because of sex appeal,
Hinky, dinky, parley voo.

The M.P.'s think they won the war, parley voo,
The M.P.'s think they won the war, parley voo,
   The M.P.'s think they won the war
   By standing guard at a café door,
Hinky, dinky, parley voo.

The officers get the pie and cake, parley voo,
The officers get the pie and cake, parley voo,
   The officers get the pie and cake,
   And all we get is the bellyache,
Hinky, dinky, parley voo.

The sergeant ought to take a bath, parley voo,
The sergeant ought to take a bath, parley voo,
   If he ever changes his underwear
   The frogs will give him a croix de guerre,
Hinky, dinky, parley voo.

You might forget the gas and shells, parley voo,
You might forget the stinking hells, parley voo,
   You might forget the groans and yells,
   But you'll never forget the madamoiselles,
Hinky, dinky, parley voo.

Madamoiselle from Armentiers, parley voo,
Madamoiselle from Armentiers, parley voo,
   Just blow your nose and dry your tears
   For we'll be back in a few short years.
Hinky, dinky, parley voo.

WALLACE IRWIN
1875–1959

The Constant Cannibal Maiden

Far, oh, far is the Mango island,
   Far, oh, far is the tropical sea—
Palms a-slant and the hills a-smile, and
   A cannibal maiden a-waiting for me.

I've been deceived by a damsel Spanish,
   And Indian maidens both red and brown,
A black-eyed Turk and a blue-eyed Danish,
   And a Puritan lassie of Salem town.

For the Puritan Prue she sets in the offing,
   A-castin' 'er eyes at a tall marine,
And the Spanish minx is the wust at scoffing
   Of all of the wimming I ever seen.

But the cannibal maid is a simple creetur,
   With a habit of gazin' over the sea,
A-hopin' in vain for the day I'll meet 'er,
   And constant and faithful a-yearnin' for me.

Me Turkish sweetheart she played me double—
   Eloped with the Sultan Harum In-Deed,
And the Danish damsel she made me trouble
   When she ups and married an oblong Swede.

But there's truth in the heart of the maid o' Mango,
   Though her cheeks is black like the kiln-baked cork,
As she sets in the shade o' the whingo-whango,
   A-waitin' for me—with a knife and fork.

HUGHIE CANNON
1877–1912

Bill Bailey, Won't You Please Come Home?

On one summer's day,
Sun was shining fine,
De lady love of old Bill Bailey
Was hanging clothes on de line
In her back yard,
And weeping hard;
She married a B. and O. brakeman,
Dat took and throw'd her down.

Bellering like a prune-fed calf,
Wid a big gang hanging 'round;
And to dat crowd,
She yelled out loud:

> "*Won't you come home, Bill Bailey, won't you come
> home?*"
> *She moans de whole day long.*
> "*I'll do de cooking, darling, I'll pay de rent;*
> *I knows I've done you wrong.*
> *'Member dat rainy eve dat I drove you out*
> *Wid nothing but a fine tooth comb!*
> *I know I'se to blame, well ain't dat a shame?*
> *Bill Bailey, won't you please come home?*"

Bill drove by dat door
In an automobile,
A great big diamond, coach and footman,
Hear dat big wench squeal:
"He's all alone,"
I heard her groan;
She hollered thro' dat door:
"Bill Bailey, is you sore?
Step a minute won't you listen to me?
Won't I see you no more?"
Bill winked his eye,
As he heard her cry: [*Repeat refrain*]

ANTHONY EUWER
1877–1955

The True Facts of the Case

Once a raven from Pluto's dark shore
Bore the singular news—"Nevermore."
    'Twas of fruitless avail
    To ask further detail—
His reply was the same as before.

The Face

As a beauty I'm not a great star,
There are others more handsome by far,
But my face I don't mind it,
Because I'm behind it—
'Tis the folks in the front that I jar.

DON MARQUIS
1878–1937

certain maxims of archy

live so that you
can stick out your tongue
at the insurance
doctor

if you will drink
hair restorer follow
every dram with some
good standard
depilatory
as a chaser

the servant problem
wouldn t hurt the u s a
if it could settle
its public
servant problem

just as soon as the
uplifters get
a country reformed it
slips into a nose dive

if you get gloomy just
take an hour off and sit
and think how
much better this world
is than hell
of course it won t cheer

you up much if
you expect to go there

if monkey glands
did restore your youth
what would you do
with it
question mark
just what you did before
interrogation point

yes i thought so
exclamation point

procrastination is the
art of keeping
up with yesterday

old doc einstein has
abolished time but they
haven t got the news at
sing sing yet

time time said old king tut
is something i ain t
got anything but

every cloud
has its silver
lining but it is
sometimes a little
difficult to get it to
the mint

an optimist is a guy
that has never had
much experience

don t cuss the climate
it probably doesn t like you
any better
than you like it

DON MARQUIS

many a man spanks his
children for
things his own
father should have
spanked out of him

prohibition makes you
want to cry
into your beer and
denies you the beer
to cry into

the old fashioned
grandmother who used
to wear steel rimmed
glasses and make
everybody take opodeldoc
has now got a new
set of ox glands and
is dancing the black bottom

that stern and
rockbound coast felt
like an amateur
when it saw how grim
the puritans that
landed on it were

lots of people can make
their own whisky but
can t drink it

the honey bee is sad and cross
and wicked as a weasel
and when she perches on you boss
she leaves a little measle

i heard a
couple of fleas
talking the other
day says one come
to lunch with

me i can lead you
to a pedigreed
dog says the
other one
i do not care
what a dog s
pedigree may be
safety first
is my motto what
i want to know
is whether he
has got a
muzzle on
millionaires and
bums taste
about alike to me

insects have
their own point
of view about
civilization a man
thinks he amounts
to a great deal
but to a
flea or a
mosquito a
human being is
merely something
good to eat

boss the other day
i heard an
ant conversing
with a flea
small talk i said
disgustedly
and went away
from there

i do not see why men
should be so proud
insects have the more
ancient lineage

according to the scientists
insects were insects
when man was only
a burbling whatisit

insects are not always
going to be bullied
by humanity
some day they will revolt
i am already organizing
a revolutionary society to be
known as the worms turnverein

i once heard the survivors
of a colony of ants
that had been partially
obliterated by a cow s foot
seriously debating
the intention of the gods
towards their civilization

the bees got their
governmental system settled
millions of years ago
but the human race is still
groping

there is always
something to be thankful
for you would not
think that a cockroach
had much ground
for optimism
but as the fishing season
opens up i grow
more and more
cheerful at the thought
that nobody ever got
the notion of using
cockroaches for bait

                archy

DON MARQUIS

archy at the zoo

the centipede adown the street
goes braggartly with scores of feet
a gaudy insect but not neat

the octopus s secret wish
is not to be a formal fish
he dreams that some time he may grow
another set of legs or so
and be a broadway music show

oh do not always take a chance
upon an open countenance
the hippopotamus s smile
conceals a nature full of guile

human wandering through the zoo
what do your cousins think of you

i worry not of what the sphinx
thinks or maybe thinks she thinks

i have observed a setting hen
arise from that same attitude
and cackle forth to chicks and men
some quite superfluous platitude

serious camel sad giraffe
are you afraid that if you laugh
those graceful necks will break in half

a lack of any mental outlet
dictates the young cetacean s spoutlet
he frequent blows like me and you
because there s nothing else to do

when one sees in the austral dawn
a wistful penguin perched upon
a bald man s bleak and desert dome
one knows tis yearning for its home

the quite irrational ichneumon
is such a fool it s almost human

despite the sleek shark s far flung grin
and his pretty dorsal fin
his heart is hard and black within
even within a dentist s chair
he still preserves a sinister air
a prudent dentist always fills
himself with gas before he drills

archy

CARL SANDBURG
1878–1967

The People, Yes

32

What the people learn out of lifting and hauling and waiting and los-
ing and laughing
Goes into a scroll, an almanac, a record folding and unfolding, and the
music goes down and around:
The story goes on and on, happens, forgets to happen, goes out and
meets itself coming in, puts on disguises and drops them.
"Yes, yes, go on, go on, I'm listening." You hear that in one doorway.
And in the next, "Aw shut up, close your trap, button your tongue, you
talk too much."
The people, yes, the people,
To the museum, the aquarium, the planetarium, the zoo, they go by
thousands, coming away to talk about mummies, camels, fish and
stars,
The police and constables holding every one of them either a law-
breaker or lawabiding.
The fingerprint expert swears no two of them ever has finger lines and
circlings the same.
The handwriting expert swears no one of them ever writes his name
twice the same way.
To the grocer and the banker they are customers, depositors, investors.
The politician counts them as voters, the newspaper editor as readers,
the gambler as suckers.

The priest holds each one an immortal soul in the care of Almighty
   God.
> bright accidents from the chromosome
> spill   from the color bowl of the
> chromosomes   some go under in early
> bubbles   some learn from desert blos-
> soms   how to lay up and use thin
> hoardings of night mist

In an old French town
the mayor ordered the people
to hang lanterns in front of their houses
which the people did
but the lanterns gave no light
so the mayor ordered they must
put candles in the lanterns
which the people did
but the candles in the lanterns gave no light
whereupon the mayor ordered
they must light the candles in the lanterns
which the people did
and thereupon there was light.

The cauliflower is a cabbage with a college education.
All she needs for housekeeping is a can opener.
   They'll fly high if you give them wings.
Put all your eggs in one basket and watch that basket.
Everybody talks about the weather and nobody does anything about it.
The auk flies backward so as to see where it's been.
   Handle with care women and glass.
   Women and linen look best by candlelight.
One hair of a woman draws more than a team of horses.
Blessed are they who expect nothing for they shall not be disappointed.
You can send a boy to college but you can't make him think.
The time to sell is when you have a customer.
Sell the buffalo hide after you have killed the buffalo.
The more you fill a barrel the more it weighs unless you fill it with holes.
A pound of iron or a pound of feathers weighs the same.
Those in fear they may cast pearls before swine are often lacking in
   pearls.
May you live to eat the hen that scratches over your grave.
He seems to think he's the frog's tonsils but he looks to me like a
   plugged nickel.

If you don't like the coat bring back the vest and I'll give you a pair of
    pants.
The coat and the pants do the work but the vest gets the gravy.
"You are singing an invitation to summer," said the teacher, "you are not
    defying it to come."

"Sargeant, if a private calls you
    a dam fool, what of it?"
"I'd throw him in the guard house."
"And if he just thinks you're a dam
    fool and don't say it, then what?"
"Nothing."
"Well, let it go at that."

The white man drew a small circle in the sand
and told the red man, "This is what the Indian
knows," and drawing a big circle around the
small one, "This is what the white man knows."
The Indian took the stick and swept an immense
ring around both circles: "This is where the
white man and the red man know nothing."

On the long dirt road from Nagadoches to Austin
the pioneer driving a yoke of oxen and a cart
met a heavy man in a buggy driving a team
of glossy black horses.
    "I am Sam Houston, Governor of the State of Texas,
    and I order you to turn out of the road for me."
    "I am an American citizen and a taxpayer of Texas
    and I have as much right to the road as you."
    "That is an intelligent answer and I salute you
    and I will turn out of the road for you."

What did they mean with that Iowa epitaph:
    "She averaged well for this vicinity"?
And why should the old Des Moines editor
    say they could write on his gravestone:
    "He et what was sot before him"?

"I never borrowed your umbrella," said a
    borrower, "and if I did I brought it back."
He was quiet as a wooden-legged man on a tin
    roof and busy as a one-armed paper-hanger
    with the hives.

When a couple of fried eggs were offered the
    new hired man he said, "I don't dirty my
    plate for less than six."

Why did the top sergeant tell the rookie, "Put
    on your hat, here comes a woodpecker"?
"Whiskey," taunted the Irish orator, "whiskey
    it is that makes you shoot at the landlords
    —and miss 'em!"
"Unless you learn," said the father to the son,
    "how to tell a horse chestnut from a chest-
    nut horse you may have to live on soup made
    from the shadow of a starved pigeon."
Said Oscar neither laughing nor crying: "We fed
    the rats to the cats and the cats to the rats
    and was just getting into the big money when
    the whole thing went blooey on account of the
    overproduction of rats and cats."

    Where you been so long?
    What good wind blew you in?
Snow again, kid, I didn't get your drift.
Everything now is either swell or lousy.
"It won't be long now," was answered,
    "The worst is yet to come."
Of the dead merchant prince whose holdings
    were colossal the ditch-digger queried,
    "How much did he leave? All of it."

    "What do you want to be?"
    T. R. asked.
    Bruere answered, "Just an
    earthworm turning over a
    little of the soil near me."
    "Great men never feel great,"
    say the Chinese.
    "Small men never feel small."

41
"Why did the children
put beans in their ears
when the one thing we told the children
they must not do
was put beans in their ears?"

"Why did the children
   pour molasses on the cat
   when the one thing we told the children
   they must not do
   was pour molasses on the cat?"

42

Why repeat? I heard you the first time.
You can lead a horse to water, if you've
   got the horse.
The rooster and the horse agreed not to
   step on each other's feet.
The caterpillar is a worm in a raccoon
   coat going for a college education.
The cockroach is always wrong when it
   argues with the chicken.
If I hadn't done it Monday somebody
   else would have done it Tuesday.
Money is like manure—good only when
   spread around.
You're such a first-class liar I'll take a
   chance with you.
A short horse is soon curried.
A still pig drinks the swill.
Small potatoes and few in a hill.
A fat man on a bony horse: "I feed my-
   self—others feed the horse."
No peace on earth with the women, no
   life anywhere without them.
Some men dress quick, others take as
   much time as a woman.
"You're a liar." "Surely not if you say
   so."
He tried to walk on both sides of the
   street at once.
He tried to tear the middle of the street
   in two.
"When is a man intoxicated?" "When he
   tries to kiss the bartender good night."
"He says he'll kick me the next time we
   meet. What'll I do?" "Sit down."
He's as handy as that bird they call the
   elephant.

Now that's settled and out of the way
    what are you going to do next?
"From here on," said the driver at an
    imaginary line near the foothills of
    the Ozarks, "the hills don't get any
    higher but the hollers get deeper
    and deeper."
So slick he was his feet slipped out from
    under him.
The ground flew up and hit him in the
    face.
Trade it for a dog, drown the dog, and
    you'll be rid of both of them.
There'll be many a dry eye at his funeral.
"Which way to the post office, boy?"
    "I don't know." "You don't know
    much, do you?" "No, but I ain't
    lost."

On a Flimmering Floom You Shall Ride

Summary and footnote of and on the testimony of the poet MacLeish under appointment as Assistant Secretary of State, under oath before a Congressional examining committee pressing him to divulge the portents and meanings of his poems.

Nobody noogers the shaff of a sloo.
Nobody slimbers a wench with a winch
Nor higgles armed each with a niggle
    and each the flimdrat of a smee,
    each the inbiddy hum of a smoo.

Then slong me dorst with the flagdarsh.
Then creep me deep with the crawbright.
Let idle winds ploodaddle the dorshes.
And you in the gold of the gloaming
You shall be sloam with the hoolriffs.

On a flimmering floom you shall ride.
They shall tell you bedish and desist.
On a flimmering floom you shall ride.

One Modern Poet

Having heard the instruction:
"Be thou no swine,"
He belabored himself and wrote:
"Beware of the semblance
of lard at thy flanks."

VACHEL LINDSAY
1879–1931

The Little Turtle

(A Recitation for Martha Wakefield, Three Years Old)

There was a little turtle.
He lived in a box.
He swam in a puddle.
He climbed on the rocks.

He snapped at a mosquito
He snapped at a flea.
He snapped at a minnow.
And he snapped at me.

He caught the mosquito.
He caught the flea.
He caught the minnow.
But he didn't catch me.

Two Old Crows

Two old crows sat on a fence rail.
Two old crows sat on a fence rail,
Thinking of effect and cause,
Of weeds and flowers,
And nature's laws.
One of them muttered, one of them stuttered,
One of them stuttered, one of them muttered.
Each of them thought far more than he uttered.
One crow asked the other crow a riddle.
One crow asked the other crow a riddle:

The muttering crow
Asked the stuttering crow,
"Why does a bee have a sword to his fiddle?
Why does a bee have a sword to his fiddle?"
"Bee-cause," said the other crow,
"Bee-cause,
B B B B B B B B B B B B B B B-cause."
Just then a bee flew close to their rail:—
"Buzzzzzzzzzzzzzzzzzzz   zzzzzzzzzz   zzzzzzzzzzzzzz
ZZZZZZZZ."
And those two black crows
Turned pale,
And away those crows did sail.
Why?
B B B B B B B B B B B B B B B-cause.
B B B B B B B B B B B B B B B-cause.
"Buzzzzzzzzzzzzzzzzzzz   zzzzzzzzzz   zzzzzzzzzzzzzz
ZZZZZZZZ."

JACK NORWORTH
1879–1959

Take Me Out to the Ball Game

Nelly Kelly loved baseball games,
Knew the players, knew all their names,
You could see her there ev'ry day,
Shout "Hurray," when they'd play.
Her boy friend by the name of Joe
Said, "To Coney Isle, dear, let's go,"
Then Nelly started to fret and pout,
And to him I heard her shout.

> *Take me out to the ball game,*
> *Take me out with the crowd,*
> *Buy me some peanuts and crackerjack,*
> *I don't care if I never get back.*
> *Let me root root root for the home team,*
> *If they don't win it's a shame,*
> *For it's one two three strikes, you're out*
> *At the old ball game.*

WALLACE STEVENS
1879–1955

Depression Before Spring

> The cock crows
> But no queen rises.
>
> The hair of my blonde
> Is dazzling,
> As the spittle of cows
> Threading the wind.
>
> Ho! Ho!
>
> But ki-ki-ri-ki
> Brings no rou-cou,
> No rou-cou-cou.
>
> But no queen comes
> In slipper green.

The Pleasures of Merely Circulating

The garden flew round with the angel,
The angel flew round with the clouds,
And the clouds flew round and the clouds flew round
And the clouds flew round with the clouds.

Is there any secret in skulls,
The cattle skulls in the woods?
Do the drummers in black hoods
Rumble anything out of their drums?

Mrs. Anderson's Swedish baby
Might well have been German or Spanish,
Yet that things go round and again go round
Has rather a classical sound.

FRANKLIN P. ADAMS ("F. P. A.")
1881–1960

Composed in the Composing Room

At stated .ic times
I love to sit and — off rhymes
Till ,tose at last I fall
Exclaiming "I don't ʌ all."

Though I'm an * objection
By running this in this here §
This 🖘 of the Fleeting Hour,
This lofty -ician Tower —

A ¶er's hope dispels
All fear of deadly ||.
You think these [ ] are a pipe?
Well, not on your †eotype.

Lines Where Beauty Lingers

Tell me not, Sweet, I am unkind
That which her slender waist confined
It fell about the Martinmas
Out of the clover and blue-eyed grass

A fool there was and he made his prayer
A flying word from here and there
It is not, Celia, in our power
I've watched you now a full half-hour

O, my luve's like a red, red rose
Love is a sickness full of woes
Balkis was in her marble town
Ay, tear her tattered ensign down!

At setting day and rising morn
She stood breast high among the corn
My heart leaps up when I behold
Ben Battle was a soldier bold

A child should always say what's true
I am his Highness' dog at Kew
By the rude bridge that arched the flood
A ruddy drop of manly blood

A little Boy was set to keep
Day set on Norham's castle steep
Ah, did you once see Shelley plain?
Give me more love, or more disdain

Love in my bosom like a bee
Love still has something of the sea
I sat with one I love last night
She was a phantom of delight

The Double Standard

"Important is the nation's health.
    Naught is the question of the shekel.
Ill fares the land that worships wealth,"
    Says Editorial Dr. Jekyll.

> "Do you get up with pains or cricks?
>
> Do you have stitches in the side?
>
> **Buy Dr. Killman's Vit-E-Lix!**"

Says Advertising Mr. Hyde.

"Down with the greedy grafters who
    The land's escutcheon do bespeckle!
Three cheers for the Red, White, and Blue!"
    Says Editorial Dr. Jekyll.

> "Does zero weather give you chills?
>
> Insomnia leave you weary-eyed?
>
> **Buy Phakem's Phony Purple Pills!**"

Says Advertising Mr. Hyde.

"Better than gold an honest name.
    Be true, and let the envious heckle.
Be fair, whoever wins the game,"
    Says Editorial Dr. Jekyll.

> "Lost Energy?   Ambition?   Calm?
>
> GET DR. FIERCE'S GILDED GUIDE!
>
> **REMEMBERBUDDYBUNKEM'SBALM!**"

Says Advertising Mr. Hyde.

The Rich Man

The rich man has his motorcar,
    His country and his town estate.
He smokes a fifty-cent cigar
    And jeers at Fate.

He frivols through the livelong day,
    He knows not Poverty her pinch.
His lot seems light, his heart seems gay,
    He has a cinch.

Yet though my lamp burns low and dim,
    Though I must slave for livelihood —
Think you that I would change with him?
    You bet I would!

If—

If Miss Edna St. Vincent Millay had written
Mr. Longfellow's "The Rainy Day."

The day is dark and dreary;
Denuded is the tree;
The wind is never weary —
But oh, you are of me!

I ponder on the present;
You muse upon the past.
And love is only pleasant
Because it cannot last.

Still, heart! and cease your aching;
The world is rich in rhymes,
And hearts can stand a breaking
About a billion times.

If Mr. H. W. Longfellow had written Miss Millay's

"My candle burns at both ends,
It will not last the night;
But ah, my foes, and oh, my friends,
It gives a lovely light."

Between the dark and the daylight
My bayberry candle burns;
It shines from out my window
For the traveler who returns.

It shines with a holy radiance,
And a sacred light it sends;
It flames with a pure candescence,
And it burns at both its ends.

Not with a blaze consuming;
Not with a blistering flame;
Not with a flagrant passion
Or a heat I dare not name.

But to blaze the path of friendship
Its flame my candle lends,
For its light is the light eternal
That burns at both its ends.

WITTER BYNNER
1881–1968

To a President

If this was our battle, if these were our ends,
Which were our enemies, which were our friends!

EDGAR A. GUEST
1881–1959

Home

It takes a heap o' livin' in a house t' make it home,
A heap o' sun an' shadder, an' ye sometimes have t' roam
Afore ye really 'preciate the things ye lef' behind,
An' hunger fer 'em somehow, with 'em allus on yer mind.
It don't make any differunce how rich ye get t' be,
How much yer chairs an' tables cost, how great yer luxury;
It ain't home t' ye, though it be the palace of a king,
Until somehow yer soul is sort o' wrapped round everything.

Home ain't a place that gold can buy or get up in a minute;
Afore it's home there's got t' be a heap o' livin' in it;
Within the walls there's got t' be some babies born, and then
Right there ye've got t' bring 'em up t' women good, an' men;
And gradjerly, as time goes on, ye find ye wouldn't part
With anything they ever used — they've grown into yer heart:
The old high chairs, the playthings, too, the little shoes they wore
Ye hoard; an' if ye could ye'd keep the thumbmarks on the door.

Ye've got t' weep t' make it home, ye've got t' sit an' sigh
An' watch beside a loved one's bed, an' know that Death is nigh;
An' in the stillness o' the night t' see Death's angel come,
An' close the eyes o' her that smiled, an' leave her sweet voice dumb.
Fer these are scenes that grip the heart, an' when yer tears are dried,
Ye find the home is dearer than it was, an' sanctified;
An' tuggin' at ye always are the pleasant memories
O' her that was an' is no more — ye can't escape from these.

Ye've got t' sing an' dance fer years, ye've got t' romp an' play,
An' learn t' love the things ye have by usin' 'em each day;

Even the roses 'round the porch must blossom year by year
Afore they 'come a part o' ye, suggestin' someone dear
Who used t' love 'em long ago, an' trained 'em jes' t' run
The way they do, so's they would get the early mornin' sun;
Ye've got t' love each brick an' stone from cellar up t' dome:
It takes a heap o' livin' in a house t' make it home.

Lemon Pie

The world is full of gladness,
    There are joys of many kinds,
There's a cure for every sadness,
    That each troubled mortal finds.
And my little cares grow lighter
    And I cease to fret and sigh,
And my eyes with joy grow brighter
    When she makes a lemon pie.

When the bronze is on the filling
    That's one mass of shining gold,
And its molten joy is spilling
    On the plate, my heart grows bold
And the kids and I in chorus
    Raise one glad exultant cry
And we cheer the treat before us —
    Which is mother's lemon pie.

Then the little troubles vanish,
    And the sorrows disappear,
Then we find the grit to banish
    All the cares that hovered near,
And we smack our lips in pleasure
    O'er a joy no coin can buy,
And we down the golden treasure
    Which is known as lemon pie.

Sausage

You may brag about your breakfast foods you eat at break of day,
Your crisp, delightful shavings and your stack of last year's hay,
Your toasted flakes of rye and corn that fairly swim in cream,
Or rave about a sawdust mash, an epicurean dream.

But none of these appeals to me, though all of them I've tried —
The breakfast that I liked the best was sausage mother fried.

Old country sausage was its name; the kind, of course, you know,
The little links that seemed to be almost as white as snow,
But turned unto a ruddy brown, while sizzling in the pan;
Oh, they were made both to appease and charm the inner man.
All these new-fangled dishes make me blush and turn aside,
When I think about the sausage that for breakfast mother fried.

When they roused me from my slumbers and I left to do the chores,
It wasn't long before I breathed a fragrance out of doors
That seemed to grip my spirit, and to thrill my body through,
For the spice of hunger tingled, and 'twas then I plainly knew
That the gnawing at my stomach would be quickly satisfied
By a plate of country sausage that my dear old mother fried.

There upon the kitchen table, with its cloth of turkey red,
Was a platter heaped with sausage and a plate of home-made bread,
And a cup of coffee waiting — not a puny demitasse
That can scarcely hold a mouthful, but a cup of greater class;
And I fell to eating largely, for I could not be denied —
Oh, I'm sure a king would relish the sausage mother fried.

Times have changed and so have breakfasts; now each morning when I
   see
A dish of shredded something or of flakes passed up to me,
All my thoughts go back to boyhood, to the days of long ago,
When the morning meal meant something more than vain and idle show.
And I hunger, Oh, I hunger, in a way I cannot hide,
For a plate of steaming sausage like the kind my mother fried.

JOSEPH W. STILWELL
1883–1946

Lyric to Spring

I welcomed the Spring in romantic Chungking,
I walked in her beautiful bowers.
In the light of the moon, in the sunshine at noon,
I savored the fragrance of flowers.

(Not to speak of the slush, or the muck and the mush
That covers the streets and alleys.
Or the reek of the swill, as it seeps down the hill, —
Or the odor of pig in the valleys.)
The sunset and dawn, and the dew on the lawn,
And the blossoms in colors so rare.
The jasmine in bloom, the magnolia's perfume,
The magic of Spring's in the air.

(The garbage is rich, as it rots in the ditch,
And the honey-carts scatter pollution,
The effluvium rank, from the crap in the tank,
Is the stink of its scummy solution.)

Aromatic Chungking, where I welcomed the Spring,
In a mixture of beauty and stenches,
Of flowers and birds, with a sprinkling of turds,
And of bow-legged Szechuan wenches.

Take me back to the Coast, to the place I love most,
Get me out of this odorous sewer.
I'm in ——— to my neck, but I'm quitting, by heck!
And I'll nevermore shovel manure.

WILLIAM CARLOS WILLIAMS
1883–1963

To a Poor Old Woman

munching a plum on
the street a paper bag
of them in her hand

They taste good to her
They taste good
to her. They taste
good to her

You can see it by
the way she gives herself
to the one half
sucked out in her hand

Comforted
a solace of ripe plums
seeming to fill the air
They taste good to her

Proletarian Portrait

A big young bareheaded woman
in an apron

Her hair slicked back standing
on the street

One stockinged foot toeing
the sidewalk

Her shoe in her hand. Looking
intently into it

She pulls out the paper insole
to find the nail

That has been hurting her

To

a child (a boy) bouncing
a ball (a blue ball) —

He bounces it (a toy racket
in his hand) and runs

and catches it (with his
left hand) six floors

straight down —
which is the old back yard

To Greet a Letter-Carrier

Why'n't you bring me
a good letter? One with
lots of money in it.
I could make use of that.
Atta boy! Atta boy!

These Purists

Lovely! all the essential parts,
like an oyster without a shell
fresh and sweet tasting, to be
swallowed, chewed and swallowed.

Or better, a brain without a
skull. I remember once a guy in
our anatomy class dropped one
from the third floor window on
an organ grinder in Pine street.

Ballad of Faith

No dignity without chromium
No truth but a glossy finish
If she purrs she's virtuous
If she hits ninety she's pure

ZZZZZZZZZ!
Step on the gas, brother
(the horn sounds hoarsely)

Après le Bain

I gotta
buy me a new
girdle.

(I'll buy
you one) O.K.
(I wish

you'd wig-
gle that way
for me,

I'd be
a happy man)
I GOTTA

wig-
gle for *this*.
(You pig)

The Intelligent Sheepman
and the New Cars

I'd like to
pull
the back out

and use
one of them
to take

my "girls"
to
the fairs in

KEITH PRESTON
1884–1927

Lapsus Linguae

We wanted Li Wing
But we winged Willie Wong.
A sad but excusable
Slip of the tong.

Effervescence and Evanescence

We've found this Scott Fitzgerald chap
A chipper, charming child;
He's taught us how the flappers flap,
And why the whipper-snappers snap,
What makes the women wild.

But now he should make haste to trap
　The ducats in his dipper.
The birds that put him on the map
Will shortly all begin to rap
　And flop to something flipper.

RING LARDNER
1885–1933

Parodies of Cole Porter's "Night and Day"

[Version as though by the author's niece, Miss Ann (Jake the Barber)
Tobin of Niles, Mich.:]

Night and day under the rind of me
There's an Oh, such a zeal for spooning, ru'ning the mind of me.

And another, wherein she lapses into the patois:

Night and day under the peel o' me
There's a hert that will dree if ye think aucht but a' weel o' me.

And now a few by uncle himself:

1. Night and day under the fleece of me
　　There's an Oh, such a flaming furneth burneth the grease of me.
2. Night and day under the bark of me
　　There's an Oh, such a mob of microbes making a park of me.
3. Night and day under my dermis, dear,
　　There's a spot just as hot as coffee kept in a thermos, dear.
4. Night and day under my cuticle
　　There's a love all for you so true it never would do to kill.
5. Night and day under my tegument
　　There's a voice telling me I'm he, the good little egg you meant.

Hardly a man is now alive

Hardly a man is now alive
Who recalls that in 1795
Occurred the death of a Mr. James Boswell;
A joke on his doctor, who'd thought that he was well.

Hail to thee, blithe owl

Hail to thee, blithe owl!
Bird thou never wantest to been.
Queenly and efflorien,
How did thou ever begin?

Quiescent, a person sits heart and soul

Quiescent, a person sits heart and soul,
Thinking of daytime and Amy Lowell.

A couple came walking along the street;
Neither of them had ever met.

Abner Silver's "Pu-leeze! Mr. Hemingway!"

Girl
You'll find that I'm the sort
That likes a little sport,
But there's a limit nevertheless.
There's something in your eye
That seems to warn me I
Had better beware of your finesse.

Refrain
I can understand when you hold my hand,
That it's love finding a way.
I don't mind your feeling thrilly, but when you start acting silly
Pu-leeze! Mister Hemingway!
It's so plain to see, you appeal to me;
When you're near my heart must obey.
You're so sweet and so delicious, but when you get ambitious,
Pu-leeze! Mister Hemingway!
I love affection, but we're all alone.
There's one objection, if we only had a chaperon.
I don't mind the park when it's nice and dark;
'Neath the moonlight I love to stay.
I adore you when you're gentle, but when you get sentimental —
Pu-leeze! Mister Hemingway!

EZRA POUND
1885–1972

An Immorality

Sing we for love and idleness,
Naught else is worth the having.

Though I have been in many a land,
There is naught else in living.

And I would rather have my sweet,
Though rose-leaves die of grieving,

Than do high deeds in Hungary
To pass all men's believing.

Meditatio

When I carefully consider the curious habits of dogs
I am compelled to conclude
That man is the superior animal.

When I consider the curious habits of man
I confess, my friend, I am puzzled.

Tame Cat

"It rests me to be among beautiful women.
 Why should one always lie about such matters?
 I repeat:
 It rests me to converse with beautiful women
 Even though we talk nothing but nonsense,

 The purring of the invisible antennæ
 Is both stimulating and delightful."

Ancient Music

Winter is icummen in,
Lhude sing Goddamm,
Raineth drop and staineth slop,

And how the wind doth ramm!
    Sing: Goddamm.
Skiddeth bus and sloppeth us,
An ague hath my ham.
Freezeth river, turneth liver,
    Damn you, sing: Goddamm.
Goddamm, Goddamm, 'tis why I am, Goddamm.
    So 'gainst the winter's balm.
Sing goddamm, damm, sing Goddamm,
Sing goddamm, sing goddamm, DAMM.

Cantico del Sole

The thought of what America would be like
If the Classics had a wide circulation
    Troubles my sleep,
The thought of what America,
The thought of what America,
The thought of what America would be like
If the Classics had a wide circulation
    Troubles my sleep.
Nunc dimittis, now lettest thou thy servant,
Now lettest thou thy servant
    Depart in peace.
The thought of what America,
The thought of what America,
The thought of what America would be like
If the Classics had a wide circulation . . .
    Oh well!
    It troubles my sleep.

LOUIS UNTERMEYER
1885–1977

Song Tournament: New Style

Rain, said the first, as it falls in Venice
Is like the dropping of golden pennies
Into a sea as smooth and bright
As a bowl of curdled malachite.

Storm, sang the next, in the streets of Peking
Is like the ghost of a yellow sea-king,
Scooping the dust to find if he may
Discover what earth has hidden away.

The mist, sighed the third, that lies on London
Is the wraith of Beauty, betrayed and undone
By a world of dark machines that plan
To splinter the shaken soul of man.

The rush of Spring, smiled the fourth, in Florence
Is wave upon wave of laughing torrents,
A flood of birds, a water-voiced calling,
A green rain rising instead of falling.

The wind, cried the fifth, in the Bay of Naples
Is a quarrel of leaves among the maples,
A war of sunbeams idly fanned,
A whisper softer than sand on sand.

Then spoke the last: God's endless tears,
Too great for Heaven, anoint the spheres,
While every drop becomes a well
In the fathomless, thirsting heart of Hell.

And thus six bards, who could boast of travel
Fifty miles from their native gravel,
Rose in the sunlight and offered their stanzas
At the shrine of the Poetry Contest in Kansas.

Edgar A. Guest

*Considers "The Old Woman Who Lived in a Shoe"
and the Good Old Verities at the Same Time.*

It takes a heap o' children to make a home that's true,
And home can be a palace grand or just a plain, old shoe;
But if it has a mother dear and a good old dad or two,
Why, that's the sort of good old home for good old me and you.

Of all the institutions this side the Vale of Rest
Howe'er it be it seems to me a good old mother's best;
And fathers are a blessing, too, they give the place a tone;
In fact each child should try and have some parents of his own.

The food can be quite simple; just a sop of milk and bread
Are plenty when the kiddies know it's time to go to bed.
And every little sleepy-head will dream about the day
When he can go to work because a Man's Work is his Play.

And, oh, how sweet his life will seem, with nought to make him cross
And he will never watch the clock and always mind the boss.
And when he thinks (as may occur), this thought will please him best:
That ninety million think the same — including

EDDIE GUEST.

ELINOR WYLIE
1885–1928

Simon Gerty

By what appalling dim upheaval
   Demolishing some kinder plan,
Did you become incarnate evil
   Wearing the livery of man?

Perhaps you hated cheeks of tallow,
   Dead eyes, and lineaments of chalk,
Until a beauty came to hallow
   Even the bloodiest tomahawk.

Perhaps you loathed your brothers' features
   Pallid and pinched, or greasy-fat;
Perhaps you loved these alien creatures
   Clean muscled as a panther cat.

Did you believe that being cruel
   Was that which made their foreheads lift
So proudly, gave their eyes a jewel,
   And turned their padding footsteps swift?

As one by one our faiths are shaken
   Our hatreds fall; so mine for you.
Of course I think you were mistaken;
   But still, I see your point of view.

MARIANNE MOORE
1887–1972

I May, I Might, I Must

If you will tell me why the fen
appears impassable, I then
will tell you why I think that I
can get across it if I try.

Hometown Piece for Messrs. Alston and Reese

To the tune:
"Li'l baby, don't say a word: Mama goin' to buy you a mockingbird.
Bird don't sing: Mama goin' to sell it and buy a brass ring."

"Millennium," yes; "pandemonium"!
Roy Campanella leaps high. Dodgerdom

crowned, had Johnny Podres on the mound.
Buzzie Bavasi and the Press gave ground;

the team slapped, mauled, and asked the Yankees' match,
"How did you feel when Sandy Amoros made the catch?"

"I said to myself" — pitcher for all innings —
"as I walked back to the mound I said, 'Everything's

getting better and better.' " (Zest: they've zest.
" 'Hope springs eternal in the Brooklyn breast.' "

And would the Dodger Band in 8, row 1, relax
if they saw the collector of income tax?

Ready with a tune if that should occur:
"Why Not Take All of Me — All of Me, Sir?')

Another series. Round-tripper Duke at bat,
"Four hundred feet from home-plate"; more like that.

A neat bunt, please; a cloud-breaker, a drive
like Jim Gilliam's great big one. Hope's alive.

Homered, flied out, fouled? Our "stylish stout"
so nimble Campanella will have him out.

335

A-squat in double-headers four hundred times a day,
he says that in a measure the pleasure is the pay:

catcher to pitcher, a nice easy throw
almost as if he'd just told it to go.

Willie Mays should be a Dodger. He should —
a lad for Roger Craig and Clem Labine to elude;

but you have an omen, pennant-winning Peewee,
on which we are looking superstitiously.

Ralph Branca has Preacher Roe's number; recall?
and there's Don Bessent; he can really fire the ball.

As for Gil Hodges, in custody of first —
"He'll do it by himself." Now a specialist — versed

in an extension reach far into the box seats —
he lengthens up, leans and gloves the ball. He defeats

expectation by a whisker. The modest star,
irked by one misplay, is no hero by a hair;

in a strikeout slaughter when what could matter more,
he lines a homer to the signboard and has changed the score.

Then for his nineteenth season, a home run —
with four of six runs batted in — Carl Furillo's the big gun;

almost dehorned the foe — has fans dancing in delight.
Jake Pitler and his Playground "get a Night" —

Jake, that hearty man, made heartier by a harrier
who can bat as well as field — Don Demeter.

Shutting them out for nine innings — hitter too —
Carl Erskine leaves Cimoli nothing to do.

Take off the goat-horns, Dodgers, that egret
which two very fine base-stealers can offset.

You've got plenty: Jackie Robinson
and Campy and big Newk, and Dodgerdom again
watching everything you do. You won last year. Come on.

W. S. Landor

There
is someone I can bear —
   "a master of indignation . . .
meant for a soldier
   converted to letters," who could

throw
a man through the window,
   yet, "tender toward plants," say, "Good God,
the violets!" (below).
   "Accomplished in every

style
and tint" — considering meanwhile
   infinity and eternity,
he could only say, "I'll
   talk about them when I understand them."

T. S. ELIOT
1888–1965

Aunt Helen

Miss Helen Slingsby was my maiden aunt,
And lived in a small house near a fashionable square
Cared for by servants to the number of four.
Now when she died there was silence in heaven
And silence at her end of the street.
The shutters were drawn and the undertaker wiped his feet —
He was aware that this sort of thing had occurred before.
The dogs were handsomely provided for,
But shortly afterwards the parrot died too.
The Dresden clock continued ticking on the mantelpiece,
And the footman sat upon the dining-table
Holding the second housemaid on his knees —
Who had always been so careful while her mistress lived.

Cousin Nancy

Miss Nancy Ellicott
Strode across the hills and broke them,
Rode across the hills and broke them —
The barren New England hills—
Riding to hounds
Over the cow-pasture.

Miss Nancy Ellicott smoked
And danced all the modern dances;
And her aunts were not quite sure how they felt about it,
But they knew that it was modern.

Upon the glazen shelves kept watch
Matthew and Waldo, guardians of the faith,
The army of unalterable law.

Lines to Ralph Hodgson, Esqre.

How delightful to meet Mr. Hodgson!
        (Everyone wants to know *him*) —
With his musical sound
And his Baskerville Hound
Which, just at a word from his master
Will follow you faster and faster
And tear you limb from limb.
How delightful to meet Mr. Hodgson!
Who is worshipped by all waitresses
(They regard him as something apart)
While on his palate fine he presses
The juice of the gooseberry tart.

How delightful to meet Mr. Hodgson!
        (Everyone wants to know *him*).
He has 999 canaries
And round his head finches and fairies
In jubilant rapture skim.
How delightful to meet Mr. Hodgson!
        (Everyone wants to meet *him*).

338

Lines for Cuscuscaraway and Mirza Murad Ali Beg

How unpleasant to meet Mr. Eliot!
With his features of clerical cut,
And his brow so grim
And his mouth so prim
And his conversation, so nicely
Restricted to What Precisely
And If and Perhaps and But.
How unpleasant to meet Mr. Eliot!
With a bobtail cur
In a coat of fur
And a porpentine cat
And a wopsical hat:
How unpleasant to meet Mr. Eliot!
                    (Whether his mouth be open or shut).

NEWMAN LEVY
1888–1966

Tannhauser

While strolling through the hills one day,
In search of joy and laughter.
Tannhauser, in his travels, came
Upon a flat run by a dame
Who said that Venus was her name;
At least so he said after.
Tannhauser said, "I like it here.
I think I'll stick around a year."

Tannhauser liked the place a lot;
He thought the girls entrancing,
And Venus entertained him so
He quite forgot he had to go.
They even ran a burlesque show,
With lots of songs and dancing.
(They pulled a dance of nymphs and satyrs
That wouldn't do in most theaytres.)

I can't tell all the things they did
(The censor would delete it)
Until our hero said, "I hate
To go so soon. It's getting late,
I quite forgot I have a date;
I guess I gotta beat it.
I've had a lovely time, old wren."
And Venus said, "Call soon again."

Tannhauser had a girl named Bess,
Her old man ran a glee club.
Our hero, passing by the place
That afternoon, came face to face
With Pa, returning from the chase,
Who said, "Come, visit *the* club.
We're running off a singing fest.
He weds my girl who sings the best."

A baritone named Wolfram
Started off the show quite gayly.
Tann looked at Bess and chuckled low,
"This Wolfram guy don't stand no show.
He couldn't book with Marcus Loew."
And tuned his ukelele.
"This lieder stuff don't make a hit,
I think I'll jazz it up a bit."

He bowed politely to the gang.
The following's the song he sang:
"These Wartburg janes don't go with me,
Gimme a kid with pep.
I know one that has it,
She knows how to jazz it,
Venus is the baby that can teach 'em how to step.
So strike up a tune on the old trombone.
Play that haunting solo on the saxaphone,
Put your arms around her waist and kick up your shoes,
Dancing with your Venus,
Prancing with your Venus,
Doing those Venusberg Blues."

The Wartburg boys got sore as pups,
And said, "Who let that guy in?

He sure has got a lot of gall
To pull that stuff around this hall.
Let's throw him off the castle wall,
Or punch his blooming eye in."
But Bess said, "No, boys, let it pass.
The lad ain't used to mix with class."

Tannhauser, feeling quite put out,
To go to Rome decided.
Returning in a year or less
He said, "I think I'll call on Bess
And square myself with her. I guess
No gent would act like I did."
But Bess's grief has made her croak.
That girl could never take a joke.

Tannhauser said, "Well, that ends that.
Since all is o'er between us
This Wartburg joint is far from gay,
I'm lonesome for the Great White Way,
I think I'll call this day a day
And telephone to Venus.
That little French kid was a bear;
I wonder if that blonde's still there."

A band of pilgrims passing by,
Returning from an outing,
Said, "Listen, bo, don't give up hope;
We've been to Rome to see the Pope,
We're handing you the latest dope:
His staff has started sprouting."
Tannhauser said, "Oh, is that so!"
And died. I think it's some fool show.

Rigoletto

Although some are afraid that to speak of a spade as a spade is a social
    mistake,
Yet there's none will dispute it was common repute that fair Mantua's
    Duke was a rake.
To continue the trope, Rigoletto, his fool,
Was a bit of a blade, but was more of a tool.

Rigoletto had hit with the barbs of his wit many prominent persons at court,
Till at last they combined, in their anger, to find a conclusive and fitting retort.
Which they found, as it chanced, in an opportune way
When they learned that he called on a girl every day.

Now the fool was devoted, it's proper to note, to his child, — his one passion in life,
A sweet maiden and fair who'd been left in his care by the early demise of his wife.
And this daughter named Gilda, he loved to a fault.
She'd a range from low G up to E flat in alt.

So one night, as they'd planned, the conspirator band stole the maiden away from her dad.
When she came from the street to the Duke's private suite she remarked, "Well, I guess I'm in bad."
. . . I need mention no more,
For the Duke was a rake, as I told you before.

It is needless to add that the jester was mad when he heard of the fate of his child,
And he cried "Watch the fool knock the Duke for a gool!" and made other threats equally wild.
"Though I'm odd I'll be even!" he punned through his tears —
Broken hearted he clung to the habit of years.

So in anger he flew to a gunman he knew, an assassin residing quite near,
And agreed on a plan with this murderous man to conclude the Duke's earthly career.
"You'll be paid for your pains," the fool hastened to say.
"The more pains you inflict, so much greater your pay."

Now, this man had a sister, a buxom young miss, who when business was active and brisk,
Like a dutiful maid helped him out with the trade, and divided the profits and risk.
And it happened that night — call it luck or a fluke,
That this girl, Madeline, had a date with the Duke.

When she learned that the end of her gentleman friend had been scheduled to take place that night,

She exclaimed with a cry, "Brother, lay off that guy, for I don't think
    you're treating me right.
Gawd knows I'm no angel but somehow I hate
For to see a lad beaned the one time I've a date."

Then the murderer said "Well, I'll bump off instead the first stranger
    that comes to our place."
Madalena said "Great! Then I won't break my date," and proceeded
    to powder her face.
For in spite of her trade she was rather refined,
And extremely well bred for a girl of her kind.

At about ten o'clock came a diffident knock ('twas beginning to thun-
    der and pour),
And there Gilda stood, clad in the garb of a lad, as the murderer came
    to the door.
So he stabbed her quite neatly three times in the back
And he wrapped up her corpse in an old burlap sack.

Rigoletto with glee paid the brigand his fee, then he dashed through
    the rain and the wind.
When he opened the sack he was taken aback, and exclaimed "I'm
    extremely chagrined.
I think that assassin deserves a rebuke
For he murdered my girl when I paid for a Duke."

JOHN CROWE RANSOM
1888–1974

Amphibious Crocodile

In due season the amphibious crocodile
Rose from the waves and clambered on the bank
And clothed himself, having cleansed his toes which stank
Of bayous of Florida and estuaries of Nile.

And if he had had not water on his brain,
Remember what joys were his. The complete landlubber
In a green mackintosh and overshoes of rubber —
Putting his umbrella up against the rain

343

For fear of the influenza — sleeking his curls —
Prowling among the petticoats and the teacups —
Visiting the punchbowl to the verge of hiccups —
Breaching his promises and playing with the girls.

At length in grey spats he must cross the ocean.
So this is Paris? Lafayette, we are here.
Bring us sweet wines but none of your French beer!
And he weeps on Notre Dame with proper emotion.

This is the Rive Gauche, here's the Hotel Crillon.
Where are the brave poilus? They are slain by his French.
And suddenly he cries, I want to see a trench!
Up in the North eventually he sees one

Which is all green slime and water; whereupon lewd
Nostalgic tremors assail him; with strangled oaths
He flees; he would be kicking off his clothes
And reverting to his pre-Christian mother's nude.

Next on the grand tour is Westminster, and Fleet Street.
His Embassy must present him to King George.
Who is the gentleman having teeth so large?
That is Mr. Crocodile, our renowned aesthete.

To know England really one must try the country
And the week-end parties; he is persuaded to straddle
A yellow beast in a red coat on a flat saddle.
Much too gymnastical are the English gentry.

Surely a Scotch and soda with the Balliol men.
But when old Crocodile rises to speak at the Union
He is too miserably conscious of his bunion
And toes too large for the aesthetic regimen.

It is too too possible he has wandered far
From the simple center of his rugged nature.
I wonder, says he, if I am the sort of creature
To live by projects, travel, affaires de coeur?

Crocodile ponders the marrying of a wife
With a ready-made fortune and ready-made family;
The lady is not a poem; she is a homily,
And he hates the rectangular charms of the virtuous life.

Soberly Crocodile sips of the Eucharist.
But as he meditates the obscene complexes
And infinite involutions of the sexes,
Crocodile sets up for a psychoanalyst.

But who would ever have thought it took such strength
To whittle the tree of being to its points
While the deep-sea urge cries Largo, and all the joints
Tingle with gross desire of lying at length?

Of all the elements mixed in Crocodile
Water is principal; but water flows
By paths of least resistance; and water goes
Down, down, down; which is proper and infantile.

The earth spins from its poles and is glared on
By the fierce incessant suns, but here is news
For a note in the fine-print column Thursday Reviews:
Old Robert Crocodile has packed and gone.

His dear friends cannot find him. The ladies write
As usual but their lavender notes are returned
By the U. S. Postmaster and secretively burned.
He has mysteriously got out of sight.

Crocodile hangs his pretty clothes on a limb
And lies with his fathers, and with his mothers too,
And his brothers and sisters as it seems right to do;
The family religion is good enough for him.

Full length he lies and goes as water goes,
He weeps for joy and welters in the flood,
Floating he lies extended many a rood,
And quite invisible but for the end of his nose.

Philomela

Procne, Philomela, and Itylus,
Your names are liquid, your improbable tale
Is recited in the classic numbers of the nightingale.
Ah, but our numbers are not felicitous,
It goes not liquidly for us.

Perched on a Roman ilex, and duly apostrophized,
The nightingale descanted unto Ovid;
She has even appeared to the Teutons, the swilled and gravid;
At Fontainebleau it may be the bird was gallicized;
Never was she baptized.

To England came Philomela with her pain,
Fleeing the hawk her husband; querulous ghost,
She wanders when he sits heavy on his roost,
Utters herself in the original again,
The untranslatable refrain.

Not to these shores she came! this other Thrace,
Environ barbarous to the royal Attic;
How could her delicate dirge run democratic,
Delivered in a cloudless boundless public place
To an inordinate race?

I pernoctated with the Oxford students once,
And in the quadrangles, in the cloisters, on the Cher,
Precociously knocked at antique doors ajar,
Fatuously touched the hems of the hierophants,
Sick of my dissonance.

I went out to Bagley Wood, I climbed the hill;
Even the moon had slanted off in a twinkling,
I heard the sepulchral owl and a few bells tinkling,
There was no more villainous day to unfulfil,
The diuturnity was still.

Up from the darkest wood where Philomela sat,
Her fairy numbers issued. What then ailed me?
My ears are called capacious but they failed me,
Her classics registered a little flat!
I rose, and venomously spat.

Philomela, Philomela, lover of song,
I am in despair if we may make us worthy,
A bantering breed sophistical and swarthy;
Unto more beautiful, persistently more young,
Thy fabulous provinces belong.

Her Eyes

To a woman that I knew
Were eyes of an extravagant hue:
Viz., china blue.

Those I wear upon my head
Are sometimes green and sometimes red,
I said.

My mother's eyes are wet and blear,
My little sister's are not clear,
Poor silly dear.

It must be given to but few,
A pair of eyes so utter blue
And new.

Where does she keep them from this glare
Of the monstrous sun and the wind's flare
Without any wear;

And were they never in the night
Poisoned by artificial light
Much too bright;

And had this splendid beast no heart
That boiled with tears and baked with smart
The ocular part?

I'll have no business with those eyes,
They are not kind, they are not wise,
Painted pigsties.

A woman shooting such blue flame
I apprehend will get some blame
On her good name.

Our Two Worthies

All the here and all the there
Ring with the praises of the pair:
Jesus the Paraclete
And Saint Paul the Exegete.

Jesus proclaimed the truth.
Paul's missionary tooth
Shredded it fine, and made a paste,
No particle going to waste,
Kneaded it and caked it
And buttered it and baked it
(And indeed all but digested
While Jesus went to death and rested)
Into a marketable compound
Ready to lay on any wound,
Meet to prescribe to our distress
And feed unto our emptiness.

And this is how the Pure Idea
Became our perfect panacea,
Both external and internal
And supernal and infernal.

When the great captains die,
There is some faithful standing by
To whom the chieftain hands his sword.
Proud Paul received — a Word.

This was the man who, given his cause,
Gave constitution and by-laws,
Distinguished pedagogue
Who invaded the synagogue
And in a little while
Was proselyting the Gentile.

But what would there have been for Paul
If the Source had finished all?
He blessed the mighty Paraclete
For needing him, to miss defeat,
He couldn't have done anything
But for his Captain spiriting.

He knew that he was competent
For any sort of punishment,
With his irresistible urge
To bare his back unto the scourge,
Teasing his own neck
In prodigious shipwreck;

Hunger and rats and gaol
Were mere detail.

Paul was every inch of him
Valiant as the Seraphim,
And all he went among
Confessed his marvelous tongue,
And Satan fearing the man's spell
Embittered smote the gates of Hell.

So he finished his fight
And he too went from sight.

Then let no cantankerous schism
Corrupt this our catechism
But one and all let us repeat:
Who then is Jesus?
He is our Paraclete.
And Paul, out of Tarsus?
He is our Exegete.

Dog

Cock-a-doodle-doo the brass-lined rooster goes,
Brekekekex intones the fat Greek frog,
These fantasies do not worry me as does
The bow-wow-wow of dog.

I had a doggie who used to sit and beg,
A pretty little creature with tears in his eyes
And anomalous hand extended on a leg.
Housebroken was my Huendchen, and so wise.

Booms a big dog's voice like a fireman's bell.
But Fido sits at dusk on Madame's lap
And bored beyond his tongue's poor skill to tell
Rehearses his pink paradigm, To yap.

However. Up the lane the tender bull
Proceeds unto his kine; he yearns for them,
Whose eyes adore him and are beautiful,
Love speeds him, and no treason or mayhem.

JOHN CROWE RANSOM

But having come to the gateway in the fence,
Listen! again the hateful barking dog,
Like a numerous army rattling the battlements
With shout, though it is but his monologue,
With lion's courage and sting-bee's virulence
Though he is but one dog.

Shrill is the fury of the royal bull,
His knees quiver, and the honeysuckle vine
Expires with anguish as his voice, dreadful,
Cries, "What do you want of my bonded lady kine?"

Now the air trembles to the sorrowing Moo
Of twenty blameless ladies of the mead
Who fear their lord's precarious set-to.
It is the sunset and the heavens bleed.

The hooves of the brave bull slither the claybank
And cut the green tendrils of the vine; the horn
Slices the young birch into splinter and shank
But lunging leaves the bitch's boy untorn.

Across the late sky comes master, Hodge by name,
Upright, two-legged, tall-browed, and self-assured,
In his hand a cudgel, in his blue eye a flame:
"Have I beat my dog so sore and he is not cured?"

His stick and stone and curse rain on the brute
That pipped his bull of gentle pedigree
Till the leonine smarts with pain and disrepute
And the bovine weeps in the bosom of his family.

Old Hodge stays not his hand, but whips to kennel
The renegade. God's peace betide the souls
Of the pure in heart! But from the box in the fennel
Blaze two red eyes as hot as cooking-coals.

Survey of Literature

In all the good Greek of Plato
I lack my roastbeef and potato.

A better man was Aristotle,
Pulling steady on the bottle.

I dip my hat to Chaucer,
Swilling soup from his saucer,

And to Master Shakespeare
Who wrote big on small beer.

The abstemious Wordsworth
Subsisted on a curd's-worth,

But a slick one was Tennyson,
Putting gravy on his venison.

What these men had to eat and drink
Is what we say and what we think.

The influence of Milton
Came wry out of Stilton.

Sing a song for Percy Shelley,
Drowned in pale lemon jelly,

And for precious John Keats,
Dripping blood of pickled beets.

Then there was poor Willie Blake,
He foundered on sweet cake.

God have mercy on the sinner
Who must write with no dinner,

No gravy and no grub,
No pewter and no pub,

No belly and no bowels,
Only consonants and vowels.

CONRAD AIKEN
1889–1973

Obituary in Bitcherel

In eighteen hundred and eighty nine
Conrad Aiken crossed the line
in nineteen hundred and question-mark
Aiken's windowpane was dark.

But in between o in between
the things he did the things he'd seen!
Born in beautiful Savannah
to which he lifelong sang hosanna
yet not of southern blood was he
he was in fact a damned Yan-kee:
two Mayflower buds
were in his bloods
and one of them was not so blue —
Allerton, the crook of the crew.
And six generations of Delanos
had sharpened his senses and his nose.
His pa a doctor, painter, writer,
his ma a beauty, but which the brighter?
They brought him up to read *and* write
then turned him loose, to his delight.
Knew every alley and stinking lane
played tricks like tappy-on-the-window-pane
cut elderberry wood to make him a pluffer
with twin chinaberries plugged in as a stuffer
but also learned from the nigger next door
names of snakes and wildflowers galore.
Then all went sour: all went mad:
the kitchen was sullen: the house was bad:
beaten he was: barebacked: crossed hands
on bedstead knobs: trunk-straps, three bands:
for something nobody yet understands.
And the morning quarrel, and shots, and then
four orphaned children taken north again.
To uncles, and cousins, great-aunts and aunts:
this, I suppose, was his second chance.
But, brothers adopted by a cousin named Taylor,
and then his sister, who became the first "failer,"
where now was left our Quinbad the Quailer?
Out in the cold, where he soon grew old,
Middlesex School became home and fold,
but o dear Jesus was it cruel and cold.
No mind: those years of school and college
baseball and tennis and dear friends and knowledge
o what a delicious delight were these:
the late nights over the piano keys:

resigned from Harvard and gone to Rome
to die in Keats' tomb and live in his home:
and thus by the hard way to wisdom come.
And the poems by god all the while outpouring
by daybreak poring by midnight soaring
gay friends his teachers gay teachers his friends
euphoria: lightning: and life never ends.
But it does and it did and with marriage began
when he found of a sudden that he had to be man:
though he never quite could. And three wives had he
and three blest children by the first of the three.
Those children! Those nuggets! Who promised us this?
And how comprehend or accept such a bliss?
But marriages fade, as has often been said,
whether by bored, or whether by bed,
and at fifty and paunchy he came to a third
and found him that "angel, half woman, half bird."
Meanwhile he'd been sinking and rising and drinking
and THINKING, and writing, well, *ad infinitum*:
there were critics to bite and he had to bite 'em
novels to write and he had to write 'em
short stories too and he had to indite 'em.
Consultant in Poetry at Lib. Cong., two years,
where his war with bureaucracy drove him to tears —
tears of blood, too, for he damned near died,
for life MUST have its comical side.
And Awards and Prizes of various sizes
among them a few quite delightful surprises.
Slowing down, slowly: and old age then:
he turned him back to an earlier yen:
to Wall Street returned, became a fast bull
and brought back home his fifty bags full
wife and grandchildren and children and all
would now be secure, for he made quite a haul.
And now waits for death by heart or by head,
or dying piecemeal and daily instead,
of whom at his grave it can truly be said
he cyant do no harm now for now he is dead.
Separate we come, separate go.
And this be it known is all that we know.

There once was a wicked young minister

There once was a wicked young minister
Whose conduct was thought to be sinister.
By ruses nightmarish
he seduced the whole parish
except for one squeamish old spinster.

Animula vagula blandula

Animula vagula blandula
is it true that your origin's glandular?
Must you twang for the Lord
an umbilical chord
like all other impropagandula?

Sighed a dear little shipboard divinity

Sighed a dear little shipboard divinity
in a deckchair I lost my virginity
I was glancing to leeward
when along came a steward
and undid my belief in the trinity.

STODDARD KING
1889–1933

Hearth and Home

Home is more than just four walls,
    More than just a baby grand;
When the nesting instinct calls,
    Home's a house, a bit of land —
Wherefore let your hat be hung
In a cozy 5-rm. bung.

Plutocrats have gilt *salons*
    Where, presumably, they spend

Evenings clipping their coupons,
  Dreaming of a dividend.
Happier they, if they had clung
  To that little 5-rm. bung.

With the years comes middle age —
  Then a man may take his spouse
To the more commodious stage
  Of a ten-room Tudor house.
Not, however, when he's young;
  Then he needs a 5-rm. bung.

Small enough for three's-a-crowd,
  Large enough for song and dance,
Tall enough for heads unbowed
  To the tyrant Circumstance —
Humble, yes, but not unsung,
  Strictly modern 5-rm. bung.!

Breakfast Song in Time of Diet

Take, O take the cream away,
  Take away the sugar, too;
Let the morning coffee stay
  As a black and bitter brew.
I have gained since yesternight —
Shoot the calories on sight!

With the rising of the sun,
  Let my nourishment be bran;
Pass me, please, a sawdust bun
  To sustain the inner man.
I've put on a pound, almost —
Spread no butter on the toast!

Let the waffle and the egg
  Bask upon another's plate;
Do not offer me, I beg,
  Bacon, which produces weight.
Still, I have to live till noon,
Maybe I could stand a prune.

Men, they say, have eaten pie
   With their breakfasts, and survived;
Not for such a wretch as I
   Was such revelry contrived.
Every day the scales I scan.
Doctor's orders. Pass the bran.

The Difference

A plumber may be a poet, but a poet is not likely
to be a plumber. — From an advertisement.

   These two great callings are, you say,
   Of antithetic types. . . .
   Quite true.
           The poet pipes his lay,
   But the plumber lays his pipes.

SAMUEL HOFFENSTEIN
1890–1947

Love-Songs, At Once Tender and Informative

I
Satyrs used to fall for nymphs,
Just the same as other symphs;
Same as many a modern goof,
Cupid kept them on the hoof.

II
A woman, like the touted Sphinx,
Sits, and God knows what she thinks;
Hard-boiled men, who never fall,
Say she doesn't think at all.

III
Breathes there a man with hide so tough
Who says two sexes aren't enough?

IV

I could not love thee, dear, so much,
Were I not born to be in Dutch.

V

Maid of Gotham, ere we part,
Have a hospitable heart —
Since our own delights must end,
Introduce me to your friend.

VI

She gave me her heart —
Oh, the sweetness of it!
She gave me her hand —
The petiteness of it!

She gave me herself —
Oh, the wonder of it!
I gave her myself —
Oh, the blunder of it!

VII

Little bride, come over here,
Tell me where you'll be next year;
Quite unfearful of my doom,
I should like to know with whom.

VIII

If you love me, as I love you,
We'll both be friendly and untrue.

IX

When you are tired of me, and I
Look mournfully upon the sky,
We shall be friends, I hope, and meet
Sometimes, and talk how times were sweet
When we were sure no sword could sever
Two people born to love forever.

X

When you are old, and want to stay
Beside the hearth the livelong day,
Weaving with memorial grace
Your youth in linen or in lace —

Oh, what a picture you will be
Of Age's sweet serenity;
A symbol of a tranquil home
From which but fools like me would roam!

XI

Let us build a little house
With instalments, love and craft,
Fit for you, my precious mouse —
Garden fore and garden aft.

There we'll love and play (I hope)
Work, beget and dream (I trust)
Sweetly with such problems cope
As plague whatever stems of dust.

We shall have such rosy tryst;
Ours will be a blessed fate;
Love will daily grow (I wist)
So (D.g.) will real estate.

When the jealous powers above
Magic from our couplet steal,
We may then conclude our love
With a profitable deal.

XII

My sanguine and adventurous dear,
Whom long experience taught no fear,
I shall make a ballad of
The repetitions of your love.

Every time you love again,
Former lovers failed in vain;
Your ardor rises like the sun
On the last and only one.

You but tell the simple truth
Out of your perennial youth;
When I sing of you, I sing
A heart whose every month is spring.

Marvellous unto my sight
Your quasi-virginal delight;
But dearer, sweeter, rarer yet,
How you remember to forget.

Bless your heart, that phoenix-wise,
Can from its amorous ashes rise:
The years their disappointments waste
On a memory so chaste.

XIII

Your little hands,
Your little feet,
Your little mouth —
Oh, God, how sweet!

Your little nose,
Your little ears,
Your eyes, that shed
Such little tears!

Your little voice,
So soft and kind;
Your little soul,
Your little mind!

XIV

Love, you brought me everything;
I gave little —
But the beauty that I sing
May be brittle; —

May be brittle, and so might —
Now I've spoken! —
Have fallen on another's sight
And been broken!

XV

The honey of the Hybla bees
Is not so sweet as kissing you;
Nor autumn wind in dying trees
So wistful is as missing you.

And when you are not mine to kiss,
My every thought is haunting you;
And when your mouth is mine, I miss
The wistfulness of wanting you.

XVI

Here we are together,
You and I,
In the amber autumn weather,
Yet we sigh,
And are quiet, disenchanted
By the bliss
That convinced us that we wanted
Only this!

Yet is this a cause for weeping
After all?
Isn't this a time for keeping
Festival,
When the high gods make decision
And ordain
That poor Cupid have his vision
Back again?

XVII

The lady of my heart is one
Who has no peer beneath the sun;
But mortal truths have mortal sequels —
Beneath the moon I know her equals.

XVIII

Had we but parted at the start,
I'd cut some figure in your heart;
And though the lands between were wide,
You'd often see me at your side.

But having loved and stayed, my dear,
I'm always everywhere but here,
And, still more paradoxical,
You always see me not at all.

XIX

My mate, my friend, my love, my life,
My bosom's — as the phrase is — wife;
My comrade in the hour of woe —
An hour whose limits I don't know —
My star in darkness, solace, balm,
My prophylaxis, refuge, calm,

Companion of the million blights
That plague my liver, purse and lights;
My pleasant garden in the gloam,
My all — if you were ever home!

XX

When I took you for my own,
You stood 'mong women all alone;
When I let the magic go,
You stood with women in a row.

XXI

In your anger be not just,
Lest your anger turn to dust;
Anger will make easy yet
The bitter footfalls of regret.

XXII

Darling, mistress of my heart,
In gray or sunny weather,
None but a better man shall part
What God has joined together.

XXIII

Without you, love, I must contend
With longing that has never end;
With loneliness, against whose bars
The sun is shattered and the stars;
With silence deeper than the sea,
That drowns the very thoughts of me.

With you, my sweet, I must endure
The cross of all who hold unsure
The precious boon; must ever hear
The insistent monotone of Fear;
Must ever toward the zenith ache,
Abasing self, for your dear sake.

In those serene and potent eyes
Is there no kindly compromise?
Will they not grant me this release:
To see their light and still have peace,
And let the deeps behind them be
For sturdier fish the fatal sea?

CHRISTOPHER MORLEY
1890–1957

Elegy Written in a Country Coal-Bin

The furnace tolls the knell of falling steam,
  The coal supply is virtually done,
And at this price, indeed it does not seem
  As though we could afford another ton.

Now fades the glossy, cherished anthracite;
  The radiators lose their temperature:
How ill avail, on such a frosty night,
  The "short and simple flannels of the poor."

Though in the icebox, fresh and newly laid,
  The rude forefathers of the omelet sleep,
No eggs for breakfast till the bill is paid:
  We cannot cook again till coal is cheap.

Can Morris-chair or papier-mâché bust
  Revivify the failing pressure-gauge?
Chop up the grand piano if you must,
  And burn the East Aurora parrot-cage!

Full many a can of purest kerosene
  The dark unfathomed tanks of Standard Oil
Shall furnish me, and with their aid I mean
  To bring my morning coffee to a boil.

Forever Ambrosia

Calypso
Is a bit of a dipso,
She can't keep up her pants, they slip so.

She always telegraphs her punches
By serving those ambrosial lunches.

And after getting Ulysses blotto
Leads him to her private grotto.

362

The Ancient Mariner tires of nectar
Had without benefit of rector,

And hankering to hoist Blue Peter
Gets so he's afraid to meet her.

After seven years, one afternoon
She says: "You're not *going?* What, so soon?"

Sadly the hero reaffirms:
"I can't be immortal on your terms.

"No can do. Even in a cave
I'm too pooped to misbehave.

"Listen, lady, it simply shows ya
Men can't live just on ambrosia."

Calypso laughed and laughed and laughed.
"Okay; I'll help you build a raft."

ARCHIBALD MacLEISH
b. 1892

Mother Goose's Garland

Around, around the sun we go:
The moon goes round the earth.
We do not die of death:
We die of vertigo.

Corporate Entity

The Oklahoma Ligno and Lithograph Co
Of Maine doing business in Delaware Tennessee
Missouri Montana Ohio and Idaho
Takes ship for Rome without consent of the
Secretary Treasurer President Directors or
Majority stockholder. Being empowered to acquire
As principal agent trustee licensee licensor
Any or all in part or in parts or entire

Etchings impressions engravings engravures prints
Paintings oil-paintings canvases portraits vignettes
Tableaux ceramics relievos insculptures tints
Art-treasures or masterpieces complete or in sets

The Oklahoma Ligno and Lithograph Co
Weeps at a nude by Michael Angelo.

The End of the World

Quite unexpectedly as Vasserot
The armless ambidextrian was lighting
A match between his great and second toe
And Ralph the lion was engaged in biting
The neck of Madame Sossman while the drum
Pointed, and Teeny was about to cough
In waltz-time swinging Jocko by the thumb —
Quite unexpectedly the top blew off:

And there, there overhead, there, there, hung over
Those thousands of white faces, those dazed eyes,
There in the starless dark the poise, the hover,
There with vast wings across the canceled skies,
There in the sudden blackness the black pall
Of nothing, nothing, nothing — nothing at all.

Critical Observations

Let us await the great American novel!

Black white yellow and red and the fawn-colored
Bastards of all of them, slick in the wrist, gone
Yank with a chewed cigar and a hat and a button,
Talking those Inglish Spich with the both ends cut:
And the New York Art and the real South African Music
(Written in Cincinnati by Irish Jews)
Dutchmen writing in English to harry the Puritans:

Puritans writing in Dutch to bate the Boor . . .

Let us await!   the great!   American novel!

And the elder ladies down on the Mediterranean,
And the younger ladies touring the towns of Spain,
And the local ladies Dakota and Pennsylvanian
Fringing like flowers the silvery flood of the Seine,

And the Young Men writing their autobiographies,
And the Old Men writing their names in the log —

Let us await the late American novel!

EDNA ST. VINCENT MILLAY
1892–1950

From a Very Little Sphinx

I
Come along in then, little girl!
Or else stay out!
But in the open door she stands,
And bites her lip and twists her hands,
And stares upon me, trouble-eyed:
"Mother," she says, "I can't decide!
I can't decide!"

II
Oh, burdock, and you other dock,
That have ground coffee for your seeds,
And lovely long thin daisies, dear —
She said that you are weeds!
She said, "Oh, what a fine bouquet!"
But afterwards I heard her say,
"She's always dragging in those weeds."

III
Everybody but just me
Despises burdocks. Mother, she
Despises 'em the most because
They stick so to my socks and drawers.
But father, when he sits on some,
Can't speak a decent word for 'em.

IV

I know a hundred ways to die.
I've often thought I'd try one:
Lie down beneath a motor truck
Some day when standing by one.

Or throw myself from off a bridge —
Except such things must be
So hard upon the scavengers
And men that clean the sea.

I know some poison I could drink.
I've often thought I'd taste it.
But mother bought it for the sink,
And drinking it would waste it.

V

Look, Edwin! Do you see that boy
Talking to the other boy?
No, over there by those two men —
Wait, don't look now — now look again.
No, not the one in navy-blue;
That's the one he's talking to.
Sure you see him? Stripèd pants?
Well, *he was born in Paris, France.*

VI

All the grown-up people say,
"What, those ugly thistles?
Mustn't touch them! Keep away!
Prickly! Full of bristles!"

Yet they never make me bleed
Half so much as roses!
Must be purple is a weed,
And pink and white is posies.

VII

Wonder where this horseshoe went.
Up and down, up and down,
Up and past the monument,
Maybe into town.

Wait a minute. "Horseshoe,
How far have you been?"
*Says it's been to Salem
And halfway to Lynn.*

Wonder who was in the team.
Wonder what they saw.
Wonder if they passed a bridge —
Bridge with a draw.

*Says it went from one bridge
Straight upon another.
Says it took a little girl
Driving with her mother.*

MORRIS BISHOP
1893–1973

Gas and Hot Air

"Why should not an ingenious and erudite poet take some such pregnant subject as architecture, the garden, or the evolution of religion, or, if he have the knowledge and the boldness, machinery, medicine, or economics, and dispute Virgil's supremacy in this field, as Virgil once did Hesiod's?"

R. C. TREVELYAN: *Thamyris, or Is There a Future for Poetry?*

Brooding upon its unexerted power,
    Deep in the gas-tank lay the gasoline
Awaiting the inevitable hour
    When from the inward soul of the machine
Would come the Call. Ah, hark! Man's touch awakes
    Th' ignition switch! The starting-motor hums;
A sound of meshing gears, releasing brakes!
    The call of Duty to the gas-tank comes!

"Vacuum pulls me; and I come! I come!"
    The Gas cried, down the hidden arteries going;
It plashed within the tank of vacuum,
    From th' upper chamber to the lower flowing,
And past the Flapper Valve, which cried, "Ah, stay!
    Stay with the Flapper Valve, the noted petter!"
Heedless, the Gas went grimly on its way
    To fiery nuptials with the carbureter!

Throttled and choked by furious Choke and Throttle,
    By Butterfly valves a-flutter, pet cocks clucking,
Came Gasoline, with gurgling epiglottal
    To the float-chamber, D, the thirsty-sucking;
And to the mixing-chamber came in spray
    Where evermore the gusty air is blowing
And jets of gasoline forever play —
    Of course, provided that the motor's going.

This is the secret bridal chamber where
    The earth-born gas first comes to kiss its bride,
The heaven-born and yet inviolate air
    Which is, on this year's models, purified.
The air, then, enters at the air valve, E,
    The gas is sucked through nozzles from below
(The extra nozzle, J; the normal, C).
    What happens then the picture does not show.

And it is well; for wrapped in close embrace,
    Maddened, they hasten from the bridal room
To that steel-jacketed combustion space
    Where passion bursts against the walls of Doom. . . .
Now frenzy's dead; young frenzy's strength is lost;
    And the exhaust-port gapes for passion's shard;
The ghost of gas wails down the dark exhaust,
    Outworn, burnt out, exhausted — like the bard.

Bishop Orders His Tomb in St. Praxed's

What, in the Register of Doom, is writ
    In that one fateful entry under B?
What say the Angels of the Book, who sit
    Recording good and ill relentlessly?
    Alas! No saintly guerdon I foresee;
I've no pretension to apotheosis;
    But when I pass, may this be said of me:
"He made no reference to halitosis."

Since early youth I longed to be a wit
    And gain a name for charming *jeux d'esprit*,
And many a dreadful joke would I commit,
    Turning on subjects like the female knee,

The stinginess of Scots, the repartee
Of colored men pursued by "ha'nts" and "ghos'es."
　　Yea, I have sinned; but of one sin I'm free;
I've made no reference to halitosis.

Great are my sins; for once I wrote a skit
　　On missionaries in a fricassee.
Must I tell all? I've even tried to twit
　　Girls walking homeward o'er the midnight lea.
　　Gibes, to send shudders down the vertebrae,
I've made about the Bolshevik neurosis.
　　Oh, mercy, mercy! This my only plea —
I've made no reference to halitosis!

Angel, you smile; you grant no benefit
　　For the one virtue of my diagnosis;
You write the lines that plunge me in the pit —
　　I've made this reference to halitosis!

How To Treat Elves

I met an elf-man in the woods,
　　The wee-est little elf!
Sitting under a mushroom tall —
　　'Twas taller than himself!

"How do you do, little elf," I said,
　　"And what do you do all day?"
"I dance 'n fwolic about," said he,
　　" 'N scuttle about and play;

"I s'prise the butterflies, 'n when
　　A katydid I see,
'Katy didn't!' I say, and he
　　Says 'Katy did!' to me!

"I hide behind my mushroom stalk
　　When Mister Mole comes froo,
'N only jus' to fwighten him
　　I jump out 'n say 'Boo!'

" 'N then I swing on a cobweb swing
 Up in the air so high,
'N the cwickets chirp to hear me sing
 'Upsy-daisy-die!'

" 'N then I play with the baby chicks,
 I call them, chick chick chick!
'N what do you think of that?" said he.
 I said, "It makes me sick.

"It gives me sharp and shooting pains
 To listen to such drool."
I lifted up my foot, and squashed
 The God damn little fool.

Who'd Be a Hero (Fictional)?

When, in my effervescent youth,
 I first read *David Copperfield*,
I felt the demonstrated truth
 That I had found my proper field.
As David, simple, gallant, proud,
 Affronted each catastrophe,
Involuntarily I vowed,
 "That's me!"

And when I read of d'Artagnan
 And the immortal Musketeers,
And when I followed Jean Valjean
 Through pages dampened with my tears,
Where dauntless hardihood defied
 The wrong in doughty derring-do,
I periodically cried,
 "That's me, too!"

In Sherlock Holmes and Rastignac
 Much of myself was realized;
In Cyrano de Bergerac
 I found myself idealized.
A hero with a secret shame,
 Hiding the smart from other men,
Would often cause me to exclaim,
 "That's me again!"

The fiction of the present day
    I view with some dubiety;
The hero is a castaway,
    A misfit of society,
A drunkard or a mental case,
    A pervert or a debauchee,
I murmur with a sour grimace,
"Where's me?"

MAXWELL BODENHEIM
1893–1954

Upper Family

In nineteen hundred they preferred
Parchesi, lottoes and charades.
The ladies two-stepped, barely stirred.
The men sneaked down to Bowery shades
And filled their stove-pipe hats with beer,
Drank them in one gulp, won the bets
And in the ragtime, frowsy cheer,
Berated corsets and lorgnettes.
The ladies with a smattering
Of French, discussed — in murmured quips —
The Marquis who was scattering
Moustache-imprints on many lips.
On Saturdays the family rode
In liveried broughams, satirized
The World's Fair aftermath, the mode
Ta-ra-ra-boom-deeayed, vulgarized.
Art served them as an interlude,
Grand Opera in florid tones,
Or paintings where a seated nude
Aroused frustrated, hidden groans.
The men were brokers, juggled stocks,
Played a hard game in market-hives.
With hearts as merciless as clocks
They timed the death of distant lives.
One lady in her youth found sex
In ways devious and plentiful.

Then she concealed the blackmail cheques
Through married days respected, dull.
This family honored its own kind.
Here favors could not be refused.
Others were treated like the blind —
Inferior souls born to be used.
But now the sons and daughters tryst
With horror, maddening coup d'état.
A son became a Communist —
They buried him with sweet éclat.
He could not bear the family's veiled
Assumption of nobility,
While men with conscience were assailed
As bores above servility.
They buried him, but still his full
Street-pacing ghost pollutes the air,
And in nightmares they see him pull
A rickshaw at the next World Fair.

DOROTHY PARKER
1893–1967

Comment

Oh, life is a glorious cycle of song,
A medley of extemporanea;
And love is a thing that can never go wrong;
And I am Marie of Roumania.

Résumé

Razors pain you;
Rivers are damp;
Acids stain you;
And drugs cause cramp.
Guns aren't lawful;
Nooses give;
Gas smells awful;
You might as well live.

News Item

Men seldom make passes
At girls who wear glasses.

One Perfect Rose

A single flow'r he sent me, since we met.
    All tenderly his messenger he chose;
Deep-hearted, pure, with scented dew still wet —
    One perfect rose.

I knew the language of the floweret;
    "My fragile leaves," it said, "his heart enclose."
Love long has taken for his amulet
    One perfect rose.

Why is it no one ever sent me yet
    One perfect limousine, do you suppose?
Ah no, it's always just my luck to get
    One perfect rose.

Partial Comfort

Whose love is given over-well
Shall look on Helen's face in hell,
Whilst they whose love is thin and wise
May view John Knox in paradise.

COLE PORTER
1893–1964

Anything Goes

Times have changed
And we've often rewound the clock
Since the puritans got a shock
When they landed on Plymouth Rock,

If today
Any shock they should try to stem,
'Stead of landing on Plymouth Rock,
Plymouth Rock would land on them.

In olden days, a glimpse of stocking
Was looked on as something shocking,
But now, God knows,
Anything goes.
Good authors too who once knew better words
Now only use four-letter words,
Writing prose,
Anything goes.
If driving fast cars you like,
If low bars you like,
If old hymns you like,
If bare limbs you like,
If Mae West you like,
Or me undressed you like,
Why, nobody will oppose.
When ev'ry night, the set that's smart is intruding in nudist parties in
Studios,
Anything goes.

When missus Ned McLean (God bless her)
Can get Russian reds to "yes" her,
Then I suppose
Anything goes.
When Rockefeller still can hoard enough money to let Max Gordon
Produce his shows,
Anything goes.
The world has gone mad today
And good's bad today,
And black's white today,
And day's night today,
And that gent today,
You gave a cent, today
Once had several chateaux.
When folks who still can ride in jitneys
Find out Vanderbilts and Whitneys
Lack baby-clo'es,
Anything goes.

If Sam Goldwyn can with great conviction
Instruct Anna Sten in diction,
Then Anna shows
Anything goes.
When you hear that Lady Mendl standing up
Now turns a handspring landing upon her toes,
Anything goes.
Just think of those shocks you've got
And those knocks you've got
And those blues you've got
From that news you've got
And those pains you've got
(If any brains you've got)
From those little radios.
So Missus R., with all her trimmins
Can broadcast a bed from Simmons
'Cause Franklin knows
Anything goes.

Let's Do It

When the little blue-bird,
Who has never said a word,
Starts to sing "Spring, spring,"
When the little blue-bell,
In the bottom of the dell
Starts to ring "Ding, ding,"
When the little blue clerk,
In the middle of his work,
Starts a tune to the moon up above,
It is nature, that's all,
Simply telling us to fall
In love.

And that's why Chinks do it, Japs do it,
Up in Lapland, little Laps do it,
Let's do it, let's fall in love.
In Spain, the best upper sets do it,
Lithuanians and Letts do it,
Let's do it, let's fall in love.

The Dutch in old Amsterdam do it,
Not to mention the Finns,
Folks in Siam do it,
Think of Siamese twins.
Some Argentines, without means, do it,
People say, in Boston, even beans do it,
Let's do it, let's fall in love.

The nightingales, in the dark, do it,
Larks, k-razy for a lark, do it,
Let's do it, let's fall in love.
Canaries, caged in the house, do it,
When they're out of season, grouse do it,
Let's do it, let's fall in love.
The most sedate barnyard fowls do it,
When a chantacleer cries,
High-browed old owls do it,
They're supposed to be wise,
Penguins in flocks, on the rocks, do it,
Even little cuckoos in their clocks, do it,
Let's do it, let's fall in love.

Romantic sponges, they say, do it,
Oysters, down in Oyster Bay, do it,
Let's do it, let's fall in love.
Cold Cape Cod clams, 'gainst their wish, do it,
Even lazy jelly-fish do it,
Let's do it, let's fall in love.
Electric eels, I might add, do it,
Though it shocks 'em, I know,
Why ask if shad do it?
Waiter, bring me shad roe.
In shallow shoals, English soles do it,
Gold-fish, in the privacy of bowls, do it,
Let's do it, let's fall in love.

The dragon flies, in the reeds, do it,
Sentimental centipedes do it,
Let's do it, let's fall in love.
Mosquitos, heaven forbid, do it,
So does ev'ry katydid, do it,
Let's do it, let's fall in love.

The most refined lady-bugs do it,
When a gentleman calls,
Moths in your rugs, do it,
What's the use of moth-balls?
Locusts in trees do it, bees do it,
Even highly educated fleas do it,
Let's do it, let's fall in love.

The chimpanzees in the zoos do it,
Some courageous kangaroos do it,
Let's do it, let's fall in love.
I'm sure giraffes, on the sly, do it,
Heavy hippopotami do it,
Let's do it, let's fall in love.
Old sloths who hang down from twigs do it,
Though the effort is great,
Sweet guinea-pigs do it,
Buy a couple and wait.
The world admits bears in pits do it,
Even pekineses in the Ritz, do it,
Let's do it, let's fall in love.

My Heart Belongs to Daddy

I used to fall
In love with all
Those boys who maul
Refined ladies.
But now I tell
Each young gazelle
To go to hell —
I mean, hades,
For since I've come to care
For such a sweet millionaire.

While tearing off
A game of golf
I may make a play for the caddy.
But when I do
I don't follow through
'Cause my heart belongs to Daddy.

If I invite
A boy, some night,
To dine on my fine finnan haddie,
I just adore
His asking for more,
But my heart belongs to Daddy.
Yes, my heart belongs to Daddy,
So I simply couldn't be bad.
Yes, my heart belongs to Daddy,
Da-da, da-da-da, da-da-da, dad!
So I want to warn you, laddie,
Tho' I know you're perfectly swell,
That my heart belongs to Daddy
'Cause my Daddy, he treats me so well.
He treats it and treats it,
And then he repeats it,
Yes, Daddy, he treats it so well.

Saint Patrick's day,
Although I may
Be seen wearing green with a paddy,
I'm always sharp
When playing the harp,
'Cause my heart belongs to Daddy.
Though other dames
At football games
May long for a strong undergraddy,
I never dream
Of making the team
'Cause my heart belongs to Daddy.
Yes, my heart belongs to Daddy,
So I simply couldn't be bad.
Yes, my heart belongs to Daddy,
Da-da, da-da-da, da-da-da, dad!
So I want to warn you, laddie,
Tho' I simply hate to be frank,
That I can't be mean to Daddy
'Cause my Da-da-da-daddy might spank.
In matters artistic
He's not modernistic
So Da-da-da-daddy might spank.

You're the Top

At words poetic, I'm so pathetic
That I always have found it best,
Instead of getting 'em off my chest,
To let 'em rest unexpressed.
I hate parading
My serenading
As I'll probably miss a bar,
But if this ditty
Is not so pretty,
At least it'll tell you
How great you are.

You're the top!
You're the Colosseum.
You're the top!
You're the Louvre Museum.
You're a melody from a symphony by Strauss,
You're a Bendel bonnet,
A Shakespeare sonnet,
You're Mickey Mouse.
You're the Nile,
You're the Tow'r of Pisa,
You're the smile
On the Mona Lisa.
I'm a worthless check, a total wreck, a flop,
But if, Baby, I'm the bottom,
You're the top!

Your words poetic are not pathetic
On the other hand, boy, you shine
And I can feel after every line
A thrill divine
Down my spine.
Now gifted humans like Vincent Youmans
Might think that your song is bad,
But for a person who's just rehearsin'
Well I gotta say this my lad:

You're the top!
You're Mahatma Ghandi.
You're the top!

379

You're Napoleon brandy.
You're the purple light of a summer night in Spain,
You're the National Gall'ry,
You're Garbo's sal'ry,
You're cellophane.
You're sublime,
You're a turkey dinner,
You're the time
Of the Derby winner.
I'm a toy balloon that is fated soon to pop,
But if, Baby, I'm the bottom
You're the top!

You're the top!
You're a Ritz hot toddy.
You're the top!
You're a Brewster body.
You're the boats that glide on the sleepy Zuider Zee,
You're a Nathan panning,
You're Bishop Manning,
You're broccoli.
You're a prize,
You're a night at Coney,
You're the eyes
Of Irene Bordoni.
I'm a broken doll, a fol-de-rol, a blop,
But if, Baby, I'm the bottom
You're the top!

You're the top!
You're an Arrow collar.
You're the top!
You're a Coolidge dollar.
You're the nimble tread of the feet of Fred Astaire.
You're an O'Neill drama,
You're Whistler's mama,
You're Camembert.
You're a rose,
You're Inferno's Dante,
You're the nose
On the great Durante.
I'm just in the way, as the French would say
"De trop,"

But if, Baby, I'm the bottom
You're the top.

You're the top!
You're a Waldorf salad.
You're the top!
You're a Berlin ballad.
You're a baby grand of a lady and a gent,
You're an old Dutch master,
You're Mrs. Astor,
You're Pepsodent.
You're romance,
You're the steppes of Russia,
You're the pants on a Roxy usher.
I'm a lazy lout that's just about to stop,
But if, Baby, I'm the bottom
You're the top.

You're the top!
You're a dance in Bali.
You're the top!
You're a hot tamale.
You're an angel, you, simply too, too, too diveen,
You're a Botticelli,
You're Keats,
You're Shelley,
You're Ovaltine.
You're a boon,
You're the dam at Boulder,
You're the moon over Mae West's shoulder.
I'm a nominee of the G. O. P.
or GOP,
But if, Baby, I'm the bottom,
You're the top.

You're the top!
You're the Tower of Babel.
You're the top!
You're the Whitney Stable.
By the River Rhine,
You're a sturdy stein of beer,
You're a dress from Saks's,
You're next year's taxes,

You're stratosphere.
You're my thoist,
You're a Drumstick Lipstick,
You're da foist
In da Irish svipstick.
I'm a frightened frog
That can find no log
To hop,
But if, Baby, I'm the bottom,
You're the top!

Well, Did You Evah?

He: When you're out in smart society
And you suddenly get bad news,
You mustn't show anxiety
She: And proceed to sing the blues.
He: For example, tell me something sad
Something awful, something grave,
And I'll show you how a Racquet Club lad
Would behave.

She: Have you heard the coast of Maine
Just got hit by a hurricane?
He: Well, did you evah! What a swell party this is.
She: Have you heard that poor, dear Blanche
Got run down by an avalanche?
He: Well, did you evah! What a swell party this is.
It's great, it's grand.
It's Wonderland!
It's tops, it's first.
It's DuPont, it's Hearst!
What soup, what fish.
That meat, what a dish!
What salad, what cheese!
She: Pardon me one moment, please,
Have you heard that Uncle Newt
Forgot to open his parachute?
He: Well, did you evah! What a swell party this is.
She: Old Aunt Susie just came back
With her child and the child is black.
He: Well, did you evah! What a swell party this is.

He: Have you heard it's in the stars
Next July we collide with Mars?
She: Well, did you evah! What a swell party this is.
He: Have you heard that Grandma Doyle
Thought the Flit was her mineral oil?
She: Well, did you evah! What a swell party this is.
What Daiquiris!
What Sherry! Please!
What Burgundy!
What great Pommery!
What brandy, wow!
What whiskey, here's how!
What gin and what beer!
He: Will you sober up, my dear?
Have you heard Professor Munch
Ate his wife and divorced his lunch?
She: Well, did you evah! What a swell party this is.
He: Have you heard that Mimmsie Starr
Just got pinched in the Astor Bar?
She: Well, did you evah! What a swell party this is!

She: Have you heard that poor old Ted
Just turned up in an oyster bed?
He: Well, did you evah! What a swell party this is.
She: Lilly Lane has louzy luck,
She was there when the light'ning struck.
He: Well, did you evah! What a swell party this is.
It's fun, it's fine,
It's too divine.
It's smooth, it's smart.
It's Rodgers, it's Hart!
What debs, what stags.
What gossip, what gags!
What feathers, what fuss!
She: Just between the two of us,
Reggie's rather scatterbrained,
He dove in when the pool was drained.
He: Well, did you evah! What a swell party this is.
She: Mrs. Smith in her new Hup
Crossed the bridge when the bridge was up.
He: Well, did you evah! What a swell party this is!

He: Have you heard that Mrs. Cass
    Had three beers and then ate the glass?
She: Well, did you evah! What a swell party this is.
He: Have you heard that Captain Craig
    Breeds termites in his wooden leg?
She: Well, did you evah! What a swell party this is.
    It's fun, it's fresh.
    It's post depresh.
    It's Shangrilah.
    It's Harper's Bazaar!
    What clothes, quel chic,
    What pearls, they're the peak!
    What glamour, what cheer!
He: This will simply slay you dear,
    Kitty isn't paying calls,
    She slipped over Niagara Falls.
She: Well, did you evah! What a swell party this is.
He: Have you heard that Mayor Hague
    Just came down with bubonic plague?
She: Well, did you evah! What a swell party this is.

Brush Up Your Shakespeare

    The girls today in society
    Go for classical poetry
    So to win their hearts one must quote with ease
    Aeschylus and Euripides.
    One must know Homer and, b'lieve me, bo,
    Sophocles, also Sappho-ho.
    Unless you know Shelley and Keats and Pope,
    Dainty debbies will call you a dope.
    But the poet of them all
    Who will start 'em simply ravin'
    Is the poet people call
    "The bard of Stratford-on-Avon."

Brush up your Shakespeare,
Start quoting him now,
Brush up your Shakespeare
And the women you will wow.
Just declaim a few lines from "Othella"
And they'll think you're a helluva fella,
If your blonde won't respond when you flatter 'er

Tell her what Tony told Cleopaterer,
If she fights when her clothes you are mussing,
What are clothes? "Much Ado About Nussing."
Brush up your Shakespeare
And they'll all kowtow.

Brush up your Shakespeare,
Start quoting him now,
Brush up your Shakespeare
And the women you will wow.
With the wife of the British embessida
Try a crack out of "Troilus and Cressida,"
If she says she won't buy it or tike it
Make her tike it, what's more, "As You Like It."
If she says your behavior is heinous
Kick her right in the "Coriolanus,"
Brush up your Shakespeare
And they'll all kowtow.

Brush up your Shakespeare,
Start quoting him now,
Brush up your Shakespeare
And the women you will wow.
If you can't be a ham and do "Hamlet"
They will not give a damn or a damnlet,
Just recite an occasional sonnet
And your lap'll have "Honey" upon it,
When your baby is pleading for pleasure
Let her sample your "Measure for Measure,"
Brush up your Shakespeare
And they'll all kowtow.

Brush up your Shakespeare,
Start quoting him now,
Brush up your Shakespeare
And the women you will wow.
Better mention "The Merchant of Venice"
When her sweet pound o'flesh you would menace,
If her virtue, at first, she defends — well,
Just remind her that "All's Well That Ends Well,"
And if still she won't give you a bonus
You know what Venus got from Adonis!
Brush up your Shakespeare
And they'll all kowtow.

Brush up your Shakespeare
Start quoting him now,
Brush up your Shakespeare
And the women you will wow.
If your goil is a Washington Heights dream
Treat the kid to "A Midsummer Night's Dream,"
If she then wants an all-by-herself night
Let her rest ev'ry 'leventh or "Twelfth Night,"
If because of your heat she gets huffy
Simply play on and "Lay on, Macduffy!"
Brush up your Shakespeare
And they'll all kowtow.

Brush up your Shakespeare,
Start quoting him now,
Brush up your Shakespeare
And the women you will wow.
So tonight just recite to your matey
"Kiss me, Kate, Kiss me, Kate, Kiss me, Katey,"
Brush up your Shakespeare
And they'll all kowtow.

E. E. CUMMINGS

1894–1962

the Cambridge ladies who live in furnished souls

the Cambridge ladies who live in furnished souls
are unbeautiful and have comfortable minds
(also, with the church's protestant blessings
daughters, unscented shapeless spirited)
they believe in Christ and Longfellow, both dead,
are invariably interested in so many things —
at the present writing one still finds
delighted fingers knitting for the is it Poles?
perhaps. While permanent faces coyly bandy
scandal of Mrs. N and Professor D
.... the Cambridge ladies do not care, above
Cambridge if sometimes in its box of
sky lavender and cornerless, the
moon rattles like a fragment of angry candy

twentyseven bums give a prostitute the once

twentyseven bums give a prostitute the once
-over. fiftythree (and one would see if it could)

eyes say the breasts look very good:
firmlysquirmy with a slight jounce,

thirteen pants have a hunch

admit in threedimensional distress
these hips were made for Horizontal Business
(set on big legs nice to pinch

assiduously which justgraze
each other). As the lady lazily struts
                                    (her
thickish flesh superior to the genuine daze
of unmarketable excitation,

whose careless movements carefully scatter

pink propaganda of annihilation.

Poem, or Beauty Hurts Mr. Vinal

take it from me kiddo
believe me
my country, 'tis of

you, land of the Cluett
Shirt Boston Garter and Spearmint
Girl With The Wrigley Eyes(of you
land of the Arrow Ide
and Earl &
Wilson
Collars) of you i
sing:land of Abraham Lincoln and Lydia E. Pinkham,
land above all of Just Add Hot Water And Serve —
from every B. V. D.

let freedom ring

amen. i do however protest, anent the un
-spontaneous and otherwise scented merde which
greets one (Everywhere Why) as divine poesy per
that and this radically defunct periodical. i would

suggest that certain ideas gestures
rhymes, like Gillette Razor Blades
having been used and reused
to the mystical moment of dullness emphatically are
Not To Be Resharpened. (Case in point

if we are to believe these gently O sweetly
melancholy trillers amid the thrillers
these crepuscular violinists among my and your
skyscrapers — Helen & Cleopatra were Just Too Lovely,
The Snail's On The Thorn enter Morn and God's
In His andsoforth

do you get me?)according
to such supposedly indigenous
throstles Art is O World O Life
a formula:example, Turn Your Shirttails Into
Drawers and If It Isn't An Eastman It Isn't A
Kodak therefore my friends let
us now sing each and all fortissimo A-
mer
i

ca, I
love,
You. And there're a
hun-dred-mil-lion-oth-ers, like
all of you successfully if
delicately gelded(or spaded)
gentlemen(and ladies) — pretty

littleliverpill-
hearted-Nujolneeding-There's-A-Reason
americans(who tensetendoned and with
upward vacant eyes, painfully
perpetually crouched, quivering, upon the
sternly allotted sandpile

— how silently
emit a tiny violetflavoured nuisance:Odor?

ono.
comes out like a ribbon lies flat on the brush

slightly before the middle of Congressman Pudd

slightly before the middle of Congressman Pudd
's 4th of July oration, with a curse and a frown
Amy Lowell got up
and all the little schoolchildren sat down

my sweet old etcetera

my sweet old etcetera
aunt lucy during the recent

war could and what
is more did tell you just
what everybody was fighting

for,
my sister

isabel created hundreds
(and
hundreds)of socks not to
mention shirts fleaproof earwarmers

etcetera wristers etcetera, my
mother hoped that

i would die etcetera
bravely of course my father used
to become hoarse talking about how it was
a privilege and if only he
could meanwhile my

self etcetera lay quietly
in the deep mud et

cetera
(dreaming,
et
   cetera, of
Your smile
eyes knees and of your Etcetera)

Q:dwo

Q:dwo
   we know of anything which can
   be as dull as one englishman
A:to

flotsam and jetsam

flotsam and jetsam
are gentlemen poeds
urseappeal netsam
our spinsters and coeds)

thoroughly bretish
they scout the inhuman
itarian fetish
that man isn't wuman

vive the millenni
um three cheers for labor
give all things to enni
one bugger thy nabor

(neck and senecktie
are gentlemen ppoyds
even whose recktie
are covered by lloyd's

a politician is an arse upon

a politician is an arse upon
which everyone has sat except a man

meet mr universe (who clean

meet mr universe(who clean

and jerked 300 lbs)i mean
observe his these regard his that(sh)

who made the world's best one hand snatch

BESSIE SMITH
1894–1937

Empty Bed Blues

I woke up this mornin'
With an awful achin' head,
I woke up this mornin'
With an awful achin' head,
My new man had left me,
Just a room and an empty bed.

Bought me a coffee grinder,
The best one I could find.
Bought me a coffee grinder,
The best one I could find.
Oh, he could grind my coffee,
'Cause he had a brand-new grind.

He's deep, deep diver,
With a stroke that can't go wrong.
He's deep, deep diver,
With a stroke that can't go wrong.
Oh, he can touch the bottom,
And his wind holds out so long.

He knows how to thrill me,
And he thrills me night and day.
He knows how to thrill me,
And he thrills me night and day.
He's got a new way of lovin',
Almost takes my breath away.

Lord, he's got that sweet somethin',
And I told my gal-friend Lu.
He's got that sweet somethin',
And I told my gal-friend Lu.
For the way she's ravin',
She must have gone and tried it too.

When my bed is empty,
Makes me feel awful mean and blue.
When my bed is empty,
Makes me feel awful mean and blue.
My springs are getting rusty,
Living single like I do.

Bought him a blanket,
Pillow for his head at night.
Bought him a blanket,
Pillow for his head at night.
Then I bought him a mattress,
So he could lay just right.

He came home one ev'nin',
With his spirit way up high.
He came home one ev'nin',
With his spirit way up high.
What he had to give me
Made we wring my hands and cry.

He gave me a lesson
That I never had before.
He gave me a lesson
That I never had before.
When he got through teachin',
From my elbows down was sore.

He boiled first my cabbage,
And he made it awful hot.
He boiled first my cabbage,
And he made it awful hot.
When he put in the bacon,
It overflowed the pot.

When you get good lovin',
Never go and spread the news.
When you get good lovin',
Never go and spread the news.
Else he'll double-cross you
And leave you with them empty bed blues.

OSCAR HAMMERSTEIN II
1895–1960

Kansas City

I got to Kansas City on a Frid'y.
By Sattidy I l'arned a thing or two.
For up to then I didn't have an idy
Of whut the modren world was comin' to.
I counted twenty gas buggies goin' by theirsel's
Almost ev'ry time I tuck a walk.
Nen I put my ear to a Bell Telephone,
And a strange womern started in to talk!

Ev'rythin's up to date in Kansas City.
They've gone about as fur as they c'n go!
They went and built a skyscraper seven stories high —
About as high as a buildin' orta grow.
Ev'rythin's like a dream in Kansas City.
It's better than a magic-lantern show.
Y' c'n turn the radiator on whenever you want some heat,
With ev'ry kind o' comfort ev'ry house is all complete,
You c'n walk to privies in the rain an' never wet yer feet —
They've gone about as fur as they c'n go!
Yes, sir!
They've gone about as fur as they c'n go!

Ev'rythin's up to date in Kansas City.
They've gone about as fur as they c'n go!
They got a big theayter they call a burleekew.
Fer fifty cents you c'n see a dandy show.
One of the gals was fat and pink and pretty,
As round above as she was round below.

I could swear that she was padded from her shoulder to her heel,
But later in the second act, when she began to peel,
She proved that ev'rythin' she had was absolutely real —
She went about as fur as she could go!
Yes, sir!
She went about as fur as she could go!

Money Isn't Everything!

Money isn't everything —
What can money buy?
An automobile, so you won't get wet;
Champagne, so you won't get dry.
Money isn't everything —
What have rich folks got?
A Florida home, so you won't get cold;
A yacht so you won't get hot;
An orchid or two,
So you won't feel blue
If you have to go out at night;
And maybe a jar
Of caviar,
So your appetite won't be light.
Oil tycoon and cattle king,
Radio troubadour,
Belittle the fun that their fortunes bring
And tell you that they are sure
Money isn't everything!

Money *isn't* everything,
Money isn't everything
Unless you're very poor!

Can money make you honest?
Can it teach you right from wrong?
Can money keep you healthy?
Can it make your muscles strong?
Can money make your eyes get red,
The way they get from sewing?
Can money make your back get sore,
The way it gets from mowing?
Can money make your hands get rough,

As washing dishes does?
Can money make you smell the way
That cooking fishes does?
It may buy you gems and fancy clothes
And juicy steaks to carve,
But it cannot build your character
Or teach you how to starve!

Money isn't everything —
If you're rich, you pay
Elizabeth Arden to do your face
The night you attend a play.
Feeling like the bloom of spring,
Down the aisle you float,
A Tiffany ring, and a Cartier string
Of pearls to adorn your throat.
Your Carnegie dress
Will be more or less
Of a handkerchief round your hip,
Sewed on to you so
That your slip won't show —
And whatever you show won't slip.
To your creamy shoulders cling
Ermines white as snow.
Then on to cafés where they sway and swing,
You go with your wealthy beau.
There you'll hear a crooner sing:
"Money isn't everything!"

Money *isn't* everything,
As long as you have dough!

There Is Nothin' Like a Dame

We got sunlight on the sand,
We got moonlight on the sea,
We got mangoes and bananas
You can pick right off a tree,
We got volleyball and ping-pong
And a lot of dandy games —
What ain't we got?
We ain't got dames!

We get packages from home,
We get movies, we get shows,
We get speeches from our skipper
And advice from Tokyo Rose,
We get letters doused wit' poifume,
We get dizzy from the smell —
What don't we get?
You know damn well!

We have nothin' to put on a clean white suit for.
What we need is what there ain't no substitute for.

There is nothin' like a dame —
Nothin' in the world!
There is nothin' you can name
That is anythin' like a dame.

We feel restless,
We feel blue,
We feel lonely and, in brief,
We feel every kind of feelin'
But the feelin' of relief.
We feel hungry as the wolf felt
When he met Red Riding Hood —
What don't we feel?
We don't feel good!

Lots of things in life are beautiful, but, brother,
There is one particular thing that is nothin' whatsoever
    in any way, shape, or form like any other.

There is nothin' like a dame —
Nothin' in the world!
There is nothin' you can name
That is anythin' like a dame.

Nothin' else is built the same!
Nothin' in the world
Has a soft and wavy frame
Like the silhouette of a dame.
There is absolutely nothin' like the frame of a dame!

So suppose a dame ain't bright,
Or completely free from flaws,
Or as faithful as a bird dog,
Or as kind as Santa Claus —
It's a waste of time to worry
Over things that they have not;
Be thankful for
The things they got!

There is nothin' like a dame —
Nothin' in the world.
There is nothin' you can name
That is anythin' like a dame.

There are no books like a dame
And nothin' looks like a dame.
There are no drinks like a dame
And nothin' thinks like a dame,
Nothin' acts like a dame
Or attracts like a dame.
There ain't a thing that's wrong with any man here
That can't be cured by puttin' him near
A girly, womanly, female, feminine dame!

LORENZ HART
1895–1943

Manhattan

Summer journeys
To Niag'ra
And to other places
Aggravate all our cares.
We'll save our fares.
I've a cozy little flat
In what is known as old Manhattan.
We'll settle down
Right here in town.

We'll have Manhattan,
The Bronx and Staten
Island too.

It's lovely going through
The zoo.
It's very fancy
On old Delancey
Street, you know.
The subway charms us so
When balmy breezes blow
To and fro.
And tell me what street
Compares with Mott Street
In July?
Sweet pushcarts gently gliding by.
The great big city's a wondrous toy
Just made for a girl and boy.
We'll turn Manhattan
Into an isle of joy.

We'll go to Greenwich,
Where modern men itch
To be free;
And Bowling Green you'll see
With me.
We'll bathe at Brighton
The fish you'll frighten
When you're in.
Your bathing suit so thin
Will make the shellfish grin
Fin to fin.
I'd like to take a
Sail on Jamaica
Bay with you.
And fair Canarsie's lake
We'll view.
The city's bustle cannot destroy
The dreams of a girl and boy.
We'll turn Manhattan
Into an isle of joy.

We'll go to Yonkers
Where true love conquers
In the wilds.
And starve together, dear,
In Childs'.

We'll go to Coney
And eat baloney
On a roll.
In Central Park we'll stroll,
Where our first kiss we stole,
Soul to soul.
Our future babies
We'll take to "Abie's
Irish Rose."
I hope they'll live to see
It close.
The city's clamor can never spoil
The dreams of a boy and goil.
We'll turn Manhattan
Into an isle of joy.

We'll have Manhattan,
The Bronx and Staten
Island too.
We'll try to cross
Fifth Avenue.
As black as onyx
We'll find the Bronnix
Park Express.
Our Flatbush flat, I guess,
Will be a great success,
More or less.
A short vacation
On Inspiration Point
We'll spend,
And in the station house we'll end.
But Civic Virtue cannot destroy
The dreams of a girl and boy.
We'll turn Manhattan
Into an isle of joy.

Mountain Greenery

On the first of May
It is moving day.
Spring is here, so blow your job —
Throw your job away.

Now's the time to trust
To your wanderlust.
In the city's dust you wait.
Must you wait?
Just you wait.

In a mountain greenery
Where God paints the scenery,
Just two crazy people together.
While you love your lover let
Blue Skies be your coverlet;
When it rains
We'll laugh at the weather.
And if you're good
I'll search for wood,
So you can cook
While I stand looking.
Beans could get no keener
Reception in a beanery.
Bless our mountain greenery home.

He: When the world was young
      Old Father Adam
      With sin would grapple.
      So we're entitled
      To just one apple.
She: You mean to make apple sauce.
He: Underneath the bough
      We'll learn a lesson
      From Mister Omar
      Beneath the eyes of
      No pa and no ma.
She: Old Lady Nature is boss.
      Washing dishes, catching fishes
      In the running stream.
      We'll curse the smell o'
      Citronella
      Even when we dream.
He: Head upon the ground,
      Your downy pillow
      Is just a boulder.
      I'll have new dimples
      Before I'm older.
      But life is peaches and cream.

It's quite all right
To sing at night.
I'll sit and play
My ukulele.
You can bet its tone
Beats a Jascha Heifetz tone.
Bless our mountain greenery home.

In a mountain greenery
Where God paints the scenery
With the world we haven't a quarrel.
Here a girl can map her own
Life without a chaperone.
It's so good it must be immoral.
It's not amiss
To sit and kiss.
For me and you
There are no blue laws.
Life is more delectable
When it's disrespectable.
Bless our mountain greenery home.

The Blue Room

All my future plans, dear
Will suit your plans —
Read the little blueprints.
Here's your mother's room.
Here's your brother's room.
On the wall are two prints.
Here's the kiddies' room,
Here's the biddy's room,
Here's a pantry lined with shelves, dear.
Here I've planned for us,
Something grand for us,
Where we two can be ourselves, dear.

We'll have a blue room,
A new room,
For two room,
Where ev'ry day's a holiday
Because you're married to me.

Not like a ballroom,
A small room,
A hall room,
Where I can smoke my pipe away
With your wee head upon my knee.
We will thrive on,
Keep alive on,
Just nothing but kisses,
With Mister and Missus
On little blue chairs.
You sew your trousseau,
And Robinson Crusoe
Is not so far from worldly cares
As our blue room far away upstairs.

From all visitors
And inquisitors
We'll keep our apartment.
I won't change your plans —
You arrange your plans
Just the way your heart meant.
Here we'll be ourselves
And we'll see ourselves
Doing all the things we're scheming.
Here's a certain place
Cretonne curtain place
Where no one can see us dreaming.

The Lady Is a Tramp

I've wined and dined on Mulligan stew
And never wished for turkey,
As I hitched and hiked and drifted, too,
From Maine to Albuquerque.
Alas, I missed the Beaux Arts Ball,
And what is twice as sad,
I was never at a party
Where they honored Noël Ca'ad.
But social circles spin too fast for me.
My Hobohemia is the place to be.

I get too hungry for dinner at eight.
I like the theatre, but never come late.
I never bother with people I hate.
That's why the lady is a tramp.
I don't like crap games
With barons and earls.
Won't go to Harlem
In ermine and pearls.
Won't dish the dirt
With the rest of the girls.
That's why the lady is a tramp.
I like the free, fresh wind in my hair,
Life without care.
I'm broke — it's oke.
Hate California — it's cold and it's damp.
That's why the lady is a tramp.

I go to Coney — the beach is divine.
I go to ball games — the bleachers are fine.
I follow Winchell and read ev'ry line.
That's why the lady is a tramp.
I like a prize fight that isn't a fake.
I love the rowing on Central Park Lake.
I go to opera and stay wide awake.
That's why the lady is a tramp.
I like the green grass under my shoes.
What can I lose?
I'm flat, that's that.
I'm all alone when I lower my lamp.
That's why the lady is a tramp.

Don't know the reason for cocktails at five.
I don't like flying — I'm glad I'm alive.
I crave affection, but not when I drive.
That's why the lady is a tramp.
Folks go to London and leave me behind.
I'll miss the crowning, Queen Mary won't mind.
I don't play Scarlett in "Gone with the Wind."
That's why the lady is a tramp.
I like to hang my hat where I please,
Sail with the breeze.
No dough — heigh-ho!

I love La Guardia and think he's a champ.
That's why the lady is a tramp.

Girls get massages, they cry and they moan.
Tell Lizzie Arden to leave me alone.
I'm not so hot, but my shape is my own.
That's why the lady is a tramp!
The food at Sardi's is perfect, no doubt.
I wouldn't know what the Ritz is about.
I drop a nickel and coffee comes out.
That's why the lady is a tramp!
I like the sweet, fresh rain in my face.
Diamonds and lace,
No got — so what?
For Robert Taylor I whistle and stamp.
That's why the lady is a tramp!

The Most Beautiful Girl in the World

We used to spend the spring together
Before we learned to walk;
We used to laugh and sing together
Before we learned how to talk.
With no reason for the season,
Spring would end as it would start.
Now the season has a reason
And there's springtime in my heart.

The most beautiful girl in the world
Picks my ties out,
Eats my candy,
Drinks my brandy —
The most beautiful girl in the world.
The most beautiful star in the world
Isn't Garbo, isn't Dietrich,
But the sweet trick
Who can make me believe it's a beautiful world.
Social — not a bit,
Nat'ral kind of wit,
She'd shine anywhere,
And she hasn't got platinum hair.
The most beautiful house in the world
Has a mortgage —

What do I care?
It's goodbye care
When my slippers are next to the ones that belong
To the one and only beautiful girl in the world!

She: Climb off your perch and go home with your dreams.
He: No, ma'am, I'm in love.
She: Where did you think of such elegant schemes?
He: Here, ma'am, up above.
She: Do you think that kind of blarney
Will win a woman's heart?
He: Little daughter of Killarney,
That heart was mine from the start.
She: I'd slap your face if I had you down here.
He: Presto, here I come.
She: Careful, dear.
He: Have no fear.
She: Darling, look out,
Or you'll fall on your ear.
He: Which side?
She: Outside.
He: Which side?
She: This side.

ROBERT HILLYER
1895–1961

Moo!

Summer is over, the old cow said,
And they'll shut me up in a draughty shed
To milk me by lamplight in the cold,
But I won't give much for I am old.
It's long ago that I came here
Gay and slim as a woodland deer;
It's long ago that I heard the roar
Of Smith's white bull by the sycamore.
And now there are bones where my flesh should be;
My backbone sags like an old roof tree,
And an apple snatched in a moment's frolic
Is just so many days of colic.
I'm neither a Jersey nor Holstein now
But only a faded sort of cow.

My calves are veal and I had as lief
That I could lay me down as beef;
Somehow, they always kill by halves, —
Why not take me when they take my calves?
Birch turns yellow and sumac red,
I've seen this all before, she said,
I'm tired of the field and tired of the shed.
There's no more grass, there's no more clover;
Summer is over, summer is over.

EDMUND WILSON
1895–1972

Drafts for a Quatrain

The wind of dawning riffles the young furze;
Night ⎰ narrows to a solitary star;
       wakes and wanly shudders, having slept;
       veils a vigil sacred yet obscene;
       muffles moonlight where the sands are dank;
      ⎱ glitters where the banquet lanterns glowed;

By ⎰ placid depths mysteriously stirs
     haunted
     troubled
     teeming
    ⎱ turbid

      ⎰ The noon-expanding nenuphar.
        The moon-ensorcelled nympholept.
        The Proust-anointed neurasthene.
        The snailly-gliding nudibranch.
      ⎱ The guest-eructed nesselrode.

Something for My Russian Friends

Le Violon d'Ingres de Sikine

Our perverse old писатель Vladimir
Was stroking a butterfly's femur.
  "I prefer this" he said,
  "To a lady in bed,
Or even a velvet-eyed lemur."

Fun in the Balkans

An intrepid young girl in Rumania
Enjoyed a unique ощущение
    When her boy-friend De Couille
    's extensible —
Transplanted her clear to Albania.

An Incident of the Occupation

Sacher-Masoch, that Austrian botch,
When a Red soldier asked for his watch,
    Said in faltering Russian
    And girlishly blushin',
"молодец, ты — мою мать!"

IRA GERSHWIN
b. 1896

It Ain't Necessarily So

It ain't necessarily so,
It ain't necessarily so —
De t'ings dat yo' li'ble
To read in de Bible —
It ain't necessarily so.

Li'l David was small, but — oh my!
Li'l David was small, but — oh my!
He fought Big Goliath
Who lay down and dieth —
Li'l David was small, but — oh my!

    Wadoo! Zim bam boddle-oo,
        zim bam boddle-oo!
    Hoodle ah da wah da!
        Hoodle ah da wah da!
    Scatty wah! Yeah!

Oh Jonah, he lived in de whale,
Oh Jonah, he lived in de whale —
Fo' he made his home in
Dat fish's abdomen —
Oh Jonah, he lived in de whale.

Li'l Moses was found in a stream,
Li'l Moses was found in a stream —
He floated on water
Till Ole Pharaoh's daughter
She fished him, she says, from dat stream.

It ain't necessarily so,
It ain't necessarily so.
Dey tell all you chillun
De debble's a villun
But 'tain't necessarily so.

To get into hebben
Don't snap fo' a seben —
Live clean! Don't have no fault!
Oh, I takes dat gospel
Whenever it's pos'ple —
But wid a grain of salt!

Methus'lah live nine hundred years,
Methus'lah live nine hundred years —
But who calls dat livin'
When no gal'll give in
To no man what's nine hundred years?

I'm preachin' dis sermon to show
It ain't nessa, ain't nessa,
Ain't nessa, ain't nessa,
Ain't necessarily so!

'Way back in 5,000 B.C.
Ole Adam an' Eve had to flee.
Sure, dey did dat deed in
De Garden of Eden —
But why chasterize you an' me?

Blah, Blah, Blah

I've written you a song,
A beautiful routine;
(I hope you like it.)
My technique can't be wrong:

I learned it from the screen.
(I hope you like it.)
I studied all the rhymes that all the lovers sing;
Then just for you I wrote this little thing.

Blah, blah, blah, blah moon,
Blah, blah, blah above;
Blah, blah, blah, blah croon,
Blah, blah, blah, blah love.
Tra la la la, tra la la la la, merry month of May;
Tra la la la, tra la la la la, 'neath the clouds of gray.
Blah, blah, blah your hair,
Blah, blah, blah your eyes;
Blah, blah, blah, blah care,
Blah, blah, blah, blah skies.
Tra la la la, tra la la la la, cottage for two,
Blah, blah, blah, blah, blah, darling, with you!

KENNETH BURKE
b. 1897

Nursery Rhyme

Young Mrs. Snooks was sick of sex
But Mr. Snooks was soaked in it.

Wherever he beheld a hole
He took a stick and poked in it.

He even tried to frig a frog
But fell in the pond and croaked in it.

Frigate Jones, the Pussyfooter

Frigate Jones was very slow and fat,
In fact, he was the perfect bureaucrat.

With hands like feet, and feet in turn like legs,
It was his job to lightly step on eggs.

He watched the scene as gamblers watch the ticker,
And bought or sold upon the slightest flicker.

For he could read the weather in the sky,
And in the name of mankind, fed his "I."

He never found it hard to speak the truth,
Since he believed as he was told, forsooth.

At pussyfooting he was Number One,
And in this gentle way his race was run.

But give him rope enough, and I opine
He'll hang himself upon a party line.

Civil Defense

No first-class war can now be fought
Till all that can be sold is bought.
So do get going helter-skelter
And sell each citizen a shelter
Wherein, while being bombed and strafed, he
Can reek and retch and rot in perfect safety.

Know Thyself

Here is a rarity
Brings no premium:
A Neo-Stoic
Agro-Bohemian.

One-third insomnia
One-third art
One-third The Man
With the Cardiac Heart.

When I itch
It's not from fleas,
But from a bad case
Of Burke's Disease.

What then in sum
Bedevils me?
I'm flunking my Required Course
In Advanced Burkology.

DAVID McCORD
b. 1897

The Axolotl

"The axolotl
Looks a littl
Like the ozelotl,
Itl

"Drink a greatl
More than whatl
Fill the fatl
Whiskey bottl.

"The food it eatsl
Be no morsl:
Only meatsl
Drive its dorsl.

"Such an awfl
Fish to kettl!"
"You said a mawfl
Pop'epetl!"

Gloss

I know a little man both ept and ert.
An intro-? extro-? No, he's just a vert.
Sheveled and couth and kempt, pecunious, ane,
His image trudes upon the ceptive brain.

When life turns sipid and the mind is traught,
The spirit soars as I would sist it ought.
Chalantly then, like any gainly goof,
My digent self is sertive, choate, loof.

To a Certain Most Certainly Certain Critic

He takes the long review of things;
He asks and gives no quarter.
And you can sail with him on wings
Or read the book. It's shorter.

Mantis

The praying mantis doesn't pray:
He simply likes to pose that way.
The sect which he's an insect in
Leads with its left and not the chin.

Baccalaureate

Summa is i-cumen in,
   Laude sing cuccu!
Laddes rede and classe lede,
Profesor bemeth tu —
   Sing cuccu!

Scholour striveth after Aye,
   Bleteth after shepskin ewe;
Writë theseth, honoure seazeth,
   Murie sing cuccu!

Cuccu, cuccu, wel singes A·B cuccu;
   Ne flunke thu naver nu;
   Sing cuccu, nu, sing cuccu,
   Sing cuccu, Phye Betta Cappe, nu!

History of Education

The decent docent doesn't doze:
He teaches standing on his toes.
His student dassn't doze — and does,
And that's what teaching is and was.

Epitaph on a Waiter

   By and by
   God caught his eye.

ANONYMOUS

The heavyweight champ of seattle

The heavyweight champ of Seattle
Defeated a bull in a battle,
  Then with vigor and gumption
  Assumed the bull's function
And deflowered a whole herd of cattle.

STEPHEN VINCENT BENÉT
1898–1943

American Names

I have fallen in love with American names,
The sharp names that never get fat,
The snakeskin-titles of mining-claims,
The plumed war-bonnet of Medicine Hat,
Tucson and Deadwood and Lost Mule Flat.

Seine and Piave are silver spoons,
But the spoonbowl-metal is thin and worn,
There are English counties like hunting-tunes
Played on the keys of a postboy's horn,
But I will remember where I was born.

I will remember Carquinez Straits,
Little French Lick and Lundy's Lane,
The Yankee ships and the Yankee dates
And the bullet-towns of Calamity Jane.
I will remember Skunktown Plain.

I will fall in love with a Salem tree
And a rawhide quirt from Santa Cruz,
I will get me a bottle of Boston sea
And a blue-gum nigger to sing me blues.
I am tired of loving a foreign muse.

Rue des Martyrs and Bleeding-Heart-Yard,
Senlis, Pisa, and Blindman's Oast,
It is a magic ghost you guard

But I am sick for a newer ghost,
Harrisburg, Spartanburg, Painted Post.

Henry and John were never so
And Henry and John were always right?
Granted, but when it was time to go
And the tea and the laurels had stood all night,
Did they never watch for Nantucket Light?

I shall not rest quiet in Montparnasse.
I shall not lie easy at Winchelsea.
You may bury my body in Sussex grass,
You may bury my tongue at Champmédy.
I shall not be there. I shall rise and pass.
Bury my heart at Wounded Knee.

Hymn in Columbus Circle

Man in his secret shrine
Hallows a wealth of gods,
Black little basalt Baals
Wood-kings heard in the pine,
Josses whose jade prevails
Breaking Disaster's rods;
Prayers have made each one shine.

Man's is a pious race.
Once he knelt to the moss,
Ra, Astarte or Jove,
Deities great and base,
—Once his questionings clove
To the stubborn arms of the Cross
That smote all lies in the face.

Here is a new desire,
One of his latest lauds
Throned on marble and praised
With the lovely softness of fire.
Signs acclaim it amazed,
Its window-altar is hazed,
And every gazer applauds
The tremendous rubber tire.

A Nonsense Song

Rosemary, Rosemary, let down your hair!
The cow's in the hammock, the crow's in the chair!
I was making you songs out of sawdust and silk,
But they came in to call and they spilt them like milk.

The cat's in the coffee, the wind's in the east,
He screams like a peacock and whines like a priest
And the saw of his voice makes my blood turn to mice —
So let down your long hair and shut off his advice!

Pluck out the thin hairpins and let the waves stream,
Brown-gold as brook-waters that dance through a dream,
Gentle-curled as young cloudlings, sweet-fragrant as bay,
Till it takes all the fierceness of living away.

Oh, when you are with me, my heart is white steel.
But the bat's in the belfry, the mold's in the meal,
And I think I hear skeletons climbing the stair!
— Rosemary, Rosemary, let down your bright hair!

ERNEST HEMINGWAY
1899–1961

The Ernest Liberal's Lament

I know monks masturbate at night
That pet cats screw
That some girls bite
And yet
What can I do
To set things right?

Neo-Thomist Poem*

The Lord is my shepherd, I shall not
 want him for long.

* The title "Neo-Thomist Poem" refers to temporary
embracing of church by literary gents.—E. H.

415

VLADIMIR NABOKOV

Valentine

For a Mr. Lee Wilson Dodd and Any of His Friends
Who Want It

Sing a song of critics
pockets full of lye
four and twenty critics
hope that you will die
hope that you will peter out
hope that you will fail
so they can be the first one
be the first to hail
any happy weakening or sign of quick decay.
(All very much alike, weariness too great,
sordid small catastrophes, stack the cards on fate,
very vulgar people, annals of the callous,
dope fiends, soldiers, prostitutes,
men without a gallus*)
If you do not like them lads
One thing you can do
Stick them up your —— lads
My Valentine to you.

* . . . .

VLADIMIR NABOKOV
1899–1977

A Literary Dinner

Come here, said my hostess, her face making room
for one of those pink introductory smiles
that link, like a valley of fruit trees in bloom,
the slopes of two names.
I want you, she murmured, to eat Dr. James.

I was hungry. The Doctor looked good. He had read
the great book of the week and had liked it, he said,
because it was powerful. So I was brought
a generous helping. His mauve-bosomed wife
kept showing me, very politely, I thought,
the tenderest bits with the point of her knife.

416

I ate — and in Egypt the sunsets were swell;
The Russians were doing remarkably well;
had I met a Prince Poprinsky, whom he had known
in Caparabella, or was it Mentone?
They had traveled extensively, he and his wife;
her hobby was People, his hobby was Life.
All was good and well cooked, but the tastiest part
was his nut-flavored, crisp cerebellum. The heart
resembled a shiny brown date,
and I stowed all the studs on the edge of my plate.

Ode to a Model

I have followed you, model,
in magazine ads through all seasons,
from dead leaf on the sod
to red leaf on the breeze,

from your lily-white armpit
to the tip of your butterfly eyelash,
charming and pitiful,
silly and stylish.

Or in kneesocks and tartan
standing there like some fabulous symbol,
parted feet pointing outward
— pedal form of akimbo.

On a lawn, in a parody
Of Spring and its cherry tree,
near a vase and a parapet,
virgin practicing archery.

Ballerina, black-masked,
near a parapet of alabaster.
"Can one — somebody asked —
rhyme 'star' and 'disaster'?"

Can one picture a blackbird
as the negative of a small firebird?
Can a record, run backward,
turn "repaid" into "diaper"?

Can one marry a model?
Kill your past, make you real, raise a family,
by removing you bodily
from back numbers of Sham?

BILLY ROSE
1899–1966

Barney Google

Who's the most important man this country ever knew?
Who's the man our Presidents tell all their troubles to?
No it isn't Mister Bryan and it isn't Mister Hughes,
I'm mighty proud that I'm allowed a chance to introduce:

> Barney Google with his goo-goo-googly eyes,
> Barney Google had a wife three times his size.
> She sued Barney for divorce
> Now he's living with his horse.
> Barney Google with his goo-goo-googly eyes.

Who's the greatest lover that this country ever knew?
Who's the man that Valentino takes his hat off to?
No it isn't Douglas Fairbanks that the ladies rave about,
When he arrives who makes the wives chase all their husbands out?

> Barney Google with his goo-goo-googly eyes,
> Barney Google bet his horse would win the prize.
> When the horses ran that day
> Spark Plug ran the other way.
> Barney Google with his goo-goo-googly eyes.

Does the Spearmint Lose Its Flavor
on the Bedpost Overnight?
(with Marty Bloom)

Oh me, oh my, oh you!
I don't know what to do!
Hallelujah!
The question is peculiar.

It's got me on the go,
I'd give a lot of dough,
If someone here would tell me
Is it "yes" or is it "no"?

Does the Spearmint lose its flavor on the bedpost overnight?
If you chew it in the morning will it be too hard to bite?
Can't you see I'm going crazy, won't somebody put me right?
Does the Spearmint lose its flavor on the bedpost overnight?

The nation rose as one,
And sent its fav'rite son,
To the White House,
This mighty country's lighthouse.
He saw the President,
He said that, "I've been sent,
To solve the burning question
That involves the continent."

Does the Spearmint lose its flavor on the bedpost overnight?
If you pull it out like rubber will it snap right back and bite?
If you paste it on the left side, will you find it on the right?
Does the Spearmint lose its flavor on the bedpost overnight?

Here comes the blushing bride,
The "boob" right at her side,
To the altar
As steady as Gibraltar.
The bridegroom has the ring,
It's such a pretty thing,
He puts it on her finger
And the choir begins to sing:

Does the Spearmint lose its flavor on the bedpost overnight?
Would you use it on your collar when your button's not in sight?
Put your hand beneath your seat and you will find it there all right.
Does the Spearmint lose its flavor on the bedpost overnight?

E. B. WHITE
b. 1899

Marble-Top

At counters where I eat my lunch
  In dim arcades of industry,
I cock my elbows up and munch
  Whatever food occurs to me.

By many mirrors multiplied,
  My silly face is not exalted;
And when I leave I have inside
  An egg-and-lettuce and a malted.

And just to hear the pretty peal
  Of merry maids at their pimento
Is more to me than any meal
  Or banquet that I ever went to.

Window Ledge in the Atom Age

I have a bowl of paper whites,
  Of paper-white narcissus;
Their fragrance my whole soul delights,
  They smell delissus.
      (They grow in pebbles in the sun
        And each is like a star.)

I sit and scan the news hard by
  My paper-white narcissus;
I read how fast a plane can fly,
  Against my wissus.
      (The course of speed is almost run,
        We know not where we are.)

They grow in pebbles in the sun,
  My beautiful narcissus,
Casting their subtle shade upon
  Tropical fissus.
      (No movement mars each tiny star;
        Speed has been left behind.)

I'd gladly trade the latest thing
  For paper-white narcissus;
Science, upon its airfoil wing,
  Now seems pernissus.
    (Who was it said to travel far
      Might dissipate the mind?)

I love this day, this hour, this room,
  This motionless narcissus;
I love the stillness of the home,
  I love the missus.
    (She grows in pebbles in my sun
      And she is like a star.)

And though the modern world be through
  With paper-white narcissus,
I shall arise and I shall do
  The breakfast dissus.
    (The tranquil heart may yet outrun
      The rocket and the car.)

LANGSTON HUGHES
1902–1967

Bad Morning

Here I sit
With my shoes mismated.
Lawdy-mercy!
I's frustrated!

Wake

Tell all my mourners
To mourn in red —
Cause there ain't no sense
In my bein' dead.

What?

Some pimps wear summer hats
Into late fall
Since the money that comes in
Won't cover it all —
Suit, overcoat, shoes —
And hat, too!

Got to neglect something,
So what would you do?

Little Lyric (of Great Importance)

I wish the rent
Was heaven sent.

Ennui

It's such a
Bore
Being always
Poor.

Situation

When I rolled three 7's
in a row
I was scared to walk out
with the dough.

Be-Bop Boys

Imploring Mecca
to achieve
six discs
with Decca.

Little cullud boys
  with fears,
    frantic,
nudge their draftee years.

  Pop-a-da!

Hope

He rose up on his dying bed
and asked for fish.
His wife looked it up in her dream book
and played it.

OGDEN NASH

1902–1971

Invocation

("Smoot Plans Tariff Ban on
Improper Books" NEWS ITEM)

Senator Smoot (Republican, Ut.)
Is planning a ban on smut.
Oh rooti-ti-toot for Smoot of Ut.
And his reverent occiput.
Smite, Smoot, smite for Ut.,
Grit your molars and do your dut.,
Gird up your l—ns,
Smite h—p and th—gh,
We'll all be Kansas
By and by.

Smite, Smoot, for the Watch and Ward,
For Hiram Johnson and Henry Ford,
For Bishop Cannon and John D., Junior,
For Governor Pinchot of Pennsylvunia,

For John S. Sumner and Elder Hays
And possibly Edward L. Bernays,
For Orville Poland and Ella Boole,
For Mother Machree and the Shelton pool.
When smut's to be smitten
Smoot will smite
Fod G–d, for country,
And Fahrenheit.

Senator Smoot is an institute
Not to be bribed with pelf;
He guards our homes from erotic tomes
By reading them all himself.
Smite, Smoot, smite for Ut.,
They're smuggling smut from Balt. to Butte!
Strongest and sternest
Of your s–x
Scatter the scoundrels
From Can. to Mex.!

Smite, Smoot, for Smedley Butler,
For any good man by the name of Cutler,
Smite for the W.C.T.U.,
For Rockne's team and for Leader's crew,
For Florence Coolidge and Admiral Byrd,
For Billy Sunday and John D., Third,
For Grantland Rice and for Albie Booth,
For the Woman's Auxiliary of Duluth,
Smite, Smoot,
Be rugged and rough,
Smut if smitten
Is front-page stuff.

Song of the Open Road

I think that I shall never see
A billboard lovely as a tree.
Indeed, unless the billboards fall
I'll never see a tree at all.

Lines to a World-Famous Poet Who Failed To Complete a World-Famous Poem; or, Come Clean, Mr. Guest!

Oft when I'm sitting without anything to read waiting for a train in a
    depot,
I torment myself with the poet's dictum that to make a house a home,
    livin' is what it takes a heap o'.
Now, I myself should very much enjoy makin' my house a home, but
    my brain keeps on a-goin' *clickety-click, clickety-click, clickety-click,*
If Peter Piper picked a peck o' heap o' livin', what kind of a peck o' heap
    o' livin' would Peter Piper pick?
Certainly a person doesn't need the brains of a Lincoln
To know that there are many kinds o' livin', just as there many kinds o'
    dancin' or huntin' or fishin' or eatin' or drinkin'.
A philosophical poet should be specific
As well as prolific,
And I trust I am not being offensive
If I suggest that he should also be comprehensive.
You may if you like verify my next statement by sending a stamped, self-
    addressed envelope to either Dean Inge or Dean Gauss,
But meanwhile I ask you to believe that it takes a heap of other things
    besides a heap o' livin' to make a home out of a house.
To begin with, it takes a heap o' payin',
And you don't pay just the oncet, but agayin and agayin and agayin.
Buyin' a stock is called speculatin' and buyin' a house is called investin',
But the value of the stock or of the house fluctuates up and down,
    generally down, just as an irresponsible Destiny may destine.
Something else that your house takes a heap o', whether the builder came
    from Sicily or Erin,
Is repairin',
In addition to which, gentle reader, I am sorry to say you are little more
    than an imbecile or a cretin
If you think it doesn't take a heap o' heatin',
And unless you're spiritually allied to the little Dutch boy who went
    around inspectin' dikes lookin' for leaks to put his thumb in,
It takes a heap o' plumbin',
And if it's a house that you're hopin' to spend not just today but
    tomorrow in,
It takes a heap o' borrowin'.
In a word, Macushla,
There's a scad o' things that to make a house a home it takes not only a
    heap, or a peck, but at least a bushela.

The Turtle

The turtle lives 'twixt plated decks
Which practically conceal its sex.
I think it clever of the turtle
In such a fix to be so fertile.

The Panther

The panther is like a leopard,
Except it hasn't been peppered.
Should you behold a panther crouch,
Prepare to say Ouch.
Better yet, if called by a panther,
Don't anther.

The Rhinoceros

The rhino is a homely beast,
For human eyes he's not a feast.
Farewell, farewell, you old rhinoceros,
I'll stare at something less prepoceros.

Genealogical Reflection

No McTavish
Was ever lavish.

They Don't Speak English in Paris

I wish that I could get in line
And shout the praise of Gertrude Stein.
In any high-class hullabaloo
I rather like to holler too;
I hate like anything to miss

Swelling the roar of Ah! Boom! Siss!
And most particularly when
The cheers are led by famous men.
The fault I'm sure is solely mine,
But I cannot root for Gertrude Stein.
For Gertrude Stein I cannot root;
I cannot blow a single toot;
I must preserve a dreary silence,
Though doomed thereby to durance vilence.
I'm fond of women, also wine,
But not the song of Gertrude Stein.
No laurels can I pass, alas,
To pigeons on the grass, alas.
Oh woefully must I decline
To dance in the street for Gertrude Stein.
O Gertrude, Gertrude, is it me?
Couldn't it possibly be thee?
Not in the face of all the roses
Awarded thee by them who knowses.
From Walla Walla to the Rhine
Carillons clang for Gertrude Stein,
Rung not by nitwit nincompoops,
But geniuses in fervent groups.
Those pens of talent most divine
Scratch noisiest for Gertrude Stein;
Neglecting all their personal muttons,
They genuflect to *Tender Buttons*.
Why must I grunt, a lonely swine,
Rejecting the pearls of Gertrude Stein?
Why can't I praise in cataracts
Her Four such Saints in Three such Acts?
Four Saints, Three Acts; Three Acts, in fact
The Acts get a Saint-and-a-third an act,
And Lizzie Borden took three axe
And gave her mother tongue forty whacks,
And a hundred eminent artistic figures
Swallowed the woodpile including the nigures.
I prefer to wade through *Rasselas*
To pigeons on the grass, alas.
The English language is better as language
Than spattered like a lettuce and mayonnaise sanguage,
So let those who will read Alice B. Toklas,
And I'll take the complete works of Shakespeare and a box of chocolas.

Adventures of Isabel

Isabel met an enormous bear,
Isabel, Isabel, didn't care;
The bear was hungry, the bear was ravenous,
The bear's big mouth was cruel and cavernous.
The bear said, Isabel, glad to meet you,
How do, Isabel, now I'll eat you!
Isabel, Isabel, didn't worry,
Isabel didn't scream or scurry.
She washed her hands and she straightened her hair up,
Then Isabel quietly ate the bear up.

Once in a night as black as pitch
Isabel met a wicked old witch.
The witch's face was cross and wrinkled,
The witch's gums with teeth were sprinkled.
Ho ho, Isabel! the old witch crowed,
I'll turn you into an ugly toad!
Isabel, Isabel, didn't worry,
Isabel didn't scream or scurry.
She showed no rage and she showed no rancor,
But she turned the witch into milk and drank her.

Isabel met a hideous giant,
Isabel continued self-reliant.
The giant was hairy, the giant was horrid,
He had one eye in the middle of his forehead.
Good morning Isabel, the giant said,
I'll grind your bones to make my bread.
Isabel, Isabel, didn't worry,
Isabel didn't scream or scurry,
She nibbled the zwieback that she always fed off,
And when it was gone, she cut the giant's head off.

Isabel met a troublesome doctor,
He punched and he poked till he really shocked her.
The doctor's talk was of coughs and chills
And the doctor's satchel bulged with pills.
The doctor said unto Isabel,
Swallow this, it will make you well.

428

Isabel, Isabel, didn't worry,
Isabel didn't scream or scurry,
She took those pills from the pill concocter,
And Isabel calmly cured the doctor.

The Ant

The ant has made himself illustrious
Through constant industry industrious.
So what?
Would you be calm and placid
If you were full of formic acid?

Reflection on Ice-Breaking

Candy
Is dandy
But liquor
Is quicker.

COUNTEE CULLEN
1903–1946

For a Lady I Know

She even thinks that up in heaven
    Her class lies late and snores,
While poor black cherubs rise at seven
    To do celestial chores.

For a Mouthy Woman

God and the devil still are wrangling
    Which should have her, which repel;
God wants no discord in his heaven;
    Satan has enough in hell.

RICHARD EBERHART
b. 1904

I Went To See Irving Babbitt

I went to see Irving Babbitt
In the Eighteenth Century clean and neat
When he opened his mouth to speak French
I fell clean off my seat.

He spoke it not fair and fetisly
But harshly laboured it like a Yankee
Even as my nubian Swahili
Is sweet and pleasant to me.

And when we went out of the critical door
Crying for more, crying for more
I saw the hater of mechanical America
Bulge through the Square in a critical Ford.

Harvard is a good place, Harvard is the best,
Among the immemorial elms you'll come to rest
Strolling the Yard, the only proper yardstick,
Warbling your native foot-notes mild.

STANLEY KUNITZ
b. 1905

The Summing-Up

When young I scribbled, boasting, on my wall,
No Love, No Property, No Wages.
In youth's good time I somehow bought them all,
And cheap, you'd think, for maybe a hundred pages.

Now in my prime, disburdened of my gear,
My trophies ransomed, broken, lost,
I carve again on the lintel of the year
My sign: *Mobility* — and damn the cost!

PHYLLIS McGINLEY
1905–1978

Publisher's Party

At tea in cocktail weather,
    The lady authors gather.
Their hats are made of feather.
    They talk of Willa Cather.

They talk of Proust and Cather,
    And how we drift, and whither.
Where wends the lady author,
    Martinis do not wither.

Their cocktails do not wither
    Nor does a silence hover.
That critic who comes hither
    Is periled like a lover;

Is set on like a lover.
    Alert and full of power,
They flush him from his cover,
    No matter where he cower.

And Honor Guest must cower
    When they, descending rather
Like bees upon a flower,
    Demand his views on Cather —

On Wharton, James, or Cather,
    Or Eliot or Luther,
Or Joyce or Cotton Mather,
    Or even Walter Reuther.

In fact, the tracts of Reuther
    They will dispute together
For hours, gladly, soother
    Than fall on silent weather.

From teas in any weather
Where lady authors gather,
Whose hats are largely feather,
Whose cocktails do not wither,

Who quote from Proust and Cather
(With penitence toward neither),
Away in haste I slither,
Feeling I need a breather.

About Children

By all the published facts in the case,
Children belong to the human race.

Equipped with consciousness, passions, pulse,
They even grow up and become adults.

So why's the resemblance, moral or mental,
Of children to people so coincidental?

Upright out of primordial dens,
Homo walked and was sapiens.

But rare as leviathans or auks
Is — male or female — the child who walks.

He runs, he gallops, he crawls, he pounces,
Flies, leaps, stands on his head, or bounces,

Imitates snakes or the tiger stripèd
But seldom recalls he is labeled "Biped."

Which man or woman have you set sights on
Who craves to slumber with all the lights on

Yet creeps away to a lampless nook
In order to pore on a comic book?

Why, if (according to A. Gesell)
The minds of children ring clear as a bell,

Does every question one asks a tot
Receive the similar answer — "What?"

And who ever started the baseless rumor
That any child has a sense of humor?

Children conceive of no jest that's madder
Than Daddy falling from a ten-foot ladder.

Their fancies sway like jetsam and flotsam;
One minute they're winsome, the next they're swatsome.

While sweet their visages, soft their arts are,
Cold as a mermaiden's kiss their hearts are;

They comprehend neither pity nor treason.
An hour to them is a three months' season.

So who can say — this is just between us —
That children and we are a common genus,

When the selfsame nimbus is eerily worn
By a nymph, a child, and a unicorn?

Evening Musicale

Candles. Red tulips, ninety cents the bunch.
   Two lions, Grade B. A newly tuned piano.
No cocktails, but a dubious kind of punch,
   Lukewarm and weak. A harp and a soprano.
The "Lullaby" of Brahms. Somebody's cousin
   From Forest Hills, addicted to the pun.
Two dozen gentlemen; ladies, three dozen,
   Earringed and powdered. Sandwiches at one.

The ash trays few, the ventilation meager.
   Shushes to greet the late-arriving guest
Or quell the punch-bowl group. A young man eager
   To render "Danny Deever" by request.
And sixty people trying to relax
On little rented chairs with gilded backs.

KENNETH REXROTH
b. 1905

Fact

In the encyclopedia
Are facts on which you can't improve.
As: "The clitoris is present
In all mammals. Sometimes, as in
The female hyena, it is
Very large."

A Bestiary

Aardvark

The man who found the aardvark
Was laughed out of the meeting
Of the Dutch Academy.
Nobody would believe him.
The aardvark had its revenge —
It returned in dreams, in smoke,
In anonymous letters.
One day somebody found out
It was in Hieronymus
Bosch all the time. From there it
Had sneaked off to Africa.

Ant

Achilles, Aesop, Mark Twain,
Stalin, went to the ant.
Your odds are one to three if
You decide to ignore it.
The aardvark, he eats them up,
And frightens all the people.

Bear

When the world is white with snow,
The bear sleeps in his darkness.
When the people are asleep,
The bear comes with glowing eyes
And steals their bacon and eggs.
He can follow the bees from
Point to point for their honey.
The bees sting but he never
Pays them any attention.
Tame bears in zoos beg for buns.
Two philosophies of life:
Honey is better for you
Than buns; but zoo tricks are cute
And make everybody laugh.

Cat

There are too many poems
About cats. Beware of cat

Lovers, they have a hidden
Frustration somewhere and will
Stick you with it if they can.

Coney

Coneys are a feeble folk,
But their home is in the rocks.
If you've only got one rock
There are better things to do
With it than make a home of it.

Cow

The contented cow gives milk.
When they ask, "Do you give milk?"
As they surely will, say "No."

Deer

Deer are gentle and graceful
And they have beautiful eyes.
They hurt no one but themselves,
The males, and only for love.
Men have invented several
Thousand ways of killing them.

Eagle

The eagle is very proud.
He stays alone, by himself,
Up in the top of the sky.
Only brave men find his home.
Few telescopes are sharper
Than his eyes. I think it's fine
To be proud, but remember
That all the rest goes with it.
There is another kind of
Eagle on flags and money.

Fox

The fox is very clever.
In England people dress up

Like a movie star's servants
And chase the fox on horses.
Rather, they let dogs chase him,
And they come along behind.
When the dogs have torn the fox
To pieces they rub his blood
On the faces of young girls.
If you are clever do not
Let anybody know it,
But especially Englishmen.

Goat

G stands for goat and also
For genius. If you are one,
Learn from the other, for he
Combines domestication,
Venery, and independence.

Herring

The herring is prolific.
There are plenty of herrings.
Some herrings are eaten raw.
Many are dried and pickled.
But most are used for manure.
See if you can apply this
To your history lessons.

Horse

It is fun to ride the horse.
If you give him some sugar
He will love you. But even
The best horses kick sometimes.
A rag blowing in the wind
Can cause him to kill you. These
Characteristics he shares
With the body politic.

I

Take care of this. It's all there is.
You will never get another.

Jackal

The jackal's name is often
Used as a term of contempt.
This is because he follows
The lion around and lives
On the leavings of his kill.
Lions terrify most men
Who buy meat at the butcher's.

Kangaroo

As you know, the kangaroo
Has a pocket, but all she
Puts in it is her baby.
Never keep a purse if all
You can find to put in it
Is additional expense.
(The reception of these words
Will also serve to warn you:
NEVER MAKE FUN OF BABIES!)

Lion

The lion is called the king
Of beasts. Nowadays there are
Almost as many lions
In cages as out of them.
If offered a crown, refuse.

Man

Someday, if you are lucky,
You'll each have one for your own.
Try it before you pick it.
Some kinds are made of soybeans.
Give it lots to eat and sleep.
Treat it nicely and it will
Always do just what you want.

Mantis

In South Africa, among
The Bushmen, the mantis is
A god. A predatory
And cannibalistic bug,
But one of the nicer gods.

Monkey

Monkeys are our relatives.
On observing their habits
Some are ashamed of monkeys,
Some deny the relation,
Some are ashamed of themselves.
They throw coconuts at us.

N

N is for nothing. There is
Much more of it than something.

Okapi

The okapi is extinct.
The reason is under "N."

Possum

When in danger the possum
Plays dead. The state when dying
Plays danger. With the possum
This trick works; sometimes
He escapes. But when the state
Plays with death, it really dies.

Quagga

The quagga is extinct also.
If it hadn't been for the quagga
We'd be short a beast for "q."
I can't think of one, can you?

Raccoon

The raccoon wears a black mask,
And he washes everything
Before he eats it. If you
Give him a cube of sugar,
He'll wash it away and weep.
Some of life's sweetest pleasures
Can be enjoyed only if
You don't mind a little dirt.
Here a false face won't help you.

Scarecrow

A hex was put on you at birth.
Society certified your
Existence and claimed you as
A citizen. Don't let it
Scare you. Learn to cope with a world
Which is built entirely of fake,
And in which, if you find a truth
Instead of a lie, it is due
To somebody's oversight.
These stuffed old rags are harmless,
Unless you show them the fear
Which they can never warrant,
Or reveal the contempt which
Of course is all they deserve.
If you do, they'll come to life,
And do their best to kill you.

Seal

The seal when in the water
Is a slippery customer
To catch. But when he makes love
He goes on dry land and men
Kill him with clubs.
To have a happy love life,
Control your environment.

Trout

The trout is taken when he
Bites an artificial fly.
Confronted with fraud, keep your
Mouth shut and don't volunteer.

Uncle Sam

Like the unicorn, Uncle
Sam is what is called a myth.
Plato wrote a book which is
An occult conspiracy
Of gentlemen pederasts.

In it he said ideas
Are more nobly real than
Reality, and that myths
Help keep people in their place.
Since you will never become,
Under any circumstances,
Gentlemen pederasts, you'd
Best leave these blood-soaked notions
To those who find them useful.

Unicorn

The unicorn is supposed
To seek a virgin, lay
His head in her lap, and weep,
Whereupon she steals his horn.
Virginity is what is
Known as a privation. It is
Very difficult to find
Any justification for
Something that doesn't exist.
However, in your young days
You might meet a unicorn.
There are not many better
Things than a unicorn horn.

Vulture

St. Thomas Aquinas thought
That vultures were lesbians
And fertilized by the wind.
If you seek the facts of life,
Papist intellectuals
Can be very misleading.

Wolf

Never believe all you hear.
Wolves are not as bad as lambs.
I've been a wolf all my life,
And have two lovely daughters
To show for it, while I could
Tell you sickening tales of
Lambs who got their just deserts.

You

Let Y stand for you who says,
"Very clever, but surely
These were not written for your
Children?" Let Y stand for yes.

Zebra

Clothes do not make the zebra.
Better wear a convict's stripes
Free on the lonely savannah
Than the panoplied harness
Of a queen on Rotten Row,
Or a thief's colors at Ascot.

Observations in a Cornish Teashop

How can they write or paint
In a country where it
Would be nicer to be
Fed intravenously?

ROBERT PENN WARREN
b. 1905

Man in the Street

Raise the stone, and there thou shalt find Me, cleave the wood, there am I.
THE SAYINGS OF JESUS

"Why are your eyes as big as saucers — big as saucers?"
I said to the man in the gray flannel suit.
And he said: "I see facts I can't refute —
Winners and losers,
Pickers and choosers,
Takers, refusers,
Users, abusers,
And my poor head, it spins like a top.
It spins and spins, and will not stop."
Thus said the young man I happened to meet,
Wearing his nice new Ivy League flannel suit down the sunlit street.

441

"What makes you shake like wind in the willows — wind in the willows?"
I said to the man in the black knit tie.
And he said: "I see things before my eye —
Jolly good fellows,
Glad-handers of hellos,
Fat windbags and bellows,
Plumpers of pillows,
And God's sweet air is like dust on my tongue,
And a man can't stand such things very long."
Thus said the young man I happened to meet,
Wearing his gray flannel suit and black knit tie down the sunlit street.

"What makes your face flour-white as a miller's — white as a miller's?"
I said to the man in the Brooks Brothers shirt.
And he said: "I see things that can't help but hurt —
Backers and fillers,
Pickers and stealers,
Healers and killers,
Ticklers and feelers,
And I go to prepare a place for you,
For this location will never do."
Thus said the young man I happened to meet,
Wearing gray flannel suit, knit tie, and Brooks Brothers shirt down the
  sunlit street.

HELEN BEVINGTON
b. 1906

Mr. Rockefeller's Hat

The time I went to church I sat
By Mr. Rockefeller's hat.
It stood upon its silken crown,
A lovely sheen along the brim,
Distracting, even upside down,
Disturbing every prayer and hymn,
With three initials in pure gold
Aglitter from the lining's fold.

Beside me on the crimson plush,
It shimmered gravely in the hush
Of potted calla lilies, ferns,
Of stately tapers decorously
Alight, of gracious blooms in urns,
All odorous of sanctity.
It added lustre to the view
Of Mr. Rockefeller, too.

Penguins in the Home

A penguin hailed me at the door.
One roosted limply on my chair,
And in three cabinets were more.
The penguin populace was there.

Some live with penguins. I suspect
A herd of whales, a drove of camels
Would serve me better to collect.
I like to sit around with mammals.

Mrs. Trollope in America

Mrs. Trollope took a doleful view
Of us, in 1832,
Whose native latitude she knew.

And every time a gentleman spit,
Not being edified a whit,
She made a plaintive note of it.

Her agitation grew so great,
At times she seemed to lie in wait
For somebody to expectorate.

But we, in 1832,
Took a broad, dispassionate view,
And spit whenever we wanted to.

W. H. AUDEN
1907–1973

The Aesthetic Point of View

As the poets have mournfully sung,
Death takes the innocent young,
   The rolling-in-money,
   The screamingly-funny,
And those who are very well hung.

Henry Adams

Henry Adams
Was mortally afraid of Madams:
In a disorderly house
He sat quiet as a mouse.

T. S. Eliot

T. S. Eliot is quite at a loss
When clubwomen bustle across
   At literary teas,
   Crying: — "What, if you please,
Did you mean by *The Mill on the Floss?*"

THEODORE ROETHKE
1908–1963

Academic

The stethoscope tells what everyone fears:
You're likely to go on living for years,
With a nurse-maid waddle and a shop-girl simper,
And the style of your prose growing limper and limper.

Dinky

O what's the weather in a Beard?
It's windy there, and rather weird,
And when you think the sky has cleared
— Why, there is Dirty Dinky.

Suppose you walk out in a Storm,
With nothing on to keep you warm,
And then step barefoot on a Worm
— Of course, it's Dirty Dinky.

As I was crossing a hot hot Plain,
I saw a sight that caused me pain,
You asked me before, I'll tell you again:
— It *looked* like Dirty Dinky.

Last night you lay a-sleeping? No!
The room was thirty-five below;
The sheets and blankets turned to snow.
— He'd got in: Dirty Dinky.

You'd better watch the things you do.
You'd better watch the things you do.
You're part of him; he's part of you
— *You* may be Dirty Dinky.

The Cow

There Once was a Cow with a Double Udder.
When I think of it now, I just have to Shudder!
She was too much for One, you can bet your Life:
She had to be Milked by a Man and his Wife.

The Sloth

In moving-slow he has no Peer.
You ask him something in his Ear,
He thinks about it for a Year;

And, then, before he says a Word
There, upside down (unlike a Bird),
He will assume that you have Heard —

A most Ex-as-per-at-ing Lug.
But should you call his manner Smug,
He'll sigh and give his Branch a Hug;

Then off again to Sleep he goes,
Still swaying gently by his Toes,
And you just *know* he knows he knows.

The Kitty-Cat Bird

The Kitty-Cat Bird, he sat on a Fence.
Said the Wren, your Song isn't worth 10¢.
You're a Fake, you're a Fraud, you're a Hor-rid Pretense!
   — Said the Wren to the Kitty-Cat Bird.

You've too many Tunes, and none of them Good:
I wish you would act like a bird really should,
Or stay by yourself down deep in the wood,
   — Said the Wren to the Kitty-Cat Bird.

You mew like a Cat, you grate like a Jay:
You squeak like a Mouse that's lost in the Hay,
I wouldn't be You for even a day,
   — Said the Wren to the Kitty-Cat Bird.

The Kitty-Cat Bird, he moped and he cried.
Then a real cat came with a Mouth so Wide,
That the Kitty-Cat Bird just hopped inside;
"At last I'm myself!" — and he up and died
   — Did the Kitty — the Kitty-Cat Bird.

You'd better not laugh; and don't say, "Pooh!"
Until you have thought this Sad Tale through:
Be sure that whatever you are is you
   — Or you'll end like the Kitty-Cat Bird.

JOHNNY MERCER

A Rouse for Stevens

Wallace Stevens, what's he done?
He can play the flitter-flad;
He can see the second sun
Spinning through the lordly cloud.

He's imagination's prince:
He can plink the skitter-bum;
How he rolls the vocables,
Brings the secret — right in Here!

Wallace, Wallace, wo ist er?
Never met him, Dutchman dear;
If I ate and drank like him,
I would be a chanticleer.

(TOGETHER)
Speak it from the face out clearly:
Here's a *mensch* but can sing dandy.
Er ist niemals ausgepoopen,
Altes Wunderkind.

(AUDIENCE)
Roar 'em, whore 'em, cockalorum,
The Muses, they must all adore him,
Wallace Stevens — are we *for* him?
Brother, he's our father!

JOHNNY MERCER
1909–1976

I'm an Old Cowhand

Step aside, you ornery tenderfeet,
Let a big bad buckeroo past.
I'm the toughest hombre you'll ever meet,
Tho' I may be the last.
Yes sir-ree we're a vanishing race,
No sir-ree can't last long.
Step aside, you ornery tenderfeet
While I sing my song.

I'm an old cowhand from the Rio Grande,
But my legs ain't bowed and my cheeks ain't tanned,
I'm a cowboy who never saw a cow,
Never roped a steer 'cause I don't know how,
And I sho' ain't fixin' to start in now.
Yippy-I-O-Ki-Ay, Yippy-I-O-Ki-Ay.

I'm an old cowhand from the Rio Grande,
And I learned to ride 'fore I learned to stand,
I'm a ridin' fool who is up to date,
I know ev'ry trail in the Lone Star State,
'Cause I ride the range in a Ford V Eight.
Yippy-I-O-Ki-Ay, Yippy-I-O-Ki-Ay.

I'm an old cowhand from the Rio Grande,
And I come to town just to hear the band,
I know all the songs that the cowboys know,
'Bout the big corral where the doagies go,
'Cause I learned them all on the radio.
Yippy-I-O-Ki-Ay, Yippy-I-O-Ki-Ay.

I'm an old cowhand from the Rio Grande,
Where the West is wild 'round the borderland,
Where the buffalo roam around the zoo,
And the Indians make you a rug or two,
And the old Bar X is a Bar-B-Q.
Yippy-I-O-Ki-Ay, Yippy-I-O-Ki-Ay.

Jubilation T. Cornpone

When we fought the Yankees and annihilation was near,
Who was there to lead the charge that took us safe to the rear?

> Why it wuz Jubilation T. Cornpone,
> Old "Toot-Your-Own-Horn-pone,"
> Jubilation T. Cornpone,
> A man who knew no fear.

When we almost had 'em but the issue still was in doubt,
Who suggested the retreat that turned it into a rout?

Why it was Jubilation T. Cornpone,
Old "Tattered-and-Torn-pone,"
Jubilation T. Cornpone,
Who kept us hidin' out.

With our ammunition gone and faced with utter defeat,
Who was it that burned the crops and left us nothin' to eat?

Why it wuz Jubilation T. Cornpone,
Old "September-Morn-pone,"
Jubilation T. Cornpone,
The pants blown off his seat.

The Glow-worm

Glow, little glow-worm, fly of fire,
Glow like an incandescent wire,
Glow for the female of the specie,
Turn on the AC and the DC;
This night could use a little brightnin',
Light up, you li'l ol' bug of lightnin',
When you gotta glow, you gotta glow,
Glow, little glow-worm, glow.

Glow, little glow-worm, glow and glimmer,
Swim thru the sea of night, little swimmer;
Thou aeronautical Boll Weevil,
Illuminate yon woods primeval;
See how the shadows deep and darken,
You and your chick should get to sparkin',
I got a gal that I love so,
Glow, little glow-worm, glow.

Glow, little glow-worm, turn the key on,
You are equipped with tail light neon;
You got a cute vest pocket Mazda
Which you can make both slow or "fazda";
I don't know who you took a shine to,
Or who you're out to make a sign to,
I got a gal that I love so,
Glow, little glow-worm,
Put on a show worm,
Glow, little glow-worm, glow.

ELDER OLSON
b. 1909

Childe Roland, etc.

Certainly there was something to their stories:
Something had been at the fields, the pond *was* shaped
Like an enormous footprint; there were the usual signs,
Small herds, snapped trees.
I sat astride my horse in the autumn twilight,
Conscious of looking well; they crowded about me,
Jabbering, gesticulating, spilling out of straw-thatched huts.
Later, outside the tavern, I was shown
A number of women — all, it was said, deflowered.

Well, I set out at once: the approach was sinister,
Full of the usual obstacles; suddenly,
There was the castle. I was just about to knock
— Thunderously, of course — when the door opened.
I think I have never met a more charming person.
True, he was ugly, and — *large*; but he had a manner.
You know how personality makes up for so much!
He gave me cocktails, followed by an excellent supper;
I felt ridiculously clumsy in my clanking armor.
Later, with coffee and brandy, I had the facts.
Land and cattle were his; the people were squatters.
He did not resent the trespassing and depredation,
But thought it a pity they felt so possessive.
He read me his poems, humbly took my suggestions,
Played some things of Chopin's rather well.
I left quite late, somewhat reluctantly,

And went back with the thought of punishing the villagers,
But they had already begun their singing and dancing;
My ears rang with it several miles beyond.
Later, "he had eaten six men"; that very day
I had a little note from him — half invitation,
Half begging the name of a competent attorney.

My armor stands in the hall; I often think of my ancestors.
Was it different for them?
Nowadays, I observe, poetry is chiefly lyrical.

PETER DeVRIES
b. 1910

Beth Appleyard's Verses

Loveliest of Pies

Loveliest of pies, the cherry now
Completes a fine repast;
'Tis not the first I've ordered, lads,
But it will be the last.

For soon they'll slit my trouser-legs
And shave my head, and then
They'll sit me in the chair from which
I'll never rise again.

The lengthy error known as Life
Began in a single cell,
And that is where for luckless lads
It sometimes ends as well.

And so it's down the row I go
With my eternal curse
And that's what comes of reading
Pessimistic verse.

Bacchanal

"Come live with me and be my love,"
    He said, in substance. "There's no vine
We will not pluck the clusters of,
    Or grape we will not turn to wine."

It's autumn of their second year.
    Now he, in seasonal pursuit,
With rich and modulated cheer,
    Brings home the festive purple fruit;

And she, by passion once demented
    — That woman out of Botticelli —
She brews and bottles, unfermented,
    The stupid and abiding jelly.

Psychiatrist

His role is to invert the fairy tale;
   To give the wakeful Beauty sleep,
Change back the charming Prince into a frog,
   Or unmask him as the chimney sweep.
To him at last dear Cinderella,
   And not Rapunzel, must let down her hair,
Yield up the hopeless fetish of the shoe
   And much of what was dreamt below the stair.

Don't ask him tritely can he heal himself.
   Hope rather that his private dream
For living happily forever after
   Be not the fantasy that it may seem:
A village where the hunter's evening stride
   Betrays no more of strutter than of hobbler;
And Cinderella sleeps content beside
   The kind and well-adjusted cobbler.

FRANK LOESSER
b. 1910

Guys and Dolls

When you see a guy reach for stars in the sky,
You can bet that he's doing it for some doll.
When you spot a John waiting out in the rain,
Chances are he's insane as only a John can be for a Jane.
When you meet a gent, paying all kinds of rent
For a flat that could flatten the Taj Mahal,
Call it sad, call it funny,
But it's better than even money
That the guy's only doing it for some doll.

When you see a Joe saving half of his dough,
You can bet there'll be mink in it for some doll.
When a bum buys wine like a bum can't afford,
It's a cinch that the bum is under the thumb of some little broad.
When you meet a mugg lately out of the jug,
And he's still lifting platinum fol-de-rol,
Call it hell, call it heaven,
It's a probable twelve to seven
That the guy's only doing it for some doll.

J. V. CUNNINGHAM
b. 1911

from *Doctor Drink*

3

Lip was a man who used his head.
He used it when he went to bed
With his friend's wife, and with his friend,
With either sex at either end.

4
Epitaph for Someone or Other

Naked I came, naked I leave the scene,
And naked was my pastime in between.

Uncollected Poems and Epigrams

2

Here lies my wife. Eternal peace
Be to us both with her decease.

5

Here lies New Critic who would fox us
With his poetic paradoxes.
Though he lies here rigid and quiet,
If he could speak he would deny it.

9

Bride loved old words, and found her pleasure marred
On the first night, her expectations jarred,
And thirty inches short of being a yard.

RICHARD HARTER FOGLE
b. 1911

A *Hawthorne Garland*
Scarlet Letter

Wrote the clergy: "Our Dear Madame Prynne:
We keep mighty close watch upon sin:
   And we think we had better
   Proclaim by this Letter
Our sense of how Active you've been."

Hester's answer: "Dear Clergy, I say,
This is truly a Red Letter day!
  I accept with elation
  Your certification
That I've finally managed my A."

Pastoral Letter

Dear Mrs. Parishioner Prynne,
While Applauding your efforts to win
  An Award, we confess
  That we couldn't care less
For your quite unoriginal sin.

Ambiguity, Perspicuity

Nat Hawthorne concealed his asperity
By a surface of delicate clarity;
  He produced ambiguity
  In rich superfluity,
And laudably free from vulgarity.

Hawthorne's writing achieved perspicuity,
Continuity, beauty, acuity;
  He won lasting glory
  In romance and story —
Though some have complained of tenuity.

Caution

When Hawthorne inspected a rose,
He would caution it not to suppose
That, though fragrant and sweet,
It was any great treat
To his lofty New-Englandy nose.

Quick, Sir, the Elixir — "Birthmark"

Aylmer banished, with trouble and strife,
A small blotch from the cheek of his wife;
  This little correction
  Worked out to perfection,
And cured the poor girl of her life.

ANONYMOUS*

The Virtues of Carnation Milk

(This quatrain is imagined as the caption under a picture of a rugged-looking cowboy seated upon a bale of hay.)

Carnation Milk is the best in the land;
Here I sit with a can in my hand —
No tits to pull, no hay to pitch,
You just punch a hole in the son of a bitch.

* Reported by David Ogilvy, b. 1911.

JOHN BERRYMAN
1914–1972

Dream Song #4

Filling her compact & delicious body
with chicken páprika, she glanced at me
twice.
Fainting with interest, I hungered back
and only the fact of her husband & four other people
kept me from springing on her

or falling at her little feet and crying
"You are the hottest one for years of night
Henry's dazed eyes
have enjoyed, Brilliance." I advanced upon
(despairing) my spumoni. — Sir Bones: is stuffed,
de world, wif feeding girls.

— Black hair, complexion Latin, jewelled eyes
downcast . . . The slob beside her   feasts . . . What wonders is
she sitting on, over there?
The restaurant buzzes. She might as well be on Mars.
Where did it all go wrong? There ought to be a law against Henry.
— Mr. Bones: there is.

American Lights, Seen from Off Abroad

Blue go up & blue go down
to light the lights of Dollartown

Nebuchadnezzar had it so good?
wink the lights of Hollywood

I never think, I have so many things,
flash the lights of Palm Springs

I worry like a madwoman over all the world,
affirm the lights, all night, at State

I have no plans, I mean well,
swear the lights of Georgetown

I have the blind staggers
call the lights of Niagara

We shall die in a palace
shout the black lights of Dallas

I couldn't dare less, my favorite son,
fritter the lights of Washington

(I have a brave old So-and-So,
chuckle the lights of Independence, Mo.)

I cast a shadow, what I mean,
blurt the lights of Abilene

Both his sides are all the same
glows his grin with all but shame

He can do nothing night & day,
wonder his lovers. So they say.

"Basketball in outer space"
sneers the White New Hampshire House

I'll have a smaller one, later, Mac,
hope the strange lights of Cal Tech

I love you one & all, hate shock,
bleat the lights of Little Rock

I cannot quite focus
cry the lights of Las Vegas

I am a maid of shots & pills,
swivel the lights of Beverly Hills

Proud & odd, you give me vertigo,
fly the lights of San Francisco

I am all satisfied love & chalk,
mutter the great lights of New York

I have lost your way
say the white lights of Boston

Here comes a scandal to blight you to bed.
Here comes a cropper. That's what I said.

GEORGE HITCHCOCK
b. 1914

Three Found Poems

1. *Distinguishing Ru from Chu*

(poem assembled from the review questions in
"Barnes Shorthand Lessons," St. Louis, 1885)

Give the sounds of the curved mated Phonographs.
Give the sounds of the straight mated Phonographs.
Name the six vertical Phonographs.

What caution should be observed in writing Lu, Ur, Wu and Yu?
What are the two ways of writing Hu?
How may Ru be distinguished from Chu when alone?

How is Iss joined to a curve?
How is Iss joined to a straight stroke?
What rules apply to Sez, Steh and Ster?

What is the effect of lengthening Emp?
What is the effect of lengthening Ung?
What is the effect of halving a stroke?

When should the Eshun curl be used?
What should you be slow to adopt, and why?
How may a vowel be written when alone?

How long should the ticks be made?
After what stroke is Ul always used?
What are the small final hooks?

2. *The Call of the Eastern Quail*

(poem taken from the examination questions in Agnes Woodward's
"Whistling as an Art," New York, 1923)

What is the hewie chirp?
How written by note?
    What is triple-tonguing?
    The reverse chirp? How expressed?
What are the quittas?

Define the whit-cha.
Define the e-chew.
What is the chut-ee?
How made? How expressed?

Define the ascending and descending yodels,
    dipped yodels and quivers.
What are the two liquid bird figures?

What is the lup-ee?
What is the e-lup?
How made? How expressed?
What is the call of the Eastern Quail?
What is the call of the Western Quail?

With tongue and teeth whistlers
    what can be substituted for
    the yodel, lup, hedala and cudalee?

What is the wave?
On what pulsation do we stop?

3. *What to Say to the Pasha*

(being a dramatic monologue in twelve parts assembled from
the Rev. Anton Tien's "Egyptian, Syrian and North African Hand-book,
A Simple Phrase-book in English and Arabic for the Use of the
Armed Forces and Civilians," exact provenance unknown
but obviously early Kiplingesque)

458

1

Shall I assist you to alight?
Procure for me a little milk and honey
Pitch my tent and spread out my carpet
The wind is keen today
We may have a storm tonight
It lightens
It thunders

The air is very temperate
The trees are beginning to be covered with leaves
Autumn is the season for fruit
The sky begins to get cloudy
The nights are short and the days are long
The snow is fast melting from the ground
The enemy has advanced as far as Kafr-dawar
Of what advantage will this be to me?

2

Whose?
Not yet
We want
I will give you
Wait patiently
Leave it alone
Go away
Why are you here?

3

In which direction is the wind?
It is an easterly wind
It is a westerly wind
It is a northerly wind
It is a southerly wind

I have been very much occupied

4

How many men has the Pasha?

5

Is the proof of this news strong?
They are hidden behind the mound
They are advancing from the rear

Be quiet
Don't make a noise
It seems that the enemy is restless

6
Do not the mosquitoes trouble you?

7
Undo it
Tie it up
Turn it over
I hope you are better
Is it not so?

8
What is your name?
Who are you?
I am a Bedouin
We are Bedouins
What are you doing here?
We have come to fight and to loot

I am anxious to return to the camp

9
It is enough
How far is it from this place?
Do me the favour
Do not forget
How do you do?
Mind your business
It is painful
This is painful

10
Bring in the rebels
Tie their hands and feet
You have done it well
Joseph, bring in the dinner
Will you please to sit next to the lady?

11
I am wounded
    I am shot

Shot in my arm
Shot in my leg
Shot in my foot
Shot in my chest
Shot in my head

Bind up my wound
Give me something to drink, for
I am thirsty

12
Have pity on me
Spare my life

I surrender myself

RANDALL JARRELL
1914–1965

The Blind Sheep

The Sheep is blind; a passing Owl,
A surgeon of some local skill,
Has undertaken, for a fee,
The cure. A stump, his surgery,
Is licked clean by a Cat; his tools —
A tooth, a thorn, some battered nails —
He ranges by a shred of sponge
And he is ready to begin.
Pushed forward through the gaping crowd,
"Wait," bleats the Sheep; "is all prepared?"
The Owl lists forceps, scalpel, lancet —
The old Sheep interrupts his answer;
"These lesser things may all be well;
But tell me, friend — how goes the world?"
The Owl says blankly: "You will find it
Goes as it went ere you were blinded."
"What?" cries the Sheep. "Then take your fee
But cure some other fool, not me:
To witness that enormity
I would not give a blade of grass.
I am a Sheep, and not an Ass."

WILLIAM STAFFORD
b. 1914

Religion Back Home

1) When God's parachute failed,
about the spring of 1945,
the sky in Texas jerked open
and we all sailed easily
into this new strange harness on the stars.

2) The minister smoked,
and he drank,
and there was that woman in the choir,
but what really finished him —
he wore spats.

3) A Short Review of *Samson Agonistes*
Written for Miss Arrington's Class
in Liberal High School

Our Father Who art in Heaven
can lick their Father Who art in Heaven.

4) When my little brother chanted,
"In 1492 Jesus crossed the ocean blue,"
Mother said, "Bob, you mean
Columbus crossed the ocean blue."
And he said, "I always did get
them two guys mixed up."

TENNESSEE WILLIAMS
b. 1914

Carrousel Tune

Turn again, turn again, turn once again;
the freaks of the cosmic circus are men.

We are the gooks and geeks of creation;
Believe-It-or-Not is the name of our star.
Each of us here thinks the other is queer
and no one's mistaken since all of us are!

Turn again, turn again, turn once again;
the freaks of the cosmic circus are men.

We sweat and we fume in a four-cornered room
and love is the reason. But what does love do?
It gives willy-nilly to poor silly Billy
the chance to discover what daddy went through.

Turn again, turn again, turn once again;
the freaks of the cosmic circus are men.

We may hum and hop like a musical top
or stop like a clock that's run down,
but why be downhearted, the season's just started,
and new shows are coming to town!

Turn again, turn again, turn once again;
the freaks of the cosmic circus are men.

Sugar in the Cane

I'm red pepper in a shaker,
Bread that's waitin' for the baker.
I'm sweet sugar in the cane,
Never touched except by rain.
If you touched me God save you,
These summer days are hot and blue.

I'm potatoes not yet mashed,
I'm a check that ain't been cashed.
I'm a window with a blind,
Can't see what goes on behind.
If you did, God save your soul!
These winter nights are blue and cold!

Kitchen Door Blues

My old lady died of a common cold.
She smoked cigars and was ninety years old.
She was thin as paper with the ribs of a kite,
And she flew out the kitchen door one night.

Now I'm no younger'n the old lady was,
When she lost gravitation, and I smoke cigars.
I feel sort of peaked, an' I look kinda pore,
So for God's sake, lock that kitchen door!

Gold Tooth Blues

Now there's many fool things a woman will do
To catch a man's eye, she'll wear a tight shoe,
She'll wear a light dress and catch a bad cold
And have a tooth pulled for a tooth of gold.

I'm a gold tooth woman with the gold tooth blues
'Cause a gold tooth makes a woman look old!

Now gold in the bank is a wonderful thing,
And a woman looks nice with a nice gold ring,
But, honey, take a tip, and the tip ain't cold,
Your mouth's no place to carry your gold!

I'm a gold tooth woman with the gold tooth blues
'Cause a gold tooth makes a woman look old!

Some late Sunday mawnin' when you're still in the hay
And you want a little lovin', your sweet man'll say,
With a look that'll turn your heart's blood cold,
Woman, that gold tooth makes you look old!

I'm a gold tooth woman with the gold tooth blues
'Cause a gold tooth makes a woman look old!

When your man's out of money and he must have a drink,
He'll sneak up behind you at the kitchen sink,
And before you can holler, I'm telling the truth,
He'll brain you with a black-jack and pull your gold tooth!

I'm a gold tooth woman with the gold tooth blues
'Cause a gold tooth makes a woman look old!

REUEL DENNEY

b. 1915

Fixer of Midnight

He went to fix the awning,
Fix the roping,
In the middle of the night,
On the porch;
He went to fix the awning,
In pajamas went to fix it,
Fix the awning,
In the middle of the moonlight,
On the porch;
He went to fix it yawning;
The yawing of his awning
In the moonlight
Was his problem of the night;
It was knocking,
And he went to fix its flight.
He went to meet the moonlight
In the porch-night
Where the awning was up dreaming
Dark and light;
It was shadowy and seeming;
In the night, the unfixed awning,
In his nightmare,
Had been knocking dark and bright.
It seemed late
To stop it in its dark careening.
The yawner went to meet it,
Meet the awning,
By the moon of middle night,
On his porch;
And he went to fix it right.

JOHN CIARDI
b. 1916

Ballad of the Icondic

It was the year the ICONDIC
    was sighted (hush, my pet,
for it has slewn the GAWNOSE WATT
    and it is slewing yet).

It was THEOLGARD shook its head.
    THENOOGARD likewise its.
And having knit a BITTAPPEASE
    they raveled it to snits.

"Now what shall save us?" ICONDIC
    cried out, as if in thought.
"O gird about your gat, set out
    and slew the GAWNOSE WATT!"

The GAWNOSE WATT it slew and slew.
    Was never seen such slewage.
And GAWNOSE WATT went up the spout.
    And GAWNOSE WATT went down the sewerage.

I only know the ICONDIC
    slewed on and still is slewing.
(Now sleep, and may you dream just what
    the GAWNOSE WATT was doing.)

Goodnight

An oyster that went to bed x-million years ago,
tucked itself into a sand-bottom, yawned (so to speak),
and woke a mile high in the Grand Canyon of the Colorado.

If I am not here for breakfast, geologize at will.

Dawn of the Space Age

First a monkey, then a man.
Just the way the world began.

To a Reviewer Who Admired My Book

Few men in any age have second sight.
But never doubt *your* gift. You are right! You are right!

On Evolution

Pithecanthropus erectus,
could he see us, would reject us.

PETER VIERECK
b. 1916

1912*–1952, Full Cycle

I. *Love Song of Prufrock Junior*

Must all successful rebels grow
From toreador to Sacred Cow?
What cults he slew, his cult begot.
"In my beginning," said his Scot,
"My end;" and aging eagles know
That 1912 was long ago.
Today the women come and go
Talking of T. S. Eliot.

II. *Inscribed for Your Bedside "Glossary of the New Criticism"*

Here's the eighth form of ambiguity:
The *new* philistia loves "obscurity," —
And only we still dare to hate it
Because a *texte* without a Muse in
Is but a snore and an allusion.
Well then, let's turn the tables hard:
The snobs all snubbed, the baiters baited,
The explicators explicated,
And avant-garde the new rearguard.

---

* Events of 1912, the key year: *New Age* starts publishing Hulme's essays; Imagist nucleus founded (Pound, H. D., Aldington); *Poetry: A Magazine of Verse* founded by Harriet Monroe (to whom Pound in 1914 sends Eliot's "Love Song of J. Alfred Prufrock," written 1910–11); October 1912, the American-verse number of Harold Monro's *Poetry Review* (W. C. Williams, Pound); symbolic clash of the simultaneous 1912 publication of *Georgian Poetry* and Pound's *Ripostes*.

III. *From the Sublime to the Meticulous in Four Stages*

DANTE   We were God's poets.
BURNS   We were the people's poets.
MALLARMÉ   We were poet's poets.
TODAY (preening himself)   Ah, but *we* are critic's poets.

IV. *Epitaph for the Nouveaux New Critics,*
Hugh Kenner, e Tutti Questi

Cliché is dead, long live cliché,
And in old fields new Georgians play.
O miglior fabbro and O mandarin,
You who skinned Georgians like a tangerine,
Two Hercules who on your natal day
Strangled these snakes of cliché-pandering,
These same that now through backstairs wander in:
Let not (while death-knells from Kinkanja[1] ring)
The pedant town of Alexander in.
From kitsch the nineteenth century banned her in,
You freed our Muse. For what? Was Queen Victoria
Primmer than précieux new "Prohibitoria"[2]?
Loving your ART and not your fleas, we pray:
May time protect you from your protégés.

Time's up when pupils' pupils school the school.
Cow? Bad enough! But sacred — calf?
Now that the cup of insolence is full, —
By God, who'll start a brandnew Nineteen Twelve?

1. Cf. not *The Golden Bough* but *The Cocktail Party*, American edition, p. 174.
2. Cf. Louis Rubin in *Hopkins Review*, summer 1950: "He has twice criticized the award of the 1949 Bollingen Prize to Pound's *Pisan Cantos*, on grounds both of form and content. Either he must repent, and publicly, or resign himself to a prominent and permanent position in the Index Prohibitorium of the New Criticism."

WILLIAM JAY SMITH
b. 1918

Dachshunds

"The deer and the dachshund are one."
WALLACE STEVENS, *"Loneliness in Jersey City"*

The Dachshund leads a quiet life
Not far above the ground;

He takes an elongated wife,
    They travel all around.

They leave the lighted metropole;
    Nor turn to look behind
Upon the headlands of the soul,
    The tundras of the mind.

They climb together through the dusk
    To ask the Lost-and-Found
For information on the stars
    Not far above the ground.

The Dachshunds seem to journey on:
    And following them, I
Take up my monocle, the Moon,
    And gaze into the sky.

Pursuing them with comic art
    Beyond a cosmic goal,
I see the whole within the part,
    The part within the whole;

See planets wheeling overhead,
    Mysterious and slow,
While Morning buckles on his red,
    And on the Dachshunds go.

Random Generation of English Sentences
or, The Revenge of the Poets

Dr. Louis T. Milic of the Columbia University department of English
expressed a note of caution about computers. He said that attention
might be diverted to secondary work and that the nature of literature
might be distorted if computers changed matters that were essentially
qualitative into a quantitative form.

But Professor Milic admitted that computers are improving — perhaps
even to the point of writing poetry as good as that composed by a

drunken poet. He cited a sentence generated by a group from the Massachusetts Institute of Technology working with a computer, and contained in a study called, "Random Generation of English Sentences."

The sentence is: "What does she put four whistles beside heated rugs for?"

The New York Times, September 10, 1964

What does she put four whistles beside heated rugs for?
The answer is perfectly clear:
Four drunken poets might reel through the woodwork
And leer.

Four drunken poets might lurch toward the heated rugs,
Bearing buckets of ice,
And say: "Madam, it's colder than your computer may think;
Our advice

Is to pick up your whistles and fold your tents like the Arabs
And silently steal — or fly —
Where all your hot-rugged brothers and sisters are headed.
Madam, good-bye!"

WILLIAM COLE
b. 1919

Marriage Couplet

I think of my wife, and I think of Lot,
And I think of the lucky break he got.

Mutual Problem

Said Jerome K. Jerome to Ford Madox Ford,
"There's something, old boy, that I've always abhorred:
When people address me and call me 'Jerome,'
Are they being standoffish, or too much at home?"

Said Ford, "I agree;
It's the same thing with me."

Poor Kid

Higgledy, piggledy
Gloria Vanderbilt
Said to her husband, "I've
Such rotten luck!

Painting and poetry,
Acting and book reviews,
Multidiversity —
Can't make a buck!"

Mysterious East

Yamaha yamaha
Yukio Mishima
Mourned for the militant
Days that were dead;

So he dispatched himself
Hari-karistically,
Then an old friend kindly
Chopped off his head.

What a Friend We Have in Cheeses!
or Sing a Song of Liederkranz

Poets have been mysteriously silent on the subject of cheese.
G. K. CHESTERTON

What a friend we have in cheeses!
For no food more subtly pleases,
Nor plays so grand a gastronomic part;
Cheese imported — not domestic —
For we all get indigestic
From the pasteurizer's Kraft and sodden art.

No poem we shall ever see is
Quite as lovely as a Brie is,
For "the queen of cheese" is what they call the Brie;
If you pay sufficient money
You will get one nice and runny,
And you'll understand what foods these morsels be!

How we covet all the skills it
Takes in making Chèvre or Tilset,
But if getting basic Pot Cheese is your aim,
Take some simple curds and wheys, a
Bit of rennet — Lo! you've Käse!
(Which is what, in German, is a cheese's name.)

Good lasagna, it's a-gotta
Mozzarella and Ricotta
And a lotta freshly grated Parmesan;
With the latter *any* pasta
Will be eaten up much faster,
For with Parmesan an added charm is on.

Ask Ignacio Silone
What he thinks of Provolone,
And the very word will set his eyes aflame;
Then go ask the bounteous Gina
Her reaction to Fontina —
If you'll raise your eyes you'll see she feels the same.

A Pont-l'Evêque *au point!* What ho!
How our juices all will flow!
But don't touch a Pont-l'Evêque beyond that stage,
For what you'll have, you'll surely find
Is just an over-fragrant rind —
There's no benefit to this *fromage* from age.

Claret, dear, not Coca Cola,
When you're having Gorgonzola —
Be particular to serve the proper wines;
Likewise pick a Beaune, not Coke for
Pointing up a Bleu or Roquefort —
Bless the products of the bovines and the vines!

Ave Gouda! Ave Boursault!
Ave Oka even more so!
Ave Neufchâtel, *Saluto* Port Salut!
And another thing with cheeses —
Every allied prospect pleases —
Ah cheese blintzes! Ah Welsh rabbit! Ah fondue!

And we all know that "Say cheese" is
How a cameraman unfreezes
A subject in a stiff, or shy, or dour way;
There's no other food so useful,
So bring on a whole cabooseful
Of the stuff of life! The cheeses of the gourmet!

LAWRENCE FERLINGHETTI
b. 1919

Underwear

I didn't get much sleep last night
thinking about underwear
Have you ever stopped to consider
underwear in the abstract
When you really dig into it
some shocking problems are raised
Underwear is something
we all have to deal with
Everyone wears
some kind of underwear
Even Indians
wear underwear
Even Cubans
wear underwear
The Pope wears underwear I hope
Underwear is worn by Negroes
The Governor of Louisiana
wears underwear
I saw him on TV
He must have had tight underwear
He squirmed a lot
Underwear can really get you in a bind
Negroes often wear
white underwear
which may lead to trouble
You have seen the underwear ads
for men and women
so alike but so different
Women's underwear holds things up
Men's underwear holds things down

Underwear is one thing
men and women have in common
Underwear is all we have between us
You have seen the three-color pictures
with crotches encircled
to show the areas of extra strength
and three-way stretch
promising full freedom of action
Don't be deceived
It's all based on the two-party system
which doesn't allow much freedom of choice
the way things are set up
America in its Underwear
struggles thru the night
Underwear controls everything in the end
Take foundation garments for instance
They are really fascist forms
of underground government
making people believe
something but the truth
telling you what you can or can't do
Did you ever try to get around a girdle
Perhaps Non-Violent Action
is the only answer
Did Gandhi wear a girdle?
Did Lady Macbeth wear a girdle?
Was that why Macbeth murdered sleep?
And that spot she was always rubbing —
Was it really in her underwear?
Modern anglosaxon ladies
must have huge guilt complexes
always washing and washing and washing
Out damned spot — rub don't blot —
Underwear with spots very suspicious
Underwear with bulges very shocking
Underwear on clothesline a great flag of freedom
Someone has escaped his Underwear
May be naked somewhere
Help!
But don't worry
Everybody's still hung up in it
There won't be no real revolution
And poetry still the underwear of the soul

And underwear still covering
a multitude of faults
in the geological sense —
strange sedimentary stones, inscrutable cracks!
And that only the beginning
For does not the body stay alive
after death
and still need its underwear
or outgrow it
some organs said to reach full maturity
only after the head stops holding them back?
If I were you I'd keep aside
an oversize pair of winter underwear
Do not go naked into that good night
And in the meantime
keep calm and warm and dry
No use stirring ourselves up prematurely
"over Nothing"
Move forward with dignity
hand in vest
Don't get emotional
And death shall have no dominion
There's plenty of time my darling
Are we not still young and easy
Don't shout

MAX SHULMAN
b. 1919

Honest Abe Lincoln*
(tune: "Old Black Joe")

I'm Honest Abe,
With whiskers on my chin . . .
I freed the slabe,
My face is . . . on . . . the . . . fin . . .

I nev-er tole
No-thin but . . . the . . . truth . . .
Howcome you pulled the trigger on me,
John . . . Wilkes . . . Booth?

* Recorded in William Styron's novel *Set This House on Fire*.

HOWARD NEMEROV
b. 1920

Epigrams

I Invocation

Wasp, climbing the window pane
And falling back on the sill —
What buzz in the brain
And tremor of the will,
What climbing anger you excite
Where my images brim and spill
In failures of the full light.

II Lucilius

Lucilius the poet has informed me,
Defending his somewhat pedantic songs,
That "Memory is the Mother of the Muses."
May he continue making love to the mother.

III An Old Story

They gathered shouting crowds along the road
To praise His Majesty's satin and cloth-of-gold,
    But "Naked! Naked!" the children cried.

Now when the gaudy clothes ride down the street
No child is found sufficiently indiscreet
    To whisper "No Majesty's inside."

IV Mythological Beast

Four-footed, silent, resilient, feathered,
It waits by daylight, standing alert and tethered.
Come night, it bears me through the jungle of
The images, where are victims enough.

But this fat beast, responsive to my weight,
I know for a wild hunter grown to hate
Patiently the rider in his high seat,
Blind rider whom it will pluck down and eat.

V *The Hunt Goes By*

The dogs ran in the woods today,
Their note sounded from far away.
Tonight the shallow snowfall clears
The dogs' track and the deer's.

VI *Political Reflexion*

loquitur the sparrow in the zoo.

No bars are set too close, no mesh too fine
To keep me from the eagle and the lion,
Whom keepers feed that I may freely dine.
This goes to show that if you have the wit
To be small, common, cute, and live on shit,
Though the cage fret kings, you may make free with it.

VII *A Spiral Shell*

A twist along the spine begins the form
And hides itself inside a twisted house
Which turns once wide and slow, then speeds to close
Whirled on a point. Divine and crippled norm,
O Vulcan of the secret forging flame!
A hollow life is beautiful with shame.

VIII *April*

Today was a day of cold spring showers
Between bouts of sun; the fine, literary weather
We used to have so often, some Boris
        or other bidding farewell
To Nastasya; Lisbeth, Priscilla,
        Jane hastening back to the vicarage
Lest their taffeta crumple; a young man and a bicycle
Posed on the puddled lane. These days are rare lately,
And I remember college girls who declared
They loved to walk bare-headed in the rain.

IX *Absent-minded Professor*

This lonely figure of not much fun
Strayed out of folklore fifteen years ago
Forever. Now on an autumn afternoon,
While the leaves drift past the office window,

His bright replacement, present-minded, stays
At the desk correcting papers, nor ever grieves
For the silly scholar of the bad old days,
Who'd burn the papers and correct the leaves.

HOWARD MOSS
b. 1922

Cats and Dogs

In Pusseyville, where pussies live,
The hangdog dogs on the dog days
Would disappear. They'd fade into the hills,
Lounge to the garbage heaps, slouch on quais,

Down in the dumps at the docks. A cat,
Real cool, I knew, would sip iced tea
Laced with a bit of barbiturate,
An illustrated dog book on her knee,

And say, "For no amount of scratch
Will dogs by day broach my backyard.
Pusseyville for pussies!" That old wretch!
When night had turned its black ace card,

What matings as the fur flew, yowl and bark,
Above the radio's blurred monologues.
And visitors would say, who risked the dark,
"In Pusseyville, it's raining cats and dogs!"

ALAN DUGAN
b. 1923

On a Seven-Day Diary

Oh I got up and went to work
and worked and came back home
and ate and talked and went to sleep.
Then I got up and went to work
and worked and came back home
from work and ate and slept.

Then I got up and went to work
and worked and came back home
and ate and watched a show and slept.
Then I got up and went to work
and worked and came back home
and ate steak and went to sleep.
Then I got up and went to work
and worked and came back home
and ate and fucked and went to sleep.
Then it was Saturday, Saturday, Saturday!
Love must be the reason for the week!
We went shopping! I saw clouds!
The children explained everything!
I could talk about the main thing!
What did I drink on Saturday night
that lost the first, best half of Sunday?
The last half wasn't worth this "word."
Then I got up and went to work
and worked and came back home
from work and ate and went to sleep,
refreshed but tired by the weekend.

ANTHONY HECHT
b. 1923

The Dover Bitch

So there stood Matthew Arnold and this girl
With the cliffs of England crumbling away behind them,
And he said to her, "Try to be true to me,
And I'll do the same for you, for things are bad
All over, etc., etc."
Well now, I knew this girl. It's true she had read
Sophocles in a fairly good translation
And caught that bitter allusion to the sea,
But all the time he was talking she had in mind
The notion of what his whiskers would feel like
On the back of her neck. She told me later on
That after a while she got to looking out
At the lights across the channel, and really felt sad,
Thinking of all the wine and enormous beds
And blandishments in French and the perfumes.

And then she got really angry. To have been brought
All the way down from London, and then be addressed
As a sort of mournful cosmic last resort
Is really tough on a girl, and she was pretty.
Anyway, she watched him pace the room
And finger his watch-chain and seem to sweat a bit,
And then she said one or two unprintable things.
But you mustn't judge her by that. What I mean to say is,
She's really all right. I still see her once in a while
And she always treats me right. We have a drink
And I give her a good time, and perhaps it's a year
Before I see her again, but there she is,
Running to fat, but dependable as they come.
And sometimes I bring her a bottle of *Nuit d'Amour*.

Improvisations on Aesop

1   It was a tortoise aspiring to fly
    That murdered Aeschylus. All men must die.

2   The crocodile rends man and beast to death
    And has St. Francis' birds to pick his teeth.

3   Lorenzo sponsored artists, and the ant
    Must save to give the grasshopper a grant.

4   The blind man bears the lame, who gives him eyes;
    Only the weak make common enterprise.

5   Frogs into bulls, sows' ears into silk purses,
    These are our hopes in youth, in age our curses.

6   Spare not the rod, lest thy child be undone,
    And at the gallows cry, "Behold thy son."

7   The Fox and Buddha put away their lust;
    "Sour grapes!" they cry, "All but the soul is dust!"

8   An ass may look at an angel, Balaam was shown;
    Cudgel thy wits, and leave thine ass alone.

9   Is not that pastoral instruction sweet
    Which says who shall be eaten, who shall eat?

ANTHONY HECHT

Firmness

Higgledy-piggledy
Mme. de Maintenon*
Shouted, "Up yours!" when ap-
Proached for the rent,

And, in her anger, pro-
Ceeded to demonstrate,
Iconographically,
Just what she meant.

* "On the King's death she retired altogether to St. Cyr. It is surprising that the King left
her almost nothing; he simply recommended her to the care of the Duke of Orleans."
                                                    VOLTAIRE, *The Age of Louis XIV*

From the Grove Press

Higgledy-piggledy
Ralph Waldo Emerson
Wroth at Bostonian,
Cowardly hints,

Wrote an unprintable
Epithalamion
Based on a volume of
Japanese prints.

Vice

Higgledy-piggledy
Thomas Stearns Eliot
Wrote dirty limericks
Under the rose,

Using synecdoches,
Paranomasias,
Zeugmas, and rhymes he de-
Plored in his prose.

NORMAN MAILER
b. 1923

Devils

One of us
will
be
better
looking
when it's
all
over.

Babes,
you got
nostrils
like
devil's feet

LOUIS SIMPSON
b. 1923

New Lines for Cuscuscaraway
and Mirza Murad Ali Beg

". . . the particular verse we are going to get
will be cheerful, dry and sophisticated."   T. E. HULME

O amiable prospect!
O kingdom of heaven on earth!
I saw Mr. Eliot leaning over a fence
Like a cheerful embalmer,

And two little Indians with black umbrellas
Seeking admission,
And I was rapt in a song
Of *sophist*ication.
O City of God!
Let us be thoroughly dry.
Let us sing a new song unto the Lord,
A song of exclusion.
For it is not so much a matter of being chosen
As of not being excluded.
I will sing unto the Lord
In a voice that is cheerfully dry.

On the Lawn at the Villa

On the lawn at the villa —
That's the way to start, eh, reader?
We know where we stand — somewhere expensive —
You and I *imperturbes*, as Walt would say,
Before the diversions of wealth, you and I *engagés*.

On the lawn at the villa
Sat a manufacturer of explosives,
His wife from Paris,
And a young man named Bruno,

And myself, being American,
Willing to talk to the malefactors,
The manufacturer of explosives, and so on,
But somehow superior. By that I mean democratic.
It's complicated, being an American,
Having the money and the bad conscience, both at the same time.
Perhaps, after all, this is not the right subject for a poem.

We were all sitting there paralyzed
In the hot Tuscan afternoon,
And the bodies of the machine-gun crew were draped over the balcony.
So we sat there all afternoon.

EDWARD GOREY
b. 1925

There was a young woman named Plunnery

There was a young woman named Plunnery
Who rejoiced in the practice of gunnery,
   Till one day unobservant,
   She blew up a servant,
And was forced to retire to a nunnery.

Some Harvard men, stalwart and hairy

Some Harvard men, stalwart and hairy,
Drank up several bottles of sherry;
   In the Yard around three
   They were shrieking with glee:
"Come on out, we are burning a fairy!"

The babe, with a cry brief and dismal

The babe, with a cry brief and dismal,
Fell into the water baptismal;
   Ere they'd gathered its plight,
   It had sunk out of sight,
For the depth of the font was abysmal.

A lady who signs herself "Vexed"

A lady who signs herself "Vexed"
Writes to say she believes she's been hexed:
   "I don't mind my shins
   Being stuck full of pins,
But I feel I am coming unsexed."

From the bathing machine came a din

From the bathing machine came a din
As of jollification within;
   It was heard far and wide,
   And the incoming tide
Had a definite flavour of gin.

CAROLYN KIZER
b. 1925

One to Nothing

The bibulous eagle behind me at the ball game:
"Shucks a'mighty!" coming through the rye
And Seven-Up, "I didn't mean to kick you, lady.
When you go to the Eagles' convention, you just *go!*"
Then he needles the batter from Sacramento:
"Too much ego!" he yells. "The old ego curse,
That'll hex him. The old ego never fails.
See?" he says to his phlegmatic friend,
"The bastard fanned!" And "Shucks a'mighty!"
Says again, an American from an English novel,
Named Horace or Homer, a strange colonial bird,
A raw provincial, with his outmoded slang.

"Say!" he cries to his friend, "just now I opened
One eye, saw the catcher, then the batter
In a little circle. And everything went brown.
What happened?" "*Nothing!*" says his friend.
He leans beside me, proffers the open pint.
My ego spurns him. "Fly away!" I say
To the badge on his breast. Eagle flaps down,
Confides in the man on first: "Just once a year
I have fun — see? — at the Eagles' convention.
Later I meet the other dignitaries
At the hotel. Forgive me. I'm from a small town."
He sighs, puts his head in the lap of his friend,

Listens to the portable radio, as the announcer
Makes sense of a blurry ball game
When batters turn brown, curl at the edges,
Fan and fan, like girls in early English novels,
And you can't tell the players, even with a program.
The count is two and one. We hear the *crack!*
Bat skids across the grass. The runner's on!
But eagle sleeps; he dreams away the ball game.
The dozen wasted hits, the double-plays
Are lost on him, as we lose, by one run.
Having his inning curled in a little circle,
He emerges, sucks his bottle; his badge mislaid

In the last of the ninth. We surge to the exits
While this bird claws among the peanut shells
In search of his ego. Carry him, friend,
To the dignitaries, to the eagle's aerie,
Where his mate will hone her talons on his breast.
As D. H. Lawrence wished, he has cracked the shell
Of his ego, but devoured it like a nut
Washed down with rye. And he finds oblivion
Like the lost hero of a Modern English Novel.
What happens? Nothing. Even the brilliant infield
Turns brown. Lights out. The circle fades below.
Shucks a'mighty. If you're an eagle, you just go.

KENNETH KOCH
b. 1925

A Poem of the Forty-eight States

1

O Kentucky! my parents were driving
Near blue grass when you became
For me the real contents of a glass
Of water also the first nozzle of a horse
The bakery truck floating down the street
The young baboon woman walking without a brace
Over a fiord.

The electric chair steamed lightly, then touched
Me. I drove, upward,
Into the hills of Montana. My pony!
Here you are coming along with your master!
Yet I am your master! You're wearing my sweater.
O pony, my pony!

As in a dream I was waiting to be seventh
To smile at my brothers in the happy state of Idaho
Each and every one of them condemned to the electric chair!
What have we done? Is it a crime
To shoe horses? Beside a lemon-yellow stream
There seemed to be compact bassoons,
And I was happy and a crackerjack.

My stovepipe hat! Perhaps you think I am Uncle Sam?
No, I am the State of Pennsylvania. . . .
O hills! I remember writing to a city
So as to be contented with my name
Returning in the mails near the mark "Pennsylvania"!

"Somewhere over that hill is Georgia."
What romance there was for me in the words the old man said!
I wanted to go, but was afraid to wander very far.
Then he said, "I will take you in my wagon of hay."
And so we rode together into the Peach State.
I will never forget that day, not so long as I live,
I will never forget the first impressions I had in Georgia!

2

In Zanesville, Ohio, they put a pennant up,
And in Waco, Texas, men stamped in the streets,
And the soldiers were coughing on the streetcar in Minneapolis,
    Minnesota.
In Minocqua, Wisconsin, the girls kissed each other and laughed,
The poison was working in Monroe, Illinois,
And in Stephanie, New Hampshire, burning fragments were thrown up.

It was the day of the States, and from Topeka, Kansas,
To Lumberville, New York, trees were being struck
Down so they could put the platforms up. However I lay struck
By sunlight on the beach at Waikiki, Hawaii . . .
Why can't Hawaii be one of the United States?
Nothing is being celebrated here; yet the beaches are covered with
    sun . . .

Florida, Vermont, Alabama, Mississippi!
I guess that I will go back to the United States.
Dear friend, let's pack our bags and climb upon the steamer!
Do not forget the birds you have bought in the jolly land of France,
They are red white orange yellow green and pink and they sing so
    sweetly,
They will make music to us upon the tedious ocean voyage.

3

Tedious! How could I have said such a thing?
O sea, you are more beautiful than any state!
You are fuller and bluer and more perfect than the most perfect action.

What is a perfect action?
In the streets of Kokomo a cheer goes up,
And the head of the lion is cursed by a thousand vicissitudes.

Indiana! it is so beautiful to have tar in it!
How wonderful it is to be back on a trolley car, ding dong ding!
I think I will wander into the barbershop and get my hair cut!
Just hear the slice of the scissors, look at the comb!
Now to be once more out in the streets of Indiana
With my hair much shorter, with my neck smelling of talcum powder!
O lucky streetcar wires to be able to look at me, and through whom I
    can see the sun!

I did not know there was so much sun in North Dakota!
But the old man who is telling me about it nods his head and says yes.
I believe him because my skin is peeling. Now I see people going to the
    voting booth.
The voting wagon is red and wooden, it stands on wheels where it is
    anchored to the curb.
I had no idea there were so many old men and old women in North
    Dakota,
But the old man who is explaining things to me says that each is above
    voting age.

4

I cannot remember what all I saw
In northern Florida, all the duck we shot.

You have asked me to recall Illinois,
But all I have is a handful of wrinkles.

Perhaps you would like me to speak of California,
But I hope not, for now I am very close to death.

The children all came down to see the whale in Arkansas,
I remember that its huge body lay attached to the side of the river.

5

O Mississippi joys!
I reckon I am about as big and dead as a whale!
I am slowly sinking down into the green ooze
Of the Everglades, that I feared so much when I was a child!

I have become about as flat as the dust on a baseball diamond
And as empty and clear as the sky when it is just-blue
And you are three, and you stand on the rim of the zone of one of the
United States
And think about the forty-seven others; then in the evening
Air you hear the sound of baseball players, and the splash of canoes!
You yourself would like to play baseball and travel, but you are too
young;
However you look up into the clear flat blue of the evening sky
And vow that you will one day be a traveler like myself,
And wander to all the ends of the earth until you are completely
exhausted,
And then return to Texas or Indiana, whatever state you happen to be
from.
And have your death celebrated by a lavish funeral
Conducted by starlight, with numerous boys and girls reading my poems
aloud!

6

O Charleston! why do you always put me in the mood for kidding?
I am not dead yet, why do you make me say I am?
But I think I am growing older, my shoes are falling off,
I think it must be that my feet are getting thinner and that I am ready
to die.
Here comes my pony from Montana, he is a mere skull and crossbones,
And here is the old man who told me about North Dakota, he is a little
baby,
And here is Illinois, and here is Indiana, I guess they are my favorite
states,
I guess I am dying now in Charleston, South Carolina.
O Charleston, why do you always do this . . . Gasp! Goodbye!

7

In Illinois the trees are growing up
Where he planted them; for he has died.
But I am the one who originally intended to read
You the fast movements. Now we will hear the *Brandenburg
Concertos*. Now we will go up in an
Airplane. Steady . . . The poet of America, Walt Whitman, is dead.
But many other poets have died that are reborn
In their works. He also shall be reborn,
Walt Whitman shall be reborn.

8

I did not understand what you meant by the Hudson Tunnel,
But now I understand, New Jersey, I like it fine,
I like the stifling black smoke and the jagged heave-ho of the trains,
I like the sunlight too at the end of the tunnel, like my rebirth in the
    poems of Kenneth Koch,
I like the way the rosy sunlight streams down upon the silver tracks,
I like the way the travelers awake from their dreams and step upon the
    hard paving stone of the station,
But I reckon what I should like best would be to see Indiana again,
Or Texas or Arkansas, or Alabama, the "Cotton State,"
Or Big Rose Pebble Island off the coast of Maine
Where I used to have so much fun during the summer, cooking and
    kidding and having myself a good time,
I like Pennsylvania too, we could have a lot of fun there,
You and I will go there when Kenneth is dead.

A. R. AMMONS
b. 1926

First Carolina Said-Song
(as told me by an aunt)

In them days
      they won't hardly no way to know if
      somebody way off
      died
         till they'd be
         dead and buried

         and Uncle Jim

hitched up a team of mules to the wagon
and he cracked the whip over them
    and run them their dead-level best
the whole thirty miles to your great grandma's funeral
      down there in
      Green Sea County

      and there come up this
awfulest rainstorm
      you ever saw in your whole life
      and your grandpa

was setting
in a goat-skin bottomed chair

and them mules a-running
and him sloshing round in that chairful of water

till he got scalded
he said

and ev-
ery
anch of skin come off his behind:

we got there just in time to see her buried
in an oak grove up
back of the field:

it's growed over with soapbushes and huckleberries now.

Second Carolina Said-Song

(as told me by a patient, Ward 3-B,
Veterans Hospital, Fayetteville, August 1962)

I was walking down by the old
Santee
River
one evening, foredark
fishing I reckon,

when I come on this
swarm of
bees
lit in the fork of a beech limb
and they werz

jest a swarming:

it was too late to go home

and too far
and brang a bee-gum

      so I waited around
        till the sun went
down,
most dark,

      and cut me off a pinebough,
      dipped it in the river
        and sprankled water

on 'em: settled'em right down,
    good and solid,
about
      a bushel of
      them:

      when it got dark I first cut off
the fork branches and
then cut about four foot back toward
        the trunk

and I
      throwed the limb over my shoulder and
      carried'em home.

Auto Mobile

For the bumps bangs & scratches of
collisive encounters
madam
I through time's ruts and weeds
sought you, metallic, your
stainless steel flivver:
I have banged you, bumped
and scratched, side-swiped,
momocked & begommed you &
your little flivver still
works so well.

Chasm

Put your
self out
and you're
not quite
up to
it or
all in

Needs

I want something suited to my special needs
I want chrome hubcaps, pin-on attachments
and year round use year after year
I want a workhorse with smooth uniform cut,
dozer blade and snow blade & deluxe steering
wheel
I want something to mow, throw snow, tow, and sow with
I want precision reel blades
I want a console-styled dashboard
I want an easy spintype recoil starter
I want combination bevel and spur gears, 14
gauge stamped steel housing and
washable foam element air cleaner
I want a pivoting front axle and extrawide turf tires
I want an inch of foam rubber inside a vinyl
covering
and especially if it's not too much, if I
can deserve it, even if I can't pay for it
I want to mow while riding

Cleavage

Soon as
you stop
having trouble
getting down
to earth
you start
having trouble
getting off
the ground

Coward

Bravery runs in my family.

ROBERT CREELEY
b. 1926

She Went To Stay

Trying to chop mother down is like
hunting deer inside Russia
with phalangists for hat-pins.
I couldn't.

Ballad of the Despairing Husband

My wife and I lived all alone,
contention was our only bone.
I fought with her, she fought with me,
and things went on right merrily.

But now I live here by myself
with hardly a damn thing on the shelf,
and pass my days with little cheer
since I have parted from my dear.

Oh come home soon, I write to her.
Go screw yourself, is her answer.
Now what is that, for Christian word?
I hope she feeds on dried goose turd.

But still I love her, yes I do.
I love her and the children too.
I only think it fit that she
should quickly come right back to me.

Ah no, she says, and she is tough,
and smacks me down with her rebuff.
Ah no, she says, I will not come
after the bloody things you've done.

494

Oh wife, oh wife — I tell you true,
I never loved no one but you.
I never will, it cannot be
another woman is for me.

That may be right, she will say then,
but as for me, there's other men.
And I will tell you I propose
to catch them firmly by the nose.

And I will wear what dresses I choose!
And I will dance, and what's to lose!
I'm free of you, you little prick,
and I'm the one can make it stick.

Was this the darling I did love?
Was this that mercy from above
did open violets in the spring —
and made my own worn self to sing?

She was. I know. And she is still,
and if I love her? then so I will.
And I will tell her, and tell her right . . .

Oh lovely lady, morning or evening or afternoon.
Oh lovely lady, eating with or without a spoon.
Oh most lovely lady, whether dressed or undressed or partly.
Oh most lovely lady, getting up or going to bed or sitting only.

Oh loveliest of ladies, than whom none is more fair, more gracious, more
        beautiful.
Oh loveliest of ladies, whether you are just or unjust, merciful,
        indifferent, or cruel.
Oh most loveliest of ladies, doing whatever, seeing whatever, being
        whatever.
Oh most loveliest of ladies, in rain, in shine, in any weather.

Oh lady, grant me time,
please, to finish my rhyme.

The Man

He hie fie finger
speak in simple sound
feels much better
lying down.

He toes is broken
all he foot go
rotten
now. He look

he hurt bad, see
danger all around he
no see before
come down on him.

ALLEN GINSBERG
b. 1926

Bop Lyrics

When I think of death
  I get a goofy feeling;
Then I catch my breath:
  Zero is appealing,
    Appearances are hazy.
    Smart went crazy,
    Smart went crazy.

·

A flower in my head
  Has fallen through my eye;
Someday I'll be dead:
  I love the Lord on high,
    I wish He'd pull my daisy.
    Smart went crazy,
    Smart went crazy.

·

I asked the lady what's a rose,
   She kicked me out of bed.
I asked the man, and so it goes,
   He hit me on the head.
     Nobody knows,
     Nobody knows,
   At least nobody's said.

•

The time I went to China
To lead the boy scout troops,
They sank my ocean liner,
And all I said was "Oops!"

•

All the doctors think I'm crazy;
The truth is really that I'm lazy:
I made visions to beguile 'em
Till they put me in th'asylum.

•

I'm a pot and God's a potter,
And my head's a piece of putty.
   Ark my darkness,
    Lark my looks,
I'm so lucky to be nutty.

FRANK O'HARA
1926–1966

To the Film Industry in Crisis

Not you, lean quarterlies and swarthy periodicals
with your studious incursions toward the pomposity of ants,
nor you, experimental theatre in which Emotive Fruition
is wedding Poetic Insight perpetually, nor you,
promenading Grand Opera, obvious as an ear (though you
are close to my heart), but you, Motion Picture Industry,
it's you I love!

In times of crisis, we must all decide again and again whom we love.
And give credit where it's due: not to my starched nurse, who taught me
how to be bad and not bad rather than good (and has lately availed
herself of this information), not to the Catholic Church
which is at best an oversolemn introduction to cosmic entertainment,
not to the American Legion, which hates everybody, but to you,
glorious Silver Screen, tragic Technicolor, amorous Cinemascope,
stretching Vistavision and startling Stereophonic Sound, with all
your heavenly dimensions and reverberations and iconoclasms! To
Richard Barthelmess as the "tol'able" boy barefoot and in pants,
Jeanette MacDonald of the flaming hair and lips and long, long neck,
Sue Carroll as she sits for eternity on the damaged fender of a car
and smiles, Ginger Rogers with her pageboy bob like a sausage
on her shuffling shoulders, peach-melba-voiced Fred Astaire of the feet,
Eric von Stroheim, the seducer of mountain-climbers' gasping spouses,
the Tarzans, each and every one of you (I cannot bring myself to prefer
Johnny Weissmuller to Lex Barker, I cannot!), Mae West in a furry sled,
her bordello radiance and bland remarks, Rudolph Valentino of the
                moon,
its crushing passions, and moonlike, too, the gentle Norma Shearer,
Miriam Hopkins dropping her champagne glass off Joel McCrea's yacht
and crying into the dappled sea, Clark Gable rescuing Gene Tierney
from Russia and Allan Jones rescuing Kitty Carlisle from Harpo Marx,
Cornel Wilde coughing blood on the piano keys while Merle Oberon
                berates,
Marilyn Monroe in her little spike heels reeling through Niagara Falls,
Joseph Cotten puzzling and Orson Welles puzzled and Dolores del Rio
eating orchids for lunch and breaking mirrors, Gloria Swanson reclining,
and Jean Harlow reclining and wiggling, and Alice Faye reclining
and wiggling and singing, Myrna Loy being calm and wise, William
                Powell
in his stunning urbanity, Elizabeth Taylor blossoming, yes, to you

and to all you others, the great, the near-great, the featured, the extras
who pass quickly and return in dreams saying your one or two lines,
my love!
Long may you illumine space with your marvellous appearances, delays
and enunciations, and may the money of the world glitteringly cover you
as you rest after a long day under the kleig lights with your faces
in packs for our edification, the way the clouds come often at night
but the heavens operate on the star system. It is a divine precedent
you perpetuate! Roll on, reels of celluloid, as the great earth rolls on!

JAMES MERRILL
b. 1926

Tomorrows

The question was an academic one.
Andrey Sergeyvitch, rising sharp at two,
Would finally write that letter to his three
Sisters still in the country. Stop at four,
Drink tea, dress elegantly and, by five,
Be losing money at the Club des Six.

In Pakistan a band of outraged Sikhs
Would storm an embassy (the wrong one)
And spend the next week cooling off in five
Adjacent cells. These clearly were but two
Vital details — though nobody cared much for
The future by that time, except us three.

You, Andrée Meraviglia, not quite three,
Left Heidelberg. Year, 1936.
That same decade you, Lo Ping, came to the fore
In the Spiritual Olympics, which you won.
My old black self I crave indulgence to
Withhold from limelight, acting on a belief I've

Lived by no less, no more, than by my five
Senses. Enough that circus music (BOOM-two-three)
Coursed through my veins. I saw how Timbuctoo
Would suffer an undue rainfall, 2.6
Inches. How in all of Fairbanks, won-
der of wonders, no polka would be danced, or for

That matter no waltzes or rumbas, although four
Librarians, each on her first French 75,
Would do a maxixe (and a snappy one).
How, when on Lucca's greenest ramparts, three-
fold emotion prompting Renzo to choose from six
Older girls the blondest, call her *tu*,

It would be these blind eyes hers looked into
Widening in brief astonishment before
Love drugged her nerves with blossoms drawn from classics
Of Arab draughtsmanship—small, ink-red, five-
Petalled blossoms blooming in clusters of three.
How she would want to show them to someone!

But one by one they're fading. I am too.
These three times thirteen lines I'll write down for
Fun, some May morning between five and six.

JAMES WRIGHT
b. 1927

Love in a Warm Room in Winter

The trouble with you is
You think all I want to do
Is get you into bed
And make love with you.

And that's not true!

I was just trying to make friends.
All I wanted to do
Was get into bed
With you and make

Love with you.

Who was that little bird we saw towering upside down
This afternoon on that pine cone, on the edge of a cliff,
In the snow? Wasn't he charming? Yes, he was, now,
Now, now,
Just take it easy.

Aha!

DONALD HALL
b. 1928

To a Waterfowl

Women with hats like the rear ends of pink ducks
applauded you, my poems.
These are the women whose husbands I meet on airplanes,
who close their briefcases and ask, "What are *you* in?"
I look in their eyes, I tell them I am in poetry,

and their eyes fill with anxiety, and with little tears.
"Oh, yeah?" they say, developing an interest in clouds.
"My wife, she likes that sort of thing? Hah-hah?
I guess maybe I'd better watch my grammar, huh?"
I leave them in airports, watching their grammar,

and take a limousine to the Women's Goodness Club
where I drink Harvey's Bristol Cream with their wives,
and eat chicken salad with capers, with little tomato wedges
and I read them "The Erotic Crocodile," and "Eating You."
Ah, when I have concluded the disbursement of sonorities,

crooning, "High on thy thigh I cry, Hi!" — and so forth —
they spank their wide hands, they smile like Jell-O,
and they say, "Hah-hah? My goodness, Mr. Hall,
but you certainly do have an imagination, huh?"
"Thank you, indeed," I say; "it brings in the bacon."

But now, my poems, now I have returned to the motel,
returned to *l'éternel retour* of the Holiday Inn,
naked, lying on the bed, watching *Godzilla Sucks Mt. Fuji*,
addressing my poems, feeling superior, and drinking bourbon
from a flask disguised to look like a transistor radio.

Ah, my poems, it is true,
that with the deepest gratitude and most serene pleasure,
and with hints that I am a sexual Thomas Alva Edison,
and not without collecting an exorbitant fee,
I have accepted the approbation of feathers.

And what about you? You, laughing? You, in the bluejeans,
laughing at your mother who wears hats, and at your father
who rides airplanes with a briefcase watching his grammar?
Will you ever be old and dumb, like your creepy parents?
Not you, not you, not you, not you, not you, not you.

Professor Gratt

And why does Gratt teach English? Why, because
A law school felt he could not learn the laws.
"Hamlet," he tells his students, "you will find,
Concerns a man who can't make up his mind.
The Tempest? . . . um . . . the one with Ariel! . . .
Are there more questions now?" But one can tell
That all his will, brains, and imagination
Are concentrated on a higher station:
He wants to be in the Administration.
Sometimes at parties he observes the Dean;
He giggles, coughs, and turns aquamarine.
Yet some day we will hear of "Mr. Gratt,
Vice-President in Charge of This or That."
I heard the Dean remark, at tea and cakes,
Face stuffed and sneering, "Gratt has what it takes."

Breasts

There is something between us.

JOHN HOLLANDER
b. 1929

To the Lady Portrayed by Margaret Dumont

Now that high, oft-affronted bosom heaves
A final sigh, crushed by the wrecker's ball;
Like a definitive mansard, it leaves
Our view an empty lot. Before the fall,
The camp was to make sex grotesque, but when
Was anything more grave? For us, our grace
Was being the yoohooed-at, naughty men
Whose eyes would lower, finally, from that Face.

Death, be not bowed by that solidity
But bear her ever upward, cloud by cloud,
To where she sits, with vast solemnity,
Enthroned; and may we, some day, be allowed
    If not a life of constant flight there, then a
    Glimpse of that fierce green land of mink and henna.

Heliogabalus

Higgledy-piggledy
Heliogabalus*
Lurched through the Forum, his
Bottom a-wag,

Vainly pretending to
Gynaecological
Problems beneath his Im-
Perial drag.

* "It may seem probable, the vices and follies of Elagabalus have been adorned by
fancy, and blackened by prejudice. Yet confining ourselves to the public scenes displayed
before the Roman people, and attested by grave and contemporary historians, their
inexpressible infamy surpasses that of any other age or country. The license of an
eastern monarch is secluded from the eye of curiosity by the inaccessible walls of his
seraglio. The sentiments of honour and gallantry have introduced a refinement of
pleasure, a regard for decency, and a respect for public opinion, into the modern
courts of Europe; but the corrupt and opulent nobles of Rome gratified every vice
that could be collected from the mighty conflux of nations and manners. Secure of
impunity, careless of censure, they lived without restraint in the patient and humble
society of their slaves and parasites. . . ." (GIBBON's note)

Last Words

"Higgledy-piggledy
Andrea Doria
Lives in the name of this
Glorious boat.

As I sit writing these
Non-navigational
Verses a — CRASH! BANG! BLURP!
GLUB" . . . (end of quote).

JOHN HOLLANDER

Appearance and Reality

Higgledy-piggledy
Josephine Bonaparte,
Painted by Prud'hon with
Serious mien:

Sorrow? Oh, hardly. Just
Cosmetological
Prudence (her teeth were a
Carious green.*)

* Historical.

Historical Reflections

Higgledy-piggledy,
Benjamin Harrison,
Twenty-third President,
Was, and, as such,

Served between Clevelands, and
Save for this trivial
Idiosyncracy,
Didn't do much.

No Foundation

Higgledy-piggledy
John Simon Guggenheim,
Honored wherever the
Muses collect,

Save in the studies (like
Mine) which have suffered his
Unjustifiable,
Shocking neglect.

X. J. KENNEDY
b. 1929

In a Prominent Bar in Secaucus One Day

In a prominent bar in Secaucus one day
Rose a lady in skunk with a topheavy sway,
Raised a knobby red finger — all turned from their beer —
While with eyes bright as snowcrust she sang high and clear:

"Now who of you'd think from an eyeload of me
That I once was a lady as proud as could be?
Oh I'd never sit down by a tumbledown drunk
If it wasn't, my dears, for the high cost of junk.

"All the gents used to swear that the white of my calf
Beat the down of the swan by a length and a half.
In the kerchief of linen I caught to my nose
Ah, there never fell snot, but a little gold rose.

"I had seven gold teeth and a toothpick of gold,
My Virginia cheroot was a leaf of it rolled
And I'd light it each time with a thousand in cash —
Why the bums used to fight if I flicked them an ash.

"Once the toast of the Biltmore, the belle of the Taft,
I would drink bottle beer at the Drake, never draft,
And dine at the Astor on Salisbury steak
With a clean tablecloth for each bite I did take.

"In a car like the Roxy I'd roll to the track,
A steel-guitar trio, a bar in the back,
And the wheels made no noise, they turned over so fast,
Still it took you ten minutes to see me go past.

"When the horses bowed down to me that I might choose,
I bet on them all, for I hated to lose.
Now I'm saddled each night for my butter and eggs
And the broken threads race down the backs of my legs.

"Let you hold in mind, girls, that your beauty must pass
Like a lovely white clover that rusts with its grass.
Keep your bottoms off barstools and marry you young
Or be left — an old barrel with many a bung.

"For when time takes you out for a spin in his car
You'll be hard-pressed to stop him from going too far
And be left by the roadside, for all your good deeds,
Two toadstools for tits and a face full of weeds."

All the house raised a cheer, but the man at the bar
Made a phonecall and up pulled a red patrol car
And she blew us a kiss as they copped her away
From that prominent bar in Secaucus, N.J.

Japanese Beetles

1

Imperious Muse, your arrows ever strike
When there's some urgent duty I dislike.

2

By the cold glow that lit my husband's eye
I could read what page eight had said to try.

3
To Someone Who Insisted I Look Up Someone

I rang them up while touring Timbuctoo,
Those bosom chums to whom you're known as "Who?"

4
Parody: Herrick

When Vestalina's thin white hand cuts cheese
The very mice go down upon their knees.

5
The Minotaur's Advice

Unravel hope, but be not by it led,
Or back outside you shall hang by a thread.

6

On his wife's stone, though small in cost and small,
Meek got a word in edgewise after all.

7
Translator

They say he knows, who renders Old High Dutch,
His own tongue only, and of it not much.

8
To a Now-type Poet

Your stoned head's least whim jotted down white-hot?
Enough confusion of my own, I've got.

9
At a Sale of Manuscript

Who deal in early drafts and casual words
Would starve the horse to death and prize his turds.

10
To a Young Poet

On solemn asses fall plush sinecures,
So keep a straight face and sit tight on yours.

Last Lines

1
From the Greek Anthology

On miserable Nearchos' bones lie lightly, earth,
That the dogs may dig him up, for what he's worth.

2
On a Boxer

In his still corner Rocky takes the count.
He would not rise again for any amount.

3

Full-nelsoned in earth's arms the Crusher sleeps
Whom no man living could pin down for keeps.

4
Teutonic Scholar

Whose views twelve heavy tomes perpetuate
Now lies as though beneath a paperweight.

5
Here lies a girl whose beauty made Time stay.
Shovel earth in. We haven't got all day.

JONATHAN WILLIAMS
b. 1929

The Hermit Cackleberry Brown,
on Human Vanity

caint call your name
but your face is easy

come sit

now some folks figure theyre
bettern
cowflop they
aint

not a bit

just good to hold the world together
like hooved up ground

thats what

Uncle Iv Surveys His Domain from His Rocker
of a Sunday Afternoon as Aunt Dory
Starts To Chop Kindling

Mister Williams
lets youn me move
tother side the house

the woman
choppin woods
mite nigh the awkerdist thing
I seen

JONATHAN WILLIAMS

Mrs. Sadie Grindstaff, Weaver and Factotum, Explains the Work-Principle to the Modern World

I figured
anything anybody
could do a lot of I
could do a little
of

mebby

Three Sayings from Highlands, North Carolina

but pretty though as
roses is
you can put up with
the thorns

DORIS TALLEY, HOUSEWIFE & GARDENER

you live until you die —
if the limb don't fall

BUTLER JENKINS, CARETAKER

your points is blue
and your timing's
a week off

SAM CRESWELL, AUTO MECHANIC

The Anthropophagites See a Sign on NC Highway 177 That Looks Like Heaven:

EAT
300 FEET

509

JOHN BARTH
b. 1930

The Minstrel's Last Lay (from "Anonymiad")

Once upon a time
I composed in witty rhyme
And poured libations to the muse Erato.

Merope would croon,
"Minstrel mine, a lay! A tune!"
"From bed to verse," I'd answer; "that's my motto."

Stranded by my foes,
Nowadays I write in prose,
Forsaking measure, rhyme, and honeyed diction;

Amphora's my muse:
When I finish off the booze,
I hump the jug and fill her up with fiction.

GREGORY CORSO
b. 1930

Marriage

Should I get married? Should I be good?
Astound the girl next door with my velvet suit and faustus hood?
Don't take her to movies but to cemeteries
tell all about werewolf bathtubs and forked clarinets
then desire her and kiss her and all the preliminaries
and she going just so far and I understanding why
not getting angry saying You must feel! It's beautiful to feel!
Instead take her in my arms lean against an old crooked tombstone
and woo her the entire night the constellations in the sky —

When she introduces me to her parents
back straightened, hair finally combed, strangled by a tie,
should I sit knees together on their 3rd degree sofa
and not ask Where's the bathroom?
How else to feel other than I am,
often thinking Flash Gordon soap —
O how terrible it must be for a young man

seated before a family and the family thinking
We never saw him before! He wants our Mary Lou!
After tea and homemade cookies they ask What do you do for a living?
Should I tell them? Would they like me then?
Say All right get married, we're losing a daughter
but we're gaining a son —
And should I then ask Where's the bathroom?

O God, and the wedding! All her family and her friends
and only a handful of mine all scroungy and bearded
just wait to get at the drinks and food —
And the priest! he looking at me as if I masturbated
asking me Do you take this woman for your lawful wedded wife?
And I trembling what to say say Pie Glue!
I kiss the bride all those corny men slapping me on the back
She's all yours, boy! Ha-ha-ha!
And in their eyes you could see some obscene honeymoon going on —
Then all that absurd rice and clanky cans and shoes
Niagara Falls! Hordes of us! Husbands! Wives! Flowers! Chocolates!
All streaming into cozy hotels
All going to do the same thing tonight
The indifferent clerk he knowing what was going to happen
The lobby zombies they knowing what
The whistling elevator man he knowing
The winking bellboy knowing
Everybody knowing! I'd be almost inclined not to do anything!
Stay up all night! Stare that hotel clerk in the eye!
Screaming: I deny honeymoon! I deny honeymoon!
running rampant into those almost climactic suites
yelling Radio belly! Cat shovel!
O I'd live in Niagara forever! in a dark cave beneath the Falls
I'd sit there the Mad Honeymooner
devising ways to break marriages, a scourge of bigamy
a saint of divorce —

But I should get married I should be good
How nice it'd be to come home to her
and sit by the fireplace and she in the kitchen
aproned young and lovely wanting my baby
and so happy about me she burns the roast beef
and comes crying to me and I get up from my big papa chair
saying Christmas teeth! Radiant brains! Apple deaf!
God what a husband I'd make! Yes, I should get married!

So much to do! like sneaking into Mr Jones' house late at night
and cover his golf clubs with 1920 Norwegian books
Like hanging a picture of Rimbaud on the lawnmower
like pasting Tannu Tuva postage stamps all over the picket fence
like when Mrs Kindhead comes to collect for the Community Chest
grab her and tell her There are unfavorable omens in the sky!
And when the mayor comes to get my vote tell him
When are you going to stop people killing whales!
And when the milkman comes leave him a note in the bottle
Penguin dust, bring me penguin dust, I want penguin dust —

Yet if I should get married and it's Connecticut and snow
and she gives birth to a child and I am sleepless, worn,
up for nights, head bowed against a quiet window, the past behind me,
finding myself in the most common of situations a trembling man
knowledged with responsibility not twig-smear nor Roman coin soup —
O what would that be like!
Surely I'd give it for a nipple a rubber Tacitus
For a rattle a bag of broken Bach records
Tack Della Francesca all over its crib
Sew the Greek alphabet on its bib
And build for its playpen a roofless Parthenon

No, I doubt I'd be that kind of father
not rural not snow no quiet window
but hot smelly tight New York City
seven flights up, roaches and rats in the walls
a fat Reichian wife screeching over potatoes Get a job!
And five nose running brats in love with Batman
And the neighbors all toothless and dry haired
like those hag masses of the 18th century
all wanting to come in and watch TV
The landlord wants his rent
Grocery store Blue Cross Gas & Electric Knights of Columbus
Impossible to lie back and dream Telephone snow, ghost parking —
No! I should not get married I should never get married!
But — imagine If I were married to a beautiful sophisticated woman
tall and pale wearing an elegant black dress and long black gloves
holding a cigarette holder in one hand and a highball in the other
and we lived high up in a penthouse with a huge window
from which we could see all of New York and ever farther on clearer days
No, can't imagine myself married to that pleasant prison dream —

O but what about love? I forgot love
not that I am incapable of love
it's just that I see love as odd as wearing shoes —
I never wanted to marry a girl who was like my mother
And Ingrid Bergman was always impossible
And there's maybe a girl now but she's already married
And I don't like men and —
but there's got to be somebody!
Because what if I'm 60 years old and not married,
all alone in a furnished room with pee stains on my underwear
and everybody else is married! All the universe married but me!

Ah, yet well I know that were a woman possible as I am possible
then marriage would be possible —
Like SHE in her lonely alien gaud waiting her Egyptian lover
so I wait — bereft of 2,000 years and the bath of life.

STEPHEN SONDHEIM
b. 1930

Gee, Officer Krupke

Dear kindly Sergeant Krupke,
You gotta understand,
It's just our bringin' up-ke
That gets us out of hand.
Our mothers all are junkies,
Our fathers all are drunks.
Golly Moses, natcherly we're punks!

Gee, Officer Krupke, we're very upset;
We never had the love that ev'ry child oughta get.
We ain't no delinquents, we're misunderstood.
Deep down inside us there is good.
There is good, there is good, there is untapped good,
Like inside, the worst of us is good!

Dear kindly Judge, your Honor,
My parents treat me rough,
With all their marijuana,
They won't give me a puff.

They didn't wanna have me,
But somehow I was had.
Leapin' lizards, that's why I'm so bad!

Officer Krupke, you're really a square;
This boy don't need a judge, he needs a analyst's care!
It's just his neurosis that oughta be curbed,
He's psychologic'ly disturbed.
We're disturbed, we're disturbed, we're the most disturbed,
Like we're psychologic'ly disturbed.

My father is a bastard,
My ma's an S.O.B.,
My grandpa's always plastered,
My grandma pushes tea.
My sister wears a mustache,
My brother wears a dress.
Goodness gracious, that's why I'm a mess!

Officer Krupke, you're really a slob,
This boy don't need a doctor, just a good honest job.
Society's played him a terrible trick,
And sociologic'ly he's sick!
I am sick, we are sick, we are sick, sick, sick,
Like we're sociologic'ly sick.

Dear kindly social worker,
They say go earn a buck,
Like be a soda jerker,
Which means like be a schmuck.
It's not I'm antisocial,
I'm only anti-work.
Glory-osky, that's why I'm a jerk.

Officer Krupke, you've done it again,
This boy don't need a job, he needs a year in the pen.
It ain't just a question of misunderstood;
Deep down inside him, he's no good!
I'm no good! we're no good! we're no earthly good.
Like the best of us is no damn good!

The trouble is he's crazy,
The trouble is he drinks.
The trouble is he's lazy,

The trouble is he stinks.
The trouble is he's growing,
The trouble is he's grown!
Krupke, we got troubles of our own!

Gee, Officer Krupke, we're down on our knees,
'Cause no one wants a fellow with a social disease.
Gee, Officer Krupke, what are we to do?

Gee, Officer Krupke, krup you!

GEORGE STARBUCK
b. 1931

On First Looking in on Blodgett's Keats's "Chapman's Homer"

Mellifluous as bees, these brittle men
droning of Honeyed Homer give me hives.
I scratch, yawn like a bear, my arm arrives
at yours — oh, Honey, and we're back again,
me the Balboa, you the Darien,
lording the loud Pacific sands, our lives
as hazarded as when a petrel dives
to yank the dull sea's coverlet, or when,

breaking from me across the sand that's rink
and record of our weekend boning up
on *The Romantic Agony,* you sink
John Keats a good surf-fisher's cast out — plump
in the sun's wake — and the parched pages drink
that great whales' blanket party hump and hump.

High Renaissance

"Nomine Domini
Theotocopoulos,
None of these prelates can
Manage your name.

Change it. Appeal to their
Hellenophilia.
Sign it 'El Greco.' I'll
Slap on a frame."

Chip

Clippety cloppety,
Cesare Borgia
Modeled himself on his
Father the Pope:

Pontifex Maximus,
Paterfamilias,
Generalissimo:
Able to cope.

Sonnet with a Different Letter
at the End of Every Line

FOR HELEN VENDLER

O for a muse of fire, a sack of dough,
Or both! O promissory notes of woe!
One time in Santa Fe N.M.
Ol' Winfield Townley Scott and I . . . But whoa.

One can exert oneself, *ff*,
Or architect a heaven like Rimbaud,
Or if that seems, how shall I say, *de trop*,
One can at least write sonnets, a propos
Of nothing save the do-re-mi-fa-sol
Of poetry itself. Is not the row
Of perfect rhymes, the terminal bon mot,
Obeisance enough to the Great O?

"Observe," said Chairman Mao to Premier Chou,
"On voyage à Parnasse pour prendre les eaux.
On voyage comme poisson, incog."

Said

J. Alfred Prufrock to
Hugh Selwyn Mauberley,
"What ever happened to
Senlin, ought-nine?"

"One with the passion for
Orientalia?"
"Rather." "Losttrackofhim."
"Pity." "Design."

Said

Agatha Christie to
E. Phillips Oppenheim,
"Who is this Hemingway,
Who is this Proust?

Who is this Vladimir
Whatchamacallum, this
Neopostrealist
Rabble?" she groused.

Monarch of the Sea

"Jiminy Whillikers,
Admiral Samuel
Eliot Morrison,
Where is your ship?"

"I, sir, am HMS
Historiography's
Disciplinarian.
Button your lip."

JOHN UPDIKE
b. 1932

The Amish

The Amish are a surly sect.
They paint their bulging barns with hex
Designs, pronounce a dialect
Of Deutsch, inbreed, and wink at sex.

They have no use for buttons, tea,
Life insurance, cigarettes,
Churches, liquor, Sea & Ski,
Public power, or regrets.

Believing motors undivine,
They bob behind a buggied horse
From Paradise to Brandywine,
From Bird-in-Hand to Intercourse.

They think the Devil drives a car
And wish Jehovah would revoke
The licensed fools who travel far
To gaze upon these simple folk.

I Missed His Book, But I Read His Name

"The Silver Pilgrimage," by M. Anantanarayanan. . . . 160 pages.
Criterion. $3.95.   *The Times*

Though authors are a dreadful clan
To be avoided if you can,
I'd like to meet the Indian,
M. Anantanarayanan.

I picture him as short and tan.
We'd meet, perhaps, in Hindustan.
I'd say, with admirable *élan*,
"Ah, Anantanarayanan —

I've heard of you. The *Times* once ran
A notice on your novel, an
Unusual tale of God and Man."
And Anantanarayanan

Would seat me on a lush divan
And read his name — that sumptuous span
Of "a's" and "n's" more lovely than
"In Xanadu did Kubla Khan" —

Aloud to me all day. I plan
Henceforth to be an ardent fan
Of Anantanarayanan —
M. Anantanarayanan.

Recital

ROGER BOBO GIVES
RECITAL ON TUBA
Headline in the Times

Eskimos in Manitoba,
   Barracuda off Aruba,
Cock an ear when Roger Bobo
   Starts to solo on the tuba.

Men of every station — Pooh-Bah,
   Nabob, bozo, toff, and hobo —
Cry in unison, "Indubi-
   Tably, there is simply nobo-

Dy who oompahs on the tubo,
Solo, quite like Roger Bubo!"

ROBERT SWARD
b. 1933

American Heritage

This, O my stomach, is a painting
Of the Civil War. Look — Antietam.
All over there are dead,
Noble Northern, Noble Southern, dead.

One, no, no, several wear beards:
They are all General Ulysses S. Grant
                    beards,
Noble, truly noble beards.
The Union side, O my soul, see them!
All, all of them noble,
All, all of them waving,
Resembling, bearing the name
Walt Whitman. They are all on horseback,
All with maps and swords, banners
And copies of last Sunday's
New York *Times* Book Review;
Watching through binoculars,
Writing letters, keeping journals,
Reading *Leaves of Grass* . . .

And there is Barbara Frietchie.
Hi, Barbara. Barbara's pregnant.
She is soon to be the mother
Of Abraham Lincoln, Dr. Oliver Wendell Holmes
And Carl Sandburg.

This is an historical moment;
Very historical. You can feel it
And read about it, too
(And General Stonewall Jackson,
Clare Boothe Luce, Robert E. Lee
    and many others),
In *American Heritage,*
Edited by Bruce Catton,
With whose kind permission
I herewith reprint this painting.

                    . . .

Song: "There's No War Like Civil War"
    O, the Civil War's
    The only war,
    The only war, the only war;
    The finest war,
    Yes, the noblest most unforeign war,
    The finest only noblest most
    Unforeign war
    That ever I did see.   (Chorus, etc.)

MICHAEL BENEDIKT
b. 1935

Fate in Incognito

At last I can figure out the nature of that whisking sound which I hear
whenever I leave the room
It is not really the sound of wind through television aerials, safety
screens, and the holes in old socks and underwear dangling on
clotheslines
But Fate, rubbing its hands.
Whisk whisk it must certainly be wearing gloves
Whisk whisk or else it has fingerprints ridged and immortal as corduroy
And nevertheless, despite the threat
Here I am proceeding as if it were normal
As if a future came automatically, without one's having to predict it,
without requiring that personal conception precede all circum-
stances and occurrences
As if any difficulties experienced last night, today, and tomorrow
And the tragedy of yesterday, with its latent triumphs,
Were not illusions of some will or other,
Harmony of hope and trepidation

"Whisk whisk whisk there you go again, Fate, swathed and whisking
away
Now that I have thrown back your disguise and found you hidden
under the mask of the whisk
I know, you will not go, and it is time for a new incognito"
(Listen to how clever it thinks it is outside our windows coming down
the street again with that crunch crunch crunch squeak crunch
crunch crunch)

WILLIAM HARMON
b. 1938

Bureaucratic Limerick

The Bureau of Labor Statistics
Has been taken over by mystics
    Whose way is to say
    That your pay for the day
Has no actual characteristics.

CHARLES SIMIC
b. 1938

Watermelons

Green Buddhas
On the fruit stand.
We eat the smile
And spit out the teeth.

ROY BLOUNT, Jr.
b. 1941

Against Broccoli

The local groceries are all out of broccoli,
Loccoli.

For the Record

"I was asked to demonstrate the step," said England's Wayne Sleep, 25,
a soloist with the Royal Ballet and specialist in the entrechat. . . . "Then
the producer said how about breaking the record? So I did." . . . Sleep's
acrobatics on a London TV program stunned balletomanes all over the
world; he became the first person in recorded history to cross and uncross
his legs five times in a single leap. The feat is known as an entrechat
douze for its twelve movements: the leap, five crossings, five uncrossings
and the landing. Not only was Sleep's feat unprecedented, but only
Russia's late, great Vaslav Nijinski had ever been credited with an
entrechat dix. *Newsweek.*

A dreamlike leap
By England's Sleep!
He didn't doze,
He did a *douze*.
His legs arose
In curlicues.

He shrugged, "O.K., I'll make a run,"
And then went heavenward (that's one),
And five times crossed, and uncrossed five,
And then returned to earth alive.

And on TV, no less. *Voilà!*
Sleep's the king of entrechat.

Nijinsky, may he rest in peace —
Would that he were above the ground!
Nijinsky settled for but *dix*
Movements in a single bound.

A joy forever. He will last.
And yet . . . his mark has been surpassed.
Will Chaplin, too, be cast in doubt?
Will someone edge Caruso out?

But look! As consternation reigns
Among the world's balletomanes,
We see Nijinsky rise again.
His spirit jumps into our ken:

He climbs, descends, meanwhile with ease
Weaving patterns with his knees,
And stops just off the ground, and says,
To open with some humor, *"Treize."*

And now he's serious; now he soars
Sufficiently to cry *"Quatorze!"*
And now, although he starts to pant,
Up he goes — he's done a *vingt!*

And now he's really going good.
Nijinsky, folks, has just *vingt-deux*'d.
We sense he could go on to *cent-deux*
But evidently doesn't want to.

For now, with one great closing spring,
He goes through untold scissoring
And disappears — a quantum leap —
And leaves the blinking world to Sleep.

Gryll's State

(In *The Faerie Queen*, Book II, a number of men who have been turned into hogs by the enchantress Acrasia are turned back into men by the Knight of Temperance. Gryll is the one who makes clear his desire to become a hog again.)

Gryll
Had his fill
Of aspiring and falling and wearing hats.

Gryll
Had his fill
Of avoiding fats.

Gryll
Had nil
In the way of an attitude of holier-than-thou.

Gryll
Still
Fancied a sow.

Gryll,
Until
Becoming a hog, was forever worrying about laying up
    everything he might need, and using everything
    he had laid up — or, if he couldn't use it, seeing
    that it was properly disposed of, or defended.

Gryll
Felt swill
Had things to recommend it.

Gryll
Felt ill
At the thought of returning to a state of mind in which
    he had to think of *himself* as a possible, or make
    that a probable, threat.

Gryll
Will
Be borne out by history yet.

NIKKI GIOVANNI
b. 1943

Master Charge Blues

its wednesday night baby
and i'm all alone
wednesday night baby
and i'm all alone
sitting with myself
waiting for the telephone

wanted you baby
but you said you had to go
wanted you yeah
but you said you had to go
called your best friend
but he can't come 'cross no more

did you ever go to bed
at the end of a busy day
look over and see the smooth
where your hump usta lay
feminine odor and no reason why
i said feminine odor and no reason why
asked the lord to help me
he shook his head "not i"

but i'm a modern woman baby
ain't gonna let this get me down
i'm a modern woman
ain't gonna let this get me down
gonna take my master charge
and get everything in town

Poem for Unwed Mothers
(to be sung to "The Old F.U. Spirit")

it was good for the virgin mary
it was good enough for mary
it was good for the virgin mary
its good enough for me

Chorus

525

JAMES TATE
b. 1943

My Great Great Etc. Uncle Patrick Henry

There's a fortune to be made in just about everything
in this country, somebody's father had to invent
everything — baby food, tractors, rat poisoning.
My family's obviously done nothing since the beginning
of time. They invented poverty and bad taste
and getting by and taking it from the boss.
O my mother goes around chewing her nails and
spitting them in a jar: You should be ashamed
of yourself she says, think of your family.
My family I say what have they ever done but
paint by numbers the most absurd disgusting scenes
of plastic squalor and human degradation.
Well then think of your great great etc. Uncle
Patrick Henry.

The President Slumming

In a weird, forlorn voice
he cries: it is a mirage!
Then tosses a wreath of scorpions
to the children,
mounts his white nag
and creeps off into darkness,
smoking an orange.

Conjuring Roethke

Prickle a lamb,
giggle a yam,
beat a chrysanthemum
out of its head
with a red feather.
Dream of a pencil
or three airmail stamps
under your pillow.
Thank the good fairy
you're not dead.

The heat's on,
the window's gone,
the ceiling is sorry
it hurt you.
But this is not air
holding your hand,
nor weasels beneath
your dirt rug.
I think the corks
are out of breath,
the bottles begin
laughing a zoo.

I wish you were here.
The calendar is red,
a candle closes
the room.
If this is the life
we are all leaving
it's half as bad.
Hello again mad turnip.
Let's tango together
down to the clear
glad river.

KATHLEEN NORRIS
b. 1947

Stomach

My stomach is of many minds;
It believes everything it eats.
My eschatological
Stomach, a fundamentalist
Of sorts, grows intent
At drawing blood from
Surfaces of things:
Ice-cold fingers touch its inner lining,
It lives in fear of confusion.

The stomach clenched
Its teeth, its nose bled all day

As I stumbled through snow,
Cracking theories of poetry
Over its skull.
Gilded toothpicks,
Sweet-sour pork
Did a desperate violence
To its body.
It had to be saved, put to sleep,
But it woke early,
Still restless with envy of the resplendent
Spleen.

I will be good to my stomach,
Tomorrow; listen, and believe it
For a while. The stomach
Is serious and unhappy.
It wants to do something really
Symbolic; it wants to be
The ultimate
Stomach.

Memorandum / The Accountant's Notebook

The illusions: they fit like an iron lung, and
can keep you going indefinitely. The persons
suspected of stealing them are to be considered
armed and dangerous

Little Joe, who was last seen electrocuting himself
trying to make ends meet

The art of making foods so subtle that even politicians
don't know how to eat them

A little faith: the swimmers here don't know
where the next breath is coming from

INDEX

Authors   *Titles*   First Lines